BUSINESS CYCLES, PART I

F. A. HAYEK

THE COLLECTED WORKS OF

F. A. Hayek

BUSINESS CYCLES
PART I

Edited by Hansjoerg Klausinger

Liberty Fund

This book is published by Liberty Fund, Inc., a foundation established to encourage
study of the ideal of a society of free and responsible individuals.

[cuneiform logo]

The cuneiform inscription that serves as our logo and as the design motif for our
endpapers is the earliest-known written appearance of the word "freedom" (*amagi*), or "liberty."
It is taken from a clay document written about 2300 B.C. in the Sumerian city-state of Lagash.

Business Cycles, Part I is volume 7 of The Collected Works of F. A. Hayek, published by
The University of Chicago Press.

This Liberty Fund paperback edition of *Business Cycles, Part I* is published by arrangement
with The University of Chicago Press and Taylor & Francis Books, Ltd., a member of the
Taylor & Francis Group.

17 18 19 20 21   P   5   4   3   2   1

Frontispiece: Friedrich Hayek © Bettmann/CORBIS
Cover photo: Friedrich August von Hayek © Hulton-Deutsch Collection/CORBIS

Library of Congress Cataloging-in-Publication Data

Names: Hayek, Friedrich A. von (Friedrich August), 1899–1992, author. |
    Klausinger, Hansjörg, editor.
Title: Business cycles / edited by Hansjörg Klausinger.
Description: Indianapolis : Liberty Fund, 2017. | Series: The collected works of
    F.A. Hayek ; volumes 7–8 | Originally issued as a 2 volume hardback set in 2012.
    Contents: Part I – Part II. | Includes bibliographical references and index.
Identifiers: LCCN 2016020043 | ISBN 9780865979031 (part 1 : pbk. : alk. paper)
    | ISBN 9780865979048 (part 2 : pbk. : alk. paper)
Subjects: LCSH: Business cycles. | Prices. | Money.
Classification: LCC HB3711 .H349 2017 | DDC 338.5/42–dc23
LC record available at https://lccn.loc.gov/2016020043

Liberty Fund, Inc.
11301 North Meridian Street
Carmel, Indiana 46032-4564

This book is printed on paper that is acid-free and meets the requirements
of the American National Standard for Permanence of Paper for Printed
Library Materials, Z39.48-1992. ⊖

Cover design by Erin Kirk New, Watkinsville, Georgia
Printed and bound by Thomson-Shore, Dexter, Michigan

THE COLLECTED WORKS OF F. A. HAYEK

Founding Editor: W. W. Bartley III
General Editor: Bruce Caldwell

*The University of Chicago Press edition
was published with the support of*

The Hoover Institution on War, Revolution,
and Peace, Stanford University

The Cato Institute

The Earhart Foundation

The Pierre F. and Enid Goodrich Foundation

The Heritage Foundation

The Morris Foundation, Little Rock

CONTENTS

PRICES AND PRODUCTION

EDITORIAL FOREWORD

Although in my home country of Austria, Friedrich August Hayek, both as the economist and as the social philosopher, for a long time had not been recognised as a major thinker of the twentieth century, in some sense his works, first and foremost his writings on money and the cycle, were always present during my endeavours as a scholar in the history of economic thought. My first encounter with Hayek's works was when a colleague, Norbert Hentschel, to whom I am still grateful, proposed a discussion of Hayek's theory of the cycle as a theme for a doctoral thesis—a suggestion which I did not follow then, but ten years later when I chose to make a chapter on Hayek part of my habilitation. From then on my interest in Hayek never receded, and in this regard I now feel much honoured by the opportunity to present this edition of Hayek's writings on the business cycle.

The first part, in this volume, contains Hayek's two major monographs on the business cycle, *Monetary Theory and the Trade Cycle* and *Prices and Production*, while his short papers, including hitherto unpublished contributions, are collected in a companion volume (*Business Cycles, Part II*). The editorial history of both monographs necessitated the specific procedure chosen here. *Monetary Theory and the Trade Cycle* (1933) is the revised translation from the German *Geldtheorie und Konjunkturtheorie* (1929), a translation not free from shortcomings in some regards, which was highlighted recently by a novel translation of what had been in effect a preprint of the first three chapters of this monograph. Thus, in addition to reproducing the text of the 1933 translation, this edition will draw on the original German version and make use of the more recent translation for pointing out divergences—whatever their causes—between the German and the English text. *Prices and Production* was published first in 1931, in English, and then in a revised second edition in 1935; shortly after the first edition Hayek produced a German version, *Preise und Produktion* (1931). In the present volume the text will be presented as a variorum edition, based on the revised second edition and noting all deviations from the first. Where it furthers the understanding of the evolution of Hayek's thought, this edition will also supply variants taken from the German version.

Apart from this, a main task for the editor consisted in the checking of references and quotations. Here the principles of the *Collected Works* editions have been maintained with some slight modifications: The reference style keeps to the rule of citing the full reference at the first quotation and abbreviated references at the following instances, yet with the modification that the editor's introduction and the two monographs are treated as self-contained parts to which this rule applies separately. Typing errors and obvious mistakes have been silently corrected throughout; similarly, the references have been silently adapted to the style of this edition. Inaccurate quotations in Hayek's original version have been left uncorrected, with the inaccuracies pointed out differently according to whether they appear in the text or in the footnotes: inaccurate quotations in the text are pointed out in accompanying editorial notes; those in the footnotes are corrected by the use of brackets. And although incomplete references given by Hayek have been silently supplemented, brackets are used to correct references that are definitely wrong, for example, as regards the author's name, title, or pagination. Finally, if no other source is indicated, German-language writings have been translated by the editor.

At last, it is a most pleasant task to acknowledge the support of those persons and institutions without which the accomplishment of this edition would have been much more difficult if not impossible. To begin with, papers dealing with this edition, and in particular, parts of the introduction, have been presented to various audiences—the conferences of the European Society for the History of Economic Thought at Strasbourg, Prague, Thessaloniki, and Amsterdam; the meeting of the History of Economics Society at George Mason University; seminars at the University of Stuttgart-Hohenheim; the Walter Eucken Institute at Freiburg im Breisgau; in Japan at Hitotsubashi University (Tachikawa) and Yokohama National University; at the HOPE workshop of Duke University; and finally at staff seminars of the Economics Department of my home university, WU (Wirtschaftsuniversität) Vienna. I owe a debt of gratitude to the discussants and commentators at all these presentations for the immense number of useful suggestions for improvement. It is certainly impossible to give a complete list of all the individuals for whose support and help I am grateful. In any case this list must include Larry White, the editor of two capital volumes of *The Collected Works*, and Roger Garrison, from whom I took over the editor's task for these volumes; numerous useful hints and queries came from Günther Chaloupek, Susan Howson, Heinz D. Kurz, Robert Leonard, and Hans-Michael Trautwein, and from responses to queries to the SHOE mailing list by Daniele Besomi, James Forder, and Nicholas Theocarakis; among my colleagues at WU I have to mention J. Hanns Pichler, Alfred Sitz, and Herbert Walther for their support. A crucial impulse for the progress of this edition resulted from the four months I spent in 2008 at Duke University as a senior research fellow of the Center for the History of Political Economy, thanks to an invitation by Bruce Caldwell; in return Bruce

Caldwell, Harald Hagemann, and Arash Molavi Vasséi spent some time as visiting researchers at WU, and during this time commented meticulously on parts of my introduction. The comments by two anonymous readers of the original typescript proved invaluable for suggesting improvements leading to the final outcome. Ciaran Cassidy contributed the translations of the prefaces to the German editions. In addition, Bruce Caldwell, the general editor of this series, must be singled out for his inexhaustible readiness to comment on preliminary versions and for sharing his experience as an editor, and moreover for the patience with which he observed the progress of these volumes.

The preparation of this volume made use of the facilities of many libraries and archives, and I am most grateful for the assistance I have invariably experienced. In particular I visited and drew upon the cooperation of the Hoover Institution Archives at Stanford University, the Perkins Library at Duke University, the Hayek Library located at the University of Salzburg, the Austrian National Library, the library of the University of Vienna, and of course, that of my home university. For permission to quote from the unpublished correspondence and papers of Fritz Machlup I am grateful to the Hoover Institution Archives, which is the repository of the Fritz Machlup papers, and for permission to quote from the unpublished papers and correspondence of F. A. Hayek to the Estate of F. A. Hayek. Last but not least, work on both *Business Cycles* volumes has been much facilitated by financial assistance from the WU-Jubiläumsstiftung, which provided the financial means for a one-year sabbatical (*Forschungsvertrag*); and the Austrian National Bank, which I gratefully acknowledge for awarding its *Internationalisierungspreis*.

A final word of thanks is due to my family: to my wife, Claudia; and to Gerulf, Helga, Marcel, and Mario, all of whom experienced my long, drawn-out preoccupation with Hayek and its unintended consequences for private life.

Hansjoerg Klausinger

INTRODUCTION

The early fame of Friedrich August Hayek as an economic theorist, in particular as a contributor to contemporary economic debates in the English-speaking world, derived from his ventures into the theories of money and the business cycle. With the publication of *Business Cycles, Part I* and *Part II*, all of Hayek's writings on the business cycle will be assembled. This volume contains two monographs on the subject, and the companion volume contains his shorter contributions, including some material published for the first time. The editor's introductions will necessarily overlap and regularly refer to one another. Echoing Hayek's fate as a business cycle theorist, this introduction will highlight the origins and the substance of his early achievements, while the other will concentrate on the actual and apparent problems of his approach and on its evolution in general. To begin at the beginning, however, we turn first to a brief reprise of Hayek's education as a theorist within the Austrian school of economics.

Hayek in Vienna, 1924–31

Hayek's education as an economist and his eventually becoming recognised as a serious theorist of high reputation coincided with the final flourishing of the Austrian school in its centre in Vienna.[1] The last of the school's second gen-

---

[1] This section draws on a wealth of sources on the Austrian school in the 1920s. These include the various editor's introductions to volumes of *The Collected Works of F. A. Hayek* (Chicago: University of Chicago Press; London: Routledge); the recent biographies of Hayek and Ludwig von Mises by, respectively, Bruce Caldwell (*Hayek's Challenge: An Intellectual Biography of F. A. Hayek* [Chicago: University of Chicago Press, 2004]) and Jörg Guido Hülsmann (*Mises: The Last Knight of Liberalism* [Auburn, AL: Mises Institute, 2007]); Hayek's recollections in F. A. Hayek, "Nobel Prize–Winning Economist", ed. Armen Alchian (transcript of an interview conducted in 1978 under the auspices of the Oral History Program, University Library, University of California–Los Angeles [transcript 300/224, Department of Special Collections, Charles E. Young Research Library, UCLA]); *The Fortunes of Liberalism: Essays on Austrian Economics and the Ideal of Freedom*, ed. Peter G. Klein, vol. 4 (1992) of *The Collected Works of F. A. Hayek*, part 1; and *Hayek on Hayek: An Autobiographical Dialogue*, ed. Stephen Kresge and Leif Wenar (Chicago: University of

eration, Friedrich Wieser, died unexpectedly in 1926 after having vacated his chair at the University of Vienna in 1922. The next generation consisted of Hans Mayer, Ludwig von Mises, Joseph Schumpeter (all in their forties), and economists of minor stature like Richard Reisch, Richard Schüller, and Richard Strigl, followed by young academics like Gottfried Haberler, Fritz Machlup, Oskar Morgenstern, Paul Rosenstein-Rodan, and of course Friedrich August Hayek himself. Although these economists contributed to quite diverse fields not easily amalgamated to a homogeneous body of thought, their efforts created an atmosphere conducive to a renaissance of Austrian economics in the 1920s comparable to that of the founding era. Quite apart from the scientific achievements of this time period, the optimistic appraisal of the future resulted from favourable developments within the academic and professional sphere of economics in Austria.

Thus, when Mayer succeeded Wieser in 1923 at least one adherent of the Austrian school occupied an economics chair at the University of Vienna. At about the same time, the Nationalökonomische Gesellschaft (Austrian Economic Association) had been revived as a platform for discussion among academics and non-academics alike, comprising all the different strands of thought within the Austrian economics community. Moreover, the numerous interlocking circles of economists were sizzling with debate; to name just two, the Mises private seminar and the so-called Geist-Kreis provided forums for discussion with members recruited not only from the economics profession but also from other social sciences, law, and business. In 1927 Mises founded the Austrian Institute for Business Cycle Research, which would provide some employment opportunities for economists outside academia. Furthermore, in 1929 Austria's most important economic journal, the *Zeitschrift für Volkswirtschaft und Sozialpolitik*, was relaunched as the *Zeitschrift für Nationalökonomie*. It would soon prove

---

Chicago Press; London: Routledge, 1994). Cf. also Earlene Craver, "The Emigration of the Austrian Economists", *History of Political Economy*, vol. 18, Spring 1986, pp. 1–32; Stephan Boehm, "Austrian Economics between the Wars: Some Historiographical Problems", in *Austrian Economics: Tensions and New Directions*, ed. Bruce Caldwell and Stephan Boehm (Boston: Kluwer, 1992), pp. 1–30; Kurt R. Leube, "Über Diskontinuitäten und Kontinuitäten der österreichischen Schule der Nationalökonomie", in *Erkenntnisgewinne, Erkenntnisverluste*, ed. Karl Acham, Knut Wolfgang Knörr, and Bertram Schefold (Stuttgart: Steiner, 1998), pp. 301–24; Robert Leonard, "'Between Worlds', or an Imagined Reminiscence by Oskar Morgenstern on Equilibrium and Mathematics in the 1920s", *Journal of the History of Economic Thought*, vol. 26, September 2004, pp. 285–310, and "The Collapse of Interwar Vienna: Oskar Morgenstern's Community, 1925–1950", (ICER Working Paper 4, International Centre for Economic Research, Turin, 2010); Hauke Janssen, *Nationalökonomie und Nationalsozialismus. Die deutsche Volkswirtschaftslehre in den dreißiger Jahren*, 2nd ed. rev. (Marburg: Metropolis, 2000); and as a main source of biographical information, *Biographisches Handbuch der deutschsprachigen wirtschaftswissenschaftlichen Emigration nach 1933*, 2 vols., ed. Harald Hagemann and Claus-Dieter Krohn (Munich: Saur, 1999). Finally, on specific points the documents collected in the papers of Oskar Morgenstern and Gottfried Haberler proved invaluable.

itself as the most prestigious German-language economic journal, in particular after the decline of the German journals subsequent to Hitler's rise to power in 1933. Additionally, most of the younger Austrians benefited from studies and research abroad. Morgenstern and Haberler, and for a few months Mises, had spent time outside Austria, supported by grants from the Rockefeller Foundation, which later also sponsored Machlup and Rosenstein-Rodan. Hayek had been the first to visit the United States; he stayed for fifteen months on his own initiative and without external funding. These members of the fourth generation of the Austrian school now pursued their habilitation at the University of Vienna in order to acquire a readership (*venia docendi*) in economics.

Even with regard to the position of Austrian economics within the German-language community, there was room for optimism that the resistance from what still remained of the German Historical school would be overcome. The situation of the Verein für Sozialpolitik at the end of the 1920s was symptomatic. The Verein, founded in 1873 and thereafter the primary association of all German-speaking economists, had long been dominated by the adherents of the historicist tradition of Gustav von Schmoller and his successors, yet recently a countermovement of economists of a more theoretical orientation had developed.[2] This group, sometimes labeled the 'German Ricardians' and including economists of a liberal as well as of a socialist orientation,[3] for a time also entertained close contact with economists of the Austrian school. At the 1928 Zurich meeting of the Verein it appeared that eventually these theoretical economists would set the agenda. In the general session on business cycle research the theorists dominated the scene, and for the adherents of a monetary theory of the business cycle, and in particular of the variant advanced by Mises, this event marked the peak of their reception in Germany.[4] Thus there seemed ample justification for the younger Austrians to look to the future with some hope for a university career or at least for some sort of employment within their field.

However, at the same time to the perceptive observer, signals were mount-

---

[2] Cf. Janssen, *Nationalökonomie*, section 2.1.

[3] Janssen (ibid., p. 35) lists as its members, among others, Alexander and Hanns-Joachim Rüstow, Walter Eucken, Albert Hahn, Friedrich Lutz, and Wilhelm Röpke, as well as Gerhard Colm, Adolf Löwe, Emil Lederer, and Hans Neisser. The reference to Ricardo evokes a model-theoretic, deductive approach to economic theory that would have made him an obvious adversary of the German Historical school. For a slightly different characterisation of the 'Ricardians', cf. F. A. Hayek, "The Rediscovery of Freedom: Personal Recollections", in *The Fortunes of Liberalism*, pp. 187–88.

[4] For the reports and proceedings of the Zurich meeting see *Schriften des Vereins für Sozialpolitik*, vol. 173, part 2, *Beiträge zur Wirtschaftstheorie, Konjunkturforschung und Konjunkturtheorie*, ed. Karl Diehl (Munich and Leipzig: Duncker and Humblot, 1928); and *Schriften*, vol. 175, *Verhandlungen des Vereins für Sozialpolitik in Zürich 1928. Wandlungen des Kapitalismus. Auslandsanleihen. Kredit und Konjunktur*, ed. Franz Boese (Munich and Leipzig: Duncker and Humblot, 1929).

ing of the more sinister events to come. A case in point was the situation in the faculty of law and economics at the University of Vienna. The responsibility for the decisions affecting the subject of economics, such as concerning habilitations or the filling of vacant chairs, rested on the faculty as a whole, which beside the economists included sociologists, but predominantly professors in the diverse fields of law. Without being able to do justice to the various shades of contemporary Austrian conservatism—ranging from (and overlapping among) Catholic conservatives and those still loyal to the Habsburg monarchy to German nationalists and propagators of the *Anschluss*, the union with the German *Reich*—the members of the faculty were as a rule conservatives of some sort, by and large hostile towards liberalism (and socialism),[5] and many of them anti-Semitic. There existed only three chairs in economics within the faculty. Mayer, after having prevailed over both Mises and Schumpeter, had become Wieser's successor and the single heir to the Austrian tradition within the University of Vienna. However, his achievements in science as well as in academic politics were soon found wanting. Moreover, he was eager to differentiate his strand of Austrian economics from the positions represented by Mises and many of the younger generation.[6] With Schumpeter leaving in 1925 for Bonn, it was Mises who finally acquired the leadership of the school in the interwar period, at least in matters of theory and of actual economic policy-making, despite Mayer's prestigious position at the university.

Yet, in issues of academic politics the younger generation still had to address Mayer, such as for his support in mentoring their habilitations. The habilitation proceedings themselves were becoming ever more difficult. The reason lay in the personalities of the other two economists who occupied chairs in the faculty. The first one was Othmar Spann, who derived his rather idiosyncratic approach of universalism from German romanticism, in particular from Adam Müller, and who excelled in his enmity towards liberalism, democracy, and anything he considered modernist stuff.[7] Predictably, he opposed any of the habilitations for which economists close to the Austrian school applied. Moreover, at the time in question the reissue of the *Zeitschrift* had already sparked a bitter conflict between Spann and Mayer only to be settled with the outright

---

[5] Both Hayek's and Robbins's claims that the faculty would have been more ready to accommodate to a candidate with socialist than with liberal leanings is certainly incorrect for the second half of the 1920s; cf. Lionel Robbins, *Autobiography of an Economist* (London: Macmillan, 1971), p. 107, and *Hayek on Hayek*, p. 59. In fact, Hans Kelsen, the preeminent legal theorist, was in 1919 the last with a close relationship to the Socialist Party to be appointed to a chair in this faculty.

[6] For some time, at least until 1930, Morgenstern and Rosenstein-Rodan may be considered with some justification to have been disciples of Mayer.

[7] Cf. Spann's notorious attack on individualism and its consequences in *Der Wahre Staat: Vorlesungen über Abbruch und Neubau der Gesellschaft* (1921), reprinted as vol. 5 (5th ed., 1972) of the *Othmar Spann-Gesamtausgabe* (Graz: Akademische Druck- und Verlagsanstalt).

elimination of Spann from the editorial board.[8] The other person was Ferdinand Degenfeld-Schonburg, a conservative economic historian and from a scientific point of a view a nonentity. Yet, in matters concerning the chairs in economics, in order to establish a majority within the faculty Mayer had to win over Degenfeld. Indeed, Mayer regularly succeeded in persuading Degenfeld to approve the habilitation of Austrian liberals provided they were not Jewish, and in return economists of a more conservative stance were habilitated, too. Nevertheless, the habilitations of Haberler and Morgenstern in 1928 were anything but easy. In both cases Mayer accomplished by some manoeuvring a majority within the faculty to counter the opposition of Spann, yet with regard to Morgenstern, Spann was able to delay the necessary confirmation by the Ministry of Education by interventions and intrigues for almost a year, until April 1929. At the same time followers of Spann's universalism or of some variety of Catholic social teaching (for example, Walter Heinrich in 1928, and Josef Dobretsberger in 1929) were able to manage their habilitations more swiftly. In the years following, Machlup and Rosenstein-Rodan were forced to surrender in the face of insurmountable obstacles for Jews hoping to secure habilitation.[9] These experiences foreshadowed the dismal prospects for economists associated with the Austrian school applying for vacant chairs within the German-language area. Haberler and Morgenstern tried, but did not get beyond becoming listed for professorships in Prague and Königsberg, and Königsberg and the Vienna Hochschule für Welthandel, respectively, where eventually other candidates were appointed. In Austria in the course of the next several years economists of little distinction like Dobretsberger (in Graz) or Heinrich and Richard Kerschagl (at the Welthandel) became tenured as (extraordinary) professors, but no one close to the Austrian school did.[10]

Now how did Hayek fare in all this turmoil? He had received his doctorates from the University of Vienna, the first in law and then a second one in political science (*Staatswissenschaften*). Although very early as a student he had been for a short spell under the influence of Spann, he soon turned to Wieser as his teacher, whose impact is clearly visible in Hayek's thesis on the problem of imputation.[11] After Hayek had left university, Mises helped him to obtain

---

[8] Eventually, Reisch and Schüller became the co-editors, with Mayer, while the day-to-day work of the managing editor was to be placed upon Morgenstern (and for a while Rosenstein).

[9] Anti-Semitism had already played a role as a weapon against Morgenstern, as rumours had been spread of his allegedly non-Aryan origin. Cf., e.g., Rosenstein-Rodan to Morgenstern, undated [July? 1928], in Oskar Morgenstern Papers, Rare Book, Manuscript, and Special Collections Library, Duke University, box 3.

[10] Mises, Strigl, and Morgenstern ended up as 'extraordinary professors', too, yet in their case this was just a title without a remuneration.

[11] Hayek's thesis has been preserved in the Friedrich A. von Hayek Papers, box 104, folder 27, Hoover Institution Archives, Stanford University.

a job in a public office (*Abrechnungsamt*) to earn a living, and indeed Mises became an important influence on Hayek's economics.[12] In 1923–24 Hayek embarked on a trip to the United States, where he became acquainted with American economics, in particular with the type of institutionalism propagated by Wesley Clair Mitchell. Back in Vienna, he discussed this type of theory, including its relation to monetary policy, rather critically in a two-part article.[13] It was Mises who, in 1927, was responsible for Hayek's appointment as the first director of the Institute for Business Cycle Research. Although the Institute started on a rather small scale, during Hayek's directorship it became possible to hire additional personnel; thus at the end of 1928 Morgenstern joined Hayek, whom he was eventually to succeed as director in 1931.[14]

Concerning the Institute, Hayek's position was somewhat awkward.[15] For the Institute's task was not prescribed as a scientific one, but as the practical one of providing information and decision-making support to the public, in particular, serving businessmen and policy makers. In its emphasis on practical business cycle research, the Austrian Institute followed the precedent set by institutes for economic research like the Harvard Economic Service, and in Germany the recently founded institutes in Berlin and Kiel. Thus Hayek, and later on Morgenstern, was primarily occupied with the writing of monthly bulletins (the *Monatsberichte*), which included statistical tables arranged in accordance with the classification of the famous Harvard barometer. Although the Institute refrained from making its own predictions, it regularly reprinted those of the Harvard Service. However, while compelled to comply with the demands of the public in this regard, both Hayek and Morgenstern expressed their scepticism towards an empirically based type of practical business cycle research. In his habilitation thesis Hayek devoted a whole chapter to defending the primacy of theory, and he rejected "the oft-repeated assertion that statistical examination of the Trade Cycle should be undertaken without any theoretical prejudice" as "always based on self-deception".[16] From a different

[12] On Hayek and Mises cf. the editor's introduction to F. A. Hayek, *The Fortunes of Liberalism*, pp. 9–13.

[13] F. A. Hayek, "Die Währungspolitik der Vereinigten Staaten seit der Überwindung der Krise von 1920", *Zeitschrift für Volkswirtschaft und Sozialpolitik*, n.s., vol. 5, nos. 1 and 2, 1925, pp. 25–63 and 254–317, translated as "Monetary Policy in the United States after the Recovery from the Crisis of 1920", and reprinted as chapter 2 of *Good Money, Part I: The New World*, ed. Stephen Kresge, vol. 5 (1999) of *The Collected Works of F. A. Hayek*.

[14] The Institute resided in the same building as the Vienna Chamber of Commerce, so Hayek and Morgenstern were close to Mises, the Chamber's secretary, and to Haberler, who worked there as a librarian for a while.

[15] Cf. for the following Hansjoerg Klausinger, "Hayek on Practical Business Cycle Research: A Note", in *Austrian Economics in Transition: From Carl Menger to Friedrich Hayek*, ed. Harald Hagemann, Tamotsu Nishizawa, and Yukihiro Ikeda (London: Palgrave Macmillan, 2010), pp. 218–34.

[16] F. A. Hayek, *Monetary Theory and the Trade Cycle* (London: Cape, 1933), p. 38, reprinted in this volume, p. 72.

perspective Morgenstern, too, voiced criticism of economic predictions, maintaining that successful prediction was in principle impossible because of the inevitable feedback from predictions to actual behaviour.[17] Significantly, when the publisher Julius Springer in 1931 floated the idea of introducing a *Journal of Business Cycle Research* (*Zeitschrift für Konjunkturforschung*), both Hayek and Morgenstern rejected the proposal insofar as such a journal might transgress the narrow boundaries of statistics and intrude into the field of economics proper. Before this project came to naught, it was even suggested that Hayek be placed on the editorial board in order to prevent such transgressions of statisticians into economic theory.[18] In this respect, the Austrian Institute's focus on the necessity of theoretical foundations for any fruitful research on business cycles differed sharply from the approach as practiced in the Berlin Institute under the auspices of Ernst Wagemann, which was much closer to the tradition of the German Historical school and in fact the main target of the Austrians' attacks. What an irony of history that it was the same Wagemann, who after the *Anschluss* in 1938 would be commissioned with the task of directing what then was to remain of the Austrian Institute.

Thus with his directorship Hayek had finally arrived at a position that for some time at least allowed him to immerse himself deeper into economic theory. His first venture was a theoretical investigation into the fields of money and the cycle that would finally result in his habilitation.[19] In the next years this broadened into a wide-ranging and ambitious project inquiring into the theory of a money economy and the proper goals for monetary policy. Its basic idea had been outlined before, during Hayek's visit in the United States, and is captured in the title of a planned but unrealised PhD thesis: "Is the function of money consistent with an artificial stabilisation of its purchasing power?"[20] Work on this inquiry progressed for several years, possibly from 1925 onwards up to 1929. At the core of it lay the development of the notion of intertemporal equilibrium as a special case of 'static theory' and its application to a monetary capital–using economy. In 1928 Hayek's inquiry culminated in a path-breaking first statement of the concept of intertemporal equilibrium, which, even if incomplete, still stands out as a unique achievement,

---

[17] Morgenstern considered his famous Holmes-Moriarty paradox an effective refutation of the possibility of economic predictions; cf. Oskar Morgenstern, *Wirtschaftsprognose: Eine Untersuchung ihrer Voraussetzungen und Möglichkeiten* (Vienna: Springer, 1928), p. 98, and "Vollkommene Voraussicht und wirtschaftliches Gleichgewicht", *Zeitschrift für Nationalökonomie*, vol. 6, no. 3, 1935, pp. 343–44, translated as "Perfect Foresight and Economic Equilibrium", trans. Frank H. Knight, in *Selected Economic Writings of Oskar Morgenstern*, ed. Andrew Schotter (New York: New York University Press, 1976), pp. 173–74.

[18] See Morgenstern's letter to Otto Lange, director of the Vienna branch of the publishing house Springer, June 18, 1931, Morgenstern Papers, box 6.

[19] The nucleus of his theory of the cycle, inspired by Mises, can be found already in 1925. See Hayek, "Monetary Policy in the United States", pp. 105–6n.

[20] Cf. the outline in the Hayek Papers, Incremental Material, box 104, folder 26.

quite apart from its importance for his theory of the cycle.[21] In the same year, he concluded a contract with the German publisher Gustav Fischer in Jena on a planned book, to be titled *Geldtheoretische Untersuchungen* (Investigations into monetary theory), from which the article had been drawn.[22] The unfinished typescript of the first part (of three planned), on price formation in a money economy, has been preserved among Hayek's papers; even though it contains some revisions, it had not yet been brought into the final form for publication.[23] The main thrust of the existing chapters lies in the integration of the elements of time, money, and capital within an equilibrium framework, yet with a distinct focus on the complications immanent in the adjustment processes, which may (or may not) tend towards equilibrium.

Hayek remained occupied with this project well into 1929, although in parallel he directed his efforts towards his habilitation. In 1928 he had presented at the Zurich meeting of the Verein für Sozialpolitik a report and a contribution to the discussion on the relationship between monetary theory and business cycle theory. These were to become the first four chapters of his habilitation thesis, *Geldtheorie und Konjunkturtheorie*, published in 1929.[24] In spite of the difficult environment, pointed out above, Hayek and his mentor Mayer were able to overcome the usual obstacles to his habilitation. Spann again had been the main adversary. Yet his diatribe in the faculty meeting proved to be in vain after Mayer had persuaded the rather reluctant Degenfeld, who in the

---

[21] F. A. Hayek, "Das intertemporale Gleichgewichtssystem der Preise und die Bewegungen des 'Geldwertes'", *Weltwirtschaftliches Archiv*, vol. 28, July 1928, pp. 33–76, translated as "Intertemporal Price Equilibrium and Movements in the Value of Money", chapter 5 of F. A. Hayek, *Good Money, Part I: The New World*. For an evaluation in the context of modern developments cf. Murray Milgate, "On the Origin of the Notion of 'Intertemporal Equilibrium'", *Economica*, n.s., vol. 46, February 1979, pp. 1–10.

[22] Cf. Hayek to Morgenstern, March 16 and October 12, 1928, Morgenstern Papers, box 3. For a more detailed account see Hansjoerg Klausinger, "Hayek's *Geldtheoretische Untersuchungen*: New Insights from a 1925–29 Typescript", *European Journal of the History of Economic Thought*, vol. 18, October 2011, pp. 579–600.

[23] Cf. Hayek Papers, box 105, folders 1–4. A translation of the previously unpublished typescript appears as "Investigations into Monetary Theory", chapter 1 of *Business Cycles, Part II*, ed. Hansjoerg Klausinger, vol. 8 (2012) of *The Collected Works of F. A. Hayek*.

[24] The report (F. A. Hayek, "Einige Bemerkungen über das Verhältnis der Geldtheorie zur Konjunkturtheorie", in *Schriften des Vereins für Sozialpolitik*, vol. 173, part 2, pp. 247–94) is almost identical to the first three chapters of *Geldtheorie und Konjunkturtheorie*. Beiträge zur Konjunkturforschung, vol. 1, ed. Österreichisches Institut für Konjunkturforschung (Vienna: Springer, 1929; reprinted, Salzburg: Neugebauer, 1976). The discussion ("Redebeitrag", in *Schriften des Vereins für Sozialpolitik*, vol. 175, pp. 369–74) is a summary of its fourth chapter; the fifth chapter was added afterwards. Hayek's *Geldtheorie* was translated by Nicholas Kaldor and Honoria R. M. Croome as *Monetary Theory and the Trade Cycle*; there is also an independent English translation of Hayek's report as "Some Remarks on the Relation of Monetary Theory to Business Cycle Theory", trans. Vincent Homolka, in *Business Cycle Theory: Selected Texts 1860–1939*, vol. 3: *Monetary Theories of the Business Cycle*, ed. Harald Hagemann (London: Pickering and Chatto, 2002), pp. 161–97.

end acquiesced in voting for Hayek although his report on the thesis was less than enthusiastic.[25] In June 1929 the proceedings were concluded by Hayek's habilitation lecture, and in July the *venia docendi* for political economy and statistics was formally conferred. It was this lecture that after it had been published in the *Zeitschrift*[26] drew the attention of Lionel Robbins, just appointed head of the economics department at the London School of Economics and one of the rare instances of a British economist well versed in the German language. The lecture eventually would become pivotal in earning Hayek an invitation of crucial consequence for his career. First, however, in December 1929, another prestigious offer would arrive. The publisher Oskar Siebeck invited Hayek to author the final, still-missing volume on money and credit in the famous series of the *Grundriß der Sozialökonomie*.[27] This motivated Hayek to abandon his work on the "Investigations", the theoretical difficulties of which had grown out of proportion anyway. So although we still find clippings of the "Widersinn des Sparens" article pasted into the typescript and though there are references in Hayek's *Geldtheorie* to a more comprehensive work on monetary theory intended, the evidence for further activities on the project subsides after 1929. Indeed, in the following year Hayek spent much of his effort in preparing the *Grundriß* volume, in particular its first part dealing with the history of English monetary policy, on which he was able to draw later when he arrived at the British scene.

In these years, a main object of Hayek's activities was to qualify for an economics chair at a university. Although some hopeful prospects emerged in this respect, none ended in success. In 1929 Hayek had been placed on a short

[25] For the documents on Hayek's habilitation including both Mayer's and Degenfeld's reports, see Österreichisches Staatsarchiv, Bundesministerium für Unterricht (GZ. 29620, 29/1, July 31, 1929). Mayer's report was unequivocally positive although he did not concur with Hayek's main thesis of the necessarily monetary nature of cyclical fluctuations. In contrast, Degenfeld criticised the thesis for its brevity and lack of novelty, yet justified his positive report by referring to Hayek's other scientific contributions.

[26] F. A. Hayek, "Gibt es einen 'Widersinn des Sparens'?", *Zeitschrift für Nationalökonomie*, vol. 1, November 1929, pp. 387–429, translated by Nicholas Kaldor and Georg Tugendhat as "The 'Paradox' of Saving", *Economica*, no. 32, May 1931, pp. 125–69, reprinted as chapter 2, *Contra Keynes and Cambridge: Essays, Correspondence*, ed. Bruce Caldwell, vol. 9 (1995) of *The Collected Works of F. A. Hayek*; a version with minor revisions had been reprinted as an appendix to *Profits, Interest and Investment. And Other Essays on the Theory of Industrial Fluctuations* (London: Routledge, 1939).

[27] Intended as part 2 of volume 4 of *Grundriß der Sozialökonomik* (Tübingen: Mohr, 1914 and later). Among others, Max Weber, Friedrich Wieser and Joseph Schumpeter had contributed monographs to the *Grundriß*. On the Siebeck offer cf. the entries in Morgenstern's diary (December 27, 1929, and June 11, 1930, Morgenstern Papers, box 13). Four chapters from the *Grundriß* manuscript have since been translated and reprinted in part 3 of *The Trend of Economic Thinking: Essays on Political Economists and Economic History*, ed. W. W. Bartley III and Stephen Kresge, vol. 3 (1991) of *The Collected Works of F. A. Hayek*.

list for a professorship at the University of Königsberg,[28] and in 1930 another opportunity opened up when a new position for an extraordinary professor had been created at the Vienna Hochschule für Welthandel. In June 1931 the faculty agreed on a proposal to the ministry listing Strigl, Hayek, and Morgenstern, ranked in this order. Hayek, because of his new affiliation with the London School of Economics (LSE), soon dropped out, yet after two more years of delay and negotiation Heinrich, the disciple of Spann, was first moved onto the list and finally appointed in 1933. However, the experience of Vienna as, still, constituting a centre that attracted many well-known economists from abroad may have brought some consolation. To name but a few, those visitors included Dennis Robertson, John Hicks, Frank Knight, Jacob Viner, and Adolf Löwe. Among the economics students visiting Vienna was also one who would become important for Hayek in various respects, namely, Nicholas Kaldor. Kaldor came from London to Vienna in May 1931 to spend several months working on his doctoral thesis on the economics of the Danubian states, and he also participated in a seminar jointly held by Haberler, Morgenstern, and Hayek. In addition, at this time Kaldor was just preparing his translation of Hayek's "Widersinn des Sparens" and already considering that of *Geldtheorie*.[29]

The crucial turning point in Hayek's early career came with the invitation to deliver a lecture series at LSE in February 1931. Although formally offered by its director, William H. Beveridge, Hayek most probably owed the invitation to a suggestion by Lionel Robbins. Robbins may also have been the source of Kaldor's plans to translate Hayek.[30] When the invitation arrived in 1930, Hayek immediately grasped the significance of the occasion, abandoned the other projects that had occupied him, and concentrated on working out the lectures. In particular, he put his work on the *Grundriß* aside and instead of resorting to the tedious analysis already developed in the "Investigations", he opted for the alternative of a radical simplification of his approach.[31] This provided him with the means of a suggestive and, as it turned out, immensely successful framework.

---

[28] Thus, with Haberler and Morgenstern, Hayek was one of three Austrian economists listed for a chair at Königsberg, yet failing to be appointed. These listings were due to the support provided by Wilhelm Vleugels (1893–1942), a former pupil of Wieser and Mayer, and from 1928 professor of economics at Königsberg. Cf. Vleugels's correspondence with Morgenstern, in Morgenstern Papers, box 4, folder: Correspondence, 1930–1932, S–Z.

[29] For more on Kaldor's role as a friendly-turned-hostile commentator on Hayek's writings, cf. the editor's introduction to F. A. Hayek, *Business Cycles, Part II*.

[30] Cf. on this Susan Howson, "Keynes and the LSE Economists", *Journal of the History of Economic Thought*, vol. 31, September 2009, p. 272, and personal communication.

[31] Cf. his retrospective account in *Hayek on Hayek*, pp. 77–78.

The recollections of the audiences of Hayek's lectures are somewhat disparate, perhaps due to the operation of the genius loci. Hayek gave his lectures at LSE at the end of January 1931, and a few days before, he presented a highly condensed version as a talk to the Marshall Society at Cambridge.[32] Despite the shortcomings due to Hayek's less-than-perfect command of the English language and the strangeness of his Austrian approach to a British audience, the lectures at LSE have been remembered by a variety of sources as "a sensation".[33] Reactions were different, and hostile, in Cambridge, possibly foreshadowing the emergence of the alternative vision of John Maynard Keynes.[34] Soon more hostilities were to follow. With some stylistic help from Robbins, the lecture series became *Prices and Production*,[35] certainly Hayek's most successful book of technical economics. Back in Vienna Hayek had just time to prepare a revised German version,[36] before he was to receive from Beveridge the offer of a one-year visiting professorship at LSE, starting in September 1931. This position became permanent in 1932 with his appointment to the Tooke chair in economics and statistics.[37] When Hayek arrived in Great Britain, the monograph based on the lectures had made him world-famous in one stroke, and due to his first contributions to the British debate, shortly after Britain's going off gold, he was soon perceived as a counterpoise to Keynes and Cambridge. This impression was reinforced by Hayek's meticulous and sharply critical two-part review of Keynes's *Treatise*,[38] which gave rise to counterattacks by Keynes himself and Piero Sraffa, turning from the defence of the *Treatise* to a severe attack on *Prices and Production*.[39] When in 1933 *Monetary Theory and the Trade Cycle*, the English translation of *Geldtheorie*, was published,

[32] F. A. Hayek, "The Purchasing Power of the Consumer and the Depression". This previously unpublished lecture appears as chapter 2 of F. A. Hayek, *Business Cycles, Part II*.

[33] Robbins, *Autobiography*, p. 129; cf. also Ronald Coase, *Essays on Economics and Economists* (Chicago: University of Chicago Press, 1994), p. 19.

[34] Cf. the almost identical accounts by Joan Robinson and Richard F. Kahn: Robinson, *Contributions to Modern Economics* (Oxford: Basil Blackwell, 1978), pp. 2–3; and Kahn, *The Making of Keynes' General Theory* (Cambridge: Cambridge University Press, 1984), pp. 181–82.

[35] F. A. Hayek, *Prices and Production* (London: Routledge, 1931; 2nd ed. rev., 1935), reprinted in this volume.

[36] F. A. Hayek, *Preise und Produktion* (Vienna: Springer, 1931; reprinted, 1976; Düsseldorf: Verlag Wirtschaft und Finanzen, 1995).

[37] Earlier in 1930 and 1931 Hubert Henderson and Jacob Viner had declined offers to be appointed to the Tooke chair (Howson, personal communication).

[38] John Maynard Keynes, *A Treatise on Money*, 2 vols. (London: Macmillan, 1930), reprinted as vols. 5 and 6 (1971) of *The Collected Writings of John Maynard Keynes*, ed. Austin Robinson and Donald Moggridge (London: Macmillan; Cambridge: Cambridge University Press).

[39] On Hayek's debates with Keynes and his disciples see the editor's introduction to F. A. Hayek, *Contra Keynes and Cambridge* (where also the contributions by Hayek, Keynes, and Sraffa referred to above have been reprinted).

Hayek's reputation as a technical economist probably had reached its climax, yet—thanks to Sraffa's devastating criticism and Hayek's not overall fortunate response—the first signals of decline might have been envisaged, too.

The Equilibrium Approach to Money and the Cycle

As has been widely, if not always approvingly, noticed, the basic tenet for interpreting Hayek's writings on money and the cycle in the interwar period is their firm foundation on an equilibrium approach, which served as the benchmark to which cyclical movements are to be related. This section addresses Hayek's grappling with the equilibrium framework as the point of departure for the analysis of money and the cycle. This approach is pertinent to all of Hayek's work in this field, yet in differing degrees of emphasis and sophistication: while the explicit defence of equilibrium analysis and the ambitious attempt to integrate time and money into this framework dominate Hayek's early writings, in *Prices and Production* he embraced a simplified, or short-cut, version, yet subsequently turned back to these foundational issues as a part of his capital theory project.[40]

Hayek's examination—and eventually his defence—of equilibrium analysis derived from the German-language debate on the proper methods for business cycle research, where both the relevance of a *theoretical* approach in general and an *equilibrium* approach in particular were at stake. Accordingly, Hayek's *Monetary Theory and the Trade Cycle* opens with a critical examination of a series of contributions by Adolf Löwe, who unlike many of his German contemporaries did not question the use of theory and as such was a most serious challenger of the equilibrium approach to dynamic analysis.[41] Put simply, Löwe's main criticism, outlined in his 1926 article, pointed to the contradiction between the static character of the equilibrium system and the intrinsi-

---

[40] For a more thorough discussion of the continuity in Hayek's thought, cf. the editor's introduction to F. A. Hayek, *Business Cycles, Part II*, pp. 24–43.

[41] Cf. Adolf Löwe, "Der gegenwärtige Stand der Konjunkturforschung in Deutschland", in *Die Wirtschaftswissenschaft nach dem Kriege, Festgabe für Lujo Brentano zum 80. Geburtstag*, vol. 2, *Der Stand der Forschung*, ed. Moritz Julius Bonn and Melchior Palyi (Munich and Leipzig: Duncker and Humblot, 1925), pp. 331–77; "Wie ist Konjunkturtheorie überhaupt möglich?", *Weltwirtschaftliches Archiv*, vol. 24, October 1926, pp. 165–97 (translated as "How Is Business Cycle Theory Possible At All?", *Structural Change and Economic Dynamics*, vol. 8, June 1997, pp. 245–70, reprinted in *Business Cycle Theory: Selected Texts 1860–1939*, vol. 4: *Equilibrium and the Business Cycle*, ed. Hagemann, pp. 3–30); "Über den Einfluß monetärer Faktoren auf den Konjunkturzyklus", in *Schriften des Vereins für Sozialpolitik*, vol. 173, part 2, pp. 355–70 (translated as "On the Influence of Monetary Factors on the Business Cycle", in *Business Cycle Theory: Selected Texts 1860–1939*, vol. 3: ed. Hagemann, pp. 199–211); and "Redebeitrag", in *Schriften des Vereins für Sozialpolitik*, vol. 175, pp. 335–47.

cally dynamic nature of the business cycle. In specifying the precise meaning of 'static' and 'dynamic' as referring to "two structurally distinct *systems of motion*",[42] he follows Schumpeter, who had characterised the movements typical for statics and dynamics as 'adaptation' (or 'adjustment') and 'development'.[43] According to Löwe, the static (or equilibrium) approach interprets the motion of the economy through time as an adjustment towards a predetermined state of rest.[44] This is, however, not a typical feature of the cycle, which by reproducing itself does not exhibit a state to be characterised as 'normal' or 'equilibrium'. Löwe's suggested solution then is to free dynamic analysis from all static elements and to replace equilibrium with the cyclical motion of the economy as the appropriate framework of analysis. Specifically, he identifies technical progress as the driving force of the cycle responsible for transforming the 'closed system' of equilibrium economics into an 'open system'.[45]

Hayek accepts the criticism that an economic system exhibiting mere 'adaptation' is incompatible with the explanation of the business cycle, yet rejects the solution proposed by Löwe. Rather Hayek allows for dynamic features by introducing money as the crucial element for explaining those movements away from equilibrium that are incompatible with the static approach. Yet, what is most important for an understanding of Hayek's writings of this period is that in his notion of equilibrium and in his terminology he sticks closely to the terms as used by Löwe, and thus indirectly by Schumpeter.[46] Accordingly, Hayek explicitly equates the "logic of equilibrium theory" with that of "static theory",[47] which he identifies as "the main object of pure economics" or of

---

[42] Löwe, "Der gegenwärtige Stand", p. 355n.1, cf. also p. 357. In the following, if not otherwise indicated, all translations from German-language sources are my own.

[43] Cf. Joseph A. Schumpeter, *Theorie der wirtschaftlichen Entwicklung*, 2nd ed. (Munich and Leipzig: Duncker and Humblot, 1926), pp. 95–96, translated as *The Theory of Economic Development*, trans. Redvers Opie (Cambridge, MA: Harvard University Press, 1934), p. 63. In this regard Schumpeter's and Löwe's definitions go beyond the traditional ones that distinguished between statics as an analysis that abstracts from time and dynamics as that of any movements in time; cf., e.g., John Bates Clark, *The Distribution of Wealth: A Theory of Wages, Interest and Profits* (New York: Macmillan, 1899; reprinted, New York: Kelley, 1965), chapter 3.

[44] In characterising the "static system", Löwe ("On the Influence of Monetary Factors", p. 16) explicitly used the term "stability" for describing its "tendency towards equilibrium".

[45] For the significance of Löwe's challenge within the German debate cf. Harald Hagemann, "Hayek and the Kiel School: Some Reflections on the German Debate on Business Cycles in the Late 1920s and Early 1930s", in *The Economics of F. A. Hayek*, vol. 1, *Money and Business Cycles*, ed. Marina Colonna and Harald Hagemann (Aldershot: Edward Elgar, 1994), pp. 101–20; and Christian Gehrke, "Introduction to Adolf Löwe's 'How is business cycle theory possible at all?'", *Structural Change and Economic Dynamics*, vol. 8, June 1997, pp. 233–44.

[46] Hayek's notion of equilibrium appears to originate from Walras as mediated in the German literature through the works of Wieser, Schumpeter, and Cassel; cf. the editor's introduction to F. A. Hayek, *Business Cycles, Part II*, p. 31.

[47] *Monetary Theory and the Trade Cycle*, this volume, p. 75.

"pure analysis"; and he considers the "tendency towards equilibrium"[48] as the most important characteristic of static theory. Thus, although he speaks of static theory, he does not refer thereby to the timeless equilibrium of statics in the usual sense, but to equilibrium over time to which the economy would return after any disturbance.

This static equilibrium in time need not even be that of a stationary or steadily progressive economy.[49] Rather, already in 1928, Hayek had developed the notion of *intertemporal equilibrium*. Such an intertemporal equilibrium, although applying to "an economic system extended through time", he describes as "static": "All that needs to be assumed for such a static equilibrium to occur is that the wants and the means of production existing at every point in time are known to the individual economic subjects at the time they frame their economic plan for the period as a whole",[50] that is, this kind of equilibrium requires the assumption of correct anticipations.[51] Hayek carries over this notion of intertemporal equilibrium into his analysis in *Monetary Theory and the Trade Cycle*; for example, his reference to the "static course of events"[52] is to intertemporal equilibrium as equilibrium over time, or to what today would be called 'equilibrium dynamics'.

Thus, following Hayek the domain of static theory is the analysis of an economy through time in its movement along, or after a change of data in its immediate approach to, an equilibrium time path. This analysis conforms to the procedure of 'pure economic theory', whose subject is a non-monetary economy, that is, one by definition free from any possibly disturbing influences of money. Hayek denotes such an economy by the term *Naturalwirtschaft*, that is, literally, 'natural economy' (or, as translated in *Monetary Theory and the Trade Cycle*, 'barter economy').[53] The idea of such an equivalence between the equi-

---

[48] Ibid., this volume, p. 88. Cf. also the reference to "the static system as presented by pure equilibrium theory" (ibid., p. 141).

[49] The notion of a steadily progressive economy, where all the factors of production are increasing at a uniform rate, had become common in contemporary literature; cf., e.g., Gustav Cassel, *The Theory of Social Economy*, rev. ed. (London: Benn; New York: Harcourt, Brace and Co., 1932; reprinted, New York: Kelley, 1967), pp. 32–41. A stationary economy is, of course, a special case of the steadily progressive economy, where all the factors of production (and all the other data of the economy) remain unchanged so that the economy just reproduces itself over time.

[50] Hayek, "Intertemporal Price Equilibrium", p. 191.

[51] Of course, the same is tacitly assumed in the analysis of a stationary state.

[52] *Monetary Theory and the Trade Cycle*, this volume, p. 112; on the translation see the editor's note, ibid., p. 116n.41.

[53] Wicksell had introduced the notion of "natural economy" as distinct from a money economy in *Geldzins und Güterpreise: Eine Studie über die den Tauschwert des Geldes bestimmenden Ursachen* (Jena: Fischer, 1898; reprinted, Aalen: Scientia, 1968), p. 143, translated as *Interest and Prices: A Study of the Causes Regulating the Value of Money*, trans. Richard F. Kahn (London: Macmillan, 1936; reprinted, New York: Kelley, 1965; Auburn, AL: Ludwig von Mises Institute, 2007), p. 156.

librium of static theory and that ruling in a barter economy as described by pure economics is attested by numerous passages, e.g., when Hayek points out that "the equilibrium inter-relationships of barter economy . . . must always be assumed by 'pure economics.'"[54]

Hayek's solution for integrating the analysis of the business cycle into an equilibrium framework consists then in distinguishing the domain of 'dynamics' from that of 'statics', and correspondingly the money economy from the barter economy of pure economics. Ideally a money economy could be imagined so that for given real economic data, its equilibrium (with regard to real characteristics) coincided with that of a barter economy; to such a money economy the laws of statics would apply, and money could be said not to exert an influence of its own, that is, to be neutral.[55] However, due to money ever being prone to generate 'one-sided' changes in aggregate demand, not compensated for by changes in aggregate supply, money generically will become non-neutral.[56] Such a non-neutral money economy will deviate crucially from the evolution of an economy described by the laws of statics: After a change in data it will not exhibit a tendency towards equilibrium, but rather—in a 'dynamic' fashion—movements away from it, which will turn out unsustainable and thus must eventually be reversed.[57] It is such movements that Hayek associates with the business cycle, and the ultimate reversals with crisis and depression.

Although suggestive, these relationships between statics and dynamics, intertemporal equilibrium and disequilibrium, and the barter and the money economy, even in Hayek' own view were all in need of more elaborate analytical underpinnings, something that he had attempted to provide in "Investigations".[58] The crucial outcome of this enquiry was the distinction between the immediate adjustment towards equilibrium of the static system and the complicated patterns caused by the successive reactions outside statics. At best, in a dynamic system equilibrium will be arrived at asymptotically. Yet, as Hayek notes, asymptotic adjustment means that indeed equilibrium will never be arrived at in finite time and, more importantly, that the adjustment path with all its imponderables may influence the end point to which the process converges. As most of the analysis in "Investigations" remained unfinished, it is not clear which conclusions Hayek eventually did draw from his exercises in dynamic analysis. In any case, his attempt at an analytical foundation for the

---

[54] *Monetary Theory and the Trade Cycle*, this volume, p. 102; see also *Prices and Production*, this volume, pp. 279–80, for a similar passage.

[55] The term 'neutrality' originated with Wicksell, *Interest and Prices*, p. 102, from where it was taken over by Hayek in *Monetary Theory and the Trade Cycle*, this volume, p. 107.

[56] Cf., e.g., F. A. Hayek, *Monetary Theory and the Trade Cycle*, this volume, pp. 103–4.

[57] Cf. ibid., p. 116.

[58] See above; cf. also for a fuller discussion of "Investigations" the editor's introduction to F. A. Hayek, *Business Cycles, Part II*.

application of an equilibrium framework to money and the cycle could not strictly justify some of the crucial theses put forward in *Monetary Theory and the Trade Cycle*. For example, the neutral-money economy is conspicuously absent from the "Investigations"—none of the types of money economies examined represented an exact counterpart to the static system, nor were violations of the tendency towards equilibrium restricted to the case of money.

In this regard, Hayek's quest for a proper model of a neutral-money economy came to a provisional conclusion when he contented himself with the definition of a barter economy that had been introduced by Johan Koopmans in 1933. Accordingly, the reference point for neutral money is

> the ideal type of a pure barter economy to which the laws of equilibrium theories apply . . . [whose object is] a *hypothetical*, and in reality unthinkable, state where *simultaneously* the frictions which prevent full equilibrium due to the lack of a generally accepted medium of exchange are assumed to be absent, as well as those specific changes resulting from the actual introduction of such a medium of exchange.[59]

In effect, Koopmans's solution *asserts* the existence of a neutral-money economy, yet stops short of specifying the formal conditions under which its existence could be established. Hayek was apparently ready to adopt Koopmans's suggestion and repeatedly referred to it approvingly, and henceforth he identified the reference norm of "the equilibrium theory developed under the assumption of barter"[60] with Koopmans's "ideal type". However, this weak foundation of a central concept of Hayek's theory made it vulnerable to the attacks of critics.

Next, we have to reconsider the conditions for neutrality. Hayek's early investigations into intertemporal equilibrium concentrated on the concrete mechanisms of (direct or indirect) exchange as causes of an economy's deviation from the course determined by static theory, but did not address specifically the interference of money and credit with the capital market and thus with the role of the rate of interest. Yet, when turning to the business cycle the interest rate became a vital element, to such an extent that eventually all other concerns about how and why a money economy might differ from the norm of static theory fell into the background.

[59] Johan G. Koopmans, "Zum Problem des Neutralen Geldes", in *Beiträge zur Geldtheorie*, ed. F. A. Hayek (Vienna: Springer, 1933; reprinted, Berlin, Heidelberg, and New York: Springer, 2007), pp. 228 and 230; emphasis in the original.

[60] Cf. F. A. Hayek, "Über 'neutrales Geld'", *Zeitschrift für Nationalökonomie*, vol. 4, October 1933, p. 659, translated as "On Neutral Money" and reprinted as chapter 6 of F. A. Hayek, *Good Money, Part I: The New World*.

Like Mises and other adherents of the monetary approach to the business cycle, Hayek draws on Wicksell's elaboration of the interest rate criterion for monetary equilibrium, that is, the equality between the natural and the money rate of interest. Here the definition of the money rate is straightforward, as the actual rate at which the banks are ready to lend. However, there are two conflicting approaches to the definition of the natural rate. In *Interest and Prices* Wicksell defines the natural rate as "the rate that would be determined by supply and demand if real capital goods were lent in kind" and, similarly, as "the rate of interest which would be determined by supply and demand if no use were made of money and all lending were effected in the form of real capital goods".[61] Yet in the *Lectures* Wicksell restates the definition as "the rate of interest at which the demand for loan-capital and the supply of savings correspond exactly to each other . . ."[62] Crucially, in the latter definition the reference to the fiction of transactions taking place in the absence of money is omitted. According to Hayek it is this latter version that ought to be preferred.[63]

Now how did this definition of the natural rate fit into Hayek's use of the barter economy, interpreted in the sense of Koopmans, as the reference for determining the neutrality of money? A consistent solution may proceed in two steps: First, in pure theory any set of real economic data determines an equilibrium of the barter economy, and there will be, as part of that equilibrium, a structure of (present and expected future) relative prices that secures the balance between investment demand and the supply of saving in the capital market.[64] Thus, in the first step this exercise still abstracts from the

[61] Wicksell, *Interest and Prices*, pp. xxv and 102.

[62] Wicksell, *Lectures on Political Economy*, vol. 2, *Money* (London: Routledge, 1935; reprinted, New York: Kelley, 1967; Auburn, AL: Ludwig von Mises Institute, 2007), p. 193.

[63] See *Monetary Theory and the Trade Cycle*, this volume, p. 151. Ludwig von Mises stayed closer to the former, in Hayek's view inferior, definition; cf. *Theorie des Geldes und der Umlaufsmittel*, 2nd ed. rev. (Munich and Leipzig: Duncker and Humblot, 1924), p. 364, translated as *The Theory of Money and Credit*, trans. Harold E. Batson (London: Cape, 1934; reprinted, Indianapolis: Liberty Classics, 1981), p. 393; and *Geldwertstabilisierung und Konjunkturpolitik* (Jena: Fischer, 1928), translated as "Monetary Stabilization and Cyclical Policy", trans. Bettina Bien Greaves, in Ludwig von Mises, *On the Manipulation of Money and Credit*, ed. Percy L. Greaves (New York: Free Market Books, 1978), p. 122.

[64] The idea of a capital market within an intertemporal system of barter may appear awkward. Yet, technically, there are two ways to save this construction: According to Böhm-Bawerk's approach, the saving in question is to be conceived as a subsistence fund, consisting of homogeneous consumers' goods, so that indeed at such a capital market saving and investment will meet *in natura*. Or, more in conformity with Hayek's approach, the transfer of purchasing power between present and future is effected by means of a 'security' denominated in commodity terms (with perfect foresight the concrete denomination is, of course, irrelevant). Evidently, both

existence of money and wholly conforms to the strictures of pure economic theory. Second, by the assumption of neutral money there will be an equilibrium of a money economy equivalent (that is, exhibiting the same relative prices and quantities) to that of the barter economy. Then, we can identify the (uniform) equilibrium rate of interest, expressed in terms of money, of this neutral-money economy as the 'natural rate' to which the actual money rate of interest must conform.

Hayek's presentation in *Monetary Theory and the Trade Cycle* on this point may be less than crystal clear, but such a two-step derivation of the equilibrium (or natural) rate of interest is at least implicit in his argument. He is well aware of the hypothetical character of the rate of interest as derived from equilibrium in the barter economy—he speaks of an *"imaginary"* or fictitious rate,[65] and of the moneyless economy as a "hypothetical system".[66] Furthermore, he clearly states that the relevant equilibrium rate, that is, that explained by "pure interest theory" and to be compared with the actual rate, is one "which is not modified by monetary influences, *although paid, of course, on capital reckoned in money terms*"[67], and therefore is a *money* rate of interest. Due to this clarification—that the relevant equilibrium rate is a *money* rate of interest—Hayek is able to respond to the challenge, voiced among others by Georg Halm,[68] that the natural rate if defined as the rate prevailing in a barter economy cannot be meaningfully compared with a money rate. According to Halm, not only is a natural rate, defined in terms of some commodity, not commensurable with a rate defined in money terms, but there need not even be a *uniform* natural rate as the rates may differ according to the commodity in terms of which they are reckoned. Halm's main objection is thus "that a uniform rate of interest could develop only in a money economy".[69] Yet, obviously, Hayek's procedure is immune to this kind of criticism, as indeed he defines the equilibrium rate in money terms and thus as a uniform rate, even if in equilibrium the respective commodity rates differ from each other.[70]

'solutions' rely on artificial assumptions, consistent with Hayek's view of the fictitious character of the equilibrium thus arrived.

[65] *Monetary Theory and the Trade Cycle*, this volume, p. 147, emphasis in the original.

[66] "Intertemporal Price Equilibrium", p. 213.

[67] *Monetary Theory and the Trade Cycle*, this volume, pp. 148–49, emphasis added.

[68] Georg Halm, "Das Zinsproblem am Geld- und Kapitalmarkt", *Jahrbücher für Nationalökonomie und Statistik*, vol. 125 (3rd series, vol. 70), nos. 1 and 2, 1926, pp. 1–34, 97–121.

[69] *Monetary Theory and the Trade Cycle*, this volume, p. 152.

[70] Note that Hayek in his response to Halm accepted the possibility of differing *equilibrium* commodity rates, thus the equilibrium in question need not be stationary. For otherwise, indeed, Hayek's reply should have been that differing commodity rates could not exist in (stationary) equilibrium. On the importance of this observation for evaluating Hayek's position in his debate with Sraffa, see the corresponding section below.

The Monetary Causes of the Cycle

Introducing *Prices and Production* in 1935, Hayek contrasted the two main pillars of his theory of the cycle, "the monetary factors which cause the trade cycle" and "the real phenomena which constitute it".[71] In the following we will keep to this distinction and first concentrate on money as the prime cause of the cycle before turning to the changes in the structure of production as the crucial cyclical mechanism.

As already noted, Hayek maintains that cycles and crises are possible only in a money economy. The analytical force of this argument draws on the distinction between neutral and non-neutral money, epitomised in the interest rate criterion, and in the identification of violations of this criterion as the ultimate cause of the business cycle. This is the only sense in which it is proper to speak, in Hayek's view, of a *monetary* explanation of the business cycle. With the introduction of money the tendency towards equilibrium prevalent in the static economy is replaced by the more complicated adjustment patterns of dynamic theory. Yet, among the various peculiarities that make the money economy differ from its static counterpart, the most systematic, and that most pertinent to the existence of the business cycle, is the effect of credit creation (or destruction) in causing an incongruity between investment and voluntary saving.[72]

Thus, the crucial property of a money economy is that, absent neutral money, a divergence of investment from voluntary saving becomes possible. In particular, Hayek considers an excess of investment over saving, financed by

---

[71] *Prices and Production*, this volume, p. 180n.7. For modern interpretations of Austrian business cycle theory following Hayekian lines see, e.g., Gerald P. O'Driscoll, Jr., *Economics as a Coordination Problem: The Contributions of Friedrich A. Hayek* (Kansas City: Sheed Andrews and McMeel, 1977); Steven Horwitz, *Microfoundations and Macroeconomics: An Austrian Perspective* (London and New York: Routledge, 2000); and Roger W. Garrison, *Time and Money: The Macroeconomics of Capital Structure* (Abingdon and New York: Routledge, 2001).

[72] To avoid misunderstandings a few words on terminology are here in order: When Hayek used the terms 'saving' and 'investment'—or alternatively 'supply and demand of saving', or 'capital formation'—he referred to planned magnitudes, preferably including the sums destined for reinvestment. Cf., e.g., his definition of "free capital" as "consisting of earned amortization quotas (or proceeds from circulating capital which has been turned over), new savings and perhaps additional credits", F. A. Hayek, "Kapitalaufzehrung", *Weltwirtschaftliches Archiv*, vol. 36, July 1932, p. 96n.2, translated as "Capital Consumption", in *Money, Capital and Fluctuations: Early Essays*, ed. Roy McCloughry (Chicago: University of Chicago Press; London: Routledge and Kegan Paul, 1984), pp. 157–58n.9; cf. also *Monetary Theory and the Trade Cycle*, this volume, p. 150. In this sense voluntary saving corresponds to the sum of these items save the additional, that is, created credits. Given that in the market for loanable funds such credit creation or credit destruction acts as an addition to or subtraction from the supply of saving, voluntary saving and investment need not be equal in equilibrium.

credit creation (inflation[73]), as the root cause of maladjustments in the structure of production and thus ultimately of the crisis. These maladjustments will arise irrespective of whether the exogenous change that generates excessive investment originates from the monetary or the real side.[74] Or put in terms of the interest rate criterion: It does not matter if a discrepancy comes about by a fall in the money rate or a rise in the natural rate—the former resulting from a policy of monetary expansion, the latter from an increase in the (expected) rate of profit, possibly due to technical progress. Indeed, Hayek in *Monetary Theory and the Trade Cycle* stressed fluctuations in the natural rate (relative to an unchanged money rate) as the typical impulse, while later on in *Prices and Production* he started the analysis of maladjustments from assuming a fall in the money rate.[75] Framing the problem—anachronistically—in terms of Ragnar Frisch's famous distinction,[76] the type of economy—money or barter—determines the *propagation mechanism*, that is, how the economy reacts to *impulses*, be they monetary or real. According to Hayek it is the distinguishing property of a (non-neutral) money economy that it will not react to such impulses by an immediate tendency towards equilibrium.[77]

A peculiarity of Hayek's approach, at least in his early works to be considered in this volume, is the assumption of full employment of resources as the starting point of the analysis.[78] He defended this assumption primarily on methodological grounds: having subscribed both to the equilibrium approach as an indispensable tool for economic analysis in general, and to the introduction of money as the necessary ingredient for the analysis of the business

[73] In the terminology preferred by Hayek and contemporary Austrian economists 'inflation' is always used in the broad sense of an increase in the circulation of money (*not* of the price level).

[74] He thus refutes the argument that a monetary explanation of the cycle requires that the cycle be driven by monetary *impulses*.

[75] One might speculate that the reason for this change in emphasis lies in the quest for analytical simplicity, which allows the elimination of the problem of technical progress. On this issue cf. Harald Hagemann and Hans-Michael Trautwein, "Cantillon and Ricardo Effects: Hayek's Contributions to Business Cycle Theory", *European Journal of the History of Economic Thought*, vol. 5, Summer 1998, p. 302.

[76] Ragnar Frisch, "Propagation Problems and Impulse Problems in Dynamic Economics", in *Economic Essays in Honour of Gustav Cassel*, ed. Karin Kock (London: Allen and Unwin, 1933), pp. 171–205, reprinted in *Business Cycle Theory: Selected Texts 1860–1939*, vol. 4, ed. Hagemann, pp. 303–35.

[77] However, Hayek conceded exceptional cases in which cycles and crisis-like phenomena may even arise independent of monetary disturbances; cf. "Investigations", pp. 129–30, and *Monetary Theory and the Trade Cycle*, this volume, p. 92n.36. Note that in these cases the true non-monetary origin of the crisis is the falsification of expectations. See also below, p. 30n.112.

[78] In his later writings he abandoned this assumption, cf., e.g., "Profits, Interest and Investment", chapter 1 of *Profits, Interest and Investment*, reprinted as chapter 8 of F. A. Hayek, *Business Cycles, Part II*.

cycle in particular, Hayek argues that, consequently, adherence to this methodology requires taking the ('static') equilibrium as it would be established in a barter (or, that is, in a neutral-money) economy as the point of departure. Then the theorist's task consists in demonstrating that with the introduction of non-neutral money, any disturbance would not simply generate a tendency back to equilibrium, but set in motion a self-reinforcing process away from it, which only after some time would reverse itself. In contrast, starting the explanation of the business cycle from a position outside equilibrium, say, from the situation after the lower turning point, would just beg the question, in assuming beforehand what in effect had to be explained. Yet, this argument is not wholly convincing. Although it is indeed true that for a dynamic explanation of the cycle Hayek had to demonstrate the absence of a direct tendency towards equilibrium, after having done so it would have been legitimate to analyse the cycle as a phenomenon of permanent disequilibrium (or a movement permanently outside static equilibrium).[79]

Having examined equilibrium and money as the point of departure of Hayek's approach, we now turn to the role of money with respect to the cyclical mechanism, that is, to the mechanism of forced saving.[80]

The emergence of the notion of forced saving[81] was roughly concomitant with the advent of the monetary approach to the business cycle. In this context forced saving denoted the effect of credit creation (or inflation) on saving and investment. Yet, in the German literature the term 'forced saving' conveys two meanings not always clearly distinguished. On the one hand, it means the *process*, possibly just a transient one, whereby actual saving (and thereby investment) could be increased beyond what would have been forthcoming voluntarily, that is, without the instrument of credit creation. On the other hand, it refers to the successful completion of such a process, that is, to an increase of saving (and thereby investment) as a *permanent outcome* capable of sustaining the induced change in the structure of production. Yet, among those who accepted forced saving as a mechanism by which credit creation produced an increase in saving, opinions diverged as to whether this increase would be a lasting one and thus make a permanent addition to the capital stock. Phrased

---

[79] For a thorough discussion of this problem, see Daniele Besomi, "Tendency to Equilibrium, the Possibility of Crisis, and the History of Business Cycle Theories", *History of Economic Ideas*, vol. 14, no. 2, 2006, pp. 53–104.

[80] For the real aspects of the cyclical mechanism see the next section.

[81] The specific term was introduced by Wicksell and Schumpeter; cf. Wicksell, *Interest and Prices*, pp. 111 and 155; Joseph A. Schumpeter, "Zinsfuß und Geldverfassung", in *Jahrbuch der Gesellschaft Österreichischer Volkswirte* (Vienna: Manz, 1913), reprinted in *Aufsätze zur ökonomischen Theorie*, ed. Erich Schneider and Arthur Spiethoff (Tübingen: Mohr, 1952), p. 19. See also F. A. Hayek, "A Note on the Development of the Doctrine of 'Forced Saving'", *Quarterly Journal of Economics*, vol. 47, November 1932, pp. 123–33, reprinted as chapter 3 of F. A. Hayek, *Business Cycles, Part II*.

differently, the crucial question is whether equilibrium after a phase of credit creation will be re-established by the money rate of interest returning to an unchanged natural rate, or if credit creation can pull down the natural rate to the artificially lowered money rate.

Before entering into this controversy and Hayek's role in it, we look at the various *mechanisms* for eliciting forced saving. The most easily discernible effect of credit creation is that the financial means, destined for the purchases of goods, coming forth from the regular circulation of income now have to compete with those means newly injected by inflation. If credit creation favours one type of purchase over another, as is the case with producer credits used for expenditure on capital goods, then it will reallocate the resources accordingly and reduce the purchasing power of those using their income for the purchase of consumers' goods.[82] Hayek has emphasised this distribution effect due to the lags in the generation and expenditure of income almost to the exclusion of all other mechanisms, from *Geldtheorie* onwards to his final words on the business cycle.[83] In any case, the effect of a single dose of inflation will last only as long as the newly injected money has not yet completed its way through the income circuit. Another mechanism is based on the redistribution of income and wealth due to inflation. This redistribution is prone to favour entrepreneurs (or capitalists) over workers, and thereby those who are inclined to save more out of their income so that as a result the aggregate supply of saving will increase. Hayek occasionally refers to this type of effect, which can also be found in the writings of Mises and of Robertson and Pigou.[84] Furthermore, if there are unused resources at the outset, credit creation may draw them into employment and give rise to a higher income out of which more can be saved.[85]

[82] Note that, under full employment, the reallocation of resources necessitates that the prices of capital goods rise while the prices of consumers' goods fall in terms of wages currently paid, yet that when spent, the purchasing power of wages in terms of consumers' goods will have fallen due to the lags in question. For an analysis of forced saving that makes use of the concept of a production possibility frontier cf. Garrison, *Time and Money*, chapters 3 and 4.

[83] Cf. the mound-of-honey example in F. A. Hayek, "Three Elucidations of the Ricardo Effect", *Journal of Political Economy*, vol. 77, March/April 1969, p. 281, reprinted in F. A. Hayek, *Business Cycles, Part II*, p. 326.

[84] See, e.g., F. A. Hayek, "Money and Capital: A Reply", *Economic Journal*, vol. 42, June 1932, pp. 242–43, reprinted in F. A. Hayek, *Contra Keynes and Cambridge*, pp. 215–16; and "Preiserwartungen, monetäre Störungen und Fehlinvestitionen", *Nationaløkonomisk Tidsskrift*, vol. 73, no. 1, 1935, translated as "Price Expectations, Monetary Disturbances, and Malinvestments", chapter 4 of *Profits, Interest and Investment*, reprinted in F. A. Hayek, *Good Money, Part I: The New World*, p. 239; as well as Mises, "Monetary Stabilization", pp. 126–27. Cf. also the references to Robertson and Pigou in Hayek, "A Note on the Development of the Doctrine of 'Forced Saving'", reprinted, p. 170. Generally, the assumption of different saving behaviour of capitalists and workers—dating back to the classical economists—was quite common in contemporary analysis.

[85] Hayek's analysis of the mechanism of forced saving under the assumption of full employment sets him apart from most other Austrian economists in that investment can only increase at

Turning to the possible *permanent effects*, one line of reasoning pursued by advocates of forced saving was that the increases in saving produced by the above-mentioned effects would suffice for sustaining the required higher level of investment.[86] Austrian economists, Hayek in particular, objected to this view. For example, Mises held that the effect from redistribution would be much too small, and in any event only temporary.[87] The latter is also the main argument put forward by Hayek in *Monetary Theory and the Trade Cycle*. Starting from a position of equilibrium, credit creation may well bring about movements that temporarily diverge from this equilibrium, but in the end, with correct anticipations restored and given time productivity of firms and time preference of households, saving and thereby investment must re-establish themselves at their original levels. Likewise Hayek disputes the benefits from the temporary increase in capital formation due to forced saving, for not only will it be impossible to maintain the more capitalistic methods of production after the rate of saving has fallen back to its voluntary level, even the gains from the transient increase in capital intensity will not come to fruition.[88] If Hayek ever conceded anything to this type of argument, he did so only for special cases that he thought were improbable. For example, credit creation may give rise to a permanent increase in investment if it does nothing more than anticipate a future increase in voluntary saving. Additionally, under specific circumstances, such as in a growing economy where the extent of forced

---

the cost of a reduction in consumption. Accordingly, in Hayek's view it is the re-establishment of the old level of consumption that eventually necessitates the return to less roundabout methods and thereby causes the crisis. Alternatively, without a rigid barrier set by full employment the increase in investment might be accompanied by an increase in consumption, too, so that this overconsumption contributes to the scarcity of intermediate-stage capital, which precipitates the crisis. Cf. on this issue Roger W. Garrison, "Overconsumption and Forced Saving in the Mises-Hayek Theory of the Business Cycle", *History of Political Economy*, vol. 36, Summer 2004, pp. 323–49; and James C. Ahiakpor, "Garrison on Mises and Forced Saving: Arguing the Impossible?" versus Garrison, "Ahiakpor and Mises on Forced Saving: A Rejoinder", *History of Political Economy*, vol. 40, Summer 2008, pp. 383–95 and 397–405, respectively. When Hayek in "Profits, Interest and Investment" employed a scheme that allowed both increases in consumption and investment, he did so not by accepting as feasible movements beyond full employment but by taking a situation with unused resources as the starting point of the boom.

[86] The most outspoken German representative of this view in the 1920s was L. Albert Hahn.

[87] Cf. Mises, "Monetary Stabilization", pp. 126–27.

[88] This argument abstracts from the possibility of path dependence, that is, that the very equilibrium position to which the process will eventually converge may be influenced by this process itself. In addition, forced saving may impinge, not on an equilibrium position (or steady-state) already attained, but on an economy during a transition process, e.g., towards a steady state with a higher capital intensity. Then even if forced saving violated the optimal intertemporal trade-off between present and future consumption, it might still be efficient to continue the process at the level of capital brought about by forced saving instead of returning to the 'old' optimal path. Cf. on this Arash Molavi Vasséi, "Ludwig von Mises's Business Cycle Theory: Static Tools for Dynamic Analysis", in *Austrian Economics in Transition*, ed. Hagemann, Nishizawa, and Ikeda, pp. 196–217.

saving is minor relative to voluntary saving, the capital created by forced saving need not be irretrievably lost. In this case forced saving, instead of bringing about a new equilibrium at a 'higher' sustained intertemporal path, just may succeed in providing a temporary peak in the path, at best with a return to the old path not accompanied by crisis-like phenomena.[89]

Another line of reasoning in favour of forced saving maintained that credit inflation and forced saving were necessary for realising the full potential of technical progress. Due to investment that incorporates technical progress coming forward in fits and starts, or just due to the existence of external economies (in the sense of Marshall), voluntary saving would only supply inadequate funds. Thus, by relying on voluntary saving alone the introduction of technical progress might be inefficient and slow. In contrast to the former, this type of reasoning concedes that such a spurt of investment, induced by the combination of technical progress and credit creation, would as a rule end in crisis and depression. Cyclical instability must thus be considered the price of economic progress, yet a price worthwhile to pay.[90] In the 1920s when Hayek started his career as a monetary theorist this view on forced saving had become quite influential, and in his early writings he was ready to attach some weight to it; even in *Geldtheorie* he still conceded the possibility of a trade-off between cyclical stability and progress. Yet, in the following years these concessions began to disappear, and significantly, the relevant passages of *Monetary Theory and the Trade Cycle* differ from those in *Geldtheorie* by more firmly rejecting this argument.[91]

Thus Hayek concludes that the boom and the accompanying process of

[89] Cf. F. A. Hayek, "Der Stand und die nächste Zukunft der Konjunkturforschung", in *Festschrift für Arthur Spiethoff*, ed. Gustav Clausing (Munich: Duncker and Humblot, 1933), pp. 115–16, translated as "The Present State and Immediate Prospects of the Study of Industrial Fluctuations", in *Profits, Interest and Investment*, pp. 179–80; and "Capital and Industrial Fluctuations", *Econometrica*, vol. 2, April 1934, p. 162; both reprinted in F. A. Hayek, *Business Cycles, Part II*, pp. 178–79 and pp. 199–200. Among Austrian economists Haberler entertained a more optimistic view on the possibility that forced saving might be smoothly absorbed; cf. Gottfried Haberler, *Systematic Analysis of the Theories of the Business Cycle* (Geneva: League of Nations, 1934), p. 18.

[90] Among contemporary German theorists Schumpeter and Spiethoff adhered to this view; cf., e.g., Joseph A. Schumpeter, *Ten Great Economists: From Marx to Keynes* (London: Allen and Unwin, 1952), p. 252; and Arthur Spiethoff, "Krisen", in *Handwörterbuch der Staatswissenschaften*, 4th ed. rev., ed. Ludwig Elster, Adolf Weber, and Friedrich Wieser, vol. 6 (Jena: Fischer, 1925), p. 85, translated in an abridged version as "Business Cycles", in *International Economic Papers*, vol. 3, 1953, reprinted in *Business Cycle Theory: Selected Texts 1860–1939*, vol. 2: *Structural Theories of the Business Cycle*, ed. Hagemann, p. 205. In Britain, Robertson was another cautious believer in this doctrine; cf. Dennis H. Robertson, *Money*, rev. ed. (London: Nisbet, 1928), reprinted as vol. 2 of *The Development of Monetary Theory, 1920s and 1930s*, ed. Forrest Capie and Geoffrey E. Wood (London: Routledge, 2000), p. 145.

[91] See the editor's note to *Monetary Theory and the Trade Cycle*, this volume, p. 143n.67. In any case, lecture 3 of *Prices and Production* was nothing less than a rejection of the idea of benefits from forced saving, yet it excluded technical progress from the analysis.

forced saving, both signifying a deviation from equilibrium, will last only as long as credit creation persists. Indeed, when the increased money stream reaches the labour market and raises money wages, and when in addition price expectations adapt, inflation must accelerate to preserve the relative prices conducive to forced saving.[92] However, such an increase in inflation cannot go on indefinitely, so sooner or later credit creation must stop, forced saving must end, and the process be reversed—the actual time required depending on the type of monetary system. For a currency conforming to the gold standard the internal (and possibly external) drain experienced by the banks during the boom must eventually prove incompatible with an unchanged gold base and thus set a limit to monetary expansion.[93] Although this limit would not apply to a pure fiat currency (or to a pure credit instead of cash economy), even in this case an ever-increasing inflation will ultimately become self-destructive because of its fatal effect on money being accepted as a means of exchange.[94] Therefore, irrespective of the monetary system, by the time the unsustainable structure of production has been created, the crisis will become inevitable.

The Structure of Production and the Mechanism of the Cycle

"The real phenomena which constitute [the business cycle]"[95] consist in the adaptations of the structure of production to changes in relative demand. Here we will concentrate on the simplified representation of the structure of production that Hayek put forward in *Prices and Production*.

The basic idea of Austrian capital theory, as founded by Eugen von Böhm-Bawerk and elaborated by Knut Wicksell,[96] lies in the productivity of time and in the representation of the ensemble of diverse capital goods by a time structure of production. Time is treated as a factor of production, so that in a sense the time that elapses between the input of the means of production and the output of products adds to the yield of the process.[97] In the simple case pro-

[92] Cf. Hayek, "Capital and Industrial Fluctuations", reprinted, p. 198; and "Three Elucidations", reprinted, p. 327; see also the discussion of this "accelerationist hypothesis" in David Laidler, *Fabricating the Keynesian Revolution: Studies in the Inter-war Literature on Money, the Cycle, and Unemployment* (Cambridge: Cambridge University Press, 1999), pp. 42–46.

[93] Cf. Hayek, *Monetary Theory and the Trade Cycle*, this volume, pp. 136–37.

[94] Cf., e.g., Hayek, "Capital and Industrial Fluctuations", reprinted, pp. 198–99.

[95] Hayek, *Prices and Production*, this volume, p. 180n.7.

[96] F. A. Hayek, *The Pure Theory of Capital* (London: Macmillan, 1941), reprinted as vol. 12 (2007) of *The Collected Works of F. A. Hayek*, ed. Lawrence H. White, was to some extent the closure of this type of approach; for more details on its origins cf. the editor's introduction to the cited volume.

[97] Inputs and outputs may be used up and accrue, respectively, either at discrete points of time or as flows over time, so that four types of production processes can be distinguished, point-input-point-output, flow-input-point-output, point-input-flow-output, and flow-input-flow-

pounded by Böhm-Bawerk, the non-produced means of production, such as labour, are applied at an even flow for a definite time, yielding an output of consumers' goods at the end of the period of production.[98] The productivity of time then will show itself in a positive, yet diminishing, marginal product of the lengthening of this period. Measuring time in such a way that the relation between the indicator used and the resulting output would be well behaved (similar to a neoclassical production function), however, turned out to be a tricky task except for the most simplified structures of production.[99] For the representation of the production process of the economy as a whole, Böhm-Bawerk took refuge in a vertical structure of staggered stages of production. The output of each stage results from combining labour with the products of the preceding stage, except for the first stage which uses solely labour as an input. The economy thus exhibits a linear structure of production, no product of a later stage being required as an input in the production process of an earlier stage.[100] In this configuration, Böhm-Bawerk considered the 'roundaboutness' of production, showing itself in the share of labour employed in the earlier stages, as both determining the productivity of the process and again amenable to measurement by an average period. Instead of roundaboutness later authors often referred to indirect, capitalistic (or capital-intensive), or simply long processes of production.

In *Prices and Production* Hayek makes use of Böhm-Bawerk's construction of an economy partitioned into stages.[101] In the examples on which the famous diagrams, his 'triangles',[102] are based he assumes the flow input of labour to be equally distributed among a given number of stages, within each of which production takes a unit period of time. Again the roundaboutness of such an economy can be indicated by an average period of production. For simplicity Hayek restricted the analysis to stationary states so that equilibrium is characterised by zero economic profits, that is, the whole of profits, as the

---

output. Hayek attributed this distinction to Ragnar Frisch; cf. F. A. Hayek, *The Pure Theory of Capital*, reprinted, p. 85.

[98] The definition of terms follows Hayek's precedent as in *Prices and Production*, this volume, p. 220. Accordingly, we distinguish among the means of production between original means (labour or land) and produced means, which are equivalent to intermediate products in the case where capital consists only of circulating capital. 'Producers' goods' is used synonymously with 'means of production'.

[99] Cf. for a fuller discussion the editor's introduction to F. A. Hayek, *Business Cycles, Part II*, pp. 34–35.

[100] Earlier and later stages are defined by their distance from consumption, consumers' goods being produced at the final stage of production.

[101] Thus, in his business cycle theory Hayek uses as a rule production schemes of the flow-input-point-output type (with some examples provided for point-input), yet in his writings on the pure theory of capital he employed more sophisticated versions.

[102] Cf., e.g., *Prices and Production*, this volume, pp. 222–25.

excess of revenue over costs, being absorbed by interest. Then in equilibrium the rate of interest will correspond to the rate of profit and, comparing equilibria, a lower rate of interest (and of profit) will correspond to a higher real wage (along what nowadays is known as a factor price curve), to a longer process of production and thereby a higher output of consumers' goods. In particular, the lengthening of the processes will be accomplished by an increase in the number of stages, making production more roundabout, yet because of its unchanged total amount less labour will be employed in each single stage. Obviously, this is a much simplified and very special representation of a capital-using economy.[103]

After recapitulating these properties of stationary equilibrium in lecture 2 of *Prices and Production*, Hayek devotes the entirety of the third lecture to a price theoretic foundation, where he sketches how these results emanate from the decisions of profit-maximising firms. In general, he assumes that such firms are located at the individual stages of production, each demanding (besides labour) the products of the preceding stage, producing output within a unit time period and supplying its own product to the next stage.[104]

Now, what will be the situation of a firm placed at some stage of production? Profit maximisation means that for such a firm the discounted marginal product conditions for the respective inputs used must be fulfilled. For example, the expected value of the discounted marginal product of labour must be equal to the wage rate, and correspondingly the expected value of the discounted marginal product of an intermediate good equal to its price. Equivalently, at any stage the expected marginal rates of profit from the use of labour and the intermediate good, respectively, must equal the rate of interest. When the expected marginal rate of profit exceeds the rate of interest, producers have an incentive to expand their output and the demand for the means of production, labour and the intermediate product. Finally, we find that the ratio of the marginal contributions of labour applied in any two adjacent

---

[103] It is due to this simplicity that there exists an unequivocally negative relation between the rate of interest and the average period of production and the output of consumers' goods, respectively. It should also be noted that capital appears only in the form of circulating capital (intermediate goods, semi-finished products). Despite attempts (showing themselves in some revisions) in the second edition of *Prices and Production* Hayek failed to integrate fixed capital into his analysis.

[104] Occasionally Hayek also uses the assumption of full vertical integration of firms so that all stages of production are operating internally within a firm. Typically this assumption is made when considering an economy characterised by a multiplicity of consumers' goods. Yet, Hayek maintained that as regards the choice of methods of production the results would be the same as with firms differentiated by stages—although the monetary aspects might differ. Cf., e.g., the analysis of vertically integrated firms in "The 'Paradox' of Saving", reprinted, pp. 107–10; in *Prices and Production*, this volume, pp. 237–39; and in "The Ricardo Effect", *Economica*, n.s., vol. 9, May 1942, pp. 147–48, reprinted in F. A. Hayek, *Business Cycles, Part II*, pp. 279–80.

stages must equal the interest factor.[105] Again, inasmuch as the ratio of marginal products deviates from the interest factor, there will be an incentive for a reallocation of labour among stages. In any case, the simple structures of Hayek's numerical and graphical examples will emerge only under very specific assumptions; e.g., the equal distribution of labour between stages depends on the symmetry of the marginal product curves in the different stages. Of course, with more complicated structures of production the results would become less straightforward.

Turning to the market level, what are the relations between prices in equilibrium? Equilibrium in a stationary economy presupposes a distribution of demand between consumers' goods and the means of production just sufficient for sustaining the existing structure of production, that is, for replacing all the producers' goods used up during the period. Specifically, in a money economy the distribution of expenditure in terms of money must correspond to the proportions required for equilibrium. Both for the description of equilibrium and for the adjustment process, or the 'traverse'[106] towards a new equilibrium, Hayek's price theoretic foundation is most important, as he emphasised the crucial significance of relative prices. The concept used by Hayek in this respect is the so-called price fan.[107] The crucial property of this equilibrium price structure is that all the relative prices, ranging from those of the original means of production, such as labour, to prices of the intermediate products of the different stages and finally to the price of consumers' goods, are determined by the condition that the profit rate in all stages must be equal to the rate of interest. This means that the price relation between products of adjacent stages is conditioned by the rate of interest. Thus, comparing equilibria, an increase in the interest rate will decrease the prices of intermediate products and of labour relative to consumers' goods, and this decrease will be stronger the greater the distance of the respective stage to consumption, and conversely for a decrease in the interest rate. Concomitantly, by the mechanism explicated above, changes in the rate of interest will by their effects on relative prices induce a reallocation of the means of production between the different stages and thereby an adaptation of the structure of production.[108]

Following Hayek's lead we sketch as the prototype of a successful traverse the transition to a new equilibrium initiated by an increase in voluntary saving. Such a rise in saving means a redistribution of monetary demand from consumers' to producers' goods, or put differently, from the later to the earlier

[105] Hayek introduced this condition in a section added to the second edition of *Prices and Production*, this volume, pp. 249–51.

[106] The term is due to John Hicks, *Capital and Growth* (Oxford: Clarendon Press, 1965), chapter 16; cf. also his *Capital and Time: A Neo-Austrian Theory* (Oxford: Clarendon Press, 1973), which initiated a renaissance of traverse analysis.

[107] *Prices and Production*, this volume, p. 248.

[108] Hayek, ibid., illustrates the process by likening it to the 'opening' or 'closing' of the price fan.

stages of production. The amounts withdrawn from consumption (or the late stages) increase the supply (of saving) to the market for loanable funds, thereby causing a fall in the rate of interest,[109] and thus will, according to the change in price relations, spread to the earlier stages. To be more definite, let us assume that the money price of the original means of production, say, the money wage as the price of labour, will remain the same in the new equilibrium.[110] Then, due to the shift in demand the price of consumers' goods will fall. Yet, this price is linked by the price fan, and by the reactions of profit-maximising firms, to the prices of the intermediate products of the preceding stages, which will fall too, but to a lesser extent. Thus the prices of intermediate products in terms of consumers' goods will *rise*, and stronger the earlier the stage. This will induce a shift of means of production towards earlier stages and also increase the number of stages, thereby lengthening the average period of production. It should be noted that according to the assumptions we started from, there will be some stage such that for earlier stages money prices have risen and for later stages money prices have fallen. Looking at these adjustments from the point of view of an individual firm, the price mechanism works by changing the relation between the (expected) rate of profit and the rate of interest. On the one hand, the decline in the rate of interest will make it profitable to increase the supply of the product and correspondingly the demand for the means of production at all stages, if money prices remain unchanged. Yet, on the other hand, the relations between money prices will have changed in favour of earlier stages (some of which will have to be newly created). In the end, the equality between the profit rate and the interest rate will be restored in all stages so that the demand for the original means of production in the previously existing stages has been reduced to the extent necessitated by its reallocation to the newly introduced stages.

In thus pursuing the effects of the thrift-driven transition to more round-about and thus more productive methods of production, Hayek—although giving a much deeper analysis of the price theoretic foundations than his predecessors—had covered familiar ground. Yet, his main interest as a theorist of the business cycle was not in successful but in "frustrated traverses"[111] and in the crises produced by them. It is here that Hayek abandoned the highly

---

[109] It should be noted that even without monetary disturbances the rate of interest immediately determined by market clearing need not be identical with the long-run equilibrium value. In a neutral-money economy this difficulty can be neglected due to the assumption of perfect foresight.

[110] This will be the case in Hayek's model under the assumption of full vertical integration of stages. Otherwise due to the increase in cash requirements when the number of stages rises, the money wage will have to fall. See the section below on neutral money.

[111] Cf. Meghnad Desai and Paul Redfern, "Trade Cycle as a Frustrated Traverse: An Analytical Reconstruction of Hayek's Model", in *The Economics of F. A. Hayek*, vol. 1, ed. Colonna and Hagemann, pp. 121–43.

idealised picture sketched for the effect of an increase in voluntary saving and focused instead on all the multifarious problems of adjustment. In the 'realistic' analysis of the cycle, and in particular the crisis, he had to take into account a multiplicity of complicating factors and 'frictions'. In doing so he was forced to leave the narrow realm of the simplified model of the numerical and graphical examples used, where in principle the logical consistency of results can be proved, and content himself with putting forward suggestive conjectures.

What now are these frictions that Hayek glossed over in his analysis of the successful traverse, yet which he—increasingly—took into account in his writings on the business cycle? The main culprit is of course money. In describing the effects of voluntary saving within the framework of neutral money, Hayek not only abstracted from credit creation or credit destruction, but also from the redistribution of money and cash balances as between stages, firms, and households, which are alien to the frictionless adjustment presupposed by static theory, but must be taken account of by any truly dynamic analysis. Indeed, it is these properties of a money economy that in Hayek's view are the vital causes of the cycle. Another crucial complication refers to expectations. The analysis of the successful traverse assumed expectations to be correct, such as with regard to future prices or the future rate of interest. Again in contrast, Hayek's explanation of the cycle, and in particular of the inevitability of the crisis, is based on monetarily induced false prices and wrong expectations.[112] Finally, Hayek's conception of the capital structure also contains serious potential for maladjustments. As is abundantly clear from his debates with Knight, he rejected the idea of capital as being malleable, and thus capable of adapting to changes in data more or less instantaneously and without friction.[113] Therefore any adjustment in the stock of capital goods, whether they are built up or dismantled, will take time, and before equilibrium is again attained new disruptions of production may be likely to occur. As we will see, the typical crisis would be difficult to explain without some such frictions in adjustment.

The case of economic crisis is then the opposite of the successful transition to an equilibrium with longer processes and thus higher productivity due to an increase in voluntary saving. Rather the crisis results from an adaptation of the capital structure of the economy to a reverse shift in demand towards con-

---

[112] Hayek's device is to assume permanent changes in data in his analysis of the successful traverse so that to a first approximation, static expectations (e.g., of a permanent reduction in the rate of interest) may prove correct. With static expectations, however, the traverses induced both by forced saving and by fluctuations in voluntary saving—where reductions in the rate of interest eventually turn out as merely temporary—must fail due to expectational errors.

[113] Cf. in this regard Avi J. Cohen, "The Hayek/Knight Controversy: The Irrelevance of Roundaboutness, or Purging Processes in Time?", *History of Political Economy*, vol. 35, Fall 2003, pp. 469–90.

sumption. The cause of such a shift may lie in spontaneous changes in preferences, like an increase in the rate of time preference on the part of the consumers, or government policies detrimental to saving.[114] However, the same effects will be produced by the breakdown of an unsustainable boom based on the inflationary creation of credit. In all these instances, the existing capital structure can no longer be maintained by the forthcoming amount of saving, and thus resources have to be transferred from earlier to later stages of production. In each of these cases the adjustment of the structure of production will be a reaction to an increase in the rate of interest, whether caused by a draining away of saving or by the cessation of credit creation. During the transition phase the economy will experience a period of capital consumption, that is, a disinvestment of capital goods, and end up in a position with shorter and less-productive processes, and therefore a lower output of consumers' goods and a lower real wage.

Yet, with perfectly flexible prices, including wages, and a completely malleable stock of capital goods, such a transition process would exhibit a decrease in real wages, and of the standard of living in general, but not the phenomena typical of a crisis, that is, labour becoming unemployed and capital lying idle.[115] Hayek finds the solution for this paradox, which also appears to contradict Say's law of markets,[116] in a special kind of friction that prevents smooth and rapid adjustment, namely the specificity and complementarity of capital. In an economy differentiated by stages of production, specificity means that producers' goods are not perfectly mobile between stages, whereas complementarity suggests a lack of substitutability such that a minimum amount of some producers' goods is necessary for maintaining production.[117] In an extreme case a capital good may be usable only in one stage and only in combination with definite amounts of other producers' goods. Then when demand shifts between stages, evidently adjustment will become more difficult the more specific and complementary the respective capital goods used in these stages. In addition, these obstacles to smooth adjustment will be more easily overcome in a transition to longer processes, when new savings provide the means for building up a new stock of capital goods, than in the reverse case of a crisis, when such funds are lacking.

[114] Cf. Hayek, "Capital Consumption", p. 138.

[115] Cf., e.g., Fritz Machlup, "Professor Knight and the 'Period of Production'", *Journal of Political Economy*, vol. 43, October 1935, p. 624, for his response to Frank H. Knight, "Professor Hayek and the Theory of Investment", *Economic Journal*, vol. 45, March 1935, pp. 77–94.

[116] See the discussion in Hayek, "Investigations", pp. 125–32.

[117] Cf. Hayek, *Prices and Production*, this volume, pp. 243–44 and 256. Among Austrian economists Lachmann strongly emphasised the role of complementarities in the structure of capital for the trade cycle and as an explanation for the end of the boom; cf., e.g., Ludwig Lachmann, *Capital and Its Structure*, 2nd ed. (Kansas City: Sheed Andrews and McMeel, 1978), pp. 112–18.

The particular mechanism to which Hayek ascribes both unemployment and idle capital is the co-existence of specific and non-specific means of production, such as, on the one hand, machines or semi-finished products, and on the other hand, most labour and raw materials. Then, when the crisis sets in, the demand for the products of the early stages tapers off and non-specific means like labour are drawn to later stages, whereas the specific means remain in their place and lose value. This becomes a source of the idleness of capital, mainly in the early stages. Correspondingly, in the late stages the demand for non-specific means of production will be limited by the lack of specific and complementary goods. The scarcity of these specific means will make itself felt especially when, during the restructuring of the process of production, new (or new types of) specific goods must be constructed in order to employ all the non-specific means available in the late stages. This is the source of unemployment of labour set free from the early stages but not yet finding profitable employment in the late stages. So, Hayek concludes, somewhere in the process there will be both unemployed labour and idle capital co-existing in the economy. Ultimately, such unemployment need not even be the consequence of rigid wages, as even a zero wage rate might not be able to sufficiently stimulate the demand for labour[118]—although rigidities will of course aggravate the situation. Yet, fundamentally the cause of the crisis is structural—the incoherence of relative demands with the sectoral composition of the economy—giving rise to a situation of simultaneous abundance and shortage.[119]

This description also highlights the sense in which it may be legitimate to identify 'capital shortage' as the cause of crisis and unemployment. In a broader sense this shortage is just a shortage of (voluntary) saving: as the crisis is always initiated by a lack in the supply of saving (that is, of the loanable funds forthcoming to the market), it could just be avoided by a compensating increase. It is such a kind of compensation that lies behind the contention of the advocates of forced saving that the crisis will be avoided if the boom creates the saving necessary to sustain itself. In the later stage of the crisis, a different kind of shortage makes itself felt, namely, the scarcity of specific means of production to be employed in the rearranged late stages of production, the absence of which makes some labour unemployable. Of course, these two diagnoses are closely connected, for the scarcity of specific capital goods will be more rapidly remedied the greater the means of saving forthcoming. This is also the reason why in Hayek's view policies of austerity should turn out as helpful in combating the crisis: measures in favour of aggregate saving, from sound fiscal policies

[118] Cf. Hayek, "The Purchasing Power of the Consumer", p. 153; and *Preise und Produktion*, p. 91n.1, cf. this volume, p. 258n.39.

[119] In "Investigations", pp. 131–32, Hayek illustrates this, with an example borrowed from Spiethoff, as equivalent to the situation where only one of a pair of gloves is available.

to wage cuts that dampen private consumption, should in this way contribute to balancing the distribution of demand to the existing structure of capital.

Summarising, we find that Hayek's analysis of the transition involves a multiplicity of mechanisms simultaneously affecting the path of the economy: money entering the economy at a specific stage of production and then trickling down to the means of production; the (temporary) redistribution of money (or purchasing power) during this process affecting the relative demands for consumers' and producers' goods; the reaction of the prices of the means of production (intermediate products and labour) influencing the profitability of production in the different stages; the dependence of all these decisions on expectations that may be misled by false prices; the discontinuing of old and the starting of new processes, incorporating methods of production which differ in their roundaboutness; and to make things still more complicated, the presence of means of production (possibly fixed capital) specific to stages of production. All these features combine to make the process as imagined by Hayek immensely complex. Certainly, there is no way of formalising Hayek's story in a mathematical model without losing most of what makes Hayek's view different.

This complexity is, indeed, better reflected in the sophisticated stories Hayek went on to tell in the verbal descriptions of the transition than in the extreme simplification of his famous 'triangles' and numerical examples. It is also due to this complexity that Hayek hedged his conclusions by many provisos and that the tentative answers he ventured may appear based as much on his intuition (or strong prior convictions) as on rigorous analysis. Some criticisms of Hayek's analysis of the cycle as a frustrated traverse point to these residues of ambiguity. For example, Hayek's explanation depends on contingent properties of the capital stock extant at a specific time and place. While with complete malleability of capital there would be *no* unemployment, with complete specificity and complementarity *any* shock to the system would give rise to at least temporary unemployment. Thus for Hayek to come up with the results he was striving for, successful traverses when money is neutral, and frustrated traverses and unemployment as the outcome of a credit-fuelled boom, he had to rely on a special, yet never concretely defined, mix of specificity and complementarity. One may also question whether the methods of production are prone during the short run of the business cycle to vary in their capital-intensity as strongly as required, or indeed whether the actually observed co-movements conform to those predicted by Hayek's theory.[120]

---

[120] See, e.g., Nicholas Kaldor, "Capital Intensity and the Trade Cycle", *Economica*, n.s., vol. 6, February 1939, pp. 40–66, reprinted as chapter 6 of *Essays on Economic Stability and Growth*, vol. 2 of *Collected Economic Essays* (London: Duckworth, 1960; 2nd ed., 1980); or Gottfried Haberler, *Prosperity and Depression: A Theoretical Analysis of Cyclical Movements*, 3rd. ed. (Geneva: League of

Neutral Money

We have discussed earlier the notion of the neutral-money economy, the course of which depends only on 'real data' as it is assumed to be the case for an ideal barter economy. In particular, neutral money implies that the actual money rate equals the 'equilibrium' or natural rate of interest.

Hayek finds the causes of the deviation of a money economy from this norm of neutral money in the so-called one-sided influences of money, that is, changes in the demand (or supply) of some goods and services that have no counterpart in the system of 'real' demands and supplies, but instead originate from the money side. Typical examples are additions to the circulation of money by credit creation, or conversely withdrawals by hoarding. These monetary influences are non-neutral by redistributing purchasing power; for example, in the most important case credit creation is supposed to reallocate purchasing power to producers.[121] Besides, in so far as the preferences between households differ, even a mere redistribution of cash balances, without changing their aggregate sum, might result in a monetary effect on the structure of production. It is thus the injection, withdrawal, or redistribution of money that makes a money economy diverge from neutrality. Then, a policy of holding the 'effective circulation of money' constant[122] would eliminate such non-neutralities in the aggregate, and this is indeed what Hayek considers a condition for neutral money, at least as a first approximation.[123]

For money being neutral the respective money economy must exhibit a state of intertemporal equilibrium; therefore the supplementary conditions for such an equilibrium must also be fulfilled. Thus, as Hayek repeatedly points out,[124] a neutral-money economy also requires correct foresight and perfect flexibil-

---

Nations, 1941), pp. 481–91. On Hayek's neglect of what came to be known as 'effective demand failures' cf. the editor's introduction to F. A. Hayek, *Business Cycles, Part II*, pp. 5–15.

[121] Nowadays, such effects are denoted as 'Cantillon effects', cf. Hagemann and Trautwein, "Cantillon and Ricardo Effects". Hayek refers to Richard Cantillon in the introduction to the first lecture of *Prices and Production*, this volume, p. 198; for Hayek's emphasis on the place of injections of money, cf. ibid., p. 278.

[122] On the notion of the 'effective circulation of money' as equivalent to MV, the left-hand side of the quantity equation, cf. *Monetary Theory and the Trade Cycle*, this volume, p. 98n.49; see also the correspondence between Hayek and Keynes (reprinted in F. A. Hayek, *Contra Keynes and Cambridge*, p. 167).

[123] In his early writings, including *Geldtheorie* (1929), Hayek advocated a constant M instead of MV (cf. also the respective revisions in *Monetary Theory and the Trade Cycle*); the first recognition of the effects of changes in velocity may be dated with "Investigations", p. 135, and the necessity for compensation is confirmed in *Prices and Production*, this volume, pp. 274–77. Cf. on this George Selgin, "Hayek versus Keynes on How the Price Level Ought to Behave", *History of Political Economy*, vol. 31, Winter 1999, pp. 714–15.

[124] Cf., e.g., Hayek, "On Neutral Money", p. 230.

ity of all prices. Indeed, Hayek makes a connection between the injection of money (credit creation), false prices (in particular a 'false' rate of interest), and the generation of incorrect price expectations, for example, due to a confusion between temporary and permanent movements in the rate of interest.

Now in the case of a stationary economy, where there is no change in output over time, neither from endogenous nor exogenous sources, a policy of a constant circulation of money leads to stability of the price level. Such a policy had been favoured by many contemporary advocates of a monetary theory of the business cycle, which associated movements in the price level with the upswings and downswings of the cycle. Irving Fisher and John Maynard Keynes were only the two most prominent adherents to this view.[125] In contrast to this approach, which concentrated on the absolute movement of prices as the source of the cycle, Hayek emphasised that the cycle is primarily the result of movements in relative prices, and thus that some kind of average stability in absolute price movements could not safeguard against booms and crises.

The distinction between Hayek's emphasis on relative prices and the preoccupation of the 'stabilisation theorists' with the price level is brought out most clearly when considering a steadily progressive economy. Here, unlike the stationary economy, the output (of consumers' goods) is growing over time, in the simplest case due to technical progress that steadily increases the total productivity of the factors of production.[126] Then a constant circulation of money makes the price level decline inversely to the rate of productivity growth. In fact, advocacy of such a 'productivity norm' for price-level behaviour was not novel. As pointed out by Robbins, such was "not the esoteric creed of a handful of 'sadistic deflationists'", but the opinion of many economists of repute like Marshall, Edgeworth, Taussig, Hawtrey, Robertson, and Pigou.[127] Yet, it was Hayek's major and novel contribution to argue for this norm as a requirement of neutrality and thus as a means to prevent the trade cycle, whereas the older economists often had rested their case on considerations of equity.[128]

---

[125] In Hayek's writings there are numerous references to Fisher and Keynes as stabilisation theorists.

[126] Changes in total factor productivity account for changes in output not attributable to changes in the quantities of the factors of production. We ignore that different causes of growth might necessitate different reactions of the circulation of money in order to secure neutrality. A thorough contemporary discussion of this problem is Gottfried Haberler, "Die Kaufkraft des Geldes und die Stabilisierung der Wirtschaft", *Schmollers Jahrbuch für Gesetzgebung, Verwaltung und Volkswirtschaft im Deutschen Reiche*, vol. 55, no. 6, 1931, pp. 993–1023; cf. also his "Money and the Business Cycle", in *Gold and Monetary Stabilization: Lectures on the Harris Foundation 1932*, ed. Quincy Wright (Chicago: University of Chicago Press, 1932), pp. 41–74.

[127] Lionel Robbins, "Consumption and the Trade Cycle", *Economica*, no. 38, November 1932, p. 418. Cf. also George Selgin, "The 'Productivity Norm' versus Zero Inflation in the History of Economic Thought", *History of Political Economy*, vol. 27, Winter 1995, pp. 705–35.

[128] Cf., e.g., Robertson, *Money*, pp. 134–38.

Looking at the market for loanable funds, in order to keep prices stable in the face of growing output money must be injected into the circulation. In particular, when money is injected by credit creation this constitutes an additional supply of credit beyond that of voluntary saving, and for this additional supply to be absorbed by demand, the interest rate must fall below its equilibrium level. Yet, this is just the situation that will give rise to an unsustainable boom, and thus to the trade cycle.[129] In the terminology of Haberler's study this case is one of 'relative inflation'.[130] According to Hayek and the Austrians such a relative inflation characterised the American boom of the 1920s, especially after 1927, and consequently the stabilisation of the price level in the face of buoyant growth in productivity was to blame for causing the crisis of 1929 and eventually the Great Depression.[131]

The controversy of 'stable prices or neutral money?' experienced a final climax in 1934–35.[132] To no great surprise, no consensus was reached in the debate, which was also marred by conflicting definitions of saving and investment used by the participants. Yet the one significant argument, beside many

[129] Cf. Hayek, *Monetary Theory and the Trade Cycle*, this volume, p. 108.

[130] Haberler, "Die Kaufkraft des Geldes", p. 1009; "Money and the Business Cycle", p. 56.

[131] Cf., e.g., F. A. Hayek, "Das Schicksal der Goldwährung", *Der Deutsche Volkswirt*, vol. 6, February 12 and 19, 1932, pp. 642–45, 677–81, translated as "The Fate of the Gold Standard" and reprinted in F. A. Hayek, *Good Money, Part I: The New World*, pp. 153–68; and "Capital and Industrial Fluctuations", reprinted, pp. 204–5. The similarity to certain developments that occurred during the current financial and economic crisis is evident. Note that on the eve of the present crisis, warnings—against the reliance on inflation targeting as a method to secure macroeconomic stability—similar to the Hayekian diagnosis were voiced by economists of the Bank of International Settlements in a series of working papers. Also in a Hayekian vein, though from outside the Austrian camp, the danger of excessive credit booms has been pointed out by Barry Eichengreen and Kris J. Mitchener, "The Great Depression as a Credit Boom Gone Wrong", *Research in Economic History*, vol. 22, 2004, pp. 183–237.

[132] Cf. "Stable Prices or Neutral Money?", *The Economist Monthly Book Supplement*, July 21, 1934, pp. 1–2, and the ensuing contributions in *The Economist* by F. A. Hayek (July 28, 1934, p. 168), Roy F. Harrod (October 6, 1934, p. 8), and Harold Barger, Gottfried Haberler, Nicholas Kaldor, and again Harrod (November 8, 1934, pp. 7–8). Eventually the controversy swept into *Economica*: cf. Harrod, "The Expansion of Credit in an Advancing Community", n.s., vol. 1, August 1934, pp. 287–99; Dennis H. Robertson", Mr. Harrod and the Expansion of Credit", and Harrod, "Rejoinder to Mr. Robertson", n.s., vol. 1, November 1934, pp. 473–75 and 476–78; Karl Bode and Gottfried Haberler, "Monetary Equilibrium and the Price Level in a Progressive Economy: A Comment", and Harrod, "Rejoinder to Drs. Haberler and Bode", n.s., vol. 2, February 1935, pp. 75–81 and 82–84. See also Haberler's correspondence with many of the participants, in the League of Nations Archives, 33–40, section 10B, dossiers 12653/12653 and 12809/12653. On the political background of the debate, deriving from Harrod's and Barger's close affiliation to the New Fabian Research Bureau, see Elizabeth Durbin, *New Jerusalems: The Labour Party and the Economics of Democratic Socialism* (London: Routledge and Kegan Paul, 1985), chapters 5 and 6. On the theoretical aspects of the debate cf. Daniele Besomi, *The Making of Harrod's Dynamics* (Houndmills and London: Macmillan, 1999), chapter 2; and Hansjoerg Klausinger, "The Austrians on Relative Inflation as a Cause of Crisis", *Journal of the History of Economic Thought*, vol. 25, June 2003, pp. 221–37.

obscure ones, drew attention to the tendency of adherents of the productivity norm to neglect the endogeneity of hoarding. Hoarding may be considered as an endogenous response to the increase in output: if the price level is kept stable and output grows, then—given an unchanged proportion between income and desired money balances—there must be hoarding in order to increase cash holdings. In the market for loanable funds, this induced hoarding will in the aggregate be just sufficient to absorb the money injected into the economy for stabilising the price level, and thus a deviation of the money rate from its equilibrium level need not occur. Against this, the pervasiveness of Cantillon effects may be invoked as a counterargument:[133] Even if the demand and supply of additional money balance each other in the aggregate, this need not be so with regard to the specific locations where injections and hoarding take place; therefore, a redistribution of cash balances might still lead to non-neutralities. Although a systematic effect on the interest rate cannot be easily derived as such redistributions may work in arbitrary ways, it can consistently be argued that by refraining from any injections the extent of redistribution effects will be minimised.

Yet, taking the argument of induced hoarding for granted, if and insofar as Cantillon effects can be neglected, both the productivity norm and a stable price level will be compatible with an undisturbed money rate of interest. This will be so as soon as hoarding is considered as reacting to the *expected* path of the price level: if the price level is expected to remain stable, then people will be induced to hoard to provide for higher balances matching the higher money income. Alternatively, if money income is expected to remain constant and the price level to fall, then there will be no incentive to hoard, and equilibrium can be preserved without any injection of money. Mutatis mutandis, this applies for any correctly anticipated path of the price level, as among the participants in the discussion Kaldor was the only one to realise:

> When . . . banking policy coincides with people's expectations any sort of policy can be carried through (without disturbing the 'neutrality' of money) whether it implies falling, or constant, or rising prices.[134]

Accordingly, under these conditions the path of the price level, and of money in circulation, associated with neutral money is indeterminate in the sense of being non-unique.[135]

---

[133] As, e.g., by Robertson, "Mr. Harrod and the Expansion of Credit", p. 473.

[134] Kaldor to Haberler, November 13, 1934, League of Nations Archives, 33–40/10B/12653/12653.

[135] For more formal demonstrations cf. J. C. Gilbert, "The Compatibility of Any Behavior of the Price Level with Equilibrium", *Review of Economic Studies*, vol. 24, June 1957, pp. 177–84; and Lawrence H. White, "Hayek's Monetary Theory and Policy: A Critical Reconstruction", *Journal of Money, Credit and Banking*, vol. 31, February 1999, pp. 109–20.

This indeterminacy of the price-level path is only one of the examples that showed the array of problems hidden behind the seemingly simple formula of neutral money. Hayek himself dealt with many of the complications, and in doing so adapted his recommendations to the evolution of his own theory. Yet, the more the elaboration of the complexities of neutral money progressed, the less it appeared suitable as a norm for practical monetary policy. Indeed, Hayek had emphasised from the outset that the prime importance of the concept lay in its use as an instrument of theoretical analysis.[136] In contrast, as a guide for monetary policy, neutral money is bound to fail for three reasons: First, the informational requirements for the monetary authorities to implement a neutral money policy are utopian—and, of course, Hayek was all too familiar with this argument from his involvement in the debates on 'planning' and socialist economic calculation. Second, there are the problems of central banking within the institution of a multi-tiered banking system. For example, stabilisation (or control) of the effective circulation of money would also necessitate the stabilisation (or control) of the volume of banking deposits. However, Hayek considered such an interference with the workings of the banking system as both impracticable—because of the existence of money surrogates[137]—and detrimental to the function performed by the banks.[138] Finally, if correct foresight and perfect price flexibility as prerequisites for neutral money are violated, monetary policy will be forced to adapt to these imperfections and take into account the rigidity of prices or the redistribution effected between creditors and debtors by movements of the price level when contracts are fixed in money. Yet as a consequence the neutrality of money will be reduced to one among conflicting goals to be pursued, and monetary policy must content itself with facing a trade-off between them.[139]

The presence of such practical obstacles called for 'second best' solutions. Throughout the 1930s Hayek favoured adherence to the gold standard as the best of the practicable monetary standards, even though it fell short of fully conforming to the norm of neutral money by rendering the money supply too elastic.[140] Thus, Hayek saw no justification for monetary reforms that intended

---

[136] Cf. especially Hayek, "On Neutral Money".

[137] Cf., e.g., the discussion in *Prices and Production*, this volume, pp. 271–72.

[138] As proof one might point to Hayek's rejection of the Chicago Plan of 100% money, which would mean "an abolition of deposit banking as we know it"; cf. F. A. Hayek, *Monetary Nationalism and International Stability* (Geneva: Longmans, 1937), reprinted in *Good Money, Part II: The Standard*, ed. Stephen Kresge, vol. 6 (1999) of *The Collected Works of F. A. Hayek*, p. 92. Hayek had earlier called such ideas "incredibly naïve" (Hayek to Haberler, September 9, 1934, Gottfried Haberler Papers, box 66, Hoover Institution Archives, Stanford University).

[139] Hayek, "Capital and Industrial Fluctuations", reprinted, p. 204, states that "the task of monetary policy would be to find a workable compromise between the different incompatible aims"; for an early exposition of this view cf. also Hayek, "Investigations", p. 64.

[140] Cf. Hayek, "Intertemporal Price Equilibrium", p. 68.

"to replace the semi-automatic gold standard by a more or less arbitrarily managed currency".[141] In any case, due to the multitude of obstacles getting in the way of a policy of neutral money, although current policies left much to be improved, the recurrence of cycles had to be accepted. Thus "under the existing conditions, money will always exert a determining influence on the course of economic events",[142] and "even under the best practicable monetary system, the self-equilibrating mechanism of prices might be seriously disturbed by monetary causes".[143]

In the face of these limitations Hayek's actual recommendations may appear to border on a kind of policy nihilism.[144] Yet, at the time, his ultimate solution to the problems of ignorance, rigidities, and the necessity to preserve a banking system ever prone to be the cause of fluctuations tended in a different direction, namely, to a policy of extreme caution and minimal intervention.[145] Concretely, his advice centred on prescriptions of what *not* to do:

> The only practical maxim for monetary policy . . . is probably the negative one that the simple fact of an increase of production and trade forms no justification for an expansion of credit, and that—save in an acute crisis— bankers need not be afraid to harm production by overcaution.[146]
>
> We arrive at results which only confirm the old truth that we may perhaps prevent a crisis by checking expansion in time, but that we can do nothing to get out of it before its natural end, once it has come.[147]

The Hayek-Sraffa Debate Reconsidered

The significance of the debate between Hayek and Sraffa[148] and the damage it did to Hayek's reputation as an economic theorist have already been alluded

---

[141] Hayek, *Prices and Production*, this volume, p. 280.

[142] Ibid., p. 279.

[143] Hayek, "Capital and Industrial Fluctuations", reprinted, p. 204.

[144] Cf. Nicolò DeVecchi, "Whatever Happened to Dr Hayek After the Debate with Mr Sraffa? A Comment on Zappia", in *Piero Sraffa's Political Economy. A Centenary Estimate*, ed. Terenzio Cozzi and Roberto Marchionatti (London and New York: Routledge, 2001), pp. 377–85.

[145] Eventually Hayek turned to the radical proposal of *Denationalisation of Money* (London: Institute of Economic Affairs, 1978), reprinted as chapter 4 of F. A. Hayek, *Good Money, Part II: The Standard*.

[146] Hayek, *Prices and Production*, this volume, p. 278. In the first edition this was followed by the remark, "even during times of general depression".

[147] Ibid., p. 261.

[148] Cf. Piero Sraffa, "Dr. Hayek on Money and Capital", *Economic Journal*, vol. 42, March 1932, pp. 42–53; F. A. Hayek, "Money and Capital: A Reply"; and Sraffa, "A Rejoinder", *Economic Journal*, vol. 42, June 1932, pp. 249–51. Reprinted, respectively, as chapters 7, 8, and 9 in

to in the biographical section above. The main points of Sraffa's critique can be classified under three headings: the functions of money and in particular the meaning of neutral money; the nature of the natural rate of interest; and the viability of forced saving.[149] Here we try to re-evaluate the debate by bringing to bear what in the foregoing has been distilled as the essentials of Hayek's approach to money and the cycle.

With regard to the Hayekian notion of *neutral money* Sraffa objected that it described in effect a non-monetary economy and that thus its use as a measuring rod for actual monetary systems was illegitimate. Furthermore, Sraffa claimed that Hayek's treatment of money reduced it merely to a means of exchange— consequently in Hayek's suppositions, "there are no debts, no money-contracts, no wage-agreements, no sticky prices"—thus, that in short this kind of money lacks almost all the properties common in money as we know it.[150]

In his reply Hayek tried to dispel Sraffa's alleged misunderstandings by pointing to his forthcoming *Monetary Theory and the Trade Cycle*, where he indeed had addressed some of the issues raised. Accordingly, the barter economy that serves as the reference for neutral money is *not* meant to represent an actual barter economy. Rather, as Hayek had repeatedly emphasised, it is just an analytical construction of the ideal type of an economy devoid of any frictions, and thus represents the 'fictitious' economy to which the laws of 'static theory' or 'pure economics' would apply. Correspondingly, the neutral-money economy is conceived as a money economy that replicates the results of this ideal barter economy. In this sense Sraffa's identification of neutral money with a non-monetary economy was mistaken. However, it is true that Hayek failed to specify fully an analytical framework within which such a neutral money could

---

F. A. Hayek, *Contra Keynes and Cambridge*. For an overview to the debate cf. the editor's introduction, ibid., pp. 37–40.

[149] The Hayek-Sraffa debate has produced a rich secondary literature; cf., e.g., Milgate, "On the Origin of the Notion of 'Intertemporal Equilibrium'"; Meghnad Desai, "The Task of Monetary Theory: The Hayek-Sraffa Debate in a Modern Perspective", and Roy McCloughry, "Neutrality and Monetary Equilibrium: A Note on Desai", both in *Advances in Economic Theory*, ed. Mauro Baranzini (Oxford: Basil Blackwell, 1982), pp. 149–70 and 171–82; Ludwig Lachmann, "Austrian Economics under Fire: The Hayek-Sraffa Duel in Retrospect", in *Austrian Economics: Historical and Philosophical Background*, ed. Wolfgang Grassl and Barry Smith (London: Croom Helm, 1986), pp. 225–42; Michael S. Lawlor and Bobbie L. Horn, "Notes on the Sraffa-Hayek Exchange", *Review of Political Economy*, vol. 4, July 1992, pp. 317–40; Heinz D. Kurz, "The Hayek-Keynes-Sraffa Controversy Reconsidered", in *Critical Essays on Piero Sraffa's Legacy in Economics*, ed. Heinz D. Kurz (Cambridge: Cambridge University Press, 2000), pp. 257–301; and Carlo Zappia, "Sraffa on Hayek: Unexpected Influences", in *Piero Sraffa's Political Economy*, ed. Cozzi and Marchionatti, pp. 333–55.

[150] Cf. Sraffa, "Dr. Hayek on Money and Capital", reprinted, pp. 198–200; the quotation is from p. 200.

have been consistently derived.[151] Such a derivation would have faced a double task: on the one hand, to explain the use of money,[152] and on the other hand, to show that it is conceivable that money thus derived could indeed be neutral, that is, that the outcome of this money economy coincides with that of the ideal barter economy. In other words, to solve this problem it would have been necessary to introduce frictions into the static economy in order to confer to money the function of a means of exchange, yet simultaneously money thus introduced would have to be able to overcome these same frictions in their effects on the equilibrium outcome of the economy. In the end, as has already been noted, Hayek circumvented the analytical problem by simply asserting the existence of an economy exhibiting the properties of neutral money.

More generally, Hayek's investigation into neutral money was only one aspect of the much wider task he had set himself from the outset. This task consisted in developing a general theory of a money economy that included neutral money just as a limiting special case.[153] Only to this special case— which Hayek never entertained false pretensions of being accomplished in practice—would the laws of statics (or of pure theory) apply without need for further qualification. This approach is in stark contrast to the view of a money economy as essentially not amenable to the laws of pure theory. It was this latter view that Keynes at the time of this controversy was beginning to expound in his first steps towards a "monetary theory of production",[154] and it might also have coloured Sraffa's preconceptions when he entered the debate. Interestingly, Hayek's later 'transformation', his struggle to free himself from the constraints imposed by an equilibrium framework, moved him progressively away from putting too much analytical weight into constructions like neutral money, in any case.[155]

---

[151] This had been, for example, one of the main tasks he had set himself for his project of "Investigations", which he eventually abandoned.

[152] In present-day monetary theory the equivalent task consists in proving the existence of a monetary economy with a positive exchange value of a fiat-type money. The locus classicus for such an exercise is Paul A. Samuelson, "An Exact Consumption-Loan Model of Interest With and Without the Social Contrivance of Money", *Journal of Political Economy*, vol. 66, December 1958, pp. 467–82.

[153] On the task of monetary theory cf. Hayek, *Prices and Production*, this volume, pp. 279–80; cf. also earlier "Investigations", p. 134. As Hayek later put it, money within this general theory was to be considered "a loose joint in the self-equilibrating apparatus of the price mechanism" (F. A. Hayek, *The Pure Theory of Capital*, reprinted, p. 367). Cf. on this also Roger W. Garrison, "Time and Money: The Universals of Macroeconomic Theorizing", *Journal of Macroeconomics*, vol. 6, Spring 1984, pp. 197–213.

[154] Cf., e.g., John Maynard Keynes in his contribution to *Festschrift für Arthur Spiethoff*, ed. Clausing, pp. 123–25, reprinted as "A Monetary Theory of Production", in *The General Theory and After, Part 1: Preparation*, vol. 13 (1973) of *The Collected Writings of John Maynard Keynes*, pp. 408–11.

[155] For more on this see the editor's introduction to F. A. Hayek, *Business Cycles, Part II*.

The most devastating of Sraffa's attacks dealt with the meaning of *the natural rate of interest*, and it is in particular this aspect of the debate which is still well and alive in its historiography. Sraffa's criticism concentrated on the multiplicity of such rates when interpreted as 'real' or 'own rates' of interest in a barter economy. Furthermore, he identified equilibrium with a stationary state (as a species of Marshallian long-period equilibrium). This gave rise to the following much-quoted interchange.

> If money did not exist, and loans were made in terms of all sorts of commodities, there would be a single rate which satisfies the conditions of equilibrium, but there might be at any one moment as many 'natural' rates of interest as there are commodities, though they would not be 'equilibrium' rates.[156]

To which Hayek responded,

> I think it would be truer to say that, in this situation, there would be *no single rate* which, applied to all commodities, would satisfy the conditions of equilibrium rates, but there might, at any moment, be as many 'natural' rates of interest as there are commodities, *all* of which would be *equilibrium rates* . . . [157]

Which apparently allowed Sraffa the final blow: if there were many "natural" rates, how could "the money rate . . . be equal to 'the' natural rate"?[158]

The validity of both of Sraffa's assertions is obvious, if restricted to his own chosen framework of reference, that is, a barter economy in stationary equilibrium—note that his 'natural rates' stand for commodity own rates, and only in a *stationary* equilibrium with unchanging relative prices will these own rates be equal to each other and therefore represent a single equilibrium rate. However, this does not contradict Hayek's remark quoted above, as applying to a barter economy in *intertemporal* equilibrium—note that Hayek's 'natural rates' (put in quotation marks in his text) are to be interpreted as equilibrium rates of a *barter economy*. Moreover, following Hayek the natural (or equilibrium) rate of interest of a *money* economy is a rate defined in terms of *money* and therefore is a uniform rate even in the case of intertemporal equilibrium, where over time relative prices are allowed to change and commodity own rates to differ.

Those siding with Sraffa in this part of the controversy must therefore main-

---

[156] Sraffa, "Dr. Hayek on Money and Capital", reprinted, p. 205.
[157] Hayek, "Money and Capital: A Reply", reprinted, p. 218.
[158] Sraffa, "A Rejoinder", reprinted, p. 225.

tain that Hayek in this instance did not argue within an intertemporal equilibrium framework.[159] The crucial issue thus turns on the continuity in Hayek's thought with respect to this concept. Intertemporal equilibrium had been the centrepiece of Hayek's analysis in 1928–29, and in *Geldtheorie* he had encountered and refuted an argument by Halm analogous to Sraffa's.[160] Interpreting Hayek's reply to Sraffa as just a repetition of that to Halm appears perfectly consistent. In contrast, opponents of this interpretation would have to base their view on a discontinuity such that Hayek in 1931 eschewed the concept of intertemporal equilibrium he had used before and was soon to use again afterwards. The assumption of continuity appears the more convincing of the two, and as such Hayek's argument, although perhaps awkwardly formulated in his reply, certainly appears capable of vindication.

The third point of Sraffa's attack is directed towards Hayek's thesis of *the futility of forced saving*. Here Sraffa questions the non-permanence of the effects of forced saving on the stock of capital.[161] According to Sraffa forced saving may typically have both permanent and temporary effects, permanent ones if the new capital structure can be sustained, and at least temporary ones as the capital goods constructed by the means of forced saving will physically remain operative even if the new structure cannot be permanently sustained. In both cases the mechanism making the viability of forced saving possible is the redistribution of income in favour of an increase in saving.

Hayek's position in this respect has already been sketched above. It is however worthwhile to emphasise once more two aspects. On the one hand, Hayek rests his case against temporary benefits from forced saving on the non-malleability of capital goods, such that the newly created capital goods can only be used properly when they fit into an overall structure of capital. On the other hand, Sraffa's argument relies crucially on the property of path depen-

---

[159] For a typical example of the secondary literature cf. Lawlor and Horn, "Notes on the Sraffa-Hayek Exchange", p. 330: "In other words, 'natural' rates are not necessarily 'equilibrium' rates *if* by equilibrium it is meant prices equal cost of production and by 'natural' we mean barter-like (money-less) intertemporal loans" (emphasis added). True enough, but what a big 'if'! In my view, Lawlor and Horn's (ibid., p. 332n.10) arguments for ascribing to Hayek the adherence to a concept of stationary equilibrium are unconvincing, building as they do on the alleged inconsistency of Hayek not analysing the process of the business cycle by means of the method of intertemporal equilibrium. Yet Hayek in *Monetary Theory and the Trade Cycle* had always been at pains to make clear that intertemporal equilibrium denotes the state of neutral money and thus the *absence* of business cycles, whereas the phenomenon of the business cycle should be considered one of intertemporal *dis*equilibrium.

[160] Cf. Hayek, *Monetary Theory and the Trade Cycle*, this volume, p. 152. On the uniformity of the money and thus the natural rate cf. ibid., this volume, pp. 148–49, and *The Pure Theory of Capital*, reprinted, p. 57n.7, and on the distinct role of the capital market in a monetary economy cf. "Investigations", pp. 105–7.

[161] Sraffa, "Dr. Hayek on Money and Capital", reprinted, pp. 203–4.

dence, that is, that the very equilibrium position to which a process eventually converges will be influenced by this process itself. In any case, the argument of path dependence is double-edged, as it is merely a necessary, not a sufficient condition for bringing about the desired result. What it can establish is that forced saving may be able to change the ultimate equilibrium from that where the process had originally started from. What it cannot, is to guarantee that the ultimate equilibrium will be one where forced saving can be permanently maintained—on the contrary the economy might even end up in a position inferior to that from which it had departed.

Summing up, it appears that, at least in some crucial parts, the usual interpretation of the Hayek-Sraffa debate is in need of revision. With regard to the foundations of monetary theory, it is true that Hayek did not live up to his own ambitions and accomplish a full integration of money into an equilibrium framework—nor, it must be acknowledged, despite appearances to the contrary, has up to now anyone else succeeded in this task, which may well turn out as a quest for a will-o'-the-wisp. In any case, Hayek must be credited for clearly formulating the problem and for thinking it through up to the very limits set by the deficiency of contemporary analytical methods and, even more importantly, by the enigmatic nature of the problem itself. Turning to the notion of the equilibrium rate of interest, the account of the controversy given above vindicates the coherence of Hayek's position, although a more lucid formulation of his reply would have been desirable. Finally, from a theoretical point of view the dispute about the effects of forced saving centred on the issue of the determinateness of the equilibrium finally attained. Here, Hayek had never denied in principle the possibility of effects deriving from path-dependence, but only questioned their practical relevance. Important though his difference with Sraffa on this may appear, it is not an issue of 'high theory'. Thus, overall, the positions Hayek put forward in his controversy with Sraffa appear tenable.

Here we leave Hayek midway between the presentation of his first two monographs on money and the cycle and his future attempt to provide them with a capital theoretic foundation, at a time when his explanation of the cycle and the crisis was widely judged as on a par with monetary or proto-Keynesian approaches. Hayek's major accomplishments consisted in a comprehensive attempt at integrating money and the cycle into an equilibrium framework, with intertemporal equilibrium as the point of reference, departures from which characterised the cycle. He had gone beyond simple monetary explanations by emphasising the structural dimension of the cyclical process such that the advent of the crisis could be attributed to the unsustainable structures created by an inflationary-led boom. However, the acceptance of the specific structural mechanism proposed, that is, variations in the capital intensity of production, expressed in terms of Austrian capital theory, had met with some resistance, or lack of understanding, even among economists in general friendly to Hayek's view. It was due to this perceived weakness that Sraffa's critique, and soon afterwards Knight's critique of Austrian capital theory, became dangerous as a threat to Hayek's reputation as a theorist. Yet, simultaneously they provided Hayek with a fresh impetus to refine and extend his investigations into the fields of money, capital, and the cycle, which gave rise to his capital project and to a series of contributions of which some are the subjects of the companion volume.

Hansjoerg Klausinger

MONETARY THEORY AND
THE TRADE CYCLE

INTRODUCTION TO THE SERIES (1933)

The science of Economics, like all other branches of knowledge, recognises no limitation by national boundaries. Contiguity of residence may give a certain unity to the speculation of particular groups of economists, a tradition of good teaching may give a presumption of excellence to the products of particular seminars; and in this sense it is not foolish to speak of local schools of economic thought, or to attach geographical labels to particular theories. But to speak of Economics, as distinct from economists, in terms of national or municipal classifications, to distinguish an English Economics from a Continental Economics, and so on, has no more sense than to speak of English Arithmetic. The criteria of scientific validity take no account of origins, and the economist who refused to avail himself of a particular set of propositions because they were foreign would be acting no less unscientifically than the chemist or physicist who acted on similar principles. It has been well said that there are only two kinds of Economics—good Economics and bad Economics. All other classifications are misleading.

Unfortunately, the economist, far more than the practitioner of the natural sciences, is victim to the curse of Babel. The chemist and the physicist—dealing as they do with tangible and quantitative relations between easily definable things—can converse in what to all intents and purposes is an international language. A very modest linguistic equipment is sufficient to enable one to follow all the chief contributions in such branches of science. In Economics this is not so. The complicated social relationships which are its chief preoccupation lend themselves much less to merely symbolic analysis. No doubt, even here, mathematical methods can be of considerable use both in assisting thought and in securing complete precision. But the description of what the symbols represent, the delimitation and interpretation of concepts, these are

[*Monetary Theory and the Trade Cycle* (London: Cape, 1933) was published in the Economic Theory Section of the Bedford Series of Economic Handbooks, edited by Lionel Robbins. The following year it was succeeded in the series by Ludwig von Mises, *The Theory of Money and Credit* (London: Cape, 1934; reprinted, Indianapolis: Liberty Classics, 1981), the English translation of the revised second edition of *Theorie des Geldes und der Umlaufsmittel* (Munich and Leipzig: Duncker and Humblot, 1924; 1st ed., 1912).—Ed.]

matters which, in the social sciences, require a wealth of qualitative terminology and a subtlety of expression calculated to strain to the full the resources of any language. Small wonder, then, that the professional economist, with limited time and limited powers at his disposal, will often conclude that depth is to be preferred to breadth and that a more intensive exploitation of the resources available to him in his own language is likely to yield more than the attempt to assimilate material only available in foreign tongues. Small wonder too that, in consequence of these conditions, there is probably more overlapping and wasteful duplication of effort in Economics than in any other branch of scientific knowledge. I know of no natural science in which it would be possible for a man to devote years to the discovery of propositions which are already commonplaces in language areas other than his own. It is notorious that in Economics this frequently happens.

It follows, therefore, that, in Economics, even more than elsewhere, there is an urgent need for a continuous series of translations which shall make available to economists in different countries the results of investigations in languages other than their own. In England before the war this need was beginning to be met. The Bruce translation of Pantaleoni, the Wotzel translation of Pierson, the Smart translations of Böhm-Bawerk,[1] are examples of work of a high order of scholarship and literary excellence which kept us in touch with the best products of contemporary thought abroad. But the war (which upset so many good things) interrupted this process of internationalisation, and

---

[1] [Cf. Maffeo Pantaleoni, *Principii di economia pura* (Florence: Barbera, 1889), translated by T. Boston Bruce as *Pure Economics* (London: Macmillan, 1898); Nikolaas Gerard Pierson, *Leerboek der Staathuishoudkunde* (Haarlem: De Erven F. Bohn, 1884), translated by A. A. Wotzel as *Principles of Economics*, 2 vols. (London: Macmillan, 1902 and 1912); Eugen von Böhm-Bawerk, *Kapital und Kapitalzins*, 1st ed., vol. 1: *Geschichte der Kapitalzinstheorien*, and vol. 2: *Positive Theorie des Kapitales* (Innsbruck: Wagner, 1884 and 1889; reprinted, Düsseldorf: Verlag Wirtschaft und Finanzen, 1994 and 1991), translated by William Smart as *Capital and Interest*, vol. 1: *A Critical History of Economical Theory*, and vol. 2: *The Positive Theory of Capital* (London: Macmillan, 1890 and 1891; reprinted, New York: Kelley, 1970). The fourth edition of *Kapital und Kapitalzins*, in three volumes (Jena: Fischer, 1921), has been translated since then by George D. Huncke and Hans F. Sennholz as *Capital and Interest*, vol. 1: *History and Critique of Interest Theories*, vol. 2: *Positive Theory of Capital*, and vol. 3: *Further Essays on Capital and Interest* (South Holland, IL: Libertarian Press, 1959). Maffeo Pantaleoni (1857–1924), Italian economist and politician, co-editor of the *Giornale degli Economisti* (from 1890), combined in his work the tradition of classical economics with the new approach of Austrian marginalism. Nikolaas Gerard Pierson (1839–1909), economist and politician, introduced Austrian and Marshallian approaches into Dutch economic thought. Hayek chose a contribution by Pierson ("The Problem of Value in Socialist Society") for reprint in *Collectivist Economic Planning*, ed. F. A. Hayek (London: Routledge, 1935; reprinted, Clifton: Kelley, 1975), pp. 41–86. Eugen von Böhm-Bawerk (1851–1914), professor of economics at the University of Vienna and for some time minister of finance, as a member of the second generation contributed, jointly with Friedrich von Wieser, to the transformation of Carl Menger's ideas into a distinctive Austrian school. His own work focused on the time dimension in the theory of capital and interest and inspired much of Hayek's earlier writings.—Ed.]

since the war it has not been completely resumed. This series is an attempt to make good the gap—to make available to English and American readers the chief recent contributions in foreign languages to the advancement of Economic Science.

It is unnecessary to introduce at length the author of the present volume, Professor von Hayek, until recently Director of the Austrian Institut für Konjunkturforschung,[2] now Tooke Professor of Economic Science and Statistics in the University of London. Professor Hayek's *Prices and Production*[3] and his various contributions to *Economica* and the *Economic Journal* will already have made him familiar to most English readers interested in recent developments in the theory of money and credit. The present volume, *Monetary Theory and the Trade Cycle*, is a translation of a work which was published in Austria before *Prices and Production*, and which deals with the problem of trade fluctuation from a more general point of view. The preface makes clear the precise relationship between this work and the author's other investigations in the same field.

Lionel Robbins[4]
The London School of Economics
September 1932

[2] [That is, the Austrian Institute for Business Cycle Research, founded at the initiative of Ludwig von Mises in 1927.—Ed.]

[3] [F. A. Hayek, *Prices and Production* (London: Routledge, 1931; 2nd ed. rev., 1935), reprinted in this volume.—Ed.]

[4] [Lionel Robbins (1898–1984), head of the Economics Department at LSE, 1928–60, closely cooperated with Hayek in the 1930s. Unlike most contemporary British economists, his work was receptive to influences outside the Marshallian tradition, in particular to Philip Wicksteed and the Austrian school. Cf. Robbins's path-breaking *Essay on the Nature and Significance of Economic Science* (London: Macmillan, 1932; 2nd ed. rev., 1935; reprinted, Auburn, AL: Ludwig von Mises Institute, 2007).—Ed.]

PREFACE (1933)

The German essay,[1] of which the following is a translation, represents an expanded version of a paper[2] prepared for the meeting of the Verein für Sozialpolitik, held in Zurich in September 1928, and of some remarks contributed to the discussion at that meeting.[3] Although, in revising the translation, I have made numerous minor alterations and additions (mainly confined to the footnotes), the general course of the argument has been left unchanged.[4] The book, therefore, still shows signs of the particular aim with which it was written. In submitting it to a public different from that for which it was originally intended, a few words of explanation are, perhaps, required.

In Germany, somewhat in contrast to the situation in English-speaking countries, monetary explanations of the Trade Cycle were always, or at least until quite recently, regarded with some mistrust. One of the aims of this study—one on which an English reader may feel that I have wasted unnecessary energy—was to justify the monetary approach to these problems. But I hope that this more explicit statement of the role of the monetary factor

---

[1] *Geldtheorie und Konjunkturtheorie*. Beiträge zur Konjunkturforschung, vol. 1, ed. Österreichisches Institut für Konjunkturforschung (Vienna: Springer, 1929 [reprinted, Salzburg: Neugebauer, 1976]).

[2] "Einige Bemerkungen über das Verhältnis der Geldtheorie zur Konjunkturtheorie", in *Schriften des Vereins für Sozialpolitik*, vol. 173, part 2: *Beiträge zur Wirtschaftstheorie, Konjunkturforschung und Konjunkturtheorie*, ed. Karl Diehl (Munich and Leipzig: Duncker and Humblot, 1928), pp. 247–94. [For a translation see "Some Remarks on the Relation of Monetary Theory to Business Cycle Theory", trans. Vincent Homolka, in *Business Cycle Theory: Selected Texts 1860–1939*, vol. 3: *Monetary Theories of the Business Cycle*, ed. Harald Hagemann (London: Pickering and Chatto, 2002), pp. 161–97.—Ed.]

[3] "Redebeitrag", in *Schriften des Vereins für Sozialpolitik*, vol. 175: *Verhandlungen des Vereins für Sozialpolitik in Zürich 1928. Wandlungen des Kapitalismus. Auslandsanleihen. Kredit und Konjunktur*, ed. Franz Boese (Munich and Leipzig: Duncker and Humblot, 1929), pp. 369–74. [In the original this note was misplaced after "Sozialpolitik".—Ed.]

[4] [The translators were two of Lionel Robbins's favourite pupils, Nicholas Kaldor and Honoria Croome. Significant discrepancies between the German and the English version, due to Hayek's revisions, but sometimes also to shortcomings of the translation, will be taken account of in the editor's notes. In this regard, for ascertaining the accuracy of the English text, use will be made of the more recent translation, "Some Remarks".—Ed.]

will not be found quite useless, for it is not only a justification of the monetary approach but also a refutation of some over-simplified monetary explanations which are widely accepted. In order to save the sound elements in the monetary theories of the Trade Cycle, I had to attempt, in particular, to refute certain theories which have led to the belief that, by stabilising the general price level, all the disturbing monetary causes would be eliminated. Although, since this book was written, this belief has been somewhat rudely shaken by the crisis of 1929, I hope that a systematic examination of its foundations will still be found useful. The critique of the programme of the 'stabilisers', which is in many ways the central theme of this book, has now occupied me for many years, and since I deal here only with some special problems which have grown mainly out of these studies, I may perhaps be permitted to refer below to other publications, in which I have partly dealt with certain further theoretical problems and partly attempted to use these considerations for the elucidation of contemporary phenomena.[5] In particular, my *Prices and Production*, originally published in England, should be considered as an essential complement to the present publication. While I have here emphasised the *monetary causes* which *start* the cyclical fluctuations, I have, in that later publication, concentrated on the *successive changes in the real structure of production*, which *constitute* those fluctuations. This essential complement of my theory seems to me to be the more important since, in consequence of actual economic developments, the over-simplified monetary explanations have gained undeserved

---

[5] "Die Währungspolitik der Vereinigten Staaten seit der Überwindung der Krise von 1920", *Zeitschrift für Volkswirtschaft und Sozialpolitik*, n.s., vol. 5, nos. 1 and 2, 1925, pp. 25–63 and 254–317 [translated as "Monetary Policy in the United States after the Recovery from the Crisis of 1920" and reprinted as chapter 2 of *Good Money, Part I: The New World*, ed. Stephen Kresge, vol. 5 (1999) of *The Collected Works of F. A. Hayek* (Chicago: University of Chicago Press; London: Routledge)—Ed.]; "Das intertemporale Gleichgewichtssystem der Preise und die Bewegungen des 'Geldwertes'", *Weltwirtschaftliches Archiv*, vol. 28, July 1928, pp. 33–76 [translated as "Intertemporal Price Equilibrium and Movements in the Value of Money" and reprinted as chapter 5 of F. A. Hayek, *Good Money, Part I: The New World*—Ed.]; "The 'Paradox' of Saving", *Economica*, no. 32, May 1931, pp. 125–69 [reprinted as chapter 2 of *Contra Keynes and Cambridge: Essays, Correspondence*, ed. Bruce Caldwell, vol. 9 (1995) of *The Collected Works of F. A. Hayek*; a version with minor revisions had been reprinted as an appendix to *Profits, Interest and Investment. And Other Essays on the Theory of Industrial Fluctuations* (London: Routledge, 1939)—Ed.]; *Prices and Production*; "Reflections on the Pure Theory of Money of Mr. J. M. Keynes", *Economica*, no. 33, August 1931, pp. 270–95, and no. 35, February 1932, pp. 22–44 [reprinted as chapters 3 and 6 of F. A. Hayek, *Contra Keynes and Cambridge*—Ed.]; "Das Schicksal der Goldwährung", *Der Deutsche Volkswirt*, vol. 6, February 12 and 19, 1932, pp. 642–45 and 677–81 [translated as "The Fate of the Gold Standard" and reprinted as chapter 3 of F. A. Hayek, *Good Money, Part I: The New World*—Ed.]; "Kapitalaufzehrung", *Weltwirtschaftliches Archiv*, vol. 36, July 1932, pp. 86–108 [translated as "Capital Consumption" and reprinted as chapter 6 of F. A. Hayek, *Money, Capital and Fluctuations: Early Essays*, ed. Roy McCloughry (Chicago: University of Chicago Press; London: Routledge and Kegan Paul, 1984), a new translation to be included in *Capital and Interest*, ed. Lawrence White, vol. 11 (forthcoming) of *The Collected Works of F. A. Hayek*—Ed.].

prominence in recent times. And since, in all my English publications, I have purposely refrained from combining purely theoretical considerations with discussions of current events, it may be useful to add here one or two remarks on the bearing of those considerations on the problems of to-day.

It is a curious fact that the general disinclination to explain the past boom by monetary factors has been quickly replaced by an even greater readiness to hold the present working of our monetary organisation exclusively responsible for our present plight. And the same stabilisers who believed that nothing was wrong with the boom and that it might last indefinitely because prices did not rise, now believe that everything could be set right again if only we would use the weapons of monetary policy to prevent prices from falling. The same superficial view which sees no other harmful effect of a credit expansion but the rise of the price level, now believes that our only difficulty is a fall in the price level, caused by credit contraction.

There can, of course, be little doubt that, at the present time, a deflationary process is going on and that an indefinite continuation of that deflation would do inestimable harm. But this does not, by any means, necessarily mean that the deflation is the original cause of our difficulties or that we could overcome these difficulties by compensating for the deflationary tendencies, at present operative in our economic system, by forcing more money into circulation. There is no reason to assume that the crisis was started by a deliberate deflationary action on the part of the monetary authorities, or that the deflation itself is anything but a secondary phenomenon, a process induced by the mal-adjustments of industry left over from the boom. If, however, the deflation is not a cause but an effect of the unprofitableness of industry, then it is surely vain to hope that, by reversing the deflationary process, we can regain lasting prosperity. Far from following a deflationary policy, Central Banks, particularly in the United States, have been making earlier and more far-reaching efforts than have ever been undertaken before to combat the depression by a policy of credit expansion—with the result that the depression has lasted longer and has become more severe than any preceding one. What we need is a readjustment of those elements in the structure of production and of prices which existed before the deflation began and which then made it unprofitable for industry to borrow. But, instead of furthering the inevitable liquidation of the maladjustments brought about by the boom during the last three years, all conceivable means have been used to prevent that readjustment from taking place; and one of these means, which has been repeatedly tried though without success, from the earliest to the most recent stages of depression, has been this deliberate policy of credit expansion.

It is very probable that the much discussed rigidities, which had already grown up in many parts of the modern economic system before 1929, would, in any case, have made the process of readjustment much slower and more

54

painful. It is also probable that these very resistances to readjustment would have set up a severe deflationary process which would finally have overcome those rigidities. To what extent, under the given situation of a relatively rigid price and wage system, this deflationary process is perhaps not only inevitable but is even the quickest way of bringing about the required result, is a very difficult question, about which, on the basis of our present knowledge, I should be afraid to make any definite pronouncement.

It seems certain, however, that we shall merely make matters worse if we aim at curing the deflationary symptoms and, at the same time (by the erection of trade barriers and other forms of state intervention) do our best to increase rather than to decrease the fundamental maladjustments. More than that: while the advantages of such a course are, to say the least, uncertain, the new dangers which it creates are great. To combat the depression by a forced credit expansion is to attempt to cure the evil by the very means which brought it about; because we are suffering from a misdirection of production, we want to create further misdirection—a procedure which can only lead to a much more severe crisis as soon as the credit expansion comes to an end. It would not be the first experiment of this kind which has been made. We should merely be repeating, on a much larger scale, the course followed by the Federal Reserve system in 1927, an experiment which Mr. A. C. Miller, the only economist on the Federal Reserve Board and, at the same time, its oldest member, has rightly characterised as "the greatest and boldest operation ever undertaken by the Federal reserve system", an operation which "resulted in one of the most costly errors committed by it or any other banking system in the last 75 years".[6] It is probably to this experiment, together with the attempts to prevent liquidation once the crisis had come, that we owe the exceptional severity and duration of the depression. We must not forget that, for the last six or eight years, monetary policy all over the world has followed the advice of the stabilisers. It is high time that their influence, which has already done harm enough, should be overthrown.

We cannot hope for the overthrow of this alluringly simple theory until its theoretical basis is definitely refuted and something better substituted for it. The opponents of the stabilisation programme still labour—and probably always will labour—under the disadvantage that they have no equally simple and clear-cut rule to propose; perhaps no rule at all which will satisfy the eagerness

---

[6] [U.S. Congress, *Operation of the National and Federal Reserve Banking Systems*, Senate Hearings before a Subcommittee of the Committee on Banking and Currency, 71st Congress, 3rd session (Washington, DC: U.S. Government Printing Office, 1931), p. 134. Adolph C. Miller (1866–1947) was a professor at the University of Chicago and the University of California–Berkeley. When the Federal Reserve System was established in 1914, President Wilson appointed Miller to its Board of Governors, then as the sole economist among its members, a position he held for twenty-two years.—Ed.]

of those who hope to cure all evils by authoritative action. But whatever may be our hope for the future, the one thing of which we must be painfully aware at the present time—a fact which no writer on these problems should fail to impress upon his readers—is how little we really know of the forces which we are trying to influence by deliberate management; so little indeed that it must remain an open question whether we would try if we knew more.

Friedrich A. Hayek
The London School of Economics
June 1932

PREFACE TO THE GERMAN EDITION, *GELDTHEORIE UND KONJUNKTURTHEORIE* (1929)

The following essay represents an expanded version of a paper titled "Einige Bemerkungen über das Verhältnis der Geldtheorie zur Konjunkturtheorie", prepared as a report on credit and the cycle for the meeting of the Verein für Sozialpolitik in Zurich in September 1928 and published in vol. 173, part 2, of the *Schriften des Vereins*. Due to limitations of space and the short deadline for delivery, it was then not possible to carry out the original plan of providing a systematic overview of all the relations between monetary theory and business cycle theory that I deemed essential. Rather I had to content myself with pointing out the general deficiencies of the non-monetary theories and to discuss the existing approaches of a monetary explanation. After the publication of the report, I felt the need to go beyond the mere beginnings and to fulfil the promises contained in them by elaborating and refining the arguments, the result of which is this new publication. The text of the original paper, which constitutes the first three chapters, forms still the basis of this essay. The revisions which the text has undergone for the reprint have been mainly confined to the elimination of stylistic shortcomings and to some minor additions. Moreover I had to refer to various contributions that have appeared in the meantime, among them some of the other reports published in the same volume of the *Schriften des Vereins für Sozialpolitik*. For this reason in particular the fifth section of chapter 3 has been inserted. I am sincerely grateful to the publisher Duncker und Humblot (Munich and Leipzig) for permitting most complaisantly the reprint of my report originally published there.

The main ideas of the new fourth chapter have been already presented during the discussion on credit and the cycle at last year's Zurich meeting of the Verein für Sozialpolitik as an oral contribution to the debate. Instead of only the very terse suggestions possible under these circumstances I have now attempted to present a self-contained argument. Finally, the last chapter contains an overview of the most important unsettled problems for future research as derived from the approach adhered to in this work.

[This is the preface to the original German edition, *Geldtheorie und Konjunkturtheorie* (1929). The translation is by the editor.—Ed.]

Even in the expanded version of the work now presented it cannot be expected to provide an elaborate theory of the business cycle. It appears to me that a successful attempt at such a theory must be preceded by certain preparatory work on the narrower fields of the theories of money and interest, work that will by far transcend the particular problems of the theory of the cycle and require an investigation on its own. With regard to the problems of monetary theory I hope to accomplish this task in a more extensive work, the beginnings of which considerably predate these investigations into the theory of the cycle. The first volume, of which a section has been published as an article, is close to completion.[1] Jointly with this work this volume can be regarded as the foundation for the elaborate theory of the business cycle, which both are not yet able to provide.

Friedrich A. Hayek
Vienna, January 1929

[1] [The reference is to the unpublished typescript "Geldtheoretische Untersuchungen", preserved in the Friedrich A. von Hayek Papers, box 105, folders 1–4, Hoover Institution Archives, Stanford University. A translation, "Investigations into Monetary Theory", appears as chapter 1 of *Business Cycles, Part II*, ed. Hansjoerg Klausinger, vol. 8 (2012) of *The Collected Works of F. A. Hayek*. The article in question is "Das intertemporale Gleichgewichtssystem der Preise".—Ed.]

PREFACE TO THE REPRINT OF THE GERMAN EDITION (1976)

It would be desirable to introduce this new edition of a book, whose original German version has been sold out and unavailable for so long, with a few words about the history of how the book first came into being.

In the course of a study visit to New York in the years 1923 and 1924, I began to occupy myself primarily with problems of money and the trade cycle. In addition, while there, I commenced on a study of the consequences of stabilising the value of money, but this was never completed. After returning to Vienna, I reported first about the new measures then undertaken by the Federal Reserve System in attempting to stabilise the cycle, and also laid the groundwork for a major investigation into monetary theory.[1] In this article, I was obliged to address some questions concerning the causes of cyclical fluctuations. Finally, on the advice of my dear friend Gottfried von Haberler,[2] I introduced a lengthy footnote to extend the overly terse presentation of this topic in the text; in a sense, this has become the point of departure for my work on the theory of business cycles. In the text of this article, I state, *inter alia*,

> The overexpansion of raw material and capital goods industries, which recurs regularly, must be regarded as the chief culprit of the periodic economic recessions. This overexpansion in turn is contingent on the highly vaunted elasticity of our modern credit system, which is in fact its main cause. The fact that banks are in a position to extend credit exceeding the concomitant growth in savings is what sets in motion the cumulative impact of a given

[The reprint of the German edition was published in 1976 (Salzburg: Neugebauer). On this occasion Hayek added a new preface. The translation is by Ciaran Cassidy.—Ed.]

[1] The report on the Federal Reserve System was published as "Die Währungspolitik der Vereinigten Staaten". [Cf. "Monetary Policy in the United States".—Ed.]

[2] [The Austrian economist Gottfried Haberler (1900–1995) was a friend of Hayek from their days in Vienna. In the 1930s he worked temporarily in Vienna, Harvard, and Geneva, the latter of which is where he wrote his magisterial survey *Prosperity and Depression* (Geneva: League of Nations, 1937). From 1936 until his retirement in 1971 he taught as a full professor at Harvard University. Apart from his work on the business cycle he is well known for major contributions to the theory of international trade.—Ed.]

increase in demand for finished products on the output of higher-order commodities and thereby triggers the accumulation of excess inventories, the
overexpansion of capital equipment, and, above all, the disproportionate rise
in raw material and capital goods prices, whose ultimate result is a dwindling
of profits. They can supply purchasing power to the entrepreneur without a
corresponding sacrifice in purchasing power on anyone else's part, and their
willingness to extend credit is enhanced when favourable economic conditions seem to lower their risks. Since an increased demand manifests itself on
a market where supply has remained constant, prices must rise, dispropor-
tionately so for higher-order commodities. This occurs because banks can
supply money capital in excess of the real available capital and can therefore offer money capital *more cheaply* than would correspond to the relationship between the increased demand for and supply of real capital. One consequence is that economically unjustified capital investments may still seem
to be profitable and will therefore eventually turn into a loss.[3]

With these remarks I assumed that I had simply reflected the theory of Ludwig von Mises, which was widely accepted in our circle, and which I referred
to in a footnote at the end of the passage.[4] In a study on monetary policy, I
had no intention of developing my own theoretical views any further. However, in response to the urging of my colleagues I incorporated a footnote,
which presented more comprehensively the ideas I had formed in America,
in the course of discussions on the opinions which dominated there. As a better illustration, I will reproduce this footnote, word for word, in the following text:

> Inappropriately low interest rates offer the greatest advantage to those sec-
> tors of the economy whose products are farthest removed from the consump-
> tion stage. This is so because for them savings in interest payments for the
> eventual end product will accumulate over a correspondingly longer stretch
> of time and because the next purchaser at each stage can pay a higher price,
> in view of the overall savings in interest on the way to the consumer. What
> is decisive here is not so much the effect of lower interest payments on pro-
> duction costs for that sector—the savings obtained might be equally large in

---

[3] "Die Währungspolitik der Vereinigten Staaten", p. 260 [pp. 260–62, as translated in "Monetary Policy in the United States", pp. 105–6.—Ed.].

[4] Mises, *Theorie des Geldes und der Umlaufsmittel*, pp. 373–74. [Cf. *The Theory of Money and Credit*,
pp. 402–3. Ludwig von Mises (1881–1973) was widely considered the leader of the Austrian
school in the interwar period. He left Vienna 1934 for the Graduate Institute of International
Studies in Geneva and in 1940 immigrated to the United States, where he taught at New York
University (1945–69). Mises had been pivotal in Hayek's appointment as the director of the Austrian Institute for Business Cycle Research.—Ed.]

all branches of production—but rather the cumulative impact of increases in demand on the part of all participants in the subsequent stages of production in the broadest sense (including commerce) generated by the greater profit potential the lower interest rate offers all of them. There is an additional consideration. The value of fixed capital depends not on the price attained at a particular point in time, but on yield anticipated over a longer period of time. The value of fixed capital is thus much more influenced by the interest rate in effect when the yield is capitalised than is true of working capital (materials, labour), which is fully consumed in a given productive cycle and obtains a single price, which must be discounted. A relatively low interest rate therefore raises the price of fixed capital and the profitability of its production far more than is true of working capital. Since a larger proportion of fixed capital is required in the output of producer goods than in the output of consumer goods and especially in commerce, the final stage of production in a broader sense, there is an added reason why a lower interest rate triggers the greatest expansion of those economic sectors that are farthest removed from the consumption stage.

In order to prevent a disproportionate expansion of higher-order producer goods, the interest rate must always be set at a high enough level to confine the output of producer goods to a volume matching the capital required for continuing production in the later stages that can be raised at equally favourable interest rates. It is the interest paid for capital that serves as a necessary restraint against a disproportionate expansion of a capital-intensive mode of production—a point on which almost all modern (catallactic) theories agree. When the interest rate happens to be temporarily too low, it is inevitable that excess capital will accumulate. The result will be a build-up of capital at the base of the pyramidical structure of the economy, but one for which the requisite savings are not available. While demand first rises in the raw materials, etc., sector because of the improved profitability of the branches of the economy refining their products, this demand is certain to decline again when the savings that were used up in expanding producer goods of a higher order are not available for a corresponding expansion of lower-order production (i.e., under equally profitable conditions, that is, without a higher interest rate).[5]

I had no immediate intention of developing these ideas further in a special publication, not least considering that such concepts would seem to require a solid basis in monetary theory. The "Geldtheoretische Untersuchungen", with which I was occupied at that time, seemed to offer such a basis (a work from

---

[5] ["Die Währungspolitik der Vereinigten Staaten", pp. 261–62n.1; cf. "Monetary Policy in the United States", pp. 105–6n.28.—Ed.]

which only the essay on "Das intertemporale Gleichgewichtssystem der Preise und die Bewegungen des 'Geldwertes'" has ever appeared). Perhaps the circumstance that I took over the leadership of the newly established Austrian Institute for Business Cycle Research at the beginning of 1927, was the reason why I was invited to deliver not only one of the prepared reports but also an oral contribution to the debate, on the topic of business cycle theory at the 1928 meeting of the Verein für Sozialpolitik in Zurich. Such an invitation could not easily be turned down by anyone set on an academic career path. These two addresses, which I summarised in book form and published as *Geldtheorie und Konjunkturtheorie*, which now, unaltered, is being presented here, also formed the basis for my habilitation at the University of Vienna in 1929.

For my habilitation lecture, I used the critique of the under-consumption theory by W. T. Foster and W. Catchings which I had largely developed while in America. This appeared in the same year under the title "Gibt es einen 'Widersinn des Sparens?'"[6] This work, in turn, was the reason why Professor Lionel Robbins (now Lord Robbins) invited me to hold four lectures at the London School of Economics and Political Science (of the University of London). It was just at this time that I had formed a clear picture of the mechanism underlying cyclical fluctuations and this enabled me to give a relatively easy and concise presentation, without having to go into all the intricacies and problems which a complete and detailed elaboration of the train of thought would have required. This appeared in book form under the title *Prices and Production* and, as such, was unusually successful.

It is mainly thanks to the initiative of Mr. Kurt Leube, my assistant for many years at the Department of Economics, University of Salzburg, that this book is now published in its original German form. It has been extended with a bibliographical appendix, compiled by Mr. Leube.[7] My thanks are also due to the scientific publisher Wolfgang Neugebauer for their editorial cooperation and energetic support.

Friedrich A. Hayek
Salzburg, January 1976

[6] *Zeitschrift für Nationalökonomie*, vol. 1, November 1929, pp. 387–429. [Cf. the translation as "The 'Paradox' of Saving". William Trufant Foster (1879–1950), educator and first president of Reed College, and Waddill Catchings (1879–1969), businessman, both propagated an under-consumptionist explanation of crises and stagnation. From 1920 onwards the Pollak Foundation, founded and financed by Catchings and directed by Foster, served as a platform for the discussion of their ideas. Cf. Hayek, "The 'Paradox' of Saving", reprinted, pp. 76–77.—Ed.]

[7] [Not reproduced in this edition.—Ed.]

ANALYTICAL TABLE OF CONTENTS

ONE

THE PROBLEM OF THE TRADE CYCLE

1. The relation between empirical observation and theoretical explanation[1]

Any attempt either to forecast the trend of economic development, or to influence it by measures based on an examination of existing conditions, must presuppose certain quite definite conceptions as to the necessary course of economic phenomena. Empirical studies, whether they are undertaken with such practical aims in view, or whether they are confined merely to the amplification, with the aid of special statistical devices, of our knowledge of the course of particular phases of trade fluctuations, can, at best, afford merely a verification of existing theories; they cannot, in themselves, provide new insight into the causes or the necessity of the Trade Cycle.

This view has been stated very forcibly by Professor A. Löwe.[2] "Our insight into the *theoretical* interconnections of economic cycles, and into the structural laws of circulation", he says, "has not been enriched at all by descriptive work or calculations of correlations". We can entirely agree with him, moreover, when he goes on to say that "to expect an immediate furtherance of *theory* from an increase in *empirical* insight is to misunderstand the logical relationship between theory and empirical research".[3]

---

[1] [The section headings have been added from the Analytical Table of Contents; in the original text the sections are denoted by numbers only.—Ed.]

[2] In his essay "Wie ist Konjunkturtheorie überhaupt möglich?", *Weltwirtschaftliches Archiv*, vol. 24, October 1926, p. 166. [Cf. the translation by Christian Gehrke as "How Is Business Cycle Theory Possible At All?", *Structural Change and Economic Dynamics*, vol. 8, June 1997, p. 246, reprinted in *Business Cycle Theory: Selected Texts 1860–1939*, vol. 4: *Equilibrium and the Business Cycle*, ed. Hagemann, p. 6. This translation substitutes "all these phase descriptions" for the less accurate "descriptive work" in the text. The German economist Adolf Löwe (1893–1995) was appointed professor in 1926 in Kiel, where he brought together a group of economists later referred to as the Kiel school, among them Fritz Burchardt, Gerhard Colm, and Hans Neisser. Professor at Frankfurt from 1931, in 1933 he was forced to leave for Great Britain, where he anglicised his name to Adolph Lowe. From 1940 onwards he taught at the New School for Social Research in New York.—Ed.]

[3] "Wie ist Konjunkturtheorie überhaupt möglich?", p. 166. [Translated more accurately as "furtherance of the *theoretical* system" instead of "furtherance of *theory*", in "How Is Business Cycle Theory Possible At All?", p. 6.—Ed.]

The reason for this is clear. The means of perception employed in statistics are not the same as those employed in economic theory; and it is therefore impossible to fit regularities established by the former into the structure of economic laws prescribed by the latter. We cannot superimpose upon the system of fundamental propositions comprised in the theory of equilibrium, a Trade Cycle theory resting on unrelated logical foundations. All the phenomena observed in cyclical fluctuations, particularly price formation and its influence on the direction and the volume of production, have already been explained by the theory of equilibrium; they can only be integrated as an explanation of the totality of economic events by means of fundamentally similar constructions. Trade Cycle theory itself is only expected to explain how certain prices are determined, and to state their influence on production and consumption; and the determining conditions of these phenomena are already given by elementary theory. Its special task arises from the fact that these phenomena show empirically observed movements for the explanation of which the methods of equilibrium theory are as yet inadequate. One need not go so far as to say that a successful solution could be reached only in conjunction with a positive explanation[4] of elementary phenomena; but no further proof is needed that such a solution can only be achieved in association with, or by means of, a theory which explains how certain prices or certain uses of given goods are determined at all. It is not only that we lack theories which fulfil this condition and which fall outside the category best described as "equilibrium theories"[5]—theories which are characterised by taking the logic of economic action as their starting point; the point is rather that statistical method is fundamentally unsuited to this purpose. Just as no statistical investigation can prove that a given change in demand must necessarily be followed by a certain change in price, so no statistical method can explain why all economic phenomena present that regular wave-like appearance which we observe in cyclical fluctuations. This can be explained only by widening the assumptions on which our deductions are based, so that cyclical fluctuations would follow from these as a necessary consequence, just as the general propositions of the theory of price followed from the narrower assumptions of equilibrium theory.

But even these new assumptions cannot be established by statistical investigation. The statistical approach, unlike deductive inference, leaves the conditions under which established economic relations hold good fundamentally undetermined; and similarly, the objects to which they relate cannot be deter-

---

[4] [A more accurate translation of the German text is "a particular explanation" (as in "Some Remarks", p. 164; cf. "Einige Bemerkungen", p. 250; *Geldtheorie*, p. 3).—Ed.]

[5] Cf. Adolf Löwe, "Der gegenwärtige Stand der Konjunkturtheorie [Konjunkturforschung] in Deutschland", in *Die Wirtschaftswissenschaft nach dem Kriege. Festgabe für Lujo Brentano zum 80. Geburtstag*, vol. 2: *Der Stand der Forschung*, ed. Moritz J. Bonn and Melchior Palyi (Munich and Leipzig: Duncker and Humblot, 1925), p. 360.

mined as unequivocally as by theory. Empirically established relations between various economic phenomena continue to present a problem to theory until the necessity for their interconnections can be demonstrated independently of any statistical evidence.[6] The concepts on which such an explanation is based will be quite different from those by which statistical interconnections are demonstrated; they can be reached independently. Moreover, the corroboration of statistical evidence provides, in itself, no proof of correctness. A priori we cannot expect from statistics anything more than the stimulus provided by the indication of new problems.

In thus emphasising the fact that Trade Cycle theory, while it may serve as a basis for statistical research, can never itself be established by the latter, it is by no means desired to deprecate the value of the empirical method. On the contrary, there can be no doubt that Trade Cycle theory can only gain full practical importance through exact measurement of the actual course of the phenomena which it describes. But before we can examine the question of the true importance of statistics to theory, it must be clearly recognised that the use of statistics can never consist in a deepening of our theoretical insight.

2. The use of statistics in the verification of theory

Even as a means of verification, the statistical examination of the cycles has only a very limited value for Trade Cycle theory. For the latter—as for any other economic theory—there are only two criteria of correctness. Firstly, it must be deduced with unexceptionable logic from the fundamental notions of the theoretical system; and secondly, it must explain by a purely deductive method those phenomena with all their peculiarities which we observe in the actual cycles.[7] Such a theory could only be 'false' either through an inad-

---

[6] Cf. the excellent analysis given by Eugen Altschul in his well-known essay "Konjunktur-theorie und Konjunkturstatistik", *Archiv für Sozialwissenschaft und Sozialpolitik*, vol. 55, no. 1, 1926, pp. 60–90. Altschul as a statistician deserves especial credit when, recognising the limitations of statistical methods, he writes (p. 85), "In economics especially, the final decision about the significance of a certain phenomenon can never be left to mathematical and statistical analysis. The main approach to research must necessarily lie [be] through theoretically obtained knowledge." Cf. also Arthur Cecil Pigou, *Industrial Fluctuations*, 2nd ed. (London: Macmillan, 1929 [reprinted as vol. 6 of Pigou, *Collected Economic Writings* (London: Macmillan, 1999)—Ed.]), p. 37: "The absence of statistical correlation between a given series of changes and industrial fluctuations does not by itself disprove—and its presence [the presence of such correlations] does not prove—that these changes are causes of the fluctuations."

[7] Professor Adolf Löwe, in his report "Über den Einfluß monetärer Faktoren auf den Konjunkturzyklus", in *Schriften des Vereins für Sozialpolitik*, vol. 173, part 2, p. 357, expresses his views in almost the same words. [Cf. the translation "On the Influence of Monetary Factors on the Business Cycle", in *Business Cycle Theory: Selected Texts 1860–1939*, vol. 3, ed. Hagemann,

equacy in its logic or because the phenomena which it explains do not correspond with the observed facts. If, however, the theory is logically sound, and if it leads to an explanation of the given phenomena as a necessary consequence of these general conditions of economic activity, then the best that statistical investigation can do is to show that there still remains an unexplained residue of processes. It could never prove that the determining relationships are of a different character from those maintained by the theory.[8]

It might be shown, for instance, by statistical investigation that a general rise in prices is followed by an expansion of production, and a general fall in prices by a diminution of production; but this would not necessarily mean that theory should regard the movement of price as an independent cause of movements of production. So long as a theory could explain the regular occurrence of this parallelism in any other way, it could not be disproved by statistics, even if it maintained that the connection between the two phenomena was of a precisely opposite nature.[9] It is therefore only in a negative sense that it is possible to verify theory by statistics. Either statistics can demonstrate that there are phenomena which the theory does not sufficiently explain, or it is unable to discover such phenomena. It cannot be expected to confirm the theory in a positive sense. The possibility is completely ruled out by what has been said above, since it would presuppose an assertion of *necessary* interconnections, such as statistics cannot make. There is no reason to be surprised, therefore, that although nearly all modern Trade Cycle theories use statistical material as corroboration, it is only where a given theory fails to explain all the observed phenomena that this statistical evidence can be used to judge its merits.

---

pp. 199–211. In the relevant passage Löwe speaks of "a twofold criterion: impeccable derivation of the theoretical conclusion from the premises, and confirmation of the premises and conclusions by economic reality" (ibid., p. 201).—Ed.]. The above sentences first appeared in another article in the same volume [that is, in Hayek's "Einige Bemerkungen", p. 252; cf. "Some Remarks", p. 165—Ed.].

[8] Cf. the analysis concerning "Argument der Wirklichkeitswidrigkeit" [that is, "argument of being inconsistent with reality"—Ed.] in the recent book of Erich Carell, *Sozialökonomische Theorie und Konjunkturproblem* (Munich and Leipzig: Duncker and Humblot, 1929) [cf. pp. 22–41—Ed.], for a very acute methodological argument. He opposes the thesis of Löwe (which remains, however, despite his analysis, the basis of my own work) that the incorporation of cyclical phenomena into the system of economic equilibrium theory, with which they are in apparent contradiction, remains the crucial problem of Trade Cycle theory.

[9] A well-known instance of such an apparent contradiction between a correct theoretical assertion and experience is the connection between the level of interest rates and the movement of prices. Cf. Knut Wicksell, *Vorlesungen über Nationalökonomie auf Grundlage des Marginalprinzips*, vol. 2: *Geld und Kredit* (Jena: Fischer, 1922 [reprinted, Aalen: Scientia, 1969]) [cf., e.g., pp. 187 and 208. For a translation, see *Lectures on Political Economy*, trans. Ernest Classen, vol. 2: *Money* (London: Routledge, 1935; reprinted, New York: Kelley, 1967; Auburn, AL: Ludwig von Mises Institute, 2007), pp. 164 and 182.—Ed.] See also my essay "Das intertemporale Gleichgewichtssystem der Preise", pp. 63 et seq. [pp. 63–64; cf. "Intertemporal Price Equilibrium", pp. 214–16—Ed.].

3. The task of statistics is to give accurate information about events which fall within the province of theory

Thus it is not by enriching or by checking theoretical analysis that economic statistics gain their real importance. This lies elsewhere. The proper task of statistics is to give us accurate information about the events which fall within the province of theory, and so to enable us not only to connect two consecutive events as cause and effect, a posteriori, but to grasp existing conditions completely enough for forecasts of the future and, eventually,[10] appropriate action, to become possible. It is only through this possibility of forecasts of systematic action[11] that theory gains practical importance.[12] A theory might, for instance, enable us to infer from the comparative movements of certain prices and quantities an imminent change in the direction of those movements: but we should have little use for such a theory if we were unable to ascertain the *actual* movements of the phenomena in question. With regard

[10] ["Eventually" (for the German "eventuell" in *Geldtheorie*, p. 7) is a translation error; the correct translation is "perhaps" (as in "Some Remarks", p. 166; cf. "Einige Bemerkungen", p. 253).—Ed.]

[11] [According to the German version (*Geldtheorie*, p. 7; cf. also "Einige Bemerkungen", p. 253, and "Some Remarks", p. 166), the passage should read, "this possibility of forecasts and of systematic action".—Ed.]

[12] It should be noted that the idea of forecasting is by no means a new one, although it is often regarded as such. Every economic theory, and indeed all theory of whatever sort, aims exclusively at foretelling the necessary consequences of a given situation, event, or measure. The subject-matter of Trade Cycle theory being what it is, it follows that ideally it should result in a collective forecast showing the total development resulting from a given situation under given conditions. In practice, such forecasts are attempted in too unconditional a form, and on an inadmissibly over-simplified basis; and, consequently, the very possibility of scientific judgments about future economic trends to-day appears problematical, and cautious thinkers are apt to disparage any attempt at such forecasting. In contrast to this view, we have to emphasise very strongly that statistical research in this field is meaningless except in so far as it leads to a forecast, however much that forecast may have to be hedged about with qualifications. In particular any measures aimed at alleviating the Trade Cycle (and necessarily based on statistical research) must be conceived in the light of certain assumptions as to the future trend to be expected in the absence of such measures. Statistical research, therefore, serves only to furnish the bases for the utilisation of existing theoretical principles. Dr. Oskar Morgenstern's recent categorical denial (*Wirtschaftsprognose: Eine Untersuchung ihrer Voraussetzungen und Möglichkeiten*, Vienna: Springer, 1928) of the possibility of forecasting seems to be due only to the fact that he demands more from forecasting than is justifiable. Even when ability to forecast a hailstorm would not be useless— but, on the contrary, very valuable—if the latter could thereupon be averted by firing rockets at the clouds! [The term "collective forecast" refers to *Totalprognose*, a forecast of the economic system in its totality, as distinguished by Morgenstern (ibid., pp. 7 and 31–33) from the "individual forecasts" by firms and consumers. Oskar Morgenstern (1902–77) studied at the University of Vienna and in 1931 succeeded Hayek as the director of the Austrian Institute for Business Cycle Research. After his emigration to the United States in 1938 he taught at Princeton and New York University. Presently, he is best known for his collaboration with John von Neumann (1903–57) in the foundation of the theory of games.—Ed.]

to certain phenomena having an important bearing on the Trade Cycle, our position is a peculiar one. We can deduce from general insight how the majority of people will behave under certain conditions; but the actual behaviour of these masses at a given moment, and therefore the conditions to which our theoretical conclusions must be applied, can only be ascertained by the use of complicated statistical methods. This is especially true when a phenomenon is influenced by a number of partly known circumstances, such as, e.g., seasonal changes. Here very complicated statistical investigations are needed to ascertain whether these circumstances whose presence indicates the applicability of theoretical conclusions were in fact operative. Often statistical analysis may detect phenomena which have, as yet, no theoretical explanation, and which therefore necessitate either an extension of theoretical speculation or a search for new determining conditions. But the explanation of the phenomena thus detected, if it is to serve as a basis for forecasts of the future, must in every case utilise other methods than statistically observed regularities; and the observed phenomena will have to be deduced from the theoretical system, independently of empirical detection.

The dependence of statistical research on pre-existing theoretical explanation hardly needs further emphasis. This holds good not only as regards the practical utilisation of its results, but also in the course of its working, in which it must look to theory for guidance in selecting and delimiting the phenomena to be investigated. The oft-repeated assertion that statistical examination of the Trade Cycle should be undertaken without any theoretical prejudice is therefore always based on self-deception.[13]

---

[13] Prof. Bullock, the Principal of the Harvard Economic Service (now the Harvard Economic Society) constantly emphasises the complete absence of theoretical prepossession with which the work of the Institute is carried out. Sincere as this belief unquestionably is, however, one may doubt its validity when one reads, for instance, the following account given by Prof. Bullock's chief collaborator, Mr. Warren M. Persons, the inventor of the famous Harvard Barometer. Here he attempts the following popular explanation of the latter: "This account of the business cycle, based upon our statistical analysis, revolves about the fluctuation of short-time interest rates, speculation, and business. We may think of interest rates as varying inversely with the amount of the bank reserves in the credit reservoir. The flow in the supply pipe to this reservoir depends upon the volume of gold imports, gold production, and the volume of paper currency. There are two outlets from this reservoir of credit: one [One] pipe furnishes credit for speculation in securities; the other pipe is for the flow of credit into business. When the level of credit in the reservoir is high, and perhaps the outlet to business is partially clogged, the flow of funds into speculation begins. After this flow goes on for some time, however, and the flow into business increases, the level of credit in the reservoir falls. Obstruction is offered to the flow into speculative markets by the devices of higher interest rates and direct discrimination against speculation and in favour [favor] of business. The outlet into speculation therefore becomes clogged but the flow into business goes on. The level in the reservoir becomes still lower until the time is reached when bankers consider it dangerous to allow the outflow to continue. We then have a halt in further credit expansion, or to use our illustration, both outlets are clogged for a time

On the whole, one can say without exaggeration that the practical value of statistical research[14] depends primarily upon the soundness of the theoretical conceptions on which it is based. To decide upon the most important problems of the Trade Cycle remains the task of theory; and whether the money and labour so freely expended on statistical research in late years[15] will be repaid by the expected success depends primarily on whether the development of theoretical understanding keeps pace with the exploration of the facts. For we must not deceive ourselves: not only do we now lack a theory which is generally accepted by economists, but we do not even possess one which could be formulated in such an unexceptionable way, and worked out in such detail, as eventually to command such acceptance. A series of important interconnections have been established and some principles of the greatest significance expounded; but no one has yet undertaken the decisive step which creates a complete theory by using one of these principles to incorporate all the known phenomena into the existing system in a satisfactory way. To realise this, of course, does not hinder us from pursuing either economic research or economic policy; but then we must always remember that we are acting on certain theoretical assumptions whose correctness has not yet been satisfactorily established. The 'practical man' habitually acts on theories which he does not consciously realise; and in most cases this means that his theories are fallacious.[16] Using a theory consciously, on the other hand, always results in some

---

and bank reserves are brought back to normal by allowing the supply to again fill the tank" ("A Non-Technical Explanation of the Index of General Business Conditions", *Review of Economic Statistics*, vol. 2, February 1920, p. 47). [Charles Jesse Bullock (1869–1941), American economist, professor at Harvard, became famous as the founder of the Harvard Economic Service, which developed the Harvard 'three curve barometer' as a statistical instrument for predicting business activity. Warren M. Persons (1878–1937), economist and statistician, collaborated with Bullock in the Harvard Economic Service. The so-called Harvard barometer consisted of three types of indicators—leading, current, and lagging—displayed graphically as curves. These curves in turn represented indices of the stock market, the commodity market (called the Index of General Business Conditions), and the money market, respectively. Observing the relative positions of these curves was meant to give a clue on the phase of the cycle which the economy was presently in and consequently on its course in the future. In fact, the Harvard barometer has become infamous as one of the most egregious failures of economic research in *neither* predicting the crisis of 1929 *nor* the length and severity of the depression that followed. Cf., e.g., Walter A. Friedman, "The Harvard Economic Service and the Problems of Forecasting", *History of Political Economy*, vol. 41, Spring 2009, pp. 57–88.—Ed.]

[14] [Here and in the following the German *Konjunkturforschung* would be more accurately translated as "business cycle research" (as in "Some Remarks", pp. 167, 168; cf. "Einige Bemerkungen", pp. 255, 256; *Geldtheorie*, pp. 9, 10, 12).—Ed.]

[15] [That is, "in recent years" (as in "Some Remarks", p. 167; cf. "Einige Bemerkungen", p. 255; *Geldtheorie*, p. 11).—Ed.]

[16] [This appears to paraphrase a well-known remark by Schumpeter: "Whoever may deny the value of theory—the 'practical man' must not do it. For he is always theorising, and *his* theories are mostly nothing but the theories of 200 years ago." (Joseph A. Schumpeter, "Das Grund-

new attempt to clear up the interrelations which it assumes, and to bring it into harmony with which[17] theoretical assumptions; that is, it results in the pursuit of theory for its own sake.

4. The main division in Trade Cycle theory is the division between monetary and non-monetary theories.

The value of business forecasting[18] depends upon correct theoretical concepts; hence there can, at the present time, be no more important task in this field than the bridging of the gulf which divides monetary from non-monetary theories.[19] This gulf leads to differences of opinion in the front rank of economists; and is also the characteristic line of division between Trade Cycle theory in Germany and in America—where business forecasting originated. Such an analysis of the relation between these two main trends seems to me especially important because of the peculiar position of the monetary theories. Largely through the fault of some of their best-known advocates in Germany, monetary explanations became discredited, and their essentials have, moreover, been much misunderstood; while, on the other hand, the reaction

---

prinzip der Verteilungstheorie", *Archiv für Sozialwissenschaft und Sozialpolitik*, vol. 42, no. 1, 1916/ 17, p. 2n., reprinted in *Aufsätze zur ökonomischen Theorie*, p. 321n.; my translation).—Ed.]

[17] [Apparently "which" is a misprint for "other" (as in "Some Remarks", p. 168; cf. "Einige Bemerkungen", p. 256; *Geldtheorie*, p. 11).—Ed.]

[18] [Again a literal translation of the German original (*Geldtheorie*, p. 12) would be "the value of practical business cycle research".—Ed.]

[19] Since the publication of the German edition of this book, I have become less convinced that the difference between monetary and non-monetary explanations is *the most important* point of disagreement between the various Trade Cycle theories. On the one hand, it seems to me that within the monetary group of explanations the difference between those theorists who regard the superficial phenomena of changes in the value of money as decisive factors in determining cyclical fluctuations, and those who lay emphasis on the real changes in the structure of production brought about by monetary causes, is much greater than the difference between the latter group and such so-called non-monetary theorists as Prof. Spiethoff and Prof. Cassel. On the other hand, it seems to me that the difference between these explanations, which seek the cause of the crisis in the scarcity of capital, and the so-called 'under-consumption' theories, is theoretically as well as practically of much more far-reaching importance than the difference between monetary and non-monetary theories. [The German economist Arthur Spiethoff (1873–1957) was a student of Gustav Schmoller, the leader of the Younger German Historical school; he taught at the University of Prague (1908–18) and then in Bonn (until 1938), and edited the influential German journal *Schmollers Jahrbuch*, 1918–39. His most significant contributions were to the field of business cycle research. Carl Gustav Cassel (1866–1945), Swedish economist, professor at the University of Stockholm, 1903–36, was the author of a widely read textbook, *The Theory of Social Economy* (London: Unwin, 1923; rev. ed., London: Benn, and New York: Harcourt, Brace and Co., 1932; reprinted, New York: Kelley, 1967), which popularised a simplified version of Walras's system of general equilibrium.—Ed.]

against them forms the main reason for the prevailing scepticism as to the possibility of any economic theory of the Trade Cycle—a scepticism which may seriously retard the development of theoretical research.[20]

There is a fundamental difficulty inherent in all Trade Cycle theories which take as their starting point an empirically ascertained disturbance of the equilibrium of the various branches of production. This difficulty arises because, in stating the effects of that disturbance, they have to make use of the logic of equilibrium theory.[21] Yet this logic, properly followed through, can do no more than demonstrate that such disturbances of equilibrium can come only from outside—i.e. that they represent a change in the economic data[22]—and that the economic system always reacts to such changes by its well-known methods of adaptation, i.e., by the formation of a new equilibrium. No tendency towards the special expansion of certain branches of production, however plausibly adduced, no chance shift in demand, in distribution or in productivity, could adequately explain, within the framework of this theoretical system, why a general 'disproportionality' between supply and demand should arise. For the essential means of explanation in static theory, which is, at the same

---

[20] Cf. the above-mentioned essay of Löwe, "Wie ist Konjunkturtheorie überhaupt möglich?"

[21] By 'equilibrium theory' we here primarily understand the modern theory of the general interdependence of all economic quantities, which has been most perfectly expressed by the Lausanne School of theoretical economics. The significant basic concept of this theory was contained in James Mill's and J. B. Say's *Théorie des Débouchés*. Cf. Leonard Miksch, *Gibt es eine allgemeine Überproduktion?* (Jena: Fischer, 1929). [James Mill (1773–1836) and Jean-Baptiste Say (1776–1832) defended, against contemporary theories of under-consumption, the thesis of the impossibility of general overproduction, arguing that goods will only be exchanged against goods and thus the total supply of must equal the total demand for goods. This is the main argument of Say's famous *théorie des débouchés* (law of markets). Cf. James Mill, *Commerce Defended* (London: Baldwin, 1808; reprinted, New York: Kelley, 1965; and London: Routledge and Thoemmes Press, 1992, as a volume of *The Collected Works of James Mill*), and Jean-Baptiste Say, *Traité d'économie politique*, 1803, translated from the fourth edition (1819) as *A Treatise on Political Economy* (Philadelphia: Claxton, Remsen and Haggelfinger, 1880; reprinted, New York: Kelley, 1971; New Brunswick, NJ: Transactions, 2001). The characteristic of the Lausanne school was its fusion of the Marginal Revolution with a distinctly mathematical approach. Its founder, Léon Walras (1834–1910), born in France, had taught at the University of Lausanne (Switzerland), 1870–92; he developed the notion of 'general equilibrium' as a main accomplishment in the realm of economic statics. Hayek considered the necessary equality between the total demand for and supply of goods as a defining element of 'static' or 'equilibrium theory'; cf. in particular "Investigations", p. 80. This note, in particular the reference to the Lausanne school, was added in the English version of 1933.—Ed.]

[22] [For a contemporary Austrian discussion of 'data' as a basic category of economic analysis cf. Richard Strigl, *Die ökonomischen Kategorien und die Organisation der Wirtschaft* (Jena: Fischer, 1923), chapter 1. Hayek, later on, questioned the 'givenness' of the data ('given to whom?') and pointed to the crucial distinction between data as subjective perceptions and objective facts; cf. "Economics and Knowledge", *Economica*, n.s., vol. 4, February 1937, p. 36, reprinted in *Individualism and Economic Order* (Chicago: University of Chicago Press, 1948; London: Routledge and Kegan Paul, 1949), p. 36.—Ed.]

time, the indispensable assumption for the explanation of particular price variations, is the assumption that prices supply an automatic mechanism for equilibrating supply and demand.[23]

The next section will deal with these difficulties in more detail: a mere hint should therefore be sufficient at this point. At the moment we have only to draw attention to the fact that the problem before us cannot be solved by examining the effect of a certain cause within the framework, and by the methods, of equilibrium theory. Any theory which limits itself to the explanation of empirically observed interconnections by the methods of elementary theory necessarily contains a self-contradiction. For Trade Cycle theory cannot aim at the adaptation of the adjusting mechanism of static theory to a special case; this scheme of explanation must itself be extended so as to explain how such discrepancies between supply and demand can ever arise. The obvious and (to my mind) the only possible way out of this dilemma, is to explain the difference between the course of events described by static theory (which only permits movements towards an equilibrium, and which is deduced by directly contrasting the supply of and the demand for goods[24]) and the actual course of events, by the fact that, with the introduction of money (or strictly speaking with the introduction of indirect exchange[25]), a new determining cause is

[23] [With regard to the definition of 'statics' and 'dynamics' Hayek follows Löwe (and implicitly Schumpeter). Cf. the distinction in Löwe, "Der gegenwärtige Stand der Konjunkturforschung", p. 358n.1 (my translation):

> The notion of 'dynamics' is often used, following Anglo-Saxon and French terminology, for processes of economic motion *per se*, in contrast to the narrower notion of 'statics' referring to a *state* of rest. Yet I shall use these two notions, according to Schumpeter, to denote two structurally distinct *systems of motion*, the one—statics—tending towards an equilibrium at rest, while the other—dynamics—exhibits very complicated tendencies of evolution, opposed in any case to an equilibrium at rest.

In Schumpeter's terminology, of which Löwe (ibid., p. 357) approved and which Hayek used in the above paragraph, the movements typical for the static and the dynamic system were referred to as 'adaptation' (or 'adjustment') versus 'development'. "By 'development' . . . we shall understand only such changes in economic life as are not forced upon it from without but arise by its own initiative, from within. . . . [If] the data change and . . . the economy continuously adapts itself to them, then we should say that there is *no* economic development" (Schumpeter, *Theorie der wirtschaftlichen Entwicklung*, 2nd ed. (Munich and Leipzig: Duncker and Humblot, 1926), pp. 95–96, translated as *The Theory of Economic Development*, trans. Redvers Opie (Cambridge, MA: Harvard University Press, 1934), p. 63). Joseph Alois Schumpeter (1883–1950) studied at the University of Vienna and, after a short spell as Austrian Minister of Finance in 1919, taught in Graz, Bonn, and ultimately, at Harvard, 1932–50. As an economic theorist he strived for a 'dynamic' theory, incorporating entrepreneurship and innovation, as a counterpart to the 'static' system of general equilibrium.—Ed.]

[24] [A more accurate translation is, "deduced from the idea that the supply of and the demand for goods directly confront each other" (my translation; cf. "Einige Bemerkungen", pp. 257–58; *Geldtheorie*, p. 14).—Ed.]

[25] [The passage in parentheses has been added in the English version.—Ed.]

introduced. Money being a commodity[26] which, unlike all others, is incapable of finally satisfying demand, its introduction does away with the rigid interdependence and self-sufficiency of the 'closed' system of equilibrium, and makes possible movements which would be excluded from the latter. Here we have a starting-point which fulfils the essential conditions for any satisfactory theory of the Trade Cycle. It shows, in a purely deductive way, the possibility and the necessity of movements which *do not* at any given moment tend towards a situation which, in the absence of changes in the economic 'data', could continue indefinitely. It shows that, on the contrary, these movements lead to such a 'disproportionality' between certain parts of the system that the given situation cannot continue.

But while it seems that it was a sound instinct which led economists to begin by looking on the monetary side for an explanation of cyclical fluctuations, it also seems probable that the one-sided development of the theory of money has, as yet, prevented any satisfactory solution to the problem being found. Monetary theories of the Trade Cycle succeeded in giving prominence to the right questions and, in many cases, made important contributions towards their solution; but the reason why an unassailable solution has not yet been put forward seems to reside in the fact that all the adherents of the monetary theory of the Trade Cycle have sought an explanation either exclusively or predominantly in the superficial phenomena of changes in the value of money, while failing to pursue the far more profound and fundamental effects of the process by which money is introduced into the economic system, as distinct from its effect on prices in general. Nor did they follow up the consequences of the fundamental diversity between a money economy and the pure barter economy[27] which is assumed in static theory.[28]

[26] [Instead of "being a commodity", a more accurate translation of "Gegenstände des wirtschaftlichen Handelns" ("Einige Bemerkungen", p. 258; *Geldtheorie*, p. 14) is "being an object of economic action" (my translation); the translation "traded objects" in "Some Remarks", p. 170, is also misleading.—Ed.]

[27] [Here and in the following the translation renders the German term *Naturalwirtschaft* (as, e.g., in *Geldtheorie*, p. 15) by 'barter economy' instead of the alternative 'natural economy' as used, e.g., in Knut Wicksell, *Interest and Prices: A Study of the Causes Regulating the Value of Money* (London: Macmillan, 1936; reprinted, New York: Kelley, 1965; Auburn, AL: Ludwig von Mises Institute, 2007), p. 156, translated by Richard F. Kahn from *Geldzins und Güterpreise: Eine Studie über die den Tauschwert des Geldes bestimmenden Ursachen* (Jena: Fischer, 1898; reprinted, Aalen: Scientia, 1968), p. 143. The term itself derives from the German economist and member of the Older Historical school, Bruno Hildebrand ("Natural-, Geld- und Kreditwirtschaft", *Jahrbücher für Nationalökonomie und Statistik*, vol. 2, no. 1, 1864, pp. 1–24), who however thereby denoted a stage in economic development (from the natural to the money and ultimately to the credit economy). In contrast, as used by economic theorists, it served as a simplified model of an economy, short of the introduction of money usually to be treated separately.—Ed.]

[28] Similar views are expressed by Wilhelm Röpke, "Kredit und Konjunktur", *Jahrbücher für Nationalökonomie und Statistik*, vol. 124 (3rd ser., vol. 69), no. 2, 1926, pp. 264 et seq. [pp. 264–65].

5. The purpose of the following essay

Naturally it cannot be the business of this essay to remove all defects and deficiencies from the monetary theories of the Trade Cycle, or to develop a complete and unassailable theory. In these pages I shall only attempt to show the general significance for this theory of the monetary starting-point, and to refute the most important objections raised against the monetary explanation by proving that certain rightly exposed deficiencies of some monetary theories do not necessarily follow from the monetary approach. All that is wanted, therefore, is, first, a proof, using as our examples some of the best-known non-monetary theories, that the 'real' explanations adduced by them do not, in themselves, suffice to build up a complete and consistent theory; secondly, a demonstration that the existing monetary theories contain the germ of a true explanation, although all suffer, more or less, from that over-simplification of the problem which results from reducing all cyclical fluctuations to fluctuations in the value of money; finally that the monetary starting-point makes it possible, in fact, to show deductively the inevitability of fluctuation under the existing monetary system and, indeed, under almost any other which can be imagined. It will be shown, in particular, that the Wicksell-Mises[29] theory of the effects of a divergence between the 'natural' and the money rate of interest already contains the most important elements of an explanation, and has only to be freed from any direct reference to a purely imaginary 'general money value'[30] (as has already been partly done by Prof. Mises) in order to form the basis of a Trade Cycle theory sufficing for a deductive explanation of all the elements in the Trade Cycle.

[29] [In *Geldtheorie*, p. 16, the reference had been to the "Marshall-Wicksell-Mises theory". Knut Wicksell (1851–1926), Swedish economist, professor at the University of Lund, 1903–17, attempted a synthesis of Austrian capital theory and the theory of marginal productivity within Walras's general equilibrium framework. His most original contribution was to monetary theory where he emphasised the indirect mechanism of money on prices by way of its impact on the money rate of interest.—Ed.]

[30] [That is, the "general value of money" (as in "Some Remarks", p. 171; cf. "Einige Bemerkungen", p. 259; *Geldtheorie*, p. 16).—Ed.]

TWO

NON-MONETARY THEORIES OF
THE TRADE CYCLE

1. A general *refutation of such theories is difficult on account of
the absence of an adequate classification*

Any attempt at a general proof, within the compass of a short essay, of the
assertion that non-monetary theories of the Trade Cycle inevitably suffer
from a fundamental deficiency, appears to be confronted with an insuperable
obstacle by reason of the very multiplicity of such theories. If it were necessary for our purpose to show that every one of the numerous disequilibrating
forces which have been made starting-points for Trade Cycle theories was, in
fact, non-existent, then the conditions of our success would, indeed, be impossible of fulfilment; for not only would it be almost impossible to deal with
all extant theories but no conclusive answer could result, seeing that we should
still have to reckon with a new and hitherto unrefuted crop of such theories in
the future. Moreover, the existence of most of the interconnections elaborated
by the various Trade Cycle theories can hardly be denied, and our task is
rather their co-ordination in a unified logical structure than the development
of entirely new and different trains of thought. In fact, it is by no means necessary to question the material correctness of the individual interconnections
emphasised in the various non-monetary theories in order to show that they
do not afford a sufficient explanation. As has already been indicated in the
first chapter, none of them is able to overcome the contradiction between the
course of economic events as described by them and the fundamental ideas
of the theoretical system which they have to utilise in order to explain that
course. It will, therefore, be sufficient to show, by examination of some of the
best-known theories, that they do not answer this fundamental question; nor
can they ever do so by their present methods and by reference to the circumstances which they now regard as relevant to Trade Cycle theory. When, however, the question is answered on different lines, viz., by reference to *monetary*
circumstances, it can be shown that the elements of explanation adduced by
different theories lose their independent importance and fall into a subordinate position as necessary consequences of the monetary cause.

It is rather difficult to select the main types of Trade Cycle theory for this purpose, since we have no theoretically satisfactory classification. The latest attempts at such classifications, by Mr. W. M. Persons,[1] Professor W. C. Mitchell,[2] and Mr. A. H. Hansen,[3] show that the usual division, which relies on external features and hardly touches the solution of fundamental problems, gives far too wide a scope for arbitrary decisions. As Professor Löwe[4] has correctly emphasised (and as should be obvious from what has been said above) the only classification which could be really unobjectionable would be one which proceeded according to the manner in which such theories explain the absence of the 'normal course' of economic events, as presented by static theory. In fact, the various theories—as we shall hope to show later—make no attempt whatever to do this. As there is, therefore, no classification which would serve our purpose, our choice must be more or less arbitrary; but by choosing some of the best known theories and exemplifying the train of thought to which our objection particularly applies, we should be able to make the general validity of the latter sufficiently clear. The task is made rather easier by the fact that there does exist to-day, on at least one point, a far-reaching agreement among the different theories. They all regard the emergence of a *disproportionality* among the various productive groups,[5] and in particular the excessive production of capital goods, as the first and main thing to be explained. The development of theory owes a real debt to statistical research in that, to-day, there is at least no substantial disagreement as to the thing to be explained.

There is, however, a point to be emphasised here. The modern habit of going beyond the actual crisis and seeking to explain the entire cycle, suffers inherently from the danger of paying less and less attention to the crucial problem. In particular, the attempt to give the object of the theory as neutral

[1] Warren M. Persons, "Theories of Business Fluctuations: I. A Classification of the Theories", *Quarterly Journal of Economics*, vol. 41, November 1926, p. 923 [correctly, pp. 102–3—Ed.].
[2] Wesley C. Mitchell, *Business Cycles: The Problem and its Setting* (New York: National Bureau of Economic Research, 1927). [Wesley Clair Mitchell (1874–1948), American economist, professor at Columbia University (1910–44) and director of the newly founded National Bureau of Economic Research (1920–45), pioneered in his work the statistical analysis of the business cycle. From the Austrian point of view this approach looked suspiciously close to that of the German Historical economists. See Hayek's obituary, reprinted in *The Fortunes of Liberalism: Essays on Austrian Economics and the Ideal of Freedom*, ed. Peter G. Klein, vol. 4 (1992) of *The Collected Works of F. A. Hayek*, pp. 40–42.—Ed.]
[3] Alvin H. Hansen, *Business-Cycle Theory: Its Development and Present Status* (Boston: Ginn, 1927). [Alvin Harvey Hansen (1887–1975), American economist, professor at the University of Minnesota and then, 1937–57 at Harvard University; in the 1930s his main field of research was business cycle theory, yet later on he became famous for introducing Keynesian thought to the United States.—Ed.]
[4] See Löwe, "Der gegenwärtige Stand der Konjunkturforschung", pp. 359 et seq. [pp. 359–67.]
[5] [The term commonly used instead of "productive groups" would be "branches of production".—Ed.]

a name as possible (such as 'Industrial fluctuations' or 'Cyclical movements of Industry') threatens to drive the real theoretical problem more into the background than was the case in the old theory of crisis. The simple fact that economic development does not go on quite uniformly, but that periods of relatively rapid change alternate with periods of relative stagnation, does not in itself constitute a problem. It is sufficiently explained by the adjustment of the economic system to irregular changes in the data—changes whose occurrence we always have to assume and which cannot be further explained by economic science. The real problem presented to economic theory is: Why does not this adjustment come about smoothly and continuously, just as a new equilibrium is formed after every change in the data? Why is there this temporary possibility of developments leading away from equilibrium and finally, without any changes in data, necessitating a change in the economic trend? The phenomena of the upward trend of the cycle and of the culminating boom constitute a problem only because they inevitably bring about a slump in sales—i.e., a falling-off of economic activity—which is *not* occasioned by any corresponding change in the original economic data.

2. The selection of subject matter for the present enquiry

The prevailing disproportionality theories are in agreement in one respect. They all see the cause of the slump in the fact that, during the boom, for various reasons, the productive apparatus is expanded more than is warranted by the corresponding flow of consumption; there finally appears a scarcity of finished consumption goods, thus causing a rise in the price of such goods relatively to the price of production goods (which amounts to the same thing as a rise in the rate of interest)[6] so that it becomes unprofitable to employ the enlarged productive apparatus or, in many cases, even to complete it. At present there is hardly a recognised theory which does not give this idea, which we only sketch for the moment,[7] a decisive place in its argument, and we should therefore be well advised to begin by seeing how the various theories try to deal with the phenomenon in question. Apart from the monetary theories, which, as will be shown later, *can only be considered satisfactory if they explain that phenomenon*, there are two groups of explanations which can be entirely disregarded. In the first place there is nothing to be gained from an examination of those theories which seek to explain cyclical fluctuations by cor-

---

[6] [The passage beginning with "thus causing", which identifies the price margin between consumption and production goods with the rate of interest, was added in 1933 to the English version.—Ed.]

[7] Cf. below, pp. 153–55, especially p. 155.

responding cyclical changes in certain external circumstances, while merely using the unquestionable methods of equilibrium theory to explain the economic phenomena which follow from these changes. To decide on the correctness of these theories is beyond the competence of Economics. In the second place, it is best, for the moment, to exclude from consideration those theories whose argument depends so entirely on the assumption of monetary changes that when the latter are excluded no systematic explanation is left. This category includes Professor J. Schumpeter,[8] Professor E. Lederer,[9] and Professor G. Cassel,[10] and to a certain extent Professor W. C. Mitchell and Professor J. Lescure.[11] We shall have to consider later, with regard to this category, how far it is theoretically permissible to treat these monetary interconnections as determining conditions on the same footing as the other phenomena used in explanation.

It is, of course, impossible at this point to go into the peculiarities of all types of theory, as worked out by their respective authors. We must leave out of account the forms in which the various explanations are presented, and confine ourselves to certain underlying types of theory which recur in a number of different guises. Inevitably, this treatment of contemporary theories must fail to do full justice to the intellectual merits exemplified in each; but for the purposes of this chapter—that is, to show the fundamental objections to which all non-monetary theories of the Trade Cycle are open—this somewhat cursory and imperfect treatment may be enough.

We may begin our demonstration by pointing out that all those forms of disproportionality theory with which we have to deal here rest on the existence of quite irregular fluctuations of 'economic data' (that is, the external determining circumstances of the economic system, including human needs and abilities). From this assumption, they try to explain in one way or another that the fluctuations in consumption or some other element in the economic

---

[8] *Theorie der wirtschaftlichen Entwicklung*, 2nd ed. [*The Theory of Economic Development*—Ed.]

[9] "Konjunktur und Krisen", in *Grundriß der Sozialökonomik*, vol. 4, part 1 (Tübingen: Mohr, 1926 [1925; reprinted, Frankfurt: Keip, 1985]), pp. 354–413; also "Zur Morphologie der Krisen", in *Die Wirtschaftstheorie der Gegenwart*, ed. Hans Mayer, Frank A. Fetter, and Richard Reisch, vol. 4 (Vienna: Springer, 1928), pp. 1–16. [Emil Lederer (1892–1939) studied at the University of Vienna, and after a short spell in Heidelberg, although a theorist, a socialist, and a Jew, in 1925 he succeeded Werner Sombart in the economics chair at the University of Berlin. From 1921 to 1933 he co-edited, jointly with Schumpeter and Alfred Weber, the *Archiv für Sozialwissenschaft und Sozialpolitik*. Forced to leave Germany in 1933, he became the first dean of the Faculty of Political and Social Sciences at the New School of Social Research in New York.—Ed.]

[10] *The Theory of Social Economy*.

[11] *Des crises générales et périodiques de surproduction* [3rd ed.] (Paris: Recueil Sirey, 1913 [1923]); and "Krisenlehre", in *Die Wirtschaftstheorie der Gegenwart*, vol. 4, pp. 32–48. [Jean Lescure (1882–1947), French economist and a historian of economic crises, was a member of the French Historical (as opposed to the French Liberal) school.—Ed.]

system occasioned by these changes are followed by relatively greater changes in the production of production goods.[12] These wide fluctuations in the industries making production goods bring about a disproportionality between them and the consumption industries to such an extent that a reversal of the movement becomes necessary. *It is not, therefore, the simple fact of fluctuation in the production of capital goods (which is certainly inevitable in the course of economic growth) which has to be explained.* The real problem is the growth of excessive fluctuations in the capital goods industries out of the inevitable and irregular fluctuations of the rest of the economic system, and the disproportional development, arising from these, of the two main branches of production. We can distinguish three main types of non-monetary theories explaining the exaggerated effect of given fluctuations on capital goods industries. The most common, at the moment, are those explanations which try to show that, on account of the *technique of production*, an increase in the demand for consumption goods, whether expected or actual, tends to bring about a relatively larger increase in the production of goods of a higher order,[13] either generally or in a certain group of these goods. Hardly less common, and differing only in appearance, are explanations which seek to derive these augmented fluctuations from special circumstances (non-monetary in character) arising in the field of *savings*

---

[12] It should be noted here that the assumption of initial changes in the economic data, which no theory of the Trade Cycle can dispense with, in itself throws no light on the proper way of explaining cyclical fluctuations. It is not the occurrence of disturbances of equilibrium, necessitating readjustment, which presents a problem to Trade Cycle theory; it is the fact that this adjustment is brought about only after a series of movements have taken place which cannot be considered 'adjustments' in the sense used by the theory of economic equilibrium. "The phenomenon is never made clear until it is explained why its cause, whatever it may be, does not call forth a continuous equilibrating process" (Prof. J. Schumpeter, *Theorie der wirtschaftlichen Entwicklung*, 2nd ed. [p. 335; cf. the passage as translated in *The Theory of Economic Development*, p. 224: "The phenomenon is never made intelligible if it is not explained why the cause, whatever it may be, cannot act in such a way as to allow the consequences to be continuously and currently absorbed."—Ed.]). These changes of data could serve as a complete explanation only if it could be shown that the successive phases of the Trade Cycle are conditioned by a series of such changes, following each other in a certain order. [For the distinction between 'adjustment' and 'development' see the editor's note, p. 76, above.—Ed.]

[13] [This terminology dates back to Menger's distinction of goods of lower and higher order, consumers' goods being goods of first order, and accordingly the order of goods being the higher the more distant they are from the stage of consumption. Cf. Carl Menger, *Grundsätze der Volkswirtschaftslehre* (Vienna: Braumüller, 1871; reprinted, Saarbrücken: VDM, Müller, 2006), p. 11; also reprinted as vol. 1 (1934) of *The Collected Works of Carl Menger*, ed. F. A. Hayek (Reprints of Scarce Tracts in Economics, vol. 17, London: London School of Economics; 2nd ed. as *Gesammelte Werke*, vol. 1, Tübingen: Mohr, 1968). For an English translation cf. *Principles of Economics*, trans. James Dingall and Bert F. Hoselitz (New York and London: New York University Press, 1981), pp. 58–59. On Carl Menger (1840–1921), the founder of the Austrian school of economics, cf. F. A. Hayek's introduction to *The Collected Works of Carl Menger*, vol. 1, reprinted in an augmented version as chapter 2 of F. A. Hayek, *The Fortunes of Liberalism*.—Ed.]

and investment. Finally, as a third group, we must mention certain *psychological* theories, which, for the most part, have however no pretension to rank as independent explanations and which merely reinforce other arguments, and are open to the same objections as the two other main types.

3. Theories which explain the cycle in terms of the technical conditions of production

We shall mention only the most important of our objections to the first type, which is the easiest to discuss from this point of view. It is common to so many economists that it is hardly necessary to mention particular representatives. The simplest way of deductively explaining excessive fluctuations in the production of capital goods is by reference to the *long period of time* which is necessary, under modern conditions, for preparing the fixed capital goods which enable the expansion of the productive process to take place.[14] According to a widely held view, this circumstance alone is enough to make every increase in the sales of consumption goods, whether brought about by an intensification of demand or by a fall in the costs of production, capable of bringing about a more than proportional increase in the production of intermediary goods. This is explained either by the individual producer's ignorance of what his competitors are doing, or—as is common in American writings—by the 'cumulative effect' of each change in the sale of consumption goods on the higher stages of production. Owing to circumstances which will be explained later, the leading idea in all these types of explanation is that the long period which, with the present technique of production, elapses between the beginning of a productive process and the arrival of its final product at the market, prevents the gradual adjustment of production to changes in demand through the agency of prices and makes it possible, from time to time,[15] for an excessively large supply to be thrown on the market. This idea is supported by another, which, however, can be independently and more widely applied; that is, that *every change in demand,* from the moment of its appearance, *propagates itself cumulatively*

---

[14] Cf. Albert Aftalion, *Les crises périodiques de surproduction* (Paris: Librairie des Sciences Politiques et Sociales, 1913), books II–VI, chapters iii to viii [that is, correctly, vol. 2, book 6, chapters 3–7—Ed.]; and Dennis H. Robertson, *Industrial Fluctuations* [*A Study of Industrial Fluctuation*—Ed.] (London: King, 1915 [reprinted, London: Routledge and Thoemmes Press, 1996]), p. 14. [Albert Aftalion (1874–1956), Bulgarian-born economist, professor at the Universities of Lille and Paris, in the work just mentioned was the first to put forward an explanation of the cycle by means of the 'acceleration principle of derived demand'. Dennis Holme Robertson (1890–1963), Cambridge economist, developed an eclectic theory of the cycle similar in some aspects to the Austrian approach. Although in the 1920s he closely collaborated with Keynes, he eventually turned into a critic of the Keynesian revolution.—Ed.]

[15] [Instead of "from time to time", the literal translation of "mehr oder weniger plötzlich" ("Einige Bemerkungen", p. 265; *Geldtheorie,* p. 25) is "more or less suddenly" (as in "Some Remarks", p. 175).—Ed.]

through all the grades of production,[16] from the lowest to the highest. This cumulative effect arises because at each stage, besides the change which would be appropriate to the actual shift in demand, another change arises from the adjustment of stocks and of productive apparatus to the alteration in market conditions.[17] An increase in the demand for consumption goods will not merely call forth a proportional increase in the demand for goods of a higher order: the latter will also be increased by the amount needed to raise current stocks to a proportional level, and, finally, by the further amount by which the requirements for producing new means of production exceed those for keeping the existing means of production intact. (For instance, an extension of 10 per cent, in one particular year, in the machinery of a factory which normally renews 10 per cent of its machinery annually, causes an increase of 100 per cent in the production of machinery—i.e. a given increase in the demand for consumption goods occasions a tenfold increase in the production of production goods.) This idea is offered as an adequate reason not only for the relatively greater fluctuations in production-goods industries but also for their *excessive* expansion in periods of boom. Similarly, the extensive use of *durable capital equipment* in the modern economy is often singled out for responsibility.[18] Industries using heavy equipment are prone to excessive expansion in boom periods because small increments in this equipment are impossible; expansion must necessarily take place by sudden jerks. Once the new equipment is available, on the other hand, the volume of production has little influence on total costs, which go on even if no production takes place at all. New inventions and new needs, however, although they are often adduced as explaining the accelerated and excessive growth of capital goods industries, cannot be dealt with on the same footing. They only represent a special group of the many possible causes from which the cumulative processes described above may originate.

4. These all overlook the essential function of the mechanism of relative prices

There is virtually no doubt that all these interconnections, and many others which are given prominence in various Trade Cycle theories and which simi-

---

[16] [The usual translation of the Böhm-Bawerkian concept of *Stufen der Produktion* (*Geldtheorie*, p. 25) is "stages of production".—Ed.]

[17] Cf. Thomas N. Carver ["A Suggestion for a Theory of Industrial Depression"], *Quarterly Journal of Economics*, vol. 17, May 1903, p. 492 [p. 497]; Albert Aftalion, *Journal d' Economie Politique*, vol. 23, March 1909, pp. 215ff. [The reference is to "La réalité des surproductions générales", published in *Revue d' Economie Politique*, pp. 215–220, reprinted as part of *La réalité des surproductions générales: Essai d'une théorie des crises générales et périodiques* (Paris: Recueil-Sirey, 1909).—Ed.]; Mitchell, *Business Cycles*; and Robertson, *A Study of Industrial Fluctuation*, pp. 122ff. [pp. 122–25].

[18] Cf. Robertson, *A Study of Industrial Fluctuation*, pp. 31 et seq. [pp. 31–32].

larly tend to disturb economic equilibrium, do actually exist; and any Trade Cycle theory which claims to be comprehensively worked out must take them into consideration. But none of them gets over the real difficulty—namely: Why do the forces tending to restore equilibrium become temporarily ineffective and why do they only come into action again when it is too late? They all try to explain this phenomenon by a further, usually tacit, assumption, which one of the advocates of these theories, Mr. C. O. Hardy,[19] has himself put forward as their common idea, by which, in my opinion, he brings out, with the utmost clarity, their fundamental weakness.[20] He states that all those theories which are based on the length of the production-period under modern technical conditions agree in regarding these conditions as a source of difficulty to producers in adjusting production to the state of the market—producing, as they must, for a future period, the market possibilities of which are necessarily unknown to them. He then emphasises that in general it is the task of the price-mechanism to adjust supply to demand; he thinks, however, that this mechanism is imperfect, if a long period has to lapse between production and the arrival of the product at the market, because "prices and orders give information concerning the prospective state of demand compared with the known facts of the present and future supply, but they give no clue to the changes in supply which they themselves are likely to cause".[21] He tries to show how periodic over- and under-production may result from an increase in demand acting as an incentive to increased production. He here states explicitly what others assume tacitly, and thus his exposition completely gives away the question-begging nature of all such arguments. For he holds that under free competition, in the case considered, more and more people try to profit by the favourable situation, all ignoring one another's preparations, and *"no force intervenes to check the continual increase in production until it reflects itself in declining orders and falling prices"*.[22] In this statement (according to which the price-mechanism comes into action only when the products come on to the market, while, until then, producers can regulate the extent of their production solely according to the estimated *total volume of demand*) the fundamental error which can be shown to recur in all these theories is plainly revealed. It

---

[19] Charles O. Hardy, *Risk and Risk Bearing* (Chicago: University of Chicago Press, 1923), p. 72. See also Mr. Hardy's reply to the above criticism in the revised second edition (1931 [reprinted, London: Risk, 1999]) of the same book (p. 94), which, however, does not seem to solve the fundamental difficulty.

[20] [More accurately, "fundamental error" (as in "Some Remarks", p. 176; cf. "Einige Bemerkungen", p. 266; *Geldtheorie*, p. 27).—Ed.]

[21] Hardy, *Risk and Risk Bearing*, 1st ed., p. 73. [Hayek's quotation is slightly inaccurate. It should read, "the known facts of present and future supply", and then, "which they are themselves likely to cause".—Ed.]

[22] Ibid. (My italics.) [Hayek's quotation is inaccurate. It should read, *"no force intervenes to check the continued increase of production till it reflects itself in declining orders and falling prices"*.—Ed.]

arises from a misconception of the deliberations which regulate the entrepreneur's actions and of the significance of the price-mechanism.

If the entrepreneur really had to guide his decisions exclusively by his knowledge of the quantitative increase in the total demand for his product, and if the success of economic activity were really always dependent on that knowledge, no very complicated circumstances would be needed to produce constant disturbances in the relation between supply and demand. But the entrepreneur in a capitalist economy is not—as many economists seem to assume—in the same situation as the dictator of a Socialist economy. The protagonists of this view seem to overlook the fact that production is generally guided not by any knowledge of the actual size of the total demand, but by the price to be obtained in the market. In the modern exchange economy, the entrepreneur does not produce with a view to satisfying a certain demand—even if that phrase is sometimes used—but on the basis of a calculation of profitability; and it is just that calculation which will equilibrate supply and demand. He is not in the least concerned with the amount by which, in a given case, the total amount demanded will alter; he only looks at the price which he can expect to get after the change in question has taken place. None of the theories under discussion explains why these expectations should generally prove incorrect. (To deduce their incorrectness from the fact that over-production, arising from false expectations, causes prices to fall, would be mere argument in a circle.) Nor can this generalisation be theoretically established by any other method. For so long, at least, as disturbing monetary influences are not operating, we have to assume that the price which entrepreneurs expect to result from a change in demand or from a change in the conditions of production will more or less coincide with the equilibrium price.[23] For the entrepreneur, from his knowledge of the conditions of production and the market, will generally be in a position to estimate the price that will rule after the changes have taken place, as distinct from the quantitative changes in the total volume of demand. One can only say, as to this prospective price of the product concerned, that it is just as likely to be lower than the equilibrium price as to be higher and that, on the average, it should more or less coincide, since there is no reason to assume that deviations will take place only in one direction. But this prospective price only represents one factor determining the extent of production. The other factor, no less important but all too often overlooked, is the price the producer has to pay for raw materials, labour-power, tools and borrowed capital—i.e., his costs. These prices, taken together, determine the extent of production for all producers operating under conditions of competition; and the producer's decisions as to his production must be guided not

---

[23] [Note that here Hayek comes close to arguing that systematic errors of expectations will only occur in a money economy.—Ed.]

only by changes in expectations as to the price of his product, but also by changes in his costs. To show how the interplay of these prices keeps supply and demand, production and consumption, in equilibrium, is the main object of pure economics, and the analysis cannot be repeated here in detail.[24] It is, however, the task of Trade Cycle theory to show under what conditions a break may occur in that tendency towards equilibrium which is described in pure analysis—i.e., why prices, in contradiction to the conclusions of static theory, do not bring about such changes in the quantities produced as would correspond to an equilibrium situation. In order to show that the theories under discussion do not solve this problem, and only as far as is necessary for this purpose, we shall now study the most important of the interconnections which bring about equilibrium under the assumptions of static theory.

5. The way in which prices react to such changes in 'data' as are assumed in these theories further examined

We may attempt this task by asking what kind of reactions will be brought about by the original change in the economic data, which is supposed to cause the excessive extension of the production of capital goods, and how, in such cases, a new equilibrium can result. Whether the original impetus[25] comes from the demand side or the supply side, the assumption from which we have to start is always a price—or rather an expected price—which renders it profitable, under the new conditions, to extend production. As stated above, we can assume—since none of the theories in question give any reason to the contrary—that this expected price will approximate to the new equilibrium price. We can assume, that is, that if the impetus is a fall in unit costs, the producer will consider the effects of an increased supply;[26] if the impetus is an increase in demand, he will consider the increase in the cost per unit following the increase in the quantity produced. The existence of a general misconception in this respect would require a special explanation, and unless this is to rest on a circular argument, it can only be accounted for by a monetary explanation, which we cannot consider at this point.

Now the length of time required to produce modern means of production cannot induce a tendency to an excessive extension of the productive appa-

[24] [Here and in the following Hayek uses the terms 'pure theory', 'pure economics', 'equilibrium theory', and 'static theory' interchangeably. Cf. also the editor's introduction to this volume, pp. 13–14.—Ed.]

[25] [The term 'impetus' denotes a change in data operating as an 'initiating cause' or 'impulse'.—Ed.]

[26] [Here, the text deviates from the German version which reads, "the effects of the expected increase in demand", instead of "the effects of an increased supply" ("Some Remarks", p. 178; cf. "Einige Bemerkungen", p. 269; *Geldtheorie*, p. 31).—Ed.]

ratus; or, more accurately, any such tendency is bound to be effectively eliminated by the increase in price of the factors of production. Thus we cannot
give a sufficient explanation for the occurrence of the disproportionality in
these terms. This becomes obvious as soon as we drop the assumption that
the price-mechanism begins to function only from the moment at which the
increased supply comes on the market, and consider that whenever the price
obtainable for the finished product is correctly estimated, the adjustment of
the prices of factors of production must ensure that the amount produced is
limited to what can be sold at remunerative prices. The mere existence of a
lengthy production period cannot be held to impair the working of the price
mechanism, so long, at any rate, as no additional reason can be given for the
occurrence of a general miscalculation in the same direction concerning the
effect of the original change in data on the prices of the products.

We must next inquire what truth there is in the alleged tendency towards
a cumulative propagation of the effect of every increase (or decrease) of
demand from the lower to the higher stages of production. The arguments
given below against this frequently-adduced theory must serve at the same
time to refute all other theories based on similar technical considerations; for
space will not permit us to go into every one of these, and the reader can be
trusted to apply the same reasoning as is employed in this demonstration to
all similar explanations—such as those based on the necessary discontinuity
of the extension of productive apparatus. Does the cumulative effect of every
increase in demand represent a new price-determining factor, as a result of
which prices, and therefore quantities produced, will be different from those
needed to achieve equilibrium? Is the regulating effect of prices on the extent
of production really suspended by the fact that when turnover increases mer-
chants try to increase stocks, and manufacturers to extend production?[27] If
the increase in the prices of production goods were the only counterbalanc-
ing factor to set against the increase in the demand for these goods, it would
still be possible for more investments to be undertaken than would prove permanently profitable. According to the view we are considering, there will be
an increase in the quantity of factors of production demanded at any price,
as compared with the equilibrium situation, and therefore it would appear
possible that, at every price at which producers still think they can profitably
make use of this quantity, investments will be undertaken to an unwarrantable
extent. This way of stating the position, however, entirely overlooks the fact
that every attempt to extend the productive apparatus must necessarily bring
about, besides the rise in factor prices, a further checking force—viz. a rise
in the rate of interest. This greatly strengthens the effect of the rise in factor

[27] [Instead of "production" the proper translation of "Produktionsapparat" ("Einige Bemerkungen", p. 270; *Geldtheorie*, p. 33) is "the productive apparatus" as in the next paragraph (cf. also
"Some Remarks", p. 179).—Ed.]

prices. It makes a greater margin between factor-prices and product-prices necessary just when this margin threatens to diminish. The maintenance of equilibrium is thus further secured.

For we must not forget that not only the volume of current production, but also the size, at any given moment, of the productive apparatus (including stocks, which cannot be omitted) is regulated through prices, and especially— apart from the above-mentioned prices for goods and services—by the price paid for the use of capital, that is, interest. Whatever particular explanation of interest we may accept, all contemporary theories agree in regarding the function of interest as one of equalising the supply of capital and the demand arising[28] in various branches of production. Until some special reason can be adduced why it should not fulfil this function in any given case, we have to assume, in accordance with the fundamental thesis of static theory, that it always keeps the supply[29] of capital goods in equilibrium with that of consumption goods. This assumption is just as indispensable, and just as inevitable, as a starting-point, as the main assumption that the supply of and demand for any kind of goods will be equilibrated by movements in the prices of those goods. In our case, when we are considering a tendency to enlarge the productive apparatus and the size of stocks, this function must be performed in such a way as to increase the rate of interest, and hence the necessary margin of profit between the price of the products and that of the means of production. This, however, automatically excludes that part of the increase in the demand for productive goods, which would have been satisfied despite the increase in their prices if the rise in the rate of interest had not taken place. None of the various Trade Cycle theories based on some alleged peculiarity of the technique of production can even begin to explain why the equilibrium position, determined by the various above-mentioned processes of price formation, should be reached at a different point from where it would be without these peculiarities.

Now as regards the prices of goods and services used for productive purposes, there seems to be no reason why they should not fulfil their function of equilibrating supply and demand. For supply and demand are here in direct relation with one another,[30] so that any discrepancy which may arise between them at a given price must, directly and immediately, lead to a change in

---

[28] [Here the German version speaks, not of "demand arising", but of "the volume of capital used in the various branches of production" (as in "Some Remarks", p. 179; cf. "Einige Bemerkungen", p. 271; *Geldtheorie*, p. 34).—Ed.]

[29] [And here the German version refers, not to the "supply", but to the "output" (as in "Some Remarks", p. 179) or to the "production" of capital goods and consumption goods (cf. "Einige Bemerkungen", p. 271; *Geldtheorie*, p. 34).—Ed.]

[30] [More accurately, "demand and supply here directly confront each other" (my translation; cf. "Einige Bemerkungen", p. 272; *Geldtheorie*, p. 35).—Ed.]

that price. Only when we come to consider the second group of prices (those paid for borrowed capital or, in other words, interest) is it conceivable that disturbances might creep in, since, in this case, price formation does not act directly, by equalising the marginal demand for and supply of capital goods, but indirectly, through its effect on money capital, whose supply need not correspond to that of real capital.[31] But the process by which divergences can arise between these two is left unexplained by all the theories with which we have hitherto dealt. Yet before going on to see how far interest may present such a breach in the strict system of equilibrium as may serve to explain cyclical disturbances, we must briefly examine the explanation offered by the second important group of non-monetary theories, which attempt to explain the origin of periodical disturbances of equilibrium purely through the phenomena arising out of the accumulation and investment of saving.[32]

6. Theories which explain fluctuations with reference to phenomena arising out of the process of saving and investment

The earlier versions of these theories start from the groundless and inadmissible assumption that unused savings are accumulated for a time and then suddenly invested, thus causing the productive apparatus to be extended in jerks. Such versions can be passed over without further analysis. For one thing, it is impossible to give any plausible explanation why unused savings should accumulate for a time;[33] for another thing, even if such an explanation were forthcoming, it would provide no clue to the disproportional development in the production of capital goods. The fact that the mere existence of fluctuations

---

[31] [The translation of this sentence appears misleading. Correcting for a misprint in the German version, a conjectural translation might read as follows: "since, in this case, price formation is not the result of directly balancing the capital goods that are ultimately demanded with their supply, because capital is only indirectly traded in the form of money capital the supply of which need not correspond to that of real capital" (my translation, drawing on "Some Remarks", p. 180; cf. "Einige Bemerkungen", p. 272; *Geldtheorie*, p. 35). Note, in particular, that "marginal" for "endgültig" is a translation error and should read, "ultimate".—Ed.]

[32] In revising the above paragraphs [for the 1929 German edition—Ed.] my notice has been called to the fact that they are in many respects in accordance with the reasoning of Siegfried Budge in his *Grundzüge der theoretischen Nationalökonomie* (Jena: Fischer, 1925), pp. 201 et seq. [pp. 201–25], to which I should therefore like to call attention.

[33] Cf. the very effective remarks of Walter Eucken in his interesting viva-voce report to the Zurich Assembly of the Verein für Sozialpolitik ("Kredit und Konjunktur", in *Schriften des Vereins für Sozialpolitik*, vol. 175, pp. 295 et seq. [pp. 295–97]). [Walter Eucken (1891–1950), professor at the University of Freiburg, 1927–50, became one of the founders of the Freiburg school of economics and law, and of ordoliberalism. In the 1930s, besides "Kredit und Konjunktur", Eucken's *Kapitaltheoretische Untersuchungen* (Jena: Fischer, 1934; 2nd ed., Tübingen: Mohr, 1954) were highly appreciated by the Austrian economists.—Ed.]

in saving activity does not in itself explain this problem is realised (in contrast to many other economists) by the most distinguished exponent of these theories, Prof. A. Spiethoff. This is plain from his negative answer to the analogous question, whether in a barter economy an increase in saving can create the necessary conditions for depression.[34] Indeed, it is difficult to see how spontaneous variations in the volume of saving (which are not themselves open to further economic explanation, and must therefore be regarded as changes of data) within the limits in which they are actually observed[35] can possibly create the typical disturbances with which Trade Cycle theory is concerned.[36]

Where, then, according to these theories, may we find the reason for this genesis of disequilibrating disturbances in the processes of saving and investment? We will keep to the basis of Spiethoff's theory, which is certainly the most complete of its kind. We may disregard his simple reference to the "complexity of capital relations",[37] for it does not in itself provide an explanation. The main basis of his explanation is to be found in the following sentence: "If capitalists and producers of immediate consumption goods want to keep their production in step with the supply of acquisitive loan capital, these processes should be *consciously adjusted to one another*".[38] But the creation of acquisitive

---

[34] Arthur Spiethoff, "Krisen", in *Handwörterbuch der Staatswissenschaften*, 4th ed. rev., ed. Ludwig Elster, Adolf Weber, and Friedrich Wieser, vol. 6 (Jena: Fischer, 1925), p. 81. [For an abridged translation, see "Business Cycles", in *International Economic Papers*, vol. 3, 1953, reprinted in *Business Cycle Theory: Selected Texts 1860–1939*, vol. 2: *Structural Theories of the Business Cycle*, ed. Hagemann, pp. 198–99.—Ed.]

[35] [Hayek's view of this case underwent some change; whereas in *Geldtheorie*, p. 37, he denied that fluctuations of saving "of whatever extent" could bring about a crisis, in the above passage he restricts this judgment to fluctuations "within the limits in which they are actually observed". The following note, added in 1933, indicates this revision; cf. also the editor's introduction to this volume, p. 20n.77.—Ed.]

[36] It is, however, not inconceivable, theoretically, that sudden and violent fluctuations in the volume of saving might give rise to the phenomena of a crisis during their downward swings. On this point, see below, chapter 5, p. 149.

[37] Spiethoff, "Krisen", p. 76 [cf. "Business Cycles", p. 190—Ed.].

[38] Ibid. My italics. [Cf. the translation in "Business Cycles", p. 191: "If the makers of indirect consumption goods and the potential investors wanted to make production and the formation of savings keep pace with each other, then the two processes would have to be adjusted to each other, in mutual knowledge." This translation improves upon that in the text by identifying "capitalists" with "potential investors" and "the supply of acquisitive loan capital" with "the formation of savings", and it corrects the translation error "immediate" for "indirect" consumption goods. According to Spiethoff (ibid.), indirect consumption goods (like iron and coal) are goods that "cannot be consumed directly, but serve to satisfy wants by means of intermediary goods (machines, dwelling-houses) which furnish [consumption] goods or long-lasting services".—Ed.] The same general view, though in a somewhat different connection, has since been expressed by Mr. J. M. Keynes in several passages of his *A Treatise on Money*, 2 vols. (London: Macmillan, 1930) [reprinted as vols. 5 and 6 (1971) of *The Collected Writings of John Maynard Keynes*, ed. Austin Robinson and Donald Moggridge (London: Macmillan; Cambridge: Cambridge University Press)—Ed.]. Cf., for example, vol. 1, p. 175 and especially p. 279 [cf. reprinted., vol. 5,

loan capital ensues independently of the production of intermediate goods and durable capital goods; and conversely, the latter can be produced without the entrepreneur knowing the extent to which acquisitive capital (i.e., savings) exists and is available for investment; and thus there is always a danger that one of these processes may lag behind while the other hastens forward. This reference to the entrepreneur's ignorance of the situation belongs, however, to that category of explanation which we had to reject earlier. Instead of showing why prices—and in this case, particularly, the price of capital, which is interest—do not fulfil, or fail to fulfil adequately, their normal function of regulating the volume of production, it unexpectedly overlooks the fact that the extent of production is regulated on the basis not of a knowledge of demand but through price determination. Assuming that the rate of interest always determines the point to which the available volume[39] of savings enables productive plant to be extended—and it is only by this assumption that we can explain what determines the rate of interest at all—any allegations of a discrepancy between savings and investments[40] must be backed up by a demonstration why, in the given case, interest does not fulfil this function.[41] Professor Spiethoff, like most of the theorists of this group, evades this necessary issue—as we shall see later—by introducing another assumption of crucial importance. It is only by means of this assumption that the causes which he particularly enumerates in his analysis gain significance as an explanation; and therefore it should not have been treated as a self-evident condition, to be casually mentioned, but as the starting-point of the whole theoretical analysis.

7. Psychological theories

Before going into this question, however, we must turn our attention to the importance in Trade Cycle theory of *errors of forecast*, and, in connection with

---

pp. 157–58 and 251—Ed.]: "There is, indeed, no possibility of intelligent foresight designed to equate savings and investment unless it is exercised by the banking system".

[39] [More accurately, "supply" (as in "Some Remarks", p. 181; cf. "Einige Bemerkungen", p. 274; *Geldtheorie*, p. 38) instead of "volume".—Ed.]

[40] [A literal translation of the German text (as in *Geldtheorie*, p. 38; cf. "Einige Bemerkungen", p. 274) would be "between the supply and the use of savings".—Ed.]

[41] Elements of the same reasoning can also be found in Cassel, *The Theory of Social Economy*, 4th German edition [that is, *Theoretische Sozialökonomie*—Ed.] (Leipzig: Winter, 1927), p. 575, when he derives high-conjuncture from an overestimate of the supply of capital (i.e., savings) which is available to take over the supply of real capital produced. [Cf. the passage, almost literally quoted, in *The Theory of Social Economy*, new rev. ed., p. 649: "The typical modern trade boom [means] an over-estimate of the supply of capital, or of the amount of savings available for taking over the real capital produced." In *Geldtheorie*, p. 38n., the passage was put in quotation marks. Note that "high-conjuncture" (as a too-literal translation of the German *Hochkonjunktur*) refers to the boom.—Ed.]

these, to a third group of theories which have not been considered up to now—the *psychological theories*. Here, as elsewhere in our investigations, we shall only be concerned with those theories which are *endogenous*—i.e., which explain the origin of general under- and over-estimation from the economic situation itself, and not from some external circumstance such as weather changes, etc. As we said earlier, fluctuations of economic activity which merely represent an adjustment to corresponding changes in external circumstances present no problem to economic theory. The various psychological factors cited are only relevant to our analysis in so far as they can cast light on its central problem: that is, how an over-estimate of future demand can occasion a development of the productive apparatus so excessive as automatically to lead to a reaction, unprecipitated by other psychological changes. Those who are familiar with the most distinguished of these theories, that of Professor A. C. Pigou (which, owing to lack of space, cannot be reproduced here),[42] will see at once that the endogenous psychological theories are open to the same objections as the two groups of theories which we have already examined. Professor Pigou does not explain why errors should arise in estimating the effect, on the price of the final product, of an increase in demand or a fall in cost; or, if the estimate is correct, why the readjustment of the prices of means of production should not check the expansion of production at the right point. No one would deny, of course, that errors can arise as regards the future movements of particular prices. But it is not permissible to assume without further proof that the equilibrating mechanism of the economic system will begin its work only when the excessively increased product due to these mistaken forecasts actually comes on the market, the disproportional development continuing undisturbed up to that time. At one point or another, all theories which start to explain cyclical fluctuations by miscalculations or ignorance as regards the economic situation fall into the same error as those naive explanations which base themselves on the 'planlessness' of the economic system. They overlook the fact that, in the exchange economy, production is governed by prices, independently of any knowledge of the whole process on the part of individual producers, so that it is only when the pricing process is itself disturbed that a misdirection of production can occur. The 'wrong' prices, on the other hand, which lead to 'wrong' dispositions, cannot in turn be explained by a mistake. Within the framework of a system of explanations in which, as in all modern economic theory, prices are merely expressions of a necessary tendency towards a state of equilibrium, it is not permissible to reintroduce the old Sismondian idea

---

[42] Cf. Pigou, *Industrial Fluctuations*; also Oskar Morgenstern, "Qualitative und quantitative Konjunkturforschung", *Zeitschrift für die gesamte Staatswissenschaft*, vol. 84 [vol. 85], no. 1, 1928, pp. 54–88. [Arthur Cecil Pigou (1877–1959), Cambridge economist and the successor of Alfred Marshall as professor of political economy, 1908–43, combined in his theory of the business cycle monetary and psychological factors.—Ed.]

of the misleading effect of prices on production[43] without first bringing it into line with the fundamental system of explanation.

8. All these theories assume the variability of credit

It is, perhaps, scarcely necessary to point out that all the objections raised against the non-monetary theories, already cited in our investigations, are justified by one particular assumption which we had to make in order to examine the independent validity of the so-called 'real' explanations. In order to see whether the 'real' causes (whose effect is always emphasised as a proof that monetary changes are not the cause of cyclical fluctuations) can provide a sufficient explanation of the cycle, it has been necessary to study their operation under conditions of pure barter. And even if it were impossible to prove fully that, under these conditions, no non-monetary explanation is sufficient, enough has been said, I think, to indicate the general trend of thought which would refute all theories based exclusively on productive, market, financial, or psychological phenomena. None of these phenomena can help us to dissolve the fundamental equilibrium-relationships which form the basis of all economic explanation. And this dissolution is indispensable if we are to protect ourselves against objections such as those outlined above.

If the various theories comprised in these groups are still able to offer a plausible explanation of cyclical fluctuations, and if their authors do not realise the contradictions involved, this is due to the unconscious importation of an assumption incompatible with a purely 'real' explanation. This assumption is adequate to dissolve the rigid reaction-mechanisms of barter-economy, and thus makes possible the processes described; but for this very reason it should not be treated as a self-evident condition, but as the basis of the explanation itself. The condition thus tacitly assumed—and one can easily prove that it is in fact assumed in all the theories examined above—is *the existence of credit* which, within reasonable limits, is always at the entrepreneur's disposal at an unchanged price. This, however, assumes the absence of the most important controls which, in the barter economy, keep the extension of the productive apparatus within economically permissible limits. *Once we assume that, even at a single point, the pricing process fails to equilibrate supply and demand, so that over a more or less long period demand may be satisfied at prices at which the available supply is inad-*

---

[43] [The idea of the 'planlessness of the modern economy' may be found in J. C. L. Simonde de Sismondi, *Nouveaux principes d'économie politique*, 2 vols. (Paris: Delauney, 1819; 2nd ed., 1827), livre IV, chapitre ii; cf. the translation *New Principles of Political Economy*, trans. Richard Hyse (New Brunswick and London: Transaction, 1991), pp. 253–60 ("On Knowledge of the Market"). Jean Charles Leonard Simonde de Sismondi (1773–1842), Swiss historian and economist, criticised the new industrial system for its tendency towards underconsumption.—Ed.]

equate to meet total demand, then the march of economic events loses its determinateness and a range of indeterminateness appears, within which movements can originate leading away from equilibrium. And it is rightly assumed, as we shall see later on, that it is precisely the behaviour of interest, the price of credit, which makes possible these disturbances in price formation. We must not, however, overlook the fact that the range of indeterminateness thus created is 'indeterminate' only in relation to the absolute determinateness of barter economy.[44] The new price formation, together with the new structure of production determined by it, must in turn conform to certain laws, and the apparent indeterminateness does not imply unfettered mobility of prices and production. On the contrary, *every departure from the original equilibrium position is definitely determined by the new conditioning factor.* But if it is the existence of credit which makes these various disturbances possible, and if the volume and direction of new credits determines the extent of deviations from the equilibrium position, it is clearly not permissible to regard credit as a kind of passive element, and its presence as a self-evident condition. One must regard it rather as the new determining factor whose appearance causes these deviations and whose effects must form our starting-point when deducing all those phenomena which can be observed in cyclical fluctuations. Only when we have succeeded in doing this can we claim to have explained the phenomena described.

The neglect to derive the appearance of disproportionality from this condition, which must be assumed in order to keep the argument within the framework of equilibrium theory, leads to certain consequences which are best exemplified in the work of Professor Spiethoff. For, in his theory, all important interconnections are worked out in the fullest detail and none of the observed phenomena remains unaccounted for. But he is not able to deduce the various phenomena described from the single factor which, by virtue of its role in disturbing the inter-relationships of general equilibrium, should form the basis of his explanation. At each stage of his exposition he calls in experience to back him up and to show what deviations from the equilibrium position actually occur within the given range of indeterminateness. Consequently it never becomes clear why these phenomena *must* always occur as they are described; and there always remains a possibility that, on some other occasion, they may occur in a different way, or in a different order, without his being able to account for this difference on the basis of his exposition. In other words the latter, however accurately and pertinently it describes the observed phenom-

---

[44] [In contemporary literature equilibrium was denoted as 'determinate' if stable and independent of initial conditions; see Nicholas Kaldor, "A Classificatory Note on the Determinateness of Equilibrium", *Review of Economic Studies*, vol. 1, February 1934, pp. 122–36, reprinted as chapter 1 of *Essays on Value and Distribution*, vol. 1 of *Collected Economic Essays* (London: Duckworth, 1960; 2nd ed., 1980). Cf. also the discussion of indeterminacy in Hayek's "Investigations", pp. 79–80.—Ed.]

ena, does not qualify as a theory in the rigid sense of the word, for it does not set out those conditions in whose presence events *must* follow a scientifically determined course.[45]

9. *The main difference between monetary and other changes in economic 'data'*

Although there is no doubt that all non-monetary Trade Cycle theories tacitly assume that the production of capital goods has been made possible by the creation of new credit, and although this condition is often emphasised in the course of the exposition,[46] no one has yet proved that this circumstance should form the exclusive basis of the explanation. As far as strict logic is concerned, it would not be impossible for such theories to make use of some other assumption which is capable of dissolving the rigid inter-relationships of equilibrium and, therefore, of forming the basis of an exact theoretical analysis. But once we assume the existence of credit in our explanation, we can attack the problem by seeing how far the objections which were raised earlier against the validity of the various theories under a barter economy are invalidated when the new assumption is made. Then we shall also be able to determine whether this assumption has necessarily to be made in the usual form, or whether it only represents a special instance of a far more widely significant extension of the assumptions of elementary theory.

The question we have to ask ourselves is: What new price-determining factor is introduced by the assumption of a credit supply which can be enlarged while other conditions remain unchanged—a factor capable of deflecting the tendency towards the establishment of equilibrium between supply and demand? Whether we necessarily accept that answer which, to my mind, is the only possible one depends on whether we agree with a certain basic proposition, which could only be briefly outlined here and whose full proof could only be given within the framework of a complete system of pure economics; namely, the proposition that, in a barter economy, interest forms a sufficient regulator for the proportional development of the production of capital goods and consumption goods, respectively. If it is admitted that, in the absence of money, interest would effectively prevent any excessive extension of the production of production goods, by keeping it within the limits of the available supply of savings, and that an extension of the stock of capital goods which is based on a voluntary postponement of consumers' demand into the future

---

[45] [In "Einige Bemerkungen", p. 278, and *Geldtheorie*, p. 44, there is no equivalent to the word "scientifically".—Ed.]

[46] Cf. Spiethoff, "Krisen", pp. 77–78 and 81. [Cf. "Business Cycles", pp. 192–93 and 198—Ed.]

can never lead to disproportionate extensions, then it must also necessarily be admitted that disproportional developments in the production of capital goods can arise only through the independence of the supply of free money capital[47] from the accumulation of savings; which in turn arises from the elasticity[48] of the volume of money.[49] Every change in the volume of means of circulation is, in fact, an event to be distinguished from all other real causes, for the purpose of theoretical reasoning; for, unlike all others, it implies a loosening of the inter-relationships of equilibrium. No change in 'real' factors, whether in the amount of available means of production, in consumers' preferences, or elsewhere, can do away with that final identity of total demand and total supply on which every conception of economic equilibrium is based. A change in the volume of money, on the other hand, represents as it were a one-sided change in demand, which is not counterbalanced by an equivalent change in supply. Money, being a pure means of exchange, not being wanted by anyone for purposes of consumption, must by its nature always be re-exchanged without ever having entirely fulfilled its purpose; thus when it is present it loosens that finality and 'closedness'[50] of the system which is the fundamental assumption of static theory, and leads to phenomena which the closed system of static equilibrium renders inconceivable.[51]

[47] [In "Capital Consumption", pp. 157–58, Hayek defines "free capital" as "consisting of earned amortization quotas (or proceeds from circulating capital which has been turned over), new savings and perhaps additional credits".—Ed.]

[48] [Here and in the following, "Veränderlichkeit" ("Einige Bemerkungen", p. 279; *Geldtheorie*, p. 46) is translated as "elasticity" instead of literally "variability" (as in "Some Remarks", p. 185). See also p. 120n.2 below.—Ed.]

[49] 'Volume of money', in this connection, does not mean merely the quantity of money in circulation but the volume of the money stream or the effective circulation (in the usual terminology—quantity *times* velocity of circulation). Even so, certain changes in the effective circulation may have no disturbing effect because of certain compensating changes in business organisation. On this point see my *Prices and Production*, lecture 4. [This note, which takes account of changes in velocity, was added to the 1933 edition. Obviously, here all references to *Prices and Production* are to the first edition.—Ed.]

[50] [Instead of "entirely" and "finality", more literal translations are "ultimately" and "finiteness" (cf. "Some Remarks", p. 186; "Einige Bemerkungen", p. 280; and *Geldtheorie*, p. 47). Cf. in this regard also the notion of a closed period characteristic of the analysis of static theory, which Hayek emphasised in "Investigations", pp. 78–79.—Ed.]

[51] This dissolution of the 'closedness' of the system, arising because a change in the volume of money is a one-sided change in demand unaccompanied by an equivalent change in supply, does not mean of course that Löwe's plea for an 'open' system ("Wie ist Konjunkturtheorie überhaupt möglich?" [pp. 185–92; cf. "How Is Business Cycle Theory Possible At All?", pp. 20–26—Ed.]) has been granted. (Löwe thinks of a system [that is, of 'an open system'—Ed.] when one or several 'independent variables' are drawn in for explanation.) This plea, which one is tempted to believe has been dictated by a desire to free theory from the trammels of exact deduction, has been justly and strongly criticised by Carell, *Sozialökonomische Theorie und Konjunkturproblem*, pp. 2 et seq. [pp. 2–15] and 115.

Together with the 'closedness' of the system there necessarily disappears the interdependence of all its parts, and thus prices become possible which do not operate according to the self-regulating principles of the economic system described by static theory. On the contrary, these prices may elicit movements which not only do not lead to a new equilibrium position but which actually create new disturbances of equilibrium. In this way, through the inclusion of money among the basic assumptions of exposition, it becomes possible to deduce a priori phenomena such as those observed in cyclical fluctuations. One instance of these disturbances in the price mechanism, brought about by monetary influences—and the one which is most important from the point of view of Trade Cycle theory—is that putting out of action of the 'interest brake' which is taken for granted by the Trade Cycle theories examined above. How far this circumstance forms a sufficient basis for a theory of the Trade Cycle is a problem of the concrete elaboration of monetary explanation, and will, therefore, be dealt with in the next chapter, where we shall examine how far existing monetary theories have already tackled those problems which are relevant to a theory of the Trade Cycle.

10. The existence of monetary disturbances having been assumed, the first task of theory is to examine all the deviations from the system contemplated by the pure theory of equilibrium which must necessarily follow this assumption

The purpose of the foregoing chapter was to show that only the assumption of primary monetary changes can fulfil the fundamentally necessary condition of any theoretical explanation of cyclical fluctuations—a condition which is not fulfilled by any theory based exclusively on 'real' processes. If this is true, then, at the outset of theoretical exposition, those monetary processes must be recognised as decisive causes. *For we can gain a theoretically unexceptionable explanation of complex phenomena only by first assuming the full activity of the elementary economic interconnections as shown by the equilibrium theory, and then introducing, consciously and successively, just those elements which are capable of relaxing these rigid inter-relationships.* All the phenomena which become possible only as a result of this relaxation must then be explained as consequences of the particular elements, through whose inclusion among the elementary assumptions they become explicable within the framework of general theory. In place of such a theoretical deduction, we often find an assertion, unfounded on any system, of a far-reaching indeterminacy in the economy. Paradoxically stated[52] as it is, this thesis is

[52] [Instead of "paradoxically stated", a more accurate translation of "schlagwortartige Form" ("Einige Bemerkungen", p. 281; *Geldtheorie*, p. 49) is "in a slogan-like form" (as in "Some Remarks", p. 187).—Ed.]

bound to have a devastating effect on theory; for it involves the sacrifice of any exact theoretical deduction, and the very possibility of a theoretical explanation of economic phenomena is rendered problematic.

Similar objections of a general nature must be levelled against another large group of theories which we have not yet mentioned. This group pays close attention to the monetary inter-connections and expressly emphasises them as a necessary condition for the occurrence of the processes described. But they fail to pass from this realisation to the necessary conclusion; to make it a starting-point for their theoretical elaboration, from which all other particular phenomena have to be deduced. To this group belongs the theory of Professor J. Schumpeter, and certain 'under-consumption theories',[53] notably that of Professor E. Lederer, and, similarly, the various 'realistic' theories— that is, those which renounce any unified theoretical deduction, such as those of Professors G. Cassel, J. Lescure, and Wesley Mitchell. With regard to all these semi-monetary explanations, we must ask whether—once we have been compelled to introduce new assumptions foreign to the static system—it is not the first task of a theoretical investigation to examine all the consequences which must necessarily ensue from this new assumption, and, in so far as any phenomena are thus proved to be logically derivable from the latter, to regard them in the course of the exposition as effects of the new condition introduced. Only in this way is it possible to incorporate Trade Cycle theory into the static system which is the basis of all theoretical economics; and, for this very reason, the monetary elements must be regarded as decisive factors in the explanation of cyclical fluctuations. The contrast therefore can be reduced to a question of theoretical presentation, and it may even seem, when comparing these theories, that the matter of the express recognition of the monetary starting-point is one of purely methodological or even terminological importance, having no bearing on the essential solution of the problem. But the same procedure which in one case may only lead to a lapse from theoretical elegance, breaking the unity of the theoretical structure, may in another case lead to the introduction of thoroughly faulty reasoning, against which only a rigid systematical procedure provides an effective security.

[53] For a detailed criticism of a representative specimen of modern under-consumption theories, that of Messrs. W. T. Foster and W. Catchings [cf., e.g., William Trufant Foster and Waddill Catchings, *Profits*, Publications of the Pollak Foundation, no. 8 (Boston and New York: Houghton Mifflin, 1925)—Ed.], see my article on "The 'Paradox' of Saving".

THREE

MONETARY THEORIES OF
THE TRADE CYCLE

1. The main tasks of a monetary theory of the Trade Cycle

The argument of the foregoing chapters has demonstrated the main reason for the necessity of the monetary approach to Trade Cycle theory. It arises from the circumstance that the automatic adjustment of supply and demand can only be disturbed when money is introduced into the economic system. This adjustment must be considered, according to the reasoning which is most clearly expressed in Say's *Théorie des Débouchés*, as being always present in a state of natural economy.[1] Every explanation of the Trade Cycle which uses the methods of economic theory—which of course is only possible through systematic co-ordination of the former with the fundamental propositions of the latter—must, therefore, start by considering the influences which emanate from the use of money. By following up their results it should be possible to demonstrate the total effect on the economic system, and formulate the result into a co-ordinated whole. This must be the aim of all theories which set out to explain disturbances in equilibrium which, by their very nature, cannot be regarded as immediate consequences of changes in data, but only as arising out of the development of the economic system itself. For that typical form of disturbance, which experience shows to be regularly recurrent and which can properly be called the Trade Cycle, the influence of money should be sought in the fact that when the volume of money is elastic, there may exist a lack of rigidity in the relationship between saving and the creation of real capital.[2] This is a fact which nearly all the theories of the disproportional production of capital goods are agreed in emphasising. It is, therefore, the first task of monetary Trade Cycle theory to show why, and how, monetary influ-

---

[1] [Here and in the following the text occasionally translates *Naturalwirtschaft* as "natural" instead of "barter economy". See p. 77n.27 above.—Ed.]

[2] [A more accurate and intelligible translation instead of "a lack of rigidity in the relationship between saving and the creation of capital" is the literal "a relative independence of real capital formation from saving activity" (as in "Some Remarks", p. 188; cf. "Einige Bemerkungen", p. 283; *Geldtheorie*, p. 52). Note, in particular, that in most other instances *Kapitalbildung* has been translated as "capital formation".—Ed.]

ences directly bring about regular disturbances in just this part of the economic system.

2.[3]

Naturally no attempt will be made at this stage to present such a theory systematically. This chapter is concerned with one particular task: it attempts to show how far existing monetary theories have already gone towards a satisfactory solution of the problem of the Trade Cycle, and what corrections are needed in order to invalidate certain objections which, up to the present, have appeared well founded.

It should already be clear that what we expect from a monetary Trade Cycle theory differs considerably from what most of the monetary Trade Cycle theories regard as the essential aim of their explanation. We are in no way concerned to explain the effect of the monetary factor on trade fluctuations through changes in the value of money and variations in the price level—subjects which form the main basis of current monetary theories. We expect such an explanation to emerge rather from a study of all the changes originating in the monetary field—more especially variations in its quantity—changes which are bound to disturb the equilibrium inter-relationships existing in the natural economy, *whether the disturbance shows itself in a change in the so-called 'general value of money' or not.* Our plea for a monetary approach to all Trade Cycle theory does not, therefore, imply that henceforward such theories should be exclusively, or even principally, based on those arguments which usually predominate in writings on money, and which set out to explain the general level of prices and alterations in the 'value of money'. On the contrary, monetary theory should not merely be concerned with money for its own sake, but should also study those phenomena which distinguish the money economy from the equilibrium inter-relationships of barter economy which must always be assumed by 'pure economics'.

It must of course be admitted that many Trade Cycle theorists regard the importance of monetary theory as residing precisely in its ability to explain the cause of fluctuations by reference to changes in the general price level. Hence, it is not difficult to understand why certain economists believe that, once they have

---

[3] [Due to an apparent editing error, in this chapter the section headings (taken from the Analytical Table of Contents above, pp. 63–65) do not correctly match the actual sections. In particular, compared with the German edition, although the first section was split up into two, this was not taken into account by changing section headings; furthermore, to make good for this oversight an additional section heading was introduced for the final section. In this edition, the proper correspondence between headings and sections has been restored. Thus, there is no heading for section 2, while the redundant heading of the penultimate section has been dropped.—Ed.]

rejected this view, they have settled once and for all with the monetary explanations of the Trade Cycle. It is not surprising that monetary theories of the Trade Cycle should be rejected by those who, like Professor A. Spiethoff in his well-known work on the Quantity Theory as '*Haussetheorie*',[4] identify them with the naive quantity-theory explanations which derive fluctuations from changes in the price level.[5] Against such a conception it can rightly be urged that there are a number of phenomena tending to bring about fluctuations, which certainly do not depend on changes in the value of money, and which can, in fact, exert a disturbing effect on the economic equilibrium without these changes occurring at all. Again, in spite of many assertions to the contrary, fluctuations in the general price level need not always be ascribed to monetary causes.[6]

3. Monetary explanations should not proceed from changes in the general level of prices

But theories which explain the Trade Cycle in terms of fluctuations in the general price level must be rejected not only because they fail to show why the monetary factor disturbs the general equilibrium, but also because their fundamental hypothesis is, from a theoretical standpoint, every bit as naive as that of those theories which entirely neglect the influence of money. They start off with a 'normal position' which, however, has nothing to do with the normal position obtaining in the static state;[7] and they are based on a pos-

---

[4] "Die Quantitätstheorie, insbesondere in ihrer Verwertbarkeit als Haussetheorie", in *Festgaben für Adolph Wagner zur 70. Wiederkehr seines Geburtstages*, ed. Georg Adler et al. (Leipzig: Winter, 1905 [reprinted, Frankfurt am Main: Keip, 1989]), pp. 299ff. [pp. 249–66; *Haussetheorie* is a theory of the boom.—Ed.]

[5] F. Burchardt, A. Löwe, and other more recent critics of monetary trade cycle theory also fall within this category. They recognise no other kind of monetary influence than that which manifests itself through changes in the price level; and as a result of this undoubtedly false conception they quite definitely conclude that there can be no such thing as pure monetary trade cycle theory. In their view the theories which are usually so called nearly always depend, in fact, on what they regard as non-monetary factors. [The German economist Fritz (later Frank A.) Burchardt (1902–58) cooperated with Löwe in Kiel and Frankfurt; after his 1935 emigration he taught at the University of Oxford.—Ed.]

[6] The assertion that changes in the *general* level of prices must always originate on the monetary side, as is argued for example by Professors G. Cassel and Irving Fisher, obviously depends on circular reasoning. It starts from the postulate that the amount of money must be adjusted to changes in the volume of trade in such a way that the price level shall remain unchanged. *If it is not, and the volume of money remains unaltered, then*, according to this remarkable argument, *the latter becomes the cause* (!) of changes in the price level. This statement is made quite baldly by Professor G. Cassel in his book *Money and Foreign Exchange After 1914* (London: Constable, 1922 [reprinted, New York: Arno Press, 1972]). [Cf. the passages on pp. 52–53.—Ed.]

[7] [Cf. the more intelligible translation, "described in the static system", in "Some Remarks", p. 189 (cf. "Einige Bemerkungen", p. 284; *Geldtheorie*, p. 55).—Ed.]

tulate, the postulate of a constant price level, which, if fulfilled, suffices in itself to break down the inter-relationships of equilibrium. All these theories, indeed, are based on the idea—quite groundless but hitherto virtually unchallenged—that if only the value of money does not change it ceases to exert a direct and independent influence on the economic system. But this assumption (which is present, more or less, in the work of all monetary theorists), so far from being the necessary starting-point for all Trade Cycle theory, is perhaps the greatest existing hindrance to a successful examination of the course of cyclical fluctuations. It forces us to assume variations in the effective quantity of money as given. Such variations, however, always dissolve the equilibrium inter-relationships described by static theory; but they must necessarily be assumed if the value of money is to remain constant despite changes in data; and therefore they cannot be used to explain deviations from the course of events which static theory lays down. The only proper starting-point for any explanation based on equilibrium theory must be the effect of a change in the volume of money; for this, in itself, constitutes a new state of affairs, entirely different from that generally treated within the framework of static theory.

In complete contrast to those economic changes conditioned by 'real' forces, influencing simultaneously total supply and total demand, changes in the volume of money have, so to speak, a one-sided influence which elicits no reciprocal adjustment in the economic activity of different individuals. By deflecting a single factor, without simultaneously eliciting corresponding changes in other parts of the system, it dissolves its 'closedness', makes a breach in the rigid reaction mechanism of the system (which rests on the ultimate identity of supply and demand), and opens a way for tendencies leading away from the equilibrium position.[8] As a theory of these one-sided influences, the theory of monetary economy should, therefore, be able to explain the occurrence of phenomena which would be inconceivable in the barter economy, and notably the disproportional developments which give rise to crises.[9] A starting-point for such explanations should be found in the possibility of alterations in the quantity of money occurring automatically and in the normal course of events, under the present organisation of money and credit, without the need for violent or artificial action by any external agency.

---

[8] [On the notions of 'simultaneous decisions' within a 'closed system' versus 'successive decisions' characterising an 'open system', cf. the relevant passages in "Investigations", pp. 80–82.—Ed.]

[9] Friedrich von Wieser, "Der Geldwert und seine geschichtlichen Veränderungen", *Zeitschrift für Volkswirtschaft, Sozialpolitik und Verwaltung*, vol. 13, no. 1, 1907, p. 57 [p. 54], reprinted in Wieser, *Gesammelte Abhandlungen*, ed. F. A. Hayek (Tübingen: Mohr, 1929 [reprinted, Saarbrücken: VDM Verlag Müller, 2006]), p. 178, has dealt with the special effects of a "one-sided money supply".

4. The essential point is the effect on the structure of production of changes in the volume of money

Even if a systematic treatment of the Trade Cycle problem has not yet been forthcoming, it should be noted that, throughout the different attempts at monetary explanation, there runs a secondary idea which is closely allied to that of the direct dependence of fluctuations on changes in the value of money. It is true that this idea is used merely as a subordinate device of technique to assist in the explanation of fluctuations in the value of money. But its development included the analysis of the most important elements in the monetary factors chiefly connected with the Trade Cycle. This was done in the teaching which began with H. Thornton[10] and D. Ricardo[11] and was taken up again by H. D. Macleod,[12]

[10] *An Enquiry into the Nature and Effects of the Paper Credit of Great Britain* (London: J. Hatchard, F. and C. Rivington, 1802), especially pp. 287 et seq. [pp. 287–88; cf. the American edition (Philadelphia: J. Humphreys, 1807), p. 183, reprinted in *A Select Collection of Scarce and Valuable Tracts and Other Publications on Paper Currency and Banking*, ed. James Ramsey McCulloch (London: Murray, 1857), which is reprinted as vol. 3 of *Classical Writings on Economics* (London: Pickering and Chatto, 1995), p. 319; cf. also the reprint *An Enquiry into the Nature and Effects of the Paper Credit of Great Britain together with his Evidence given before the Committee of Secrecy of the Two Houses of Parliament in the Bank of England, March and April 1797, some Manuscript Notes, and his Speeches on the Bullion Report, May 1811*, ed. F. A. Hayek (London: Allen and Unwin, 1939; reprinted, New York: Kelley, 1991), pp. 253–54.—Ed.] This is one of the most remarkable accomplishments in monetary theory, and still commands great attention; cf. the references to it by K. Wicksell in the preface to the second volume of his *Vorlesungen*, p. xii [not reproduced in *Lectures*, vol. 2—Ed.], and Fritz Burchardt ["Entwicklungsgeschichte der monetären Konjunkturtheorie", *Weltwirtschaftliches Archiv*, vol. 28, July 1928, pp. 77–143; Burchardt's article is mistakenly referred to by "op. cit." although there is no prior citation—Ed.]. For a fuller discussion of these earlier theories, see my *Prices and Production*, pp. 11ff. [pp. 11–19; this volume, pp. 200–210. Henry Thornton (1760–1815) was an outstanding monetary theorist of the nineteenth century, famous for his contribution to the debates during the restriction period and, jointly with Francis Horner (1778–1817) and William Huskisson (1770–1830), for the authorship of the Bullion Report.—Ed.]

[11] Cf. *The High Price of Bullion: A Proof of the Depreciation of Banknotes* [4th ed., 1811], reprinted in *Economic Essays*, ed. Edward C. K. Gonner (London: Bell, 1923), p. 35 [cf. *The Works and Correspondence of David Ricardo*, ed. Piero Sraffa, vol. 3: *Pamphlets and Papers, 1809–1811* (Cambridge: Cambridge University Press, 1951; reprinted, Indianapolis: Liberty Press, 2004), p. 91—Ed.], where Ricardo says that "interest would, during that interval[,] be *under its natural level*" [emphasis added by Hayek—Ed.], and also chapter 27 of his *On the Principles of Political Economy and Taxation* [1817; 3rd ed., 1821], reprinted in *The Works of David Ricardo*, ed. John Ramsey McCulloch (London: Murray, 1846), p. 220 [cf. *Works and Correspondence*, ed. Sraffa, vol. 1, pp. 363–64—Ed.], which for a long time have passed almost unnoticed but which already contained much of what is set out in later theories. [David Ricardo (1772–1823) was the prime theorist (in the modern sense of abstract model-building) among the classical economists; in the Bullion debate his position was more radical, but less subtle, than Thornton's.—Ed.]

[12] *Theory and Practice of Banking*, 2 vols. (London: Longman, Brown, Green and Longmans, 1855 and 1856) and later editions. See particularly vol. 2, pp. 278 et seq. [Cf. pp. 278–81 in the 5th edition, 1893. Henry Dunning Macleod (1821–1902), a British banker, developed a

H. Sidgwick, R. Giffen, and J. S. Nicholson,[13] and finally developed by A. Marshall,[14] K. Wicksell,[15] and L. von Mises,[16] whose works trace the development of the effects on the structure of production of a rate of interest which alters relatively to the equilibrium rate,[17] as a result of monetary influences.

---

credit theory of money and wealth, yet never succeeded in acquiring an academic position as an economist.—Ed.]

[13] For H. Sidgwick, R. Giffen, and J. S. Nicholson, cf. James W. Angell's *Theory of International Prices: History, Criticism and Restatement* (Cambridge, MA: Harvard University Press, 1926 [reprinted, New York: Kelley, 1965]), pp. 117–22. [Indeed, Angell (ibid., pp. 117–25) refers to Sidgwick's *Principles of Political Economy*, 3rd ed. (London: Macmillan, 1901); Giffen's "Gold Supply, the Rate of Discount, and Prices", in *Essays in Finance*, 2nd series (London: Bell, 1886); Nicholson's *Treatise on Money*, 5th ed. (London: Black, 1901); and Marshall's testimony before the Gold and Silver Commission of 1888, as reprinted in his *Money, Credit, and Commerce*. On p. 123 Angell speaks of the "'indirect' chain of effects that connect money and prices". Henry Sidgwick (1838–1900), Cambridge economist and philosopher, foreshadowed in his synthesis of classical and utilitarian thought to some extent the accomplishments of Alfred Marshall. Sir Robert Giffen (1837–1910), journalist and statistician, wrote on economic and financial subjects; a fierce supporter of laissez-faire, he favoured free trade and opposed bimetallism. His present-day fame derives from his being credited by Marshall for suggesting the possibility that, in the case of some inferior goods, the effect on the marginal utility of money may be so strong that the law of demand will be violated, the so-called Giffen paradox. Joseph Shield Nicholson (1850–1927), professor of political economy at the University of Edinburgh, 1880–1925, was a supporter of bimetallism and an adherent of the quantity theory of money.—Ed.]

[14] Cf. his evidence before the various Parliamentary Commissions which is collected in the volume *Official Papers by Alfred Marshall*, ed. John M. Keynes (London: Macmillan, 1926), especially pp. 38–41, 45, 46 et seq. [46–52], 273 et seq. [273–74], as well as the later account in *Money, Credit, and Commerce* (London: Macmillan, 1923), pp. 255–56. [Both were reprinted in *The Collected Works of Alfred Marshall*, ed. Peter Groenewegen (Bristol: Overstone Press, 1997). Alfred Marshall (1842–1924), professor of political economy at Cambridge, 1884–1908, was the founder of the Cambridge school of neoclassical economics. His *Principles of Economics*, 1st ed. (London: Macmillan, 1890), was the dominant economics textbook for almost fifty years, and conveyed to his disciples the conviction that 'it's all in Marshall'. Cf. the ninth variorum edition of the *Principles* with annotations by C. W. Guillebaud (London: Macmillan, 1961), reprinted in two volumes in *The Collected Works of Alfred Marshall* (1997).—Ed.]

[15] Especially in *Geldzins und Güterpreise* [cf. *Interest and Prices*—Ed.], as well as in the second volume of his later *Vorlesungen*, already quoted [cf. *Lectures*, vol. 2—Ed.], which has not had the influence which it deserved, mainly on account of the exceedingly bad German translation in which it appeared. I had unfortunately no means of access to the other Swedish works connected with that of Wicksell, which should certainly not be overlooked if one is to achieve a complete survey of the development of this theory.

[16] *Theorie des Geldes und der Umlaufsmittel* [cf. *The Theory of Money and Credit*—Ed.]; also the more recent *Geldwertstabilisierung und Konjunkturpolitik* (Jena: Fischer, 1928) [translated as "Monetary Stabilization and Cyclical Policy", trans. Bettina Bien Greaves, in *On the Manipulation of Money and Credit*, ed. Percy L. Greaves (New York: Free Market Books, 1978), pp. 59–171—Ed.]. [At this place the editor, Lionel Robbins, added a note announcing the forthcoming translation of Mises' book in the Bedford Economic Handbook Series: "[A translation of the former will shortly appear in the present series. Ed.]"—Ed.]

[17] [That is, "a rate of interest which deviates from the equilibrium rate".—Ed.]

For the purpose of this review it is unnecessary to go back to the earlier representatives of this group; it is enough to consider the conceptions of Wicksell and Mises, since both the recent improvements which have been effected and the errors which still subsist can be best examined on the basis of these studies.[18]

It must be taken for granted that the reader is acquainted with the works of both Wicksell and Mises. Wicksell, from the outset,[19] regards the problem as concerning explicitly the *average* change in the price of goods, which from the theoretical standpoint is quite irrelevant. He starts from the hypothesis that, in the absence of disturbing monetary influences, the average price level must remain unchanged. This assumption is based on another, only incidentally expressed,[20] which is not worked out and which, from the point of view of most of the problems dealt with, is not even permissible; i.e., the assumption of a stationary state of the economy. His fundamental thesis is that when the money rate of interest coincides with the natural rate (i.e., that rate which exactly balances the demand for loan capital and the supply of savings),[21] then money bears a completely *neutral* relationship to the price of goods, and tends neither to raise nor to lower it. But, owing to the nature of his basic assumptions, this thesis enables him to show deductively only that every lag of the money rate behind the natural rate must lead to a rise in the general price level, and every increase of the money rate above the natural rate to a fall in general price level. It is only incidentally, in the course of his analysis of the effects on the price level of a money rate of interest differing from the natural rate that Wicksell touches on the consequences of such a distortion of the natural price formation (made possible by elasticity in the volume

[18] Professor A. Hahn, whose views regarding Trade Cycle theory (put forward in *Volkswirtschaftliche Theorie des Bankkredits*, Tübingen: Mohr, 1920 [3rd ed. rev., 1930—Ed.]) are in some respects similar to those of Professor Mises, cannot be considered here, since we are unable to follow him in all those points in which he differs from the latter. Similar theories have also been put forward quite recently by Professor W. Röpke and S. Budge. [Lucien Albert Hahn (1889–1968), German banker and economist, initiated a controversy among German economists on the banks' ability to 'create' credit as well as on the possibly beneficial effects of inflationary credit—Austrian economists concurred with Hahn in the former, but not in the latter issue. After his immigration to the United States 1933, he recanted his early beliefs and became a harsh critic of Keynesianism, cf. his *The Economics of Illusion* (New York: Squier, 1949). Wilhelm Röpke (1892–1966), German economist, taught in Jena, Graz, and Marburg, and after his forced emigration of 1933 in Istanbul and Geneva. In post-war Germany Röpke became an advocate of the model of the Social Market Economy. Siegfried Budge (1869–1941), an industrialist and private scholar, taught monetary theory at the University of Frankfurt until his dismissal in 1933 because of his Jewish origin.—Ed.]

[19] See, e.g., *Geldzins und Güterpreise*, p. 125 [cf. *Interest and Prices*, p. 135—Ed.].

[20] Ibid., p. 126 [cf. ibid., p. 136—Ed.].

[21] Ibid., p. 93 [cf. ibid., p. 102—Ed.] and also *Vorlesungen*, vol. 2, p. 220. [Cf. *Lectures*, vol. 2, p. 193. See below, pp. 151–52, for a discussion of these definitions.—Ed.]

of currency) on the development of particular branches of production; and it is this question which is of the most decisive importance to Trade Cycle theory. If one were to make a systematic attempt to co-ordinate these ideas into an explanation of the Trade Cycle (dropping, as is essential, the assumption of the stationary state), a curious contradiction would arise. On the one hand, we are told that *the price level remains unaltered when the money rate of interest is the same as the natural rate*; and, on the other, that *the production of capital goods is, at the same time, kept within the limits imposed by the supply of real savings*. One need say no more in order to show that there are cases—certainly all cases of an expanding economy, which are those most relevant to Trade Cycle theory—in which the rate of interest which equilibrates the supply of real savings and the demand for capital cannot be the rate of interest which also prevents changes in the price level.[22] In this case, stability of the price level presupposes changes in the volume of money: but these changes must always lead to a discrepancy between the amount of real savings and the volume of investment. *The rate of interest at which, in an expanding economy, the amount of new money entering circulation is just sufficient to keep the price level stable, is always lower than the rate which would keep the amount of available loan-capital equal to the amount simultaneously saved by the public*: and thus, despite the stability of the price level, it makes possible a development leading away from the equilibrium position. But Wicksell does not recognise here a monetary influence tending, independently of changes in the price level, to break down the equilibrium system of barter economics: so long as the stability of the price level is undisturbed, everything appears to him to be in order.[23] Obsessed by the notion that the only aim of monetary theory is to explain those phenomena which cause the value of money to alter, he thinks himself justified in neglecting all deviations of the processes of money-economy from those of barter-economy, so long as they throw no direct light on the determination of the value of money: and thus he shuts the door on the possibility of a general theory covering all the consequences of the phenomena which he indicates.[24] But although his thesis of a direct rela-

---

[22] Similarly also Eucken, "Kredit und Konjunktur", pp. 300 et seq. [pp. 300–301].

[23] Wicksell's justification of this view in *Geldzins und Güterpreise* (see p. 97 [pp. 96–97; cf. *Interest and Prices*, p. 105—Ed.]) is incomprehensible to me.

[24] Rudolf Stucken in his *Theorie der Konjunkturschwankungen* (Jena: Fischer, 1926), p. 26, was one of the first to draw attention to the fact that the relation, indicated by Wicksell, between a money rate of interest diverging from the natural rate, and movements in the price level only exists in a stationary economy; while, if the flow of goods is increasing, only an addition to purchasing power can secure stability in the price level. He remains, however, entirely steeped in the prevalent opinion that a stable price level is indispensable to undisturbed economic development, and therefore holds that the additional money necessary to secure that condition cannot be regarded as an element of disturbance in the economic process. Similarly Mr. Dennis H. Robertson pointed out at about the same time (*Banking Policy and the Price Level: An Essay in the Theory of the Trade Cycle* (London: King, 1926), p. 99 [reprinted as vol. 3 of *The Development of Monetary Theory, 1920s*

tionship between movements in the price level and deviations of the money rate of interest from its natural level, holds good only in a stationary state, and is therefore inadequate for an explanation of cyclical fluctuations, his account of the effects of this deviation on the price structure and the development of the various branches of production constitutes the most important basis for any future monetary Trade Cycle theory. But this future theory, unlike that of Wicksell, will have to examine not movements in the general price level but rather those deviations of particular prices from their equilibrium position which were caused by the monetary factor.

5. Such changes in the structure of production are fundamentally independent of changes in the value of money

The investigations of Professor Mises represent a big step forward in this direction, although he still regards the fluctuations in the value of money as the main object of his explanation, and deals with the phenomena of disproportionality only in so far as they can be regarded as consequences—in the widest sense of the term—of these fluctuations. But Professor Mises' conception of the intrinsic value of money[25] extends the notion of 'fluctuations

---

and 1930s, ed. Forrest Capie and Geoffrey E. Wood (London: Routledge, 2000)—Ed.]) that the rate of interest which keeps the price level stable need not coincide with that which equates the supply of savings with the demand for capital. [Hayek's reference is erroneous; the passage in question is in D. H. Robertson, *Money*, new rev. ed. (London: Nisbet, 1928), p. 99, which is reprinted as vol. 2 of *The Development of Monetary Theory, 1920s and 1930s.*—Ed.] I am now informed that, even before the war, this objection formed the basis of a criticism directed by Prof. David Davidson of Upsala against Wicksell's theory. Prof. Davidson's article and the subsequent discussion with Wicksell in the Swedish *Economisk Tidskrift* are, however, inaccessible to me. [The articles in question appeared between 1906 and 1909; for accounts of the controversy cf. Bertil Ohlin, introduction to Wicksell, *Interest and Prices*, pp. x–xii, and Brinley Thomas, "The Monetary Doctrines of Professor Davidson", *Economic Journal*, vol. 45, March 1935, pp. 36–50.—Ed.]

[25] [The distinction between *innerer* and *äußerer Tauschwert des Geldes* (that is, the 'inner' and 'outer exchange value of money') was introduced by Carl Menger; cf. "Geld", in *Handwörterbuch der Staatswissenschaften*, 3rd ed., vol. 4 (Jena: Fischer, 1909), reprinted in *Gesammelte Werke*, ed. F. A. Hayek, 2nd ed., vol. 4 (Tübingen: Mohr, 1970); translated by Leland B. Yeager with Monika Streissler as "Money", in *Carl Menger and the Evolution of Payments Systems*, ed. Michael Latzer and Stefan W. Schmitz (Cheltenham and Northampton: Elgar, 2002), section 11. Mises (*Theorie des Geldes und der Umlaufsmittel*, 2nd ed., pp. 103–4) defines the inner value as the objective exchange value of money as far as it is determined solely by monetary influences, whereas the outer value is determined both by monetary and nonmonetary influences. He cautions in this regard (ibid., p. 104) not to confuse his 'inner' and 'outer exchange value' with the notions of 'intrinsic' and 'extrinsic value' of ancient authors. In *The Theory of Money and Credit*, pp. 145–46, the distinction between inner and outer exchange value has been dropped, the term 'objective exchange value of money' being used synonymously with 'inner exchange value' (see ibid., p. 146, translator's note).—Ed.]

in money value' far beyond the limits of what this term is commonly understood to mean; and so he is in a position to describe within the framework,
or rather under the name, of a theory of fluctuations in the value of money,
all monetary influences on price formation.[26] His exposition already contains
an account of practically all those effects of a rate of interest altered through
monetary influences, which are important for an explanation of the course of
the Trade Cycle. Thus he describes the disproportionate development of various branches of production and the resulting changes in the income structure.
And yet this presentation of his theory under the guise of a theory of fluctuation in the value of money remains dangerous, partly because it always gives
rise to misunderstandings, but mainly because it seems to bring into the fore-
ground a secondary effect of cyclical fluctuations, an effect which generally
accompanies the latter but which need not necessarily do so.

[26] If one follows C. Menger and now Professor Mises in disregarding ordinary usage and
including in the theory of the value of money *all* influences of money on prices, instead of
restricting it to an explanation of the general purchasing power of money (by which is understood the absolute level of money prices as distinct from the relative prices of particular goods),
then it is correct to say that any economic theory of money must be a theory of the value of
money. But this use of the phrase is hardly opportune, for 'value of money' is usually taken to
mean 'general purchasing power', while *monetary theory has by no means finished its work when it has
explained the absolute level of prices (or, as Wicksell would call it, the 'concrete' level); its far more important
task is to explain those changes in the relative height of particular prices which are conditioned by the introduction of money.* [Wicksell speaks of "konkrete Geldpreise" in *Geldzins und Güterpreise*, p. 92; cf. *Interest
and Prices*, p. 100, where the phrase is translated as "actual money prices".—Ed.] On the other
hand, to avoid any possible misunderstanding we must particularly insist at this point that in the
sense of the famous contrast between such nominalistic theories as the 'state theory' of Knapp,
and the catallactic theories in general, the monetary theory which we are seeking will also have
to be exclusively a 'theory of money values'. [The distinction between catallactic and acatallactic theories of money is due to Mises, *Theorie des Geldes und der Umlaufsmittel*, 2nd ed., chapter 9 (cf.
The Theory of Money and Credit, appendix A), the former denoting those monetary doctrines that
fit into a general theory of exchange. At the time the most famous of the acatallactic theories
was Georg Friedrich Knapp's *State Theory of Money* (London: Macmillan, 1924; reprinted, New
York: Kelley, 1973), as translated by H. M. Lucas and J. Bonar from the 4th edition of *Staat-
liche Theorie des Geldes* (Munich and Leipzig: Duncker and Humblot, 1923).—Ed.] In justice to
Menger and Mises, it should be pointed out that what they mean when they speak of the stability of the 'inner' value of money has nothing to do with any measurable value, in the sense
of some price level; but is only another and, as it seems to me, misleading, expression for what
I now prefer to call neutrality of money. (Cf. my *Prices and Production*, pp. 27–28 [this volume,
p. 216—Ed.] and passim.) This expression, first used by Wicksell in the passage quoted earlier in
the text [cf. *Geldzins und Güterpreise*, p. 93; *Interest and Prices*, p. 102—Ed.], has of late become fairly
common in German and Dutch writings on money. Cf. Ladislaus von Bortkiewicz, "Die Frage
der Reform unserer Währung [und die Knappsche Geldtheorie]", *Brauns Analen [Annalen für sozi-
ale Politik und Gesetzgebung*], vol. 6, 1919 [1918], pp. 57–59; Walter G. Behrens, *Das Geldschöpfungsproblem* (Jena: Fischer, 1928), pp. 228 et seq., 286 and 312 [pp. 228–30, 286–87, 312–14];
Gerard M. Verrijn Stuart and Johan G. Koopmans in the reports and discussions of the 1929
meeting of the Vereinigung [Vereeniging] voor de Staathuishoudkunde en de Statistik. [Fur-

This is no place to examine the extent to which Professor Mises escapes from this difficulty by using the concept of the inner objective value of money. For us, the only point of importance is that the effects of an artificially lowered rate of interest, pointed out by Wicksell and Mises, exist whether this same circumstance does or does not eventually react on the general value of money, in the sense of its purchasing power. Therefore they must be dealt with independently if they are to be properly understood.[27] Increases in the volume of circulation, which in an expanding economy serve to prevent a drop in the price level, present a typical instance of a change in the monetary factor calculated to cause a discrepancy between the money and natural rate of interest without affecting the price level. These changes are consequently neglected, as a rule, in dealing with phenomena of disproportionality; but they are bound to lead to a distribution of productive resources between capital-goods and consumption-goods which differs from the equilibrium distribution, just as those changes in the monetary factor which do manifest themselves in changes in the price level. This case is particularly important, because under contemporary currency systems[28] the automatic adjustment of the value of money, in the form of a flow of precious metals, will regularly make available new supplies of purchasing power which will depress the money rate of interest below its natural level.[29]

Since a stable price level has been regarded as normal hitherto, far too little investigation has been made into the effects of these changes in the volume of money, which necessarily cause a development different from that which would be expected on the basis of static theory, and which lead to the establishment of a structure of production incapable of perpetuating itself once the change in the monetary factor has ceased to operate. Economists have over-

thermore, Koopmans's contribution "Zum Problem des Neutralen Geldes" was just to appear in *Beiträge zur Geldtheorie*, ed. F. A. Hayek (Vienna: Springer, 1933; reprinted, Berlin, Heidelberg, and New York: Springer, 2007). The second part of the note, beginning with "In justice . . .", which moderates the criticism of Menger and Mises, was added to the English version. Notably, Mises's distinction between inner and outer value of money had already been criticised in Gottfried Haberler's habilitation thesis, *Der Sinn der Indexzahlen* (Tübingen: Mohr, 1927), p. 109n.1, to which Mises reacted with a stern reprimand in *Geldwertstabilisierung*, p. 20n.1; cf. "Monetary Stabilization", p. 86n.4.—Ed.]

[27] Professor Mises recently admitted this, in principle, when he explicitly emphasised the fact that *every* new issue of circulating media brings about a lowering of the money rate of interest in relation to the natural rate (*Geldwertstabilisierung*, p. 57 [cf. "Monetary Stabilization", p. 136—Ed.]).

[28] [The German version refers more precisely to "the existing systems of tied currencies" (cf. for a similar formulation "Some Remarks", p. 194). In contemporary usage "tied currencies" (*gebundene Währungen*, cf. "Einige Bemerkungen", p. 290; *Geldtheorie*, p. 63) referred to currencies tied to gold, that is, with a fixed parity.—Ed.]

[29] Cf. also my article "Das intertemporale Gleichgewichtssystem der Preise" [pp. 58–59; cf. "Intertemporal Price Equilibrium", pp. 210–11—Ed.].

looked the fact that the changes in the volume of money, which, in an expanding economy, are necessary to maintain price stability, lead to a new state of
affairs foreign to static analysis, so that the development which occurs under a
stable price level cannot be regarded as consonant with static laws. Thus the
disturbances described as resulting from changes in the *value* of money form
only a small part of the much wider category of deviations from the static
course of events brought about by changes in the *volume* of money—which
may often exist without changes in the value of money, while they may also
fail to accompany changes in value of money when the latter occur.

6. Most criticisms of the monetary explanation are due to a misunderstanding of this point

As has been briefly indicated above, most of the objections raised against
monetary theories of cyclical fluctuations rest on the mistaken idea that their
significant contribution consists in deducing changes in the volume of production from the movement of prices en bloc. In particular, the very extensive criticism recently levelled by Dr. Burchardt and Professor Löwe against
monetary Trade Cycle theory is based throughout on the idea that this theory
must start from the wavelike fluctuations of the price level, which are conditioned mainly by monetary causes; the rise, as well as the fall, of the price
level being brought about by particular new forces originating on the side of
money. It is only through this special assumption, which is also stated explicitly, that Professor Löwe's systematic presentation of his objections in his latest
work[30] becomes comprehensible; he is completely misleading when he asserts
that, if it is to raise the monetary factor to the rank of a *conditio sine qua non* of
the Trade Cycle, monetary theory ought to prove that the effectiveness of all
non-monetary factors depends on a previous price-boom.[31] We have already
shown that it is not even necessary, in order to ascribe the cause of cyclical
fluctuations to monetary changes, to assume that these monetary causes act
through changes in the general price level. It is therefore impossible to maintain that the importance of monetary theories lies solely in an explanation of
price cycles.[32]

But even the essential point in the criticism of Löwe and Burchardt—
the assertion that all monetary theories explain the transition from boom to
depression not in terms of monetary causes but in terms of other causes super-

---

[30] "Über den Einfluß monetärer Faktoren", pp. 361–68 [cf. "On the Influence of Monetary
Factors", pp. 204–10—Ed.].

[31] Ibid., p. 366 [cf. ibid., p. 208—Ed.].

[32] As is maintained by Professor Löwe (ibid., p. 364 [cf. ibid., p. 207—Ed.]).

added to the monetary explanation—rests exclusively on the idea that only general price changes can be recognised as monetary effects. But general price changes are no essential feature of a monetary theory of the Trade Cycle; *they are not only unessential, but they would be completely irrelevant if only they were completely 'general'*—that is, if they affected all prices at the same time and in the same proportion. The point of real interest to Trade Cycle theory is the existence of certain deviations in individual price-relations occurring because changes in the volume of money appear at certain individual points; deviations, that is, away from the position which is necessary to maintain the whole system in equilibrium. Every disturbance of the equilibrium of prices leads *necessarily* to shifts in the structure of production, which must therefore be regarded as consequences of monetary change, never as additional separate assumptions. The nature of the changes in the composition of the existing stock of goods, which are effected through such monetary changes, depends of course on the point at which the money is injected into the economic system.

There is no doubt that the emphasis placed on this phenomenon marks the most important advance made by monetary science beyond the elementary truths of the quantity theory. Monetary theory no longer rests content with determining the final reaction of a given monetary cause on the purchasing power of money, but attempts instead to trace the successive alterations in particular prices, which eventually bring about a change in the whole price system.[33] The assumption of a 'time lag' between the successive changes in various prices has not been spun out of thin air solely for the purposes of Trade Cycle theory; it is a correction, based on systematic reasoning, of the mistaken conceptions of older monetary theories.[34] Of course, the expression 'time lag', borrowed from Anglo-American writers and denoting a temporary lagging behind of the changes in the price of some goods relatively to the changes in the price of other goods, is a very unsuitable expression when the shifts in relative prices are due to changes in demand which are themselves conditioned by monetary changes. For such shifts are bound to continue so long as the change in demand persists. They disappear only with the disappearance of the disturbing monetary factor. They cease when money ceases to increase or diminish further; *not*, however, when the increase or diminution has itself been wiped out. But, whatever expression we may use to denote these changes in relative prices and the changes in the structure of produc-

[33] On the development of this point of view, see lecture 1 of my *Prices and Production*.

[34] We cannot, therefore, regard Mises' pronouncement [in his "Redebeitrag"] at the Zurich debate of the Verein für Sozialpolitik as a surrender of the monetary standpoint. On this occasion, he not only admitted but indeed emphasised the fact that monetary causes can only act by producing a 'lag' between various prices, wages, and interest rates. (Cf. *Schriften des Vereins für Sozialpolitik*, vol. 175, pp. 317–26.)

tion conditioned by them, there can be no doubt that they are, in turn, conditioned by monetary causes, which alone make them possible.

The only plausible objection to this argument would be that the shifts in price-relationships occurring at any point in the economic system could not possibly cause those typical, regularly recurring shifts in the structure of production which we observe in cyclical fluctuations. In opposition to this view, as we shall show in more detail later, it can be urged that those changes which are constantly taking place in our money and credit organisation cause a certain price, the rate of interest, to deviate from the equilibrium position, and that deviations of this kind *necessarily* lead to such changes in the relative position of the various branches of production as are bound later to precipitate the crisis.[35] There is one important point, however, which must be emphasised against the above-named critics; namely, that it is not only when the crisis is directly occasioned by a new monetary factor, separate from that which originally brought about the boom,[36] that it is to be regarded as conditioned by monetary causes. Once the monetary causes have brought about that development in the whole economic system which is known as a boom, sufficient forces have already been set in motion to ensure that, sooner or later, when the monetary influence has ceased to operate, a crisis must occur. The 'cause' of the crisis is, then, the disequilibrium of the whole economy occasioned by monetary changes and maintained through a longer period, possibly, by a succession of further monetary changes—a disequilibrium the origin of which can only be explained by monetary disturbances.

Professor Löwe's most important argument against the monetary theory of the Trade Cycle—an argument which so far as most existing monetary theories are concerned is unquestionably valid—will be discussed in more detail later. The sole purpose of the next chapter of this book is to show that the cycle is not only due to "mistaken measures by monopolistic bodies" (as Professor Löwe assumes),[37] but that the reason for its continuous recurrence lies in an "immanent necessity of the monetary and credit mechanism".[38]

---

[35] It is not essential, as Burchardt maintains ("Entwicklungsgeschichte", p. 124), to base this analysis on any particular theory of interest, such as that of Böhm-Bawerk; it is equally consonant with all modern interest theories. The reason why, under the circumstances assumed, interest fails to equilibrate production for the future and production for the present, is bound up not with the special form in which interest in general is explained, but with the deviations, due to monetary causes, of the current rate of interest from the equilibrium rate.

[36] [The term used in *Geldtheorie*, p. 68, *Aufschwung*, is not exactly the equivalent of "boom" but rather of "upswing".—Ed.]

[37] "Über den Einfluß monetärer Faktoren", pp. 365 et seq. [pp. 365–66; cf. "On the Influence of Monetary Factors", p. 208—Ed.].

[38] [Ibid., p. 365 (cf. ibid., p. 208).—Ed.]

7. Changes in individual price relationships must be the main focus of attention, for such changes cause shifts in the direction of production

Among the phenomena which are fundamentally independent of changes in the value of money, we must include, first of all, the effects of a rate of interest lowered by monetary influences, which must necessarily lead to the excessive production of capital goods. Wicksell and Mises both rightly emphasise the decisive importance of this factor in the explanation of cyclical phenomena, as its effect will occur even when the increase in circulation is only just sufficient to prevent a fall in the price level. Besides this, there exist a number of other phenomena, by virtue of which a money economy (in the sense of an economy with a variable money supply) differs from a static economy, which for this reason are important for a true understanding of the course of the Trade Cycle. They have been partly described already by Mises, but they can only be clearly observed by taking as the central subject of investigation not changes in general prices but the divergences of the relation of particular prices as compared with the price system of static equilibrium. Phenomena of this sort include the changes in the relation of costs and selling prices and the consequent fluctuations in profits, which Professors Mitchell and Lescure in particular have made the starting point of their exposition; and the shifts in the distribution of incomes which Professor Lederer investigates—both of these phenomena depending for their explanation on monetary factors,[39] while neither of them can be immediately connected with changes in the general value of money. It is, perhaps, for this very reason that their authors, although perfectly realising the monetary origin of the phenomena which they described, did not present their views as monetary theories. While we cannot attempt here to show the position which these phenomena would occupy in a systematically developed Trade Cycle theory (a task which really involves the development of a new theory, and which is unnecessary for the purposes of our present argument), it is not difficult to see that all of them can be logically deduced from an initiating monetary disturbance,[40] which, in any case, we are compelled to assume in studying them. The special advantages of the monetary approach consist precisely in the fact that, by starting from a monetary disturbance, we are able to explain deductively all the different peculiarities observed in the course of the Trade Cycle, and so to protect ourselves against objections such as were raised in an earlier chapter against non-monetary

[39] That Professor Lederer himself sees this clearly is evident from his analysis, mentioned earlier, "Konjunktur und Krisen", pp. 390–91.

[40] Cf. Mises' presentation of the social effects of changes in the value of money (*Theorie des Geldes und der Umlaufsmittel*, 2nd ed., pp. 178–200 [pp. 178–99; cf. *The Theory of Money and Credit*, pp. 225–46—Ed.]).

theories. It makes it possible to look upon empirically recognised interconnections, which would otherwise rival one another as independent clues to an explanation, as necessary consequences of one common cause.

Much theoretical work will have to be done before such a theoretical system can be worked out in such detail that all the empirically observed characteristics of the Trade Cycle can find their explanation within its framework. Up to now, the monetary theories have unduly narrowed the field of phenomena to be explained, by limiting research to those monetary changes which find their expression in changes in the general value of money. Thus they are prevented from showing the deviations of a money economy from a static economy in all their multiplicity.[41] The problem of cyclical fluctuations can only be solved satisfactorily when a theory of the money economy itself—still almost entirely lacking at present—has been evolved, comprising a detailed discussion of all those points in which it differs from the equilibrium analysis worked out on the assumption of a pure barter economy. The full elaboration of this intermediate step of theoretical exposition is indispensable before we can achieve a Trade Cycle theory, which—as Böhm-Bawerk has expressed it in a phrase, often quoted but hardly ever taken to heart—must constitute the last chapter of the complete theory of social economy.[42] In my opinion, the most important step towards such a theory, which would embrace all new phenomena arising from the addition of money to the conditions assumed in elementary equilibrium theory, would be the emancipation of the theory of money from the restrictions which limit its scope to a discussion of the *value* of money.

8. Advantages of the proposed method of approach; the possibility of a rapprochement between monetary and non-monetary theories

Once, however, we have accomplished this urgently necessary displacement of the problem of monetary value[43] from its present central position in monetary theory, we find ourselves in a position to come to an understanding with the most important non-monetary theorists of the Trade Cycle; for the effect of money on the 'real' economic processes will automatically be brought more

[41] [A more accurate translation would read, "from showing the multiplicity of deviations from the static course of events, based on the ideal image of the barter economy, which money causes in the money economy" (as in "Some Remarks", p. 195; cf. "Einige Bemerkungen", p. 292; *Geldtheorie*, p. 71).—Ed.]

[42] This expression occurs in connection with a [that is, Eugen von Böhm-Bawerk's—Ed.] review of Eugen von Bergmann's [*Die Wirtschaftskrisen:*] *Geschichte der nationalökonomischen Krisentheorien. Zeitschrift für Volkswirtschaft, Sozialpolitik und Verwaltung*, vol. 7, no. 1, 1898, p. 112 [p. 132].

[43] [Instead of "monetary value" the more appropriate term is "the value of money" (cf. *Geldtheorie*, p. 72).—Ed.]

116

to the surface, while monetary theory will no longer appear to be insisting on the immediate dependence of Trade Cycle phenomena on changes in the value of money—a claim which is certainly unjustified. On the other hand, a number of non-monetary theories do not question in the least the dependence of the processes which they describe on certain monetary assumptions; and in their case the only conflict now arising concerns the systematic presentation of these. It should be the task of our analysis to show that the placing of the monetary factor in the centre of the exposition is necessary in the interest of the unity of the system, and that the various 'real' interconnections, which, in certain theories, form the main basis of the explanation, can only find place in a closed system as consequences of the original monetary influences. There can hardly be any question, in the present state of research, as to what should be the basic idea of a completely developed theory of money. One can abandon those parts of the Wicksell-Mises theory which aim at explaining the movements in the general value of money, and develop to the full the effects of all discrepancies between the natural and money rates of interest on the relative development of the production of capital goods and consumption goods—a theory which has already been largely elaborated by Professor Mises. In this way, one can achieve, by purely deductive methods, the same picture of the process of cyclical fluctuations which the more realistic theories of Spiethoff and Cassel have already deduced from experience. Wicksell himself[44] drew attention to the way in which the processes deduced from his own theory harmonise with the exposition of Spiethoff; and conversely, Spiethoff, in a statement already quoted,[45] has emphasised the fact that the phenomena which he describes are all conditioned by a change in monetary factors. But it is only by placing monetary factors first that such expositions as those of Spiethoff and Cassel can be incorporated into the general system of theoretical economics. A final point of decisive importance is that the choice of the monetary starting point enables us to deduce simultaneously all the other phenomena, such as shifts in relative prices and incomes, which are more empirically determined and utilised as independent factors; and thus the relations existing between them can be classified and their relative position and

---

[44] *Vorlesungen*, vol. 2, p. 238 [cf. *Lectures*, vol. 2, p. 209—Ed.]; Wicksell's review of Cassel's textbook [that is, *Theoretische Sozialökonomie*, 1st ed., 1918—Ed.], which has since appeared in a German translation ("Professor Cassels nationalökomisches System", *Schmollers Jahrbuch für Gesetzgebung, Verwaltung und Volkswirtschaft im Deutschen Reiche*, vol. 52, no. 5, 1928, pp. 1–38), shows that, although he rightly opposes Cassel's general system, he agrees to a large extent with his theory of the Trade Cycle. [For a translation of Wicksell's review, see "Cassel's System of Economics", in *Lectures on Political Economy*, vol. 1: *General Theory*, trans. Ernest Classen (London: Routledge, 1934; reprinted, New York: Kelley, 1967; Auburn, AL: Ludwig von Mises Institute, 2007), pp. 219–57.—Ed.]

[45] [See above, p. 97.—Ed.]

importance determined within the framework of the theory. Even when these phenomena are, as yet, much further from a satisfactory explanation than are the disproportionalities in the development of production, which are cleared up in a greater degree, there can be no doubt that it will become possible to incorporate them also into a self-sufficient theory of the effects of monetary disturbances. These effects, however, although ultimately caused by monetary factors, do not fall within the narrower field of monetary theory. A well-developed theory of the Trade Cycle ought to deal thoroughly with them; but as this book is exclusively concerned with the monetary theories[46] themselves, we shall, in the following chapters, only study the reasons why these monetary causes of the Trade Cycle inevitably recur under the existing system of money and credit organisation, and what are the main problems with which future research is faced by reason of the realisation of the determining role played by money.

[46] [According to *Geldtheorie*, p. 74, here the text should not refer to "monetary theories", but to the "monetary effects" mentioned above.—Ed.]

FOUR

THE FUNDAMENTAL CAUSE OF
CYCLICAL FLUCTUATIONS

1. The problem is to discover why certain changes in 'data' are
able to lead the system away from equilibrium

So far we have not answered, or have only hinted at an answer to the question why, under the existing organisation of the economic system, we constantly find those deviations of the money rate of interest from the equilibrium rate[1] which, as we have seen, must be regarded as the cause of the periodically recurring disproportionalities in the structure of production. The problem is, then, to discover the gap in the reaction mechanism of the modern economic system which is responsible for the fact that certain changes of data, so far from being followed by a prompt readjustment (i.e., the formation of a new equilibrium) are, actually, the cause of recurrent shifts in economic activity which subsequently have to be reversed before a new equilibrium can be established.

The analysis of the foregoing chapters has shown that when it is possible to detect, in the organisation of our economy, a dislocation in the reaction mechanism described by equilibrium theory, it should be possible (and should, indeed, be the object of a fully developed Trade Cycle theory) to describe deductively, as a necessary effect of the disturbance—quite apart from their observed occurrence—all the deviations in the course of economic events conditioned by this dislocation. It has been shown, in addition, that the primary cause of cyclical fluctuations must be sought in changes in the volume of money, which are undoubtedly always recurring and which, by their occurrence, always bring about a falsification of the pricing process, and thus a misdirection of production. The new element which we are seeking is, therefore,

---

[1] The term 'equilibrium rate of interest' which, I believe, was introduced into Germany in this connection by Karl Schlesinger in his *Theorie der Geld- und Kreditwirtschaft* (Munich and Leipzig: Duncker and Humblot, 1914), p. 128, seems to me preferable in this case to the usual expression of 'natural rate' or 'real rate'. Alfred Marshall used the term 'equilibrium level' as early as 1887 (cf. *Official Papers of Alfred Marshall*, p. 130). Cf. also chapter 5 of the present work.

to be found in the 'elasticity'[2] of the volume of money at the disposal of the economic system. It is this element whose presence forms the 'necessary and sufficient' condition for the emergence of the Trade Cycle.[3]

The question which we now have to examine is whether this elasticity in the volume of money is an immanent characteristic of our present money and credit system; whether, given certain conditions, changes in the volume of money and the resulting differences between the natural and the monetary rate[4] of interest must necessarily occur, or whether they represent, so to speak, casual phenomena arising from arbitrary interferences by the authorities responsible for the regulation of the volume of currency media.[5] Is it an inherent necessity of the existing monetary and credit system that its reaction to certain changes in data is different from what we should expect on the basis of economic equilibrium theory; or are these discrepancies to be explained by special assumptions regarding the nature of the monetary administration, i.e., by a series of what might be called 'political' assumptions?[6] The question

[2] [In the corresponding passage the German term *Elastizität* (without quotation marks) is used for the first time in *Geldtheorie*, p. 76. Possibly, here the translators put 'elasticity' between quotation marks to distinguish it from the term 'elasticity' as used before, which did not stand for 'Elastizität', but for 'Veränderlichkeit', that is, 'variability'. See above, p. 98n.48. For a similar use of the term 'elasticity' cf. also lecture 4 of *Prices and Production*.—Ed.]

[3] Mr. Ralph G. Hawtrey regards the following theses as important for monetary Trade Cycle theories: (1) That certain monetary and credit movements are necessary and sufficient [*necessary* and *sufficient*] conditions of the observed phenomena of the Trade Cycle [trade cycle]; and (2) that the periodicity of those [these] phenomena can be explained by purely monetary tendencies[,] which cause the movements to take place successively [in succession] and to be spread over a considerable period of years ("The Monetary Theory of the Trade Cycle and its Statistical Test", *Quarterly Journal of Economics*, vol. 41, May 1927, p. 472). [Although not indicated, this passage is an almost literal quotation from Hawtrey's article. In the German version (*Geldtheorie*, p. 76n.) the quotation is exact and put within quotation marks.—Ed.] This entirely correct definition of Mr. Hawtrey's should have prevented Dr. Burchardt and Prof. Löwe, who expressly fasten on this point in their criticism of monetary Trade Cycle theories, from looking from monetary influences to changes in the general value of money, while disregarding the changes in the distributive process which are conditioned by monetary causes.

[4] [Here "monetary rate" is a misnomer, instead of the correct "money rate".—Ed.]

[5] [A preferable translation of the German term *Umlaufsmittel* (as in Mises's *Theorie des Geldes und der Umlaufsmittel*) is "circulating media", which is how subsequently in most cases this term has been translated in the text. Mises defines them as money substitutes "not covered . . . by the reservation of corresponding sums of money" (*The Theory of Money and Credit*, p. 155, where *Umlaufsmittel* is rendered by "fiduciary media", see the translater's note, ibid., pp. 525–26); thus, basically, these consist of uncovered bank deposits and notes, and of token money. However, it appears that Hayek occasionally uses the term *Umlaufsmittel* in a broader sense, comprising the circulating media in the narrower sense as in Mises, *plus* money.—Ed.]

[6] [Here Hayek echoes Löwe's criticism, directed among others at Mises, that "in their view, it is not any necessity inherent to the mechanism of money and credit that triggers the cycle, but mistaken measures of a monopolistic economic agent" ("On the Influence of Monetary Factors", p. 208; cf. "Über den Einfluß monetärer Faktoren", pp. 365–66.—Ed.]

whether the recurrence of credit cycles is, or is not, due to an unavoidable characteristic of the existing economic organisation, depends on whether the existing monetary and credit organisation in itself necessitates changes in the currency media, or whether these are brought about only by the special inter- ference of external agencies. The answer to this question will also decide into which of the most commonly accepted categories a given Trade Cycle theory is to be placed. We must deal briefly with this point because a false classifica- tion, which is largely the fault of the exponents of the monetary theories, has contributed much to make them misunderstood.

2. Exogenous and endogenous monetary theories

If we are to understand the present status of monetary theories of the Trade Cycle,[7] we must pay special attention to the assumptions upon which they are based. At the present day, monetary theories are generally regarded as falling within the class of so-called 'exogenous' theories, i.e., theories which look for the cause of the cycle not in the interconnections of economic phenomena themselves but in external interferences. Now it is, no doubt, often a waste of time to discuss the merits of classifying a theory in a given category. But the question of classification becomes important when the inclusion of a theory in one class or another implies, at the same time, a judgment as to the sphere of validity of the theory in question. This is undoubtedly the case with the dis- tinction, very general to-day,[8] between *endogenous* and *exogenous* theories—a dis- tinction introduced into economic literature some twenty years ago by Bouni- atian.[9] Endogenous theories, in the course of their proof, avoid making use of assumptions which cannot either be decided by purely economic consider- ations, or regarded as general characteristics of our economic system—and hence capable of general proof. Exogenous theories, on the other hand, are based on concrete assertions whose correctness has to be proved separately in each individual case. As compared with an endogenous theory, which, if logi- cally sound, can in a sense lay claim to general validity, an exogenous theory is

---

[7] [*Geldtheorie*, p. 77, speaks, more specifically, of *Zirkulationskredittheorie*, that is, "circulation credit theory", which is how Mises preferred to denote his own theory for explaining the busi- ness cycle (see, e.g., *Theorie des Geldes und der Umlaufsmittel*, 2nd ed., p. 268, *The Theory of Money and Credit*, p. 297). It appears that in *Geldtheorie* Hayek uses the terms *Zirkulationskredittheorie* and *The- orie des zusätzlichen Kredits* (literally "theory of additional credit") interchangeably. In the follow- ing both terms are occasionally translated also by "theory of bank credit" or simply "monetary theory".—Ed.]

[8] [This should read, "very generally accepted to-day".—Ed.]

[9] Mentor Bouniatian, *Studien zur Theorie und Geschichte der Wirtschaftskrisen* [vol. 1: *Wirtschaftskrisen und Ueberkapitalisation*] (Munich: Reinhardt, 1908), p. 3.

at some disadvantage, inasmuch as it has, in each case, to justify the assumptions on which its conclusions are based.

Now as far as most contemporary monetary theories of the cycle are concerned, their opponents are undoubtedly right in classifying them, as does Professor Löwe[10] in his discussion of the theories of Professors Mises and Hahn, among the exogenous theories; for they begin with arbitrary interferences on the part of the banks. This is, perhaps, one of the main reasons for the prevailing scepticism concerning the value of such theories. A theory which has to call upon the deus ex machina[11] of a false step by bankers, in order to reach its conclusions is, perhaps, inevitably suspect. Yet Professor Mises himself—who is certainly to be regarded as the most respected and consistent exponent of the monetary theory of the Trade Cycle in Germany—has, in his latest work,[12] afforded ample justification for this view of his theory by attributing the periodic recurrence of the Trade Cycle to the general tendency of Central Banks to depress the money rate of interest below the natural rate.[13] Both the protagonists and the opponents of the Monetary Theory of the Trade Cycle thus agree in regarding these explanations as falling ultimately within the exogenous and not the endogenous group. The fact that this is not an inherent necessity of the monetary starting-point is however shown by the undoubtedly endogenous nature of the various older Trade Cycle theories, such as that of Wicksell. But since this suffers from other deficiencies, which have already been indicated, the question whether the exogenous character of modern theories is, or is not, an inherent necessity of their nature remains an open one.[14] It seems to me that this classification of monetary Trade Cycle theory depends exclusively on the fact that a single, specially striking, case is treated as the normal; while, in fact, it is quite unnecessary to adduce interference on the part of the banks in order to bring about a situation of alternating boom and crisis. By disregarding those divergencies between the natural and money rate of interest which arise automatically in the course of economic development, and by emphasising those caused by an artificial lowering of the money rate, the Monetary Theory of the Trade Cycle deprives itself of one of its strongest arguments; namely, the fact that the process which it describes *must* always recur under the existing credit organisation, and that it thus rep-

[10] "Der gegenwärtige Stand der Konjunkturforschung", p. 349.

[11] Cf. Hans Neisser, *Der Tauschwert des Geldes* (Jena: Fischer, 1928), p. 161.

[12] [The reference is to Mises, *Geldwertstabilisierung* ("Monetary Stabilization").—Ed.]

[13] While it seems to me that in the analysis of the effects of a money rate of interest diverging from the natural rate Professor Mises has made considerable progress as compared with the position adopted by Wicksell, the latter succeeded better than Mises did in explaining the origin of this divergence. We shall go into Wicksell's explanation in somewhat more detail below.

[14] Part of the two following paragraphs repeats word for word my contribution to the discussion on Credit and the Trade Cycle at the Zurich Assembly of the Verein für Sozialpolitik (cf. "Redebeitrag", pp. 370–71).

resents a tendency inherent in the economic system, and is in the fullest sense of the word an *endogenous* theory.

It is an apparently unimportant difference in exposition which leads one to this view that the Monetary Theory can lay claim to an endogenous position. The situation in which the money rate of interest is below the natural rate need not, by any means, originate in a *deliberate lowering* of the rate of interest by the banks. The same effect can be obviously produced by an improvement in the expectations of profit or by a diminution in the rate of saving, which may drive the 'natural rate' (at which the demand for and the supply of savings are equal) above its previous level; while the banks refrain from raising their rate of interest to a proportionate extent, but continue to lend at the previous rate, and thus enable a greater demand for loans to be satisfied than would be possible by the exclusive use of the available supply of savings. The decisive significance of the case quoted is not, in my view, due to the fact that it is probably the commonest in practice, but to the fact that it *must inevitably recur* under the existing credit organisation.

3. Of three possible ways of increasing the volume of money, the most important, from the present point of view, is the creation of credit by the banks

The notion that the increase in circulation is due to arbitrary interference by the banks owes its origin to the widespread view that Banks of Issue are the exclusive or predominant agencies which can change the volume of the circulation; and that they do so of their own free will. But the Central Banks are by no means the only factor capable of bringing about a change in the volume of circulating media;[15] they are, in their turn, largely dependent upon other factors, although they can influence or compensate for these to a great extent. Altogether, there are three elements which regulate the volume of circulating media within a country—changes in the volume of cash, caused by inflows and outflows of gold; changes in the note circulation of the Central Banks; and last, and in many ways most important, the often-disputed 'creation' of deposits[16] by other banks. The interrelations of these are, naturally, complicated.

As regards original changes in the first two factors—that is, changes which

[15] This fact has already been pointed out by the representatives of the Banking School, and later by Clement Juglar, *Du change et de la liberté d'emission* (Paris: Guillaumin, 1868), chapter 3, passim; and *Des crises commerciales et [de] leur retour périodique [en France, en Angleterre et aux États-Unis]*, 2nd ed. (Paris: Guillaumin, 1889), p. 57. Wicksell (*Geldzins und Güterpreise*, p. 101 [cf. *Interest and Prices*, p. 110—Ed.]) also points, first of all, to the deposit business of the banks as the cause of the 'elasticity' of the volume of currency media.

[16] [A note in the German version (*Geldtheorie*, p. 82n.1), deleted in the translation, clarifies that "deposits" refers to "deposits on current account".—Ed.]

are not set in motion by changes in one of the other factors—there is comparatively little to say. It has already been pointed out that, in principle, an increase in the volume of cash, occasioned by an increase in the volume of trade, also implies a lowering of the money rate of interest—which gives rise to shifts in the structure of production which seem, though only temporarily, to be advantageous. It must certainly appear very problematical whether the deviations in the money rate of interest thus occasioned would, as a rule, be large enough to cause fluctuations of an empirically ascertainable magnitude. Central Banks, on the other hand, are by law or custom bound to preserve such a close connection between note issues and cash holdings that we have no reason to assume that they, and they alone, provide the original impetus. Of course, it is possible to assume, with Professor Mises,[17] that the Central Banks, under the pressure of an inflationist ideology, are always trying to expand credit and thus provide the impetus for a new upward swing of the Trade Cycle; and this assumption may be correct in many cases. The credit expansion is then conditioned by special circumstances, which need not always be present; and the cyclical fluctuations caused by it are, therefore, not the necessary consequence of an inherent tendency of our credit system, for the removal of the special circumstances would eliminate them. But before deciding in favour of this special assumption—which requires a proof of its own, to be given separately in the case of each cycle—we have to ask whether, in some other part of our credit system, such extensions may not take place automatically under certain conditions—without the necessity for any special assumption of the inadequate functioning of any part of the system. To me this certainly appears to be true as regards the third factor of money expansion—the 'credit creation' of the commercial banks.

There are few questions upon which scientific literature, especially in Germany, is so lacking in clarity as on the possibility and importance of an increase in circulating media due to the granting of additional credits by the banks of deposit. To give an answer to the question whether credit creation is a regular consequence of the existing organisation of banking, we shall have to attempt to clear up our conception of the methods and extent of such credit creation by deposit banks. Besides dealing with the fundamental question of the possibility of credit creation and the limits to which it can extend, we shall have to discuss two special questions which are important for our further investigations: namely, whether the practical importance of credit creation depends upon certain practices of banking technique, as is often assumed; and secondly, whether it is, in fact, possible to determine whether a given issue of credit represents credit freshly created or not.

---

[17] [*Geldtheorie*, p. 82, included here a reference to Mises, *Geldwertstabilisierung*, p. 58 (cf. "Monetary Stabilization", pp. 136–37), and to Hayek's review of the book in *Schmollers Jahrbuch für Gesetzgebung, Verwaltung und Volkswirtschaft im Deutschen Reiche*, vol. 52, no. 6, 1928, pp. 125–28.—Ed.]

If in the course of our investigation, it is possible to prove that the rate of interest charged by the banks to their borrowers is not promptly adjusted to all changes in the economic data (as it would be if the volume of money in circulation were constant)—either because the supply of bank credits is, within certain limits, fundamentally independent of changes in the supply of savings, or because the banks have no particular interest in keeping the supply of bank credit in equilibrium with the supply of savings and because it is, in any case, impossible for them to do so—then we shall have proved that, under the existing credit organisation, monetary fluctuations[18] must inevitably occur and must represent an immanent feature of our economic system—a feature deserving of the closest examination.

4. Confusion on this point is due largely to a failure to distinguish between the possibilities open to a single bank and those open to the banking system as a whole

The main reason for the existing confusion with regard to the creation of deposits is to be found in the lack of any distinction between the possibilities open to a single bank and those open to the banking system as a whole.[19]

---

[18] [The translation is misleading. It should read, "monetarily induced fluctuations" (cf. *Geldtheorie*, p. 85).—Ed.]

[19] As it is impossible to deal exhaustively with this problem, it must be sufficient to draw attention to the main literature of the subject. The first author known to me who definitely stated that "the balances in the bank are to be considered in very much the same light with the paper circulation" [that is, correctly, "the balances at the Bank are to be considered therefore very much in the same light with the Paper circulation"—Ed.], was Henry Thornton (see his *Evidence before the Committee on the Bank Restriction*, 1797) [reprinted in *Paper Credit*, ed. Hayek, p. 282—Ed.]). The development of a more definite theory of credit creation by the banks began, however, with the criticisms levelled by the Banking School against the Currency School, and represent the former's only correct contribution to the science of economics. As Professor Theodore E. Gregory has recently shown ("Introduction" to Tooke and Newmarch's *A History of Prices and of the State of the Circulation from 1792 to 1876*, in 6 vols. (London: King; New York: Adelphi, 1928 [reprinted, London: London School of Economics and Political Science, 1962]), pp. 11 et seq. [pp. 11–12]), it was James Pennington who originally developed this thesis, first in an appendix to Thomas Tooke's *Letter to Lord Grenville on the Effects Ascribed to the Resumption of Cash Payments* (London, 1829), then in further contributions to Robert Torrens's *Letter to the Rt. Hon. Viscount Melbourne* (London, 1837) and finally in an appendix to the third volume of Tooke's *History of Prices* (1838). [James Pennington (1777–1862) was a businessman and an expert on currency questions. On the interrelationships between Pennington's writings see Richard S. Sayers, "The Life and Work of James Pennington", in *Economic Writings of James Pennington*, ed. Sayers (London: London School of Economics and Political Science, 1963; reprinted, Routledge and Thoemmes Press, 1996), pp. xiii–xvi. Some of the material cited by Hayek is reproduced in *Economic Writings*, pp. xlv–li and 91–102. Cf. also F. A. Hayek, "The Dispute between the Currency School and the Banking School, 1821–1848", chapter 12 of *The Trend of Economic Thinking: Essays on Political Economists and Economic History*, ed. W. W. Bartley III and Stephen Kresge, vol. 3 (1991) of *The Collected Works of F. A. Hayek*, pp. 224–25.—Ed.] If one wanted to trace the further progress of this theory dur-

This is connected with the fact that, in Germany, the whole theory has been taken over bodily from England, where, owing to differences in banking technique, the limits imposed on any individual bank are, perhaps, somewhat less narrow, so that the general possibilities open to the banking system as a whole have not been indicated with the degree of emphasis which their importance deserves. In Germany, following the popular exposition of Mr. Hartley

---

ing the nineteenth century, one would have to draw particular attention to the writings of Henry Dunning Macleod (cf., in particular, his *Dictionary of Political Economy* (London: Longman, Brown, Longmans and Roberts, 1863), article on "Credit", pp. 567–617), C. F. Dunbar, and F. Ferrara. [Charles Franklin Dunbar (1830–1900) was the first holder of a chair of political economy at Harvard, founder of the *Quarterly Journal of Economics*. Cf. his *Chapters on the Theory and History of Banking* (New York: Putnam, 1891; reprinted, New York: Arno Press, 1980). Francesco Ferrara (1810–1900), Italian economist and an advocate of classical liberalism, furthered Italian economic thought in the nineteenth century through the publication of the *Biblioteca dell' Economista*, of which he edited the first two series (Turin, 1850–75).—Ed.]

Modern developments follow the exposition of Herbert J. Davenport, *The Economics of Enterprise* (New York: Macmillan, 1915 [1st ed., 1913; reprinted, New York: Kelley, 1968]), pp. 250 et seq. [pp. 259–66]; and mention should, in particular, be made of Chester O. [Arthur] Phillips's *Bank Credit* (New York: Macmillan, 1920 [reprinted, New York: Arno Press, 1980]), especially chapter 3, "The Philosophy of Bank Credit"; of Wilfred F. Crick, "The Genesis of Bank Deposits", *Economica*, no. 20, June 1927, pp. 191–202; and Robert G. Rodkey, *The Banking Process* (New York: Macmillan, 1928). Apart from these, we must include in our list the well-known works of Hartley Withers [cf. *The Meaning of Money*, 3rd ed. (London: Smith, Elder, 1909)—Ed.], Irving Fisher [cf. *The Purchasing Power of Money* (New York: Macmillan, 1911), 2nd ed. rev. (1913) reprinted as vol. 4 of *The Works of Irving Fisher*, ed. William Barber (London: Pickering and Chatto, 1997)—Ed.], and Ralph G. Hawtrey [cf. *Currency and Credit*, 3rd ed. (London: Longmans, Green, 1928)—Ed.], and in German literature, Wicksell, *Geldzins und Güterpreise*, p. 101 [cf. *Interest and Prices*, p. 110], Adolf Weber, *Depositenbanken und Spekulationsbanken: Ein Vergleich deutschen und englischen Bankwesens*, 2nd [3rd] ed. (Munich and Leipzig: Duncker and Humblot, 1922), the works which we have already mentioned of Mises and Hahn, Gottfried Haberler's essay on the latter ("Albert Hahns *Volkswirtschaftliche Theorie des Bankkredits*", *Archiv für Sozialwissenschaften* [*Sozialwissenschaft und Sozialpolitik*], vol. 57, no. 3, 1927, pp. 803–19), and, finally, Neisser, *Der Tauschwert des Geldes*. [Of the more important authors mentioned, Herbert Joseph Davenport (1861–1931) was an American economist, professor at the University of Missouri and Cornell University. He shared with the Austrians the belief in the banks' ability to bring about changes in the volume of money and credit as a major cause of the cycle. Hartley Withers (1867–1950), British financial journalist, was the editor of the *Economist*, 1916–21. The American economist Irving Fisher (1867–1947), professor at Yale University and an ardent adherent of the quantity theory, untiringly advocated price level stabilisation (and other schemes for social reform). Ralph George Hawtrey (1879–1971), a long-term civil servant at the Treasury, was representative of an almost exclusively monetary, price level oriented approach to the cycle. Adolf Weber (1876–1950), German economist, held various chairs, ultimately and most importantly from 1921 to 1948 as professor of economics and public finance at the University of Munich. Leaning towards a liberal and theoretical approach, he was one of the editors of the influential *Handwörterbuch der Staatswissenschaften*. Hans Philipp Neisser (1895–1975), German economist, worked at the Kiel Institute for the World Economy under the directorship of Löwe, 1928–33, when he was forced to emigrate. In the United States he taught at the University of Pennsylvania and eventually, 1943–65,

Withers,[20] the most generally accepted view starts from English banking practice which (except in the case of 'overdrafts') credits the account of the customer with the amount borrowed before the latter is actually utilised. Granted this assumption, the process leading to an increase of circulating media is comparatively easy to survey and therefore hardly ever disputed. So long and in so far as the credits which a bank is able to grant, considering its cash position, remain on current account—and in the United States, for example, it is a regular condition for the granting of a loan that the current account of the borrower shall never fall below a certain relatively high percentage of the sum borrowed[21]—every new grant of credit must, of course, bring about an equivalent increase of deposits and a proportionately smaller diminution of cash reserves. Against these "deduced deposits" (Phillips)[22] which regularly occur in the normal course of business, the banks naturally have to keep only a certain percentage of cash reserve; and thus it is clear that every bank can, on the basis of a given increase of deposits resulting from public payments,[23] grant new credits to an amount exceeding this increase in deposits.

Against this method of proof it can rightly be objected that, while banking practices of this kind may well lead to the possibility of credit creation, the conditions which this argument assumes are not present on the Continent. It has been justifiably and repeatedly emphasised that there is no reason why the borrower, so long as he is not forced to do so, should borrow money at a higher rate of interest merely to leave that money on deposit at a lower rate.[24]

---

at the New School for Social Research in New York. A translation of Hayek's review of Neisser's *Tauschwert des Geldes* appears as an addendum to chapter 1 of *Business Cycles, Part II.*—Ed.]

The theory has been severely criticised especially by Professor Edwin Cannan [cf. his "Limitation of Currency or Limitation of Credit?", *Economic Journal*, vol. 34, March 1924, pp. 65–68, reprinted in *An Economist's Protest* (London: King, 1927), pp. 370–84, which is reprinted as vol. 6 of *The Collected Works of Edwin Cannan* (London: Routledge and Thoemmes Press, 1997)—Ed.], Walter Leaf [cf. his *Banking*, Home University Library, vol. 124 (New York: Holt; London: Williams and Norgate, 1926), the 3rd edition (1937) reprinted as vol. 7 of *Banking Theory, 1870–1930*, ed. Forrest Capie and Geoffrey Edward Wood (London: Routledge, 1999)—Ed.], and more recently by Richard Reisch, "Die 'Deposit'-Legende in der Banktheorie", *Zeitschrift für Nationalökonomie*, vol. 1, January 1930, pp. 489–533. [Edwin Cannan (1861–1935) was professor of economics at LSE, 1895–1926, and thus for a short time a highly appreciated colleague of Hayek. Cf. Hayek's obituary, translated and reprinted in F. A. Hayek, *Contra Keynes and Cambridge*, pp. 64–73. On Leaf and Reisch see below.—Ed.]

[20] [Notably the German translation of *The Meaning of Money* by Hans Patzauer as *Geld und Kredit in England* (Jena: Fischer, 1911).—Ed.]

[21] Cf. Phillips, *Bank Credit*, p. 50.

[22] [Actually, Phillips (ibid., p. 40 and passim) referred to "derivative deposits".—Ed.]

[23] [The translation "public payments" is misleading: it should read, "cash payments [by the public]" (cf. *Geldtheorie*, p. 87).—Ed.]

[24] Richard Reisch in "Die wirtschaftliche Bedeutung des Kredites im Lichte von Theorie und Praxis", *Mitteilungen des Verbandes österreichischer Banken und Bankiers*, vol. 10, nos. 2–3, 1928, p. 38, and

If the possibility of creating credit depended only on the fact that borrowers leave part of their loans on current account for a time, then credit creation would be practically impossible on the Continent;[25] while even in England and the United States it would have only a very secondary importance. It should be noted that this applies to the case in which the borrower pays the sum borrowed into another account in the *same* bank, so that it is transferred from one to the other without diminishing the total volume of deposits in the bank concerned. We need not, therefore, go separately into this case.

But, in adopting this line of argument, by far the most important process by which deposits are created in the course of current banking business even in Anglo-Saxon countries is neglected, and the sole way in which they are created on the Continent is left entirely out of consideration. The latter could easily be overlooked, since the ability of individual banks to make an increase in their deposits the basis of a far greater amount of new credit can only be accounted for by means of the assumptions used above, while in the banking system as a whole the same process occurs independently. In the following pages, therefore, we shall examine how an increase in deposits, paid in cash, influences the lending capacity of the whole banking system; starting from the assumption, more appropriate to Continental conditions, that the sums granted will be credited to the account of the borrower only at the time when, and to the extent that, he makes use of them.

5. The actual origin of additional credits

We may start as before by examining the procedure of a single bank. At this bank a certain amount of cash is newly deposited; a sum, let us say, equal to 5 per cent of its previous total deposits. If the policy of the bank was to keep a reserve of 10 per cent against deposits, that ratio has now been increased, by the new deposit, to 14.3 per cent,[26] and the bank is therefore in a position, in accordance with its policy, to grant new credits. If we assume further that it re-lends 90 per cent of the newly deposited money and that the whole of this is immediately utilised by the borrower (in order, let us say, to increase his purchases of raw materials), then the ratio of cash to deposits has again sunk to

---

Adolf Jöhr in his verbal report on Credit and the Cycle ["Kredit und Konjunktur"—Ed.], in the Zurich Assembly of the Verein für Sozialpolitik (*Schriften des Vereins für Sozialpolitik*, vol. 175, p. 311).

[25] As Bouniatian, evidently for this reason, actually assumes (cf. his essay "Industrielle Schwankungen, Bankkredit und Warenpreise", *Archiv für Sozialwissenschaft und Sozialpolitik*, vol. 58, no. 3, 1927, p. 463).

[26] [As deposits have increased by 5 percent and cash reserves by 50 percent, thus the new ratio is $105/15 \approx 14.3$ percent.—Ed.]

10 per cent. In so far as the bank does not change its policy its individual lending capacity is exhausted, in these circumstances, before it has even re-lent the whole of the amount newly deposited.

The effect of the sums newly deposited at one bank on the lending capacity of the whole banking system is, however, not exhausted by this transaction. If the borrower does not use the credit in a way which leads quickly to the market for consumers' goods, such as wage payments, but devotes it instead to the purchase of raw materials or half-finished products, then it is to be assumed that payment will be made by cheque and that the seller will hand over the sum received to his own bank for encashment, the amount being credited to his own account. The next consequence must be that the clearing-house position of this bank improves by exactly the amount transferred, and it therefore obtains an equivalent amount of cash from the bank which originally granted the credit. For the second bank, therefore, the sum originating in the granting of credit and paid into its accounts (representing, as we remember, 90 per cent of the original deposit) is just as much an original deposit, based on cash payments, as it was to the bank which we originally considered. It will, therefore, be regarded as a basis for additional lending and used in just the same way as any other new deposit. If the second bank also keeps 10 per cent of its deposits as cash reserves, it too will be in a position to lend 90 per cent of the new deposit, and the same process will be continued as long as the amounts are merely transferred from bank to bank and are not taken out in cash. As every bank re-lends 90 per cent of the amount paid into it and thus causes an equivalent increase in deposits for some other bank, the original deposit will give rise to credits representing $0.9 + 0.9^2 + 0.9^3 + 0.9^4 \ldots$ times the original amount. As the sum of this converging infinite series is 9, the banks will be enabled, in an extreme case, to create, against an amount of cash flowing in from an outside source, credits equal to nine times that amount. This becomes clear when we consider that the process can only stop when the last part of this cash is required for the 10 per cent reserve of the deposits.

For simplicity's sake we have made use of an assumption which is undoubtedly incorrect, but which affects our conclusion only in so far as it reduces the actual amount of new credit which the banks can create with a reserve ratio of 10 per cent. Its omission leaves our fundamental conclusion intact; i.e. that they can grant credit to an amount several times greater than the sum originally deposited. In fact some part of the credit at least, if not on the first then on subsequent occasions, will always be withdrawn in cash and not deposited with other banks. For example, if 70 per cent is always redeposited instead of the full 90 per cent this amount being re-lent by every bank and the remainder being used in cash transactions, then the increase in deposits will give rise to additional credits equal to only $0.7 + 0.7^2 + 0.7^3 \ldots$ times (i.e., two and one-third times) the original. So long as any part of the credits granted are not withdrawn in cash but redeposited with the banks, the latter will be able to create additional credits, of a larger or smaller amount, as a consequence of every increase in their cash holdings.[27] The lifetime of this pyramid of credit is limited to that of the first credit granted, save in the case (which can be assumed as long as there are no withdrawals from deposits) where it is immediately replaced by a fresh credit. If, however, deposits unexpectedly diminish at any part of the banking system, the process will be reversed, and the original diminution of deposits will occasion a contraction of credit correspondingly exceeding the amount withdrawn.[28]

In this connection we must note for further emphasis later the fact that the proportion in which the credits granted are transferred to other accounts—and not paid out in cash—must be regarded as subject to very wide fluctuations as between different individuals at a given moment, as well as between various periods of time for the economic system as a whole. We return later to the significance of this fact.

What has been said above should be sufficient to show that the possibility of creating credits over and above the sums deposited—which, under Continental banking conditions, is not open to any individual bank—is, however, open to the whole banking system of the country to a considerable extent. The fact that a single bank cannot do what is automatically done by the banking system as a whole also explains another circumstance, which might otherwise easily be cited as a proof of the impossibility of additional credit creation. If every bank could re-lend several times the amount deposited, there would be no reason against its offering a much higher rate of interest on deposits than it actually does, or, in particular, under the existing discount rates of the Central Banks, against its procuring cash in unlimited quantities by way of re-

[27] The maximum amount of credit, to the creation of which the increase in the cash holdings of the banks may give rise under such an assumption, is easily found by inserting the factor representing the proportion of the original deposit which is re-lent and redeposited with another bank into the mathematical formula expressing the limit which a convergent geometrical series approaches, viz., $1/(x-1)$. [This formula is incorrect; with x the proportion in question it should read instead $1/(1-x)$.—Ed.] The result gives the total of credits which originate in the series of transactions, including the original deposit; and, in order to arrive at the amount of additional credits, 1 has to be subtracted from the result. It is thus easily seen that even if, for example, only 1–9th of the 90 per cent re-lent by the first bank, or 10 per cent of the original deposit, is redeposited with another bank—and this process is repeated, *additional* credits amounting to 0.111 times the original deposit will be created. [This note was added in 1933. In *Geldtheorie*, pp. 90–91, Hayek was mistaken in believing that the creation of additional credits would only be possible if x be greater than 0.5.—Ed.]

[28] On this question, and on the interesting effects of a transference of deposits from one bank to another, cf. the more elaborate treatment of Phillips, *Bank Credit*, pp. 64 et seq. [pp. 64–66]; also the remarks of Crick, "The Genesis of Bank Deposits", p. 196.

discount; for it would only have to charge its customers a small part of the rate of interest charged by the banks[29] in order to make the business pay. This apparent contradiction between theory and practice is cleared up as soon as one realises that an increase of deposits by a single bank only offers possibilities for credit creation to the banking system as a whole. But the importance of this circumstance transcends the mere clearing up of this difficulty.

6. The possibility of bankers arbitrarily *creating credits is ruled out because, in individual cases, it is impossible to distinguish between those deposits which arose through cash payments and those which find their origin in credit*

As credits created on the basis of additional deposits do not normally appear in the accounts of the same bank which granted the credit, it is fundamentally impossible to distinguish, in individual cases, between "those deposits which arose through cash payment and those which find their origin in credit".[30] But this consideration rules out, a priori, the possibility of bankers limiting the amount of credit granted by them to the amount of 'real' accumulated deposits[31]—that is, those arising from the accommodation of temporarily unused money. The same fact enables us to understand why it is generally just those economic writers who are also practical bankers who are most unwilling to admit in any circumstances that they are in a position to create credits.[32] "The

[29] [This formulation is misleading: What is meant is, "charged to the banks by the Central Bank" (cf. *Geldtheorie*, p. 92).—Ed.]

[30] Neisser (*Der Tauschwert des Geldes*, p. 53) deserves credit for clearing up an untenable conception, which was quite recently held by no less an authority than Professor J. Schumpeter (*Theorie der wirtschaftlichen Entwicklung*, 2nd ed., p. 144 [cf. *The Theory of Economic Development*, p. 99n.—Ed.]).

[31] ["Real deposits" is the term used by Schumpeter, ibid.—Ed.]

[32] Cf., for example, Walter Leaf, the late chairman of the Westminster Bank, in his book *Banking*, or the contributions of A. Jöhr ("Kredit und Konjunktur") and B. Dernburg ("Redebeitrag") to the Zurich Debate on the Trade Cycle (*Schriften des Vereins für Sozialpolitik*, vol. 175, pp. 311 and 329). These arguments were perfectly correctly answered by another 'practical' banker, Karl Schlesinger ("Redebeitrag", ibid., p. 355 [pp. 355–56]). Professor A. Hahn, on the other hand, falls into the opposite error. The standpoint of Professor R. Reisch will be discussed later. [Walter Leaf (1852–1927), an English banker and scholar, was one of the founders of the International Chamber of Commerce. Adolf Jöhr (1878–1953), from 1907 to 1915 general secretary of the Swiss National Bank, and from 1918 to 1939 general director of the Schweizerische Kreditanstalt. Bernhard Dernburg (1865–1937), German politician and banker, was from 1901 to 1906 director of the Darmstädter Bank, and from 1907 to 1910 deputy minister for Colonial Affairs. After World War I, for a short time in 1919 he was minister of finance, and he represented the liberal German Democratic Party in the Reichstag, 1920–30. Karl Schlesinger (1889–1938) was a Hungarian-born banker and author of *Theorie der Geld- und Kreditwirtschaft*. After his flight in 1919 from Budapest to Vienna, he participated in the Mises-*Kreis* and in Karl Menger's Mathematical Colloquium, where he directed Abraham Wald's attention to the mathe-

banker simply does not notice that through this process there is an increase
in the amount of money in circulation".[33] Once the impetus has been given
to any part of the banking system, mere adherence to the routine of banking technique will lead to the creation of additional deposits without the
possibility arising, at any point, of determining whether any particular credit
should properly be regarded as 'additional'. Every time money which has
been deposited is re-lent—provided that the depositor is not prevented from
using his deposits for making payments—this process is to be regarded as the
creation of additional purchasing power; and it is merely this comparatively
simple operation which is at the root of the banks' ability to create purchasing
power—although the process appears so mysterious to many people. It is thus
by no means necessary that the banks should grant these credits, as Dr. Dernburg seems to assume, in an "improper or wanton" way.[34]

It is of course quite another question whether bankers can, or do, create
additional credits of their own free will. The objections to this theory of additional credits, which are levelled against the statement that the banks create
credit 'as they please', although holding good at a given rate of interest, do
not in the least affect that part of the theory which we need for our analysis. If Professor Reisch, for example, emphasises that bank deposits generally
increase only "according to the needs of business",[35] or if Prof. Bouniatian
objects that "it does not depend on the banks, but on the demands made by
commerce and industry, how far banks expand credit",[36] then these assertions,
coming as they do from opponents of the theory of bank credits,[37] already
contain all that is needed for a deductive proof of the necessity for the recurrence of credit cycles. What interests us is precisely the question whether the
banks are able to satisfy the increased demands of business men for credits

---

matics of general equilibrium. Schlesinger committed suicide on the day of Austria's *Anschluss* to
Hitler's Germany. Richard Reisch (1866–1938), public servant and banker, after studying law at
the University of Vienna, worked at the Ministry of Finance, eventually in 1919–20 succeeding
Schumpeter as minister. After a short spell at the Viennese Bodencreditanstalt, Reisch became in
1922 president of the newly founded Austrian National Bank, from which he resigned in 1932 as
a consequence of the Creditanstalt crisis. He co-edited the *Zeitschrift für Nationalökonomie*, 1929–
38.—Ed.]

[33] Neisser, *Der Tauschwert des Geldes*, p. 54 [in the original "banker" is emphasised—Ed.]. He
goes on to say, quite correctly, that "the mere fact that cheque-deposits represent money, without
being covered by cash up to 100 per cent, already explains the money-creating nature of bank
credit" [ibid., pp. 54–55—Ed.].

[34] [Dernburg, "Redebeitrag", p. 328.—Ed.]

[35] Reisch, "Die wirtschaftliche Bedeutung des Kredites", p. 39. [Hayek's quotation is inaccurate insofar as it should read, "according to the increase in the needs of trade".—Ed.]

[36] Bouniatian, "Industrielle Schwankungen", p. 465.

[37] [Here "theory of bank credits" refers to the "theory of additional credits" (cf. *Geldtheorie*,
p. 94), as indicated above, p. 121n.7.—Ed.]

without being obliged immediately to raise their interest charges—as would be the case if the supply of savings and the demand for credits were to be in direct contact, without the agency of the banks (as for example in the hypothetical 'savings market' of theory); or whether it is even possible for the banks to raise their interest charges immediately the demand for credits increases. Even the bitterest opponents of this theory of bank credit are forced to admit that "there can be no doubt that, with the upward swing of the Trade Cycle, a certain expansion of bank credits takes place".[38]

We must not, however, be satisfied with registering the general agreement of opinion on this point. Before passing on to analyse the consequences of this phenomenon we must ask whether the causes which bring it about that banks increase their deposits through additional credits in periods of boom and thus postpone, at any rate temporarily, the rise in the rate of interest which would otherwise necessarily take place, are inherent in the nature of the system, or not.

7. The reaction of the banks to an increased demand for credit

So far, the starting point of our argument concerning the origin of additional credits has been the assumption that the banks receive an increased in-flow of cash which they then use as a basis for new credits on a much larger scale. We must now inquire how banks behave when an increased demand for credit makes itself felt. Assuming, as is preferable, that this increased demand was not caused by a lowering of their own interest rates, this additional demand is always a sign that the natural rate of interest has risen—that is, that a given amount of money can now find more profitable employment than hitherto. The reasons for this can be of very different kinds.[39] New inventions or discoveries, the opening up of new markets, or even bad harvests,[40] the appearance of entrepreneurs of genius who originate "new combinations" (Schumpeter),[41] a fall in wage rates due to heavy immigration, and the destruction of great blocks of capital by a natural catastrophe, or many others. We have already seen that none of these reasons is in itself sufficient to account for an *excessive*

---

[38] Dernburg, "Redebeitrag", p. 329. He merely adds to this statement the remark that the banks and the Central Bank should see to it that this expansion is "kept in order"!

[39] "A great variety of causes", observes Ralph G. Hawtrey, very correctly (*Trade and Credit* (London: Longmans, Green, 1928), p. 175).

[40] Regarding the influence of harvests on the Trade Cycle, cf. the useful compilation of various contradictory theories by Vladimir P. Timoshenko, *The Role of Agricultural Fluctuations in the Business Cycle*, Michigan Business Studies, vol. 2, no. 9 (Ann Arbor: University of Michigan, 1930).

[41] [Cf., e.g., *The Theory of Economic Development*, p. 74.—Ed.]

increase of investing activity, which necessarily engenders a subsequent crisis; but that they can lead to this result only through the increase in the means of credit which they inaugurate.

But how is it possible for the banks to extend credit, as they undoubtedly do, following an increase in demand, when no additional cash is flowing into their vaults? There is no reason to assume that the same cause which has led to an increased demand for credit will also influence another factor, the cash position of the banks—which as we know is the only factor determining the extent to which credit can be granted.[42] So long as the banks maintain a constant proportion between their cash reserves and their deposits it would be impossible to satisfy the new demand for credit. The fact that in reality deposits always do expand relatively to cash reserves, in the course of the boom, so that the liquidity of the banks is always impaired in such periods, does not of course constitute a sufficient starting point for an argument in which the increase in credits is regarded as *the* decisive factor determining the course and extent of the cyclical movement. We must attempt to understand fully the causes and nature of this credit expansion and in particular, its limits.

The key to this problem can only be found in the fact that the ratio of reserves to deposits does not represent a constant magnitude, but, as experience shows, is itself variable. But we shall achieve a satisfactory solution only by showing that the reason for this variability in the reserve is not based on the arbitrary decisions of the bankers, but is itself conditioned by the general economic situation. Such an examination of the causes determining the size of the reserve ratio desired by the banks is all the more important since we had no theoretical warrant for our previous assumption that it always tends to be constant.

It is best to begin our investigation by considering once again the situation of a single bank, and asking how the manager will react when the credit requirements of the customers increase in consequence of an all-round improvement in the business situation.[43] For reasons which will shortly become clear, we must assume that the bank under consideration is the first to feel the new credit requirements of industry, because, let us say, its customers are drawn from just those industries which first feel the effects of the new recovery. Among the fac-

---

[42] It is of course possible that an improvement in the conditions of production and profit-making will also indirectly cause an increased flow of cash to the banks, for a flow of funds for investment, as well as an increased flow of payments for goods, can be expected from abroad. But, in the first place, this increased flow of cash can only be expected in a comparatively late stage of the boom, so that it can hardly explain the latter's origin; and in the second place, such an explanation could only be adduced in the case of a single country, and not for the world economy as a whole, or in a closed system.

[43] The problems with which the manager of a single bank is confronted in deciding the bank's credit policy are very neatly analysed by Mr. W. F. Crick, "The Genesis of Bank Deposits", pp. 197 et seq. [pp. 197–98].

tors which determine the volume of loans granted by the bank, only one has changed; whereas previously, at the same rate of interest and with the same security, no new borrowers came forward, now, under the same conditions of borrowing, more loans can be placed. On the other hand, the cash holdings of the bank remain unchanged. This does not mean, however, that the considerations of liquidity which dictate the amount of loans to be granted will lead to the same result now as when fresh loans could only have been placed at a lower rate of interest or with inferior security than was the case with loans already granted. In this connection, finally, we must mention that the sums which we have, for simplicity's sake, hitherto called cash balances, and which form the bank's liquid reserve, are by no means exclusively composed of cash—and are not even of a constant magnitude, unrelated to the size of the profits which they make possible. The danger that, in case of need, the reserves may have to be replenished by rediscounting bills through the Central Bank;[44] or that, in order to correct an unfavourable clearing-house balance, day-money may have to be borrowed at a given rate of interest, is far less abhorrent when it is possible to extend credits at an undiminished rate of interest than when such an extension would involve a lowering of that rate. But even disregarding this possibility and assuming that the bank recognises that it can satisfy its eventual need for cash only at correspondingly higher rates, we can see that the greater loss of profit entailed by keeping the cash reserve intact will, as a rule, lead the bank to a policy which involves diminishing the size of this non-earning asset. Besides this, we have the consideration that, in the upward phase of the cycle, the risks of borrowing are less; and therefore a smaller cash reserve may suffice to provide the same degree of security. But it is above all for reasons of competition that the bank which first feels the effect of an increased demand for credits cannot afford to reply by putting up its interest charges; for it would risk losing its best customers to other banks which had not yet experienced a similarly increased demand for credits. There can be little doubt, therefore, that the bank or banks which are the first to feel the effects of new credit requirements will be forced to satisfy these even at the cost of reducing their liquidity.

8. The process of credit expansion and its cessation

But once one bank or group of banks has started the expansion, then all the other banks receive, as already described, a flow of cash which at first enables

---

[44] On this point see J. S. Lawrence, "Borrowed Reserves and Bank Expansion", *Quarterly Journal of Economics*, vol. 42, August 1928, pp. 593–626, where Mr. Phillips's exposition, mentioned above, is extensively criticised; also the rejoinder of Mr. Frederick A. Bradford, published under the same title in the next volume (vol. 43, November 1928, pp. 179–84) of the same journal.

them to expand credit on their own account without impairing their liquidity. They make use of this possibility the more readily since they, in turn, soon feel the increased demand for credit. Once the process of expansion has become general, however, the banks soon realise that, for the moment at any rate, they can safely modify their ideas of liquidity. While expansion by a single bank will soon confront it with a clearing-house deficit of practically the same magnitude as the original new credit, a general expansion carried on at about the same rate by all banks will give rise to clearing-house claims which, although larger, mainly compensate one another and so induce only a relatively unimportant cash drain. If a bank does not at first keep pace with the expansion it will, sooner or later, be induced to do so, since it will continue to receive cash at the clearing house as long as it does not adjust itself to the new standard of liquidity.

So long as this process goes on, it is practically impossible for any single bank, acting alone, to apply the only control by which the demand for credit can, in the long run, be successfully kept within bounds; that is, an increase in its interest charges. Concerted action in this direction, which for competitive reasons is the only action possible, will ensue only when the increased cash requirements of business compel the banks to protect their cash balances by checking further credit expansion, or when the Central Bank has preceded them by raising its discount rate. This, again, will only happen, as a rule, when the banks have been induced by the growing drain on their cash to increase their re-discount. Experience shows, moreover, that the relation between cheque-payments and cash payments alters in favour of the latter as the boom proceeds, so that an increased proportion of the cash is finally withdrawn from the banks.[45]

This phenomenon is easily explained in theory by the fact that a low rate of interest first raises the prices of capital goods and only subsequently those of consumption goods, so that the first increases occur in the kind of payments which are effected in large blocks.[46] It may lead to the consequence

[45] Cf. the statements contained in the well-known *10th* [*Tenth*] *Yearly* [*Annual*] *Report of the Federal Reserve Board*, [Covering Operations] for [the Year] 1923 (Washington, DC: Government Printing Office, 1924), p. 25: "This is the usual sequence—an increase in [of] deposits followed by an increase in [of the] currency. Ordinarily the first effect of an increase in business activity [up] on the banking position is a growth in loans and deposits . . . Then [There] comes a time when the increase in [of] business activity and the fuller employment of labour and increased payroll [pay rolls] call for an increase in [of] actual pocket money to support the increased wage disbursements and the increased volume of purchases in detail [at retail]." [Hayek had quoted this passage more extensively, and accurately, in "Die Währungspolitik der Vereinigten Staaten", pp. 269–70n.2; cf. "Monetary Policy in the United States", p. 113.—Ed.]

[46] Neisser (*Der Tauschwert des Geldes*, p. 162) doubts this, but his criticism results from an inadequate grasp of the effects of an unduly low money rate of interest. But even if he were right on this point, the arguments of monetary Trade Cycle theory would remain unaffected, since the latter, as is shown in the text, does not depend on this assumption for its proof.

that banks are not only prevented from granting new credits, but even forced to diminish credits already granted. This fact may well aggravate the crisis; but it is by no means necessary in order to bring it about. For this *it is quite enough that the banks should cease to extend the volume of credit*, and sooner or later this must happen. Only so long as the volume of circulating media is increasing can the money rate of interest be kept below the equilibrium rate; once it has ceased to increase, the money rate must, despite the increased total volume in circulation,[47] rise again to its natural level and thus render unprofitable (temporarily, at least)[48] those investments which were created with the aid of additional credit.[49]

9. Elasticity *in the volume of circulating media is a sufficient cause of cyclical fluctuation*

The assertion which forms the starting point of the 'Additional Credit Theory of the Trade Cycle',[50] and whose proof has been attempted in the preceding pages, has never in fact been seriously questioned; but hardly any attempts have been made to follow up all the unpleasant consequences of the state of affairs it indicates. Yet what is implied when the beneficial effects of bank credits are praised but that thanks to the activities of banks an increased demand for credit is followed by a greater increase in its supply than would be warranted by the supply of contemporary saving? Wherein lie the often praised effects of credit, if not in the fact that it provides means for enterprises for which no provision could be found if the choices of the different economic subjects were strictly followed? By creating additional credits in response to an increased demand, and thus opening up new possibilities of improving and extending production, the banks ensure that impulses towards expansion of the productive apparatus shall not be so immediately and insuperably balked by a rise of interest rates as they would be if progress were limited by the slow increase in the flow of savings.[51] But this same policy stultifies the automatic mechanism of adjustment which keeps the various parts of the system in equilibrium, and makes possible disproportionate developments which must, sooner or later, bring about a reaction.

---

[47] [That is, "volume of money in circulation" (cf. *Geldtheorie*, p. 101).—Ed.]

[48] [Note that the qualification, "temporarily, at least", has been added in 1933.—Ed.]

[49] We need not stay to examine the case of a continuous increase in circulating media, which can only occur under a free paper standard. [In *Geldtheorie*, p. 101n.2, this note continues: "It should just be noted that—as experience has amply demonstrated—even in this case the banks will not succeed in keeping the rate of interest at an artificially low level by increasing credit creation, but that the rate of interest will be compensated by the movement of prices."—Ed.]

[50] [That is, "circulation credit theory" (cf. *Geldtheorie*, p. 102); see above, p. 121n.7.—Ed.]

[51] [*Geldtheorie*, p. 102, does not refer to "a slow increase in the flow of savings" but characterises the flow of savings as only "slightly variable".—Ed.]

Elasticity in the credit supply of an economic system is not only universally demanded but also—as the result of an organisation of the credit system which has adapted itself to this requirement—an undeniable fact, whose necessity or advantages are not discussed here.[52] But we must be quite clear on one point. *An economic system with an elastic currency must, in many instances, react to external influences quite differently from an economy in which economic forces impinge on goods in their full force*[53]—*without any intermediary; and we must, a priori, expect any process started by an outside impulse to run an entirely different course in such an economy from that described by a theory which only takes into account changes originating on the side of goods.* Once, owing to the disturbing influence of money, even a single price has been fixed at a different level from that which it would have formed in a barter economy, a shift in the whole structure of production is inevitable; and this shift, so long as we make use of static theory and the methods proper to it, can only be explained as an exclusive consequence of the peculiar influence of money. The immediate consequence of an adjustment of the volume of money to the 'requirements' of industry is the failure of the 'interest brake' to operate as promptly as it would in an economy operating without credit. This means, however, that new adjustments[54] are undertaken on a larger scale than can be completed; a boom is thus made possible, with the inevitably recurring 'crisis'. *The determining cause of the cyclical fluctuation is, therefore, the fact that on account of the elasticity of the volume of currency media the rate of interest demanded by the banks is not necessarily always equal to the equilibrium rate, but is, in the short run, determined by considerations of banking liquidity.*[55]

---

[52] Cf. Wicksell, *Geldzins und Güterpreise*, p. 101: "The more elastic is the currency system [. . .] the longer can a more or less constant difference persist between the two interest rates and the greater, therefore, will be the influence of this discrepancy on prices." [Cf. the translation of the paragraph in *Interest and Prices*, p. 110: " . . . in an elastic monetary system . . . a fairly constant difference between the two rates of interest could be maintained for a long time, and the effect on prices might be considerable."—Ed.]

[53] [The corresponding formulation "hart im Raume stoßen sich die Güter", put between quotation marks in *Geldtheorie*, p. 103, alludes to a dictum of the German poet Friedrich Schiller (*Wallensteins Tod*, act 2, scene 2, 102–5): "Eng ist die Welt, und das Gehirn ist weit; / leicht beieinander wohnen die Gedanken, / doch hart im Raume stoßen sich die Sachen." For an English translation cf. *Schiller's Wallenstein*. Rendered in English verse by Alexander Falconer Murison (London, New York, and Toronto: Longmans, Green and Co., 1931), p. 263: "The world is narrow, and the brain is wide, / With ease by one another dwell the thoughts, / And rudely clash the things in space together."—Ed.]

[54] [Most probably, this is a misprint and should read, "new investments" (cf. *Geldtheorie*, p. 103).—Ed.]

[55] In a previous work ("Die Währungspolitik der Vereinigten Staaten", p. 260 [pp. 260–62; cf. "Monetary Policy in the United States", pp. 105–7—Ed.]), I have already dealt with the elasticity of bank credit as *the* cause of cyclical fluctuations. This view of its determining importance is now also put forward by Professor Frank A. Fetter in a very interesting essay, "Interest Theories [Theory] and Price Movements", *American Economic Review*, vol. 17, supplement, March

The main question set by this inquiry is thus answered. A deductive explanation embracing all the phenomena of the Trade Cycle would require far-reaching logical investigations entirely transcending the scope of this work, which aims merely at an exposition of the monetary basis of Trade Cycle theory. For the present, we must content ourselves with a reference to existing literature on the subject.[56] In the present work we shall only draw a few con-

---

1927, see especially, pp. 95 et seq. [pp. 95–96]). Prof. Fetter, of course, is also under the influence of the prevailing dogma which holds that the existence of a stable price level is sufficient proof of the absence of all monetary influences. The crucial part of his argument, not having received the attention which it deserves in recent monetary literature, is reprinted here:

"The foregoing presents the extreme case of the expansion and contraction of bank loans in relation to prices, but [prices *but*] *in principle quite small changes in the loan policies of banks affecting the volume of commercial loans,* discount rates, and percentages of reserves, *are of the same nature.* They cause and constitute inflation and deflation of the exchange medium and of commercial purchasing power, not originating in [changes in] the amount of standard money but in the elasticity of banking loan funds. *This word 'elasticity' has long been used in discussions [discussion] of banking policy to designate a quality assumed to be [highly and] wholly desirable in bank note issues and [in] customers' credits,* but with only vague suggestions as to what is the need, standard, or means, with reference to which bank loans should expand and contract.

"Rather, it may be more exact to say, the tacit assumption has been that the bank loan funds should be elastic in response to the 'needs ['the needs] of business'. But *'the needs of business' appears to be nothing but another name for changes in customers' eagerness for loans;* and this eagerness increases when prices are beginning, or are expected, to rise and [are beginning or are expected to rise, and] often continues to gather momentum while prices rise and until, because of vanishing reserve percentages (and other factors), the limit of this elasticity and also the limit of price increase are in sight. In this situation[,] the most conservative business operations become intermixed with elements of investment[s] speculation, motivated by the rise of prices and the hope of profit that will be made possible by a further rise. *Throughout this process the much-esteemed [much esteemed] elasticity of bank funds is the very condition causing, or making possible, the rising prices which stimulate the so-called 'needs of business'. Truly a vicious circle, to be broken only by crisis and collapse when bank loans reach a limit and prices fall.*" (My italics.) [Frank Albert Fetter (1863–1949), an exponent of the Austrian view among American economists, taught at Indiana, Stanford, Cornell, and finally, 1911–33, at Princeton.—Ed.]

Further, we should point out the connection between our theory and a famous thesis of Mr. R. G. Hawtrey. The phrase "so long as credit is regulated with reference to reserve proportions, the trade cycle is bound to recur" (*Monetary Reconstruction*, 2nd ed. (London: Longmans, 1926), p. 135) is undoubtedly correct, though perhaps in a sense somewhat different from that intended by the author; for a regulation of this volume of loans exclusively from the point of view of liquidity can never effect a prompt adjustment of the rates charged on loans to the changes in the equilibrium rate, and thus cannot help providing opportunities for the temporary creation of additional credits as soon as (at a given rate of interest) the demand for credit surpasses the accumulation of savings; that is, when the natural rate of interest has risen. See, finally, the remarks of Professor W. Röpke, "Kredit und Konjunktur", p. 274.

[56] Besides Professor Mises' *Theorie des Geldes und der Umlaufsmittel* we must mention the last chapter of Budge's *Grundzüge der theoretischen Nationalökonomie*, and Prof. Richard Strigl's paper on "Die Produktion unter dem Einfluß einer Kreditexpansion", in *Schriften des Vereins für Sozialpolitik*, vol. 173, part 2, pp. 185–211, a volume which has been repeatedly quoted above. Since the above was written, I have tried to carry the analysis of these phenomena a step further in *Prices*

clusions which follow from our previous arguments, some with regard to practical policy, some with regard to further scientific research. Before going on to this, however, we shall venture a few remarks on the question whether the result of our investigations unequivocally settles the controversy between the protagonists and opponents of the monetary Trade Cycle theory in favour of the former.

10. The significance of these monetary influences from the point of view of Trade Cycle theory

It must be emphasised first and foremost that there is no necessary reason why the initiating change, the original disturbance eliciting a cyclical fluctuation in a stationary economy, should be of monetary origin. Nor, in practice, is this even generally the case. The initial change need have no specific character at all, it may be any one among a thousand different factors which may at any time increase the profitability of any group of enterprises. For it is not the occurrence of a 'change of data' which is significant, but the fact that the economic system, instead of reacting to this change with an immediate 'adjustment' (Schumpeter)[57]—i.e., the formation of a new equilibrium—begins a particular movement of 'boom' which contains, within itself, the seeds of an inevitable reaction. This phenomenon, as we have seen, should undoubtedly be ascribed to monetary factors, and in particular to 'additional credits' which also necessarily determine the extent and duration of the cyclical fluctuation. Once this point is agreed upon, it naturally becomes quite irrelevant whether we label this explanation of the Trade Cycle as a monetary theory or not. What is important is to recognise that it is to monetary causes that we must ascribe the divergences of the pricing process, during the Trade Cycle, from the course deduced in static theory.

From the particular point of view from which we started, our theory must be regarded most decisively as a monetary one. As to the incorporation of Trade Cycle theory into the general framework of static equilibrium theory (for the clear formulation of which we are indebted to Professor A. Löwe, one of the strongest opponents of monetary Trade Cycle theory), we must maintain, in opposition to his view, not only that our own theory is undoubtedly a

---

and Production. [Richard Strigl (1891–1942), economist and public servant; a student of Böhm-Bawerk, contributed to the Austrian theory of capital and the cycle and taught at the University of Vienna and the Hochschule für Welthandel. See Hayek's obituary "Richard von Strigl", reprinted in F. A. Hayek, *The Fortunes of Liberalism*, pp. 168–70.—Ed.]

[57] [Cf. *The Theory of Economic Development*, p. 224, as quoted above, p. 83n.12.—Ed.]

monetary one but that a theory other than monetary is hardly conceivable.[58] It must be conceded that the monetary theory as we have presented it—whether one prefers to call it a monetary theory or not, and whether or not one finds it a sufficient explanation of the empirically determined fluctuations—has this definite advantage: *it deals with problems which must, in any case, be dealt with for they are necessarily given when the central apparatus of economic analysis is applied to the explanation of the existing organisation of exchange. Even if we had never noticed cyclical fluctuations, even if all the actual fluctuations of history were accepted as the consequences of natural events, a consequential analysis of the effects which follow from the peculiar workings of our existing credit organisation would be bound to demonstrate that fluctuations caused by monetary factors are unavoidable.*

It is, of course, an entirely different question whether these monetary fluctuations would, if not reinforced by other factors, attain the extent and duration which we observe in the historical cycles; or whether in the absence of these supplementary factors they would not be much weaker and less acute than they actually are. Perhaps the empirically observed strength of the cyclical fluctuations is really only due to periodic changes in external circumstances, such as short-period variations of climate, or changes in subjective data (as, e.g., the sudden appearance of entrepreneurs of genius) or perhaps the interval between individual cyclical waves may be due to some natural law.[59] Whatever further hypothetical causes are adduced to explain the empirically observed course of the fluctuations, there can be no doubt (and this is the important and indispensable contribution of monetary Trade Cycle theory) that the modern economic system cannot be conceived without fluctuations ascribable to monetary influences; and therefore any other factors which may be found necessary to explain the empirically observed phenomena will have to be regarded as causes *additional* to the monetary cause. In other words, any non-monetary Trade Cycle theory must superimpose its system of explanation on that of the monetarily determined fluctuations; it cannot start simply from the static system as presented by pure equilibrium theory.[60]

Once this is admitted, however, the question whether the monetary theory of the Trade Cycle is correct or not must, at any rate, be presented in a different form. For if the correctness of the interconnections described by mone-

---

[58] Cf. my report: "Über den Einfluß monetärer Faktoren", pp. 362 et seq. [pp. 362–63; cf. "On the Influence of Monetary Factors", pp. 205–6. The attribution of the report to Hayek is a mistake; its author was, of course, Adolf Löwe.—Ed.]

[59] From now to the end of the section the exposition follows, in part word for word, my contribution to the Zurich discussion of the Verein für Sozialpolitik ("Redebeitrag", pp. 372 et seq. [pp. 372–73]).

[60] [In *Geldtheorie*, p. 108, the corresponding passage reads, "the stationary economy as presented by general equilibrium theory".—Ed.]

tary theory is unquestioned, there still remains the problem whether it is also sufficient to explain all those phenomena which are observed empirically in the course of the Trade Cycle; it may perhaps need supplementing in order to make it an instrument suitable to explain the working of the modern economic system. It seems to me, however, that before we can successfully tackle this problem we ought to know exactly how much of the empirically observed fluctuations is due to the monetary factor, which is actually always at work; and therefore we shall have to work out in the fullest detail the theory of monetary fluctuations. It is hardly permissible, methodologically speaking, to go in search of other causes whose existence we may conjecture, before ascertaining exactly how far, and to what extent, the monetary factors are operative. It is our duty to work out in detail the necessary consequences of those causes of disturbance which we know, and to make this train of thought a definite part of our logical system, before attempting to incorporate any other factors which may come into play.

11. Their bearing on policy

The fact, simple and indisputable as it is, that the 'elasticity' of the supply of currency media, resulting from the existing monetary organisation, offers a sufficient reason for the genesis and recurrence of fluctuations in the whole economy is of the utmost importance—for it implies that no measure which can be conceived in practice would be able entirely to suppress these fluctuations.[61]

It follows particularly from the point of view of the monetary theory of the Trade Cycle that it is by no means justifiable to expect the total disappearance of cyclical fluctuations to accompany a stable price level—a belief which Professor Löwe[62] seems to regard as the necessary consequence of the Monetary Theory of the Trade Cycle. Professor Röpke is undoubtedly right when he emphasises the fact that "even if a stable price level could be successfully imposed on the capitalist economy the causes making for cyclical fluctuations would not be removed".[63] But to realise this, as the preceding argument shows,

---

[61] [This is one of the numerous occasions where Hayek is explicit in his rejection of neutral money as a norm for monetary policy in practice. Cf. similarly F. A. Hayek, "Über 'neutrales Geld'", *Zeitschrift für Nationalökonomie*, vol. 4, October 1933, pp. 659–61, translated as "On Neutral Money" and reprinted as chapter 6 of F. A. Hayek, *Good Money, Part I: The New World*.—Ed.]

[62] "Über den Einfluß monetärer Faktoren", p. 369 [cf. "On the Influence of Monetary Factors", p. 211. It should be noted that in *Geldtheorie*, p. 110, Hayek attributed this belief—erroneously—also to Mises, cf. *Geldwertstabilisierung*, p. 36 (note that the corresponding passage in "Monetary Stabilization", p. 107, diverges from the German version).—Ed.]

[63] Röpke, "Kredit und Konjunktur", p. 265 [pp. 265–66].

is by no means "equivalent to a rejection of a 100 per cent monetary Trade Cycle theory".[64] On the contrary, on this view, we must regard Professor Röpke's theory, which coincides in the more important points with our own,[65] as itself constituting such a 100 per cent monetary Trade Cycle theory.

Once this is realised, we can also see how nonsensical it is to formulate the question of the causation of cyclical fluctuations in terms of 'guilt', and to single out, e.g., the banks as those 'guilty' of causing fluctuations in economic development.[66] Nobody has ever asked them to pursue a policy other than that which, as we have seen, gives rise to cyclical fluctuations; and it is not within their power to do away with such fluctuations,[67] seeing that the latter originate not from their policy but from the very nature of the modern organisation of credit. So long as we make use of bank credit as a means of furthering economic development we shall have to put up with the resulting trade cycles. They are, in a sense, the price we pay for a speed of development exceeding that which people would voluntarily make possible through their savings, and which therefore has to be extorted from them.[68] And even if it is a mistake—as the recurrence of crises would demonstrate—to suppose that we can, in this way, overcome all obstacles standing in the way of progress, it is at least conceivable[69] that the non-economic factors of progress, such as technical and commercial knowledge, are thereby benefited in a way which we should be reluctant to forgo.

If it were possible, as has been repeatedly asserted in recent English literature,[70] to keep the total amount of bank deposits entirely stable, that would constitute the only means of getting rid of cyclical fluctuations. This seems to us purely

[64] Ibid., p. 278.

[65] Cf. especially pp. 274 et seq. [pp. 274–75] of the work mentioned.

[66] As Prof. S. Budge seems inclined to do (*Grundzüge der theoretischen Nationalökonomie*, p. 216). His exposition in other respects largely coincides with ours.

[67] [Here and in the following the text deviates from that in *Geldtheorie*, which (p. 111) continues with the following passage, "nor for reasons to be explained below would it probably not be desirable that they abandon this policy" (my translation). The new formulation is most probably due to a revision by Hayek himself, prompted by his change of mind with regard to the potential benefits derived from forced saving. Cf. on this Hansjoerg Klausinger, "Hayek Translated: Some Words of Caution", *History of Economics Review*, vol. 37, Winter 2003, pp. 78–79.—Ed.]

[68] [Instead of "has to be extorted from them", *Geldtheorie*, p. 111, reads, "has to be tricked out of them" (my translation).—Ed.]

[69] [Instead of "it is at least conceivable", *Geldtheorie*, p. 111, reads, "there is hardly any doubt" (my translation).—Ed.]

[70] Certain statements of Mr. R. G. Hawtrey seem to point to this, especially *Monetary Reconstruction*, p. 121. [This passage might also be read as a comment on the Chicago Plan of 100% money, cf., e.g., Henry C. Simons, "Banking and Currency Reform", Memorandum (with Supplement and Appendix), dated November 17, 1933, published in *Research in the History of Economic Thought and Methodology*, Archival Supplement, vol. 4, 1994, pp. 31–49. On Hayek's rejection of the plan cf. also the editor's introduction, p. 38n.138.—Ed.]

Utopian. It would necessitate the complete abolition of all bank-money—i.e., notes and cheques—and the reduction of the banks to the role of brokers, trading in savings. But even if we assume the fundamental possibility of this state of things, it remains very questionable whether many would wish to put it into effect if they were clear about its consequences. The stability of the economic system would be obtained at the price of curbing economic progress. The rate of interest would be constantly above the level maintained under the existing system (for, generally speaking, even in times of depression some extension of credit takes place).[71] The utilisation of new inventions and the 'realisation of new combinations' would be made more difficult, and thus there would disappear a psychological incentive towards progress, whose importance cannot be judged on purely economic grounds. It is no exaggeration to say that not only would it be impossible to put such a scheme into practice in the present state of economic enlightenment of the public, but even its theoretical justification would be doubtful.[72]

As regards the practical bearing of our analysis on the Trade Cycle policy of the banks, all that can be deduced from it is that bankers will have to weigh carefully the relative advantages and disadvantages of granting credits on an increasing scale, and to take into account the demand, now fairly widespread, for the early application of a check to credit expansion. But the utmost that can be achieved on these lines is only a mitigation, never the abolition, of the Trade Cycle. Apart from this, the only way of minimising damage is through a far-reaching adjustment of the economic system to the recognised existence of cyclical movements; and for this purpose the most important condition is an increased insight into the nature of the Trade Cycle and a knowledge of its actual phase at any particular moment.[73]

---

[71] Cf. Professor A. C. Pigou, *Industrial Fluctuations*, p. 145: "Banks do not in bad times reduce the amount [stream] of new real capital flowing to business men below what it would have been had there been no banks, but merely increase it to a smaller extent than they do in good times." [The passage in the text apparently implies that the money rate—"under the existing system"—will not converge to the natural rate and is thus difficult to reconcile with Hayek's writings on money and the cycle from this period. Possibly it should be a considered a relic of his earlier views; see p. 143n.67 above.—Ed.]

[72] [*Geldtheorie*, p. 112, refers to the "enlightenment of the public and of scholarship", and instead of "would be doubtful" reads, "would be hardly justifiable".—Ed.]

[73] In this connection, apart from empirical research, the greatest consideration should be given to the plea made by Morgenstern (*Wirtschaftsprognose*, pp. 123 et seq. [pp. 123–24]) for giving increased publicity to company developments.

FIVE

UNSETTLED PROBLEMS OF
TRADE CYCLE THEORY

*1. All variations in the volume of effective circulation necessarily involve
movements other than those which can be immediately
deduced from the propositions of static theory*

So much has already been said[1] about the most important of the outstanding
problems of monetary influences on economic phenomena that only a brief
supplement is needed at this point. With regard to the problems of monetary
theory in the narrower sense I may restrict myself chiefly to what has been
said above, as I hope to publish the results of a separate investigation concerning this problem elsewhere.[2] A few remarks may, however, be ventured
merely as a summing-up of what has already been said, and in doing this we
shall touch on a number of other important problems. The most significant
result of our investigation must be the grasp of the elementary fact that *we
have no right to assume that an economic system with an 'elastic' currency will ever exhibit
those movements which can be immediately deduced from the propositions of static theory.*
On the contrary, it is to be expected that movements will arise which would
not be possible under the conditions usually assumed by that theory. It is particularly important to realise that this proposition is true whether the changes
in the volume of money also effect changes in the so-called 'general value of
money' or not. With the disappearance of the idea that money can only exert
an active influence on economic movement[3] when the value of money (as
measured by one kind of price level) is changing, the theory that the general
value of money is the sole object of explanation for monetary theory must fall

---

[1] In chapter 3, sections 4 and 6.

[2] Cf. "Das intertemporale Gleichgewichtssystem der Preise" ["Intertemporal Price Equilibrium"]; and more especially *Prices and Production*, where I have attempted to develop some of
the points touched upon in this chapter. [In the German version of 1929 the "separate investigation" referred to the book project of *Geldtheoretische Untersuchungen*, which Hayek had already
abandoned before he turned to *Prices and Production*. See also the editor's introduction to this volume, p. 9.—Ed.]

[3] [More accurately, "the economic processes" or "the course of economic events" (cf. *Geldtheorie*, p. 115).—Ed.]

to the ground. Its place must, henceforth, be taken by an analysis of *all* the effects of money on the course of economic development. All changes in the *volume* of effective monetary circulation,[4] and only such changes, will therefore rank for consideration as changes in economic data capable of originating 'monetary influences'.

The next task of monetary theory is, therefore, a systematic investigation of the effects of changes in the volume of money. In the course of this approach, relationships will inevitably be contemplated which do not have the permanence of the equilibrium relationships. All these results, however (and this must be emphasised to prevent misunderstanding) will be reached by the aid of the methods of static analysis, for these are the only instruments available to economic theory. The only difference is that these methods will be applied to an entirely new set of circumstances which have never, up till now, received the attention they deserve. It is vitally necessary that such an investigation should keep clear of the notion that the adjustment of the supply of money to changes in 'money requirements' is an essential condition for the smooth working of the equilibrating process of the system, as presented in equilibrium theory.[5] It must always start from the assumption that the natural determining factors[6] will exert their full effect only when the effective volume of money remains unchanged, whatever may be the actual changes in the extent of economic activity.

Precise propositions as to the effects of changes in the volume of money can be laid down only when accurate information is available both as to the genesis of the change and the part of the economic system where it took place. For this reason little can be said about changes resulting from the decumulation of hoarded treasure or the discovery of new gold deposits. The way in which an individual will elect to spend money coming to him as a gift or as a result of other non-economic motives cannot be determined from deductive considerations. Similarly, little can be said a priori about bank credits granted to the State,[7] so long as we have no information as to how they are to be used. The

---

[4] [Here the deviation from *Geldtheorie*, p. 115, replacing "volume of money" by "volume of effective monetary circulation", is significant as it explicitly takes account of changes in the velocity of money as a monetary influence principally on a par with changes in the volume of money.—Ed.]

[5] This notion rests on a confusion between the demand for money and the demand for cash, i.e., that portion of the total amount of money which at any given moment is utilised in cash, and which undergoes sharp seasonal fluctuations. This phenomenon, however, is itself a consequence of the use of bank credit. For a somewhat more detailed discussion of these problems, cf. lecture 4 of *Prices and Production*. [Note once more that here 'bank credit' is used synonymously for 'circulation credit'; cf. *Geldtheorie*, p. 116n.1.—Ed.]

[6] [That is, "the determining factors operating in a natural (or barter) economy" (cf. *Geldtheorie*, p. 116).—Ed.]

[7] [In *Geldtheorie*, p. 116, Hayek made clear that "bank credits granted to the State" are a special case of "credits granted for purposes of consumption".—Ed.]

situation is different, however, when we are dealing with productive credits granted by the banks to industry—which constitute the most frequent form of increase in the volume of circulating media. These credits are only given when and where their utilisation is profitable, or at least appears to be so. Profitability is determined, however, by the ratio of the interest paid on these credits to the profits earned by their use. So long as the amount of credit obtainable at any given rate of interest is limited, competition will ensure that only the most profitable employments are financed out of a given amount of credit. The uses to which the additional money can be put are thus determined by the rate of interest, and the amount which can be said about those uses[8] will therefore depend, in turn, on how much is known about the importance and the effects of interest. Whatever may have been written or thought on this old problem of theoretical economics, it is undeniable that those particular aspects of interest theory which are important for our analysis have so far received less attention and even less recognition than is their due. It is not practicable to work out, within the limits of this essay, the supplementary analysis which seems to me to be necessary in this field; but I should like, at least, to indicate, before I conclude, some angles of approach which appear to have been unduly neglected hitherto. Needless to say, the sections which follow have even less claim than their predecessors to be regarded as comprehensive.

2. The most important effects are via movements in the structure of the money rates of interest—which thus present a series of important problems

In the economic system of to-day, interest does not exist in the form in which it is presented by pure economic theory. Not only do we find, instead of one uniform rate, a great number of differing rates, but, beyond this, none of the various rates of interest existing is entitled to rank as *the* rate of interest described by static theory, on which all other rates depend, differing only to the extent to which they are affected by special circumstances. The process of interest fixation,[9] which is at the basis of pure theory, never in fact follows the same course in a modern credit economy; for in such an economy the supply of, and the demand for, savings never directly confront each other.

All existing theories of interest, with a few not very successful exceptions, restrict themselves to the explanation of that *imaginary* rate of interest which would result from such an immediate confronting of supply and demand. The fact that the rate of interest which these theories explain is one never found in practice does not mean that they are of no importance, or even that any explanation of the actual rates can afford to ignore them. On the contrary, an ade-

---

[8] [That is, "what can be said about . . ."—Ed.]

[9] [A more accurate translation of *Zinsbildung* (*Geldtheorie*, p. 118) is "interest formation".—Ed.]

quate explanation of that 'natural rate' is the indispensable starting point for any realisation of the conditions necessary to the achievement of equilibrium, and for an understanding of the effects which every rate of interest actually in force exerts on the economic system. It is true that it does not suffice to explain all empirically observed rates since it takes into consideration only one of the factors determining those rates (though that factor is, of course, the one which is always operative); but any consideration of ruling interest rates which did not relate its analysis to that of the imaginary interest rate of static theory would hang entirely in the air. For the most part, however, no solution has been found to the wider problem of building up on the basis of the theory of an equilibrium rate of interest, which can be deduced from the credit-less economy, the structure of different rates which can be simultaneously observed in a modern economy. The solution of this particular problem should provide a most valuable contribution to a deeper insight into cyclical fluctuations.

But before we set out to explore on the one hand the difference between the natural rate of interest and the actual rate, and on the other hand that between the various kinds of the latter, we must say something about the importance of changes in the equilibrium rate itself, since some very confused ideas prevail as to the function of the equilibrium rate of interest in a dynamic economy. This is not very surprising since, as we have seen above, an insufficient appreciation of the role of interest is the cause of most misunderstanding in Trade Cycle theory. Perhaps it is not too much to say that the importance which an economist attaches to interest as a regulator of economic development is the best criterion of his theoretical insight. It is therefore all the more regrettable that recent economic literature has been quite fruitless so far as the theory of interest is concerned.[10] This too is, perhaps, due in part to the fact that the earlier economists, to whom we owe our present knowledge of interest theory, stopped short in their investigations and never came to the point of explaining the actual rates.

3. The significance of fluctuations in the natural rate of interest

Under the rubric of *pure interest theory* (by which we understand the explanation of that rate of interest which is not modified by monetary influences,

---

[10] The best confirmation of this view is given by Mr. Gerhard Heinze, who, in his recent study, *Static or Dynamic Interest Theory* [*Statische oder dynamische Zinstheorie? Versuch einer kritischen Beleuchtung der Casselschen und Schumpeterschen Zinstheorie*—Ed.] (Leipzig: Scholl, 1928), comes to the correct conclusion that: "In spite of all the partly justified criticism which was levelled against the interest theory of Böhm-Bawerk, the latter still represents the most logically perfect economic explanation of the phenomenon of interest, and is, moreover, the one which comes nearest to the observed facts" (p. 165).

although paid, of course, on capital reckoned in money terms) we shall have to deal briefly with the question of the effect of transitory fluctuations in the natural rate of interest, conditioned by 'real' factors. This question is of great importance, taking as it does a decisive place in some of the best known Trade Cycle theories of our day. In particular Professor Cassel's view[11] that the real cause of cyclical fluctuations lies in an over-estimate of the supply of new capital, is based on the assumption that a temporary fall in the rate of interest conditioned by real causes can bring about over-investment in the same way as a rate of interest artificially lowered by monetary factors. This view, which seems to be supported by a considerable body of experts, has to be judged quite differently according as the changes which elicit fluctuations in the rate of interest originate on the demand or the supply side. Fluctuations caused by changes on the demand side, which Professor Cassel uses as an explanation in his trade cycle theory, certainly cannot be regarded as an adequate explanation of the cycle; for, as Professor Amonn has already pointed out,[12] this is no reason why entrepreneurs should (assuming an unchanged rate of interest) expect to obtain more credits in the future than they can now. However there can be no doubt that violent fluctuations in savings and the consequent temporary changes in the equilibrium rate of interest act similarly to an artificial lowering of the money rate of interest in causing an extension of capital investments which cannot be maintained later owing to the diminished supply of savings.[13] In this case, therefore, it is permissible to speak of non-monetary cyclical fluctuations.[14] This differs, however, from the conception of cyclical fluctuations employed hitherto, in that the passage from boom into depression is not a necessary consequence of the boom itself, but is conditioned by 'exter-

[11] Mentioned above, p. 93n.41 [cf. Cassel, *The Theory of Social Economy*—Ed.].

[12] Alfred Amonn, "Cassels System der Theoretischen Nationalökonomie, II", *Archiv für Sozialwissenschaft und Sozialpolitik*, vol. 51, no. 2, 1924, pp. 348 et seq. [pp. 348–54]. In order to remain within the scope of our work we have to forgo the very alluring task of criticising Professor Cassel's argument. Such a criticism would also have to deal with the very ingenious theoretical interpretation of this argument by Dr. Georg Halm, "Das Zinsproblem am Geld- und Kapitalmarkt", *Jahrbücher für Nationalökonomie und Statistik*, vol. 125 (3rd series, vol. 70), no. 1, 1926, pp. 16 et seq. [pp. 16–29]. Here we may only point out that in this study Halm is driven to make use of the old hypothesis that savings accumulate for a time and are then suddenly utilised "at the moment when the real boom begins" (p. 21). [Note that Halm speaks of *Aufschwung*, that is, "upswing" instead of "boom". In his review of *Geldtheorie*, in *Zeitschrift für Nationalökonomie*, vol. 1, January 1930, p. 606, Halm interpreted the accumulation of capital disposal as bringing about an increase in inventories that could be utilised in the upswing; Hayek presented a similar view in his "Profits, Interest and Investment", in *Profits, Interest and Investment*, p. 42, reprinted as chapter 8 in F. A. Hayek, *Business Cycles, Part II*, p. 237.—Ed.]

[13] Cf. Dr. Adolf Lampe, *Zur Theorie des Sparprozesses und der Kreditschöpfung* (Jena: Fischer, 1926), pp. 67 et seq. [pp. 67–68].

[14] [A more accurate translation is "non-monetarily induced cyclical fluctuations" (cf. *Geldtheorie*, p. 121).—Ed.]

nal circumstances'. A downward turn of this sort can occur just as well in a hitherto stationary economy or during a depression as at the end of a boom; and it should therefore be regarded less as an example of a cyclical movement than as a particularly complicated case of the direct process of adjustment to changes in data. In any case, for reasons given above, such an explanation, as compared with an endogenous theory, would only come into play when the latter had proved insufficient to explain a given concrete phenomenon.

But there can be no doubt that such fluctuations in the natural rate, conditioned by changes in the rate of saving activity, present some very important problems in interest theory, the solution of which would be an important aid in estimating the effect of fluctuations conditioned by monetary changes. We have entirely disregarded the circumstances determining the supply of savings and the fluctuations in this supply; and the examination of these is a promising field for future research. It might even be possible to show that fluctuations in saving activity are a necessary concomitant of economic progress, and thus to give a firm basis to the theories which we have mentioned. This is, perhaps, not very probable.

In direct relation to the above problem stands the question of the effects of alterations in the rate of interest on the price system as a whole. An examination of this subject should throw light on the point of view, emphasised by Professor Fetter,[15] that the height of interest rate, at any given moment expresses itself in the whole structure of price relationships, while every change in that rate must pari passu bring about changes in the relation between particular prices and thus in the quantitative relationships of the whole economy.

But here we must content ourselves with drawing attention to the problems arising out of the changes in the natural rate of interest, without contributing further to their solution. We shall only venture a further remark on a question concerning not the consequences but the causes of these changes, since this is important in what follows. This is the question whether the rate of interest at any moment depends on the total amount of capital existing at that moment or only on *the amount of free capital available for new investment*.[16] We mention this here only in order to emphasise the untenability of the widespread view that the determining factor, on the supply side, is the whole existing stock of capital. If that were so it would hardly be possible to explain any

---

[15] Fetter, "Interest Theory and Price Movements", especially p. 78. Cf. also lecture 3 of *Prices and Production.*

[16] 'Capital disposable for investment' was the phrase usually employed by the classical writers to distinguish this free capital from the stock of real capital. Cf., e.g., John Stuart Mill, *Essays on Some Unsettled Questions of Political Economy* (London: Parker, 1844), pp. 113ff. [Mill used the phrase "disposable capital" on pp. 113 and 115; cf. the reprint in *Essays on Economics and Society*, Part 1, ed. John M. Robson, vol. 4 (1967) of the *Collected Works of John Stuart Mill* (Toronto: University of Toronto Press; London: Routledge and Kegan Paul; reprinted, Indianapolis: Liberty Fund, 2006), pp. 304–5.—Ed.]

large fluctuations of the rate of interest, since the *relative* changes which the existing capital stock undergoes within brief periods and under normal circumstances is insignificant. A thorough investigation of the interconnections in this field must show that the actual rate of interest depends (apart from the demand for loan capital) only on the supply of newly produced or reproduced capital.[17] The existing stock of fixed capital affects only the demand side, by determining the yields to be expected from new investments. This explains how, in a country which is well equipped with fixed capital, the rate of interest can temporarily rise higher than that obtainable in a country which is poorly equipped, provided that there is relatively more free capital available for *new* investment in the latter than in the former. This fact has some significance in connection with the phenomenon of enforced saving with which we shall deal later.

4. The concept of a natural *or* equilibrium *rate of interest*

As regards the relationship of the natural or equilibrium rate of interest to the actual rate, it should be noted, in the first place, that even the existence of this distinction is questioned. The objections, however, mainly arise from a misunderstanding which occurred because K. Wicksell, who originated the distinction, made use in his later works of the term 'real rate' (which to my mind is less suitable than 'natural rate') and this expression became more widespread than that which we have used.[18] The expression 'real rate of interest' is also unsuitable, since it coincides with Professor Fisher's 'real interest',[19] which, as is well known, denotes the actual rate plus the rate of appreciation or minus the rate of depreciation of money, and is thus in accordance with common usage, which employs the term 'real wages' or 'real income' in the same sense. Unfortunately Wicksell's change in terminology is also linked up with a certain ambiguity in his definition of the 'natural rate'. Having correctly defined it once as "that rate at which the demand for loan capital just equals the supply of savings"[20] he redefines it, on another occasion, as that rate which would rule

---

[17] [In *Geldtheorie*, p. 124, Hayek refers to the "Angebot von neugebildetem und reproduziertem Kapital", that is, "the supply from new capital formation and from reproduced capital [that is, earned amortisations]". Note that Hayek speaks of funds, not of capital goods.—Ed.]

[18] Cf. the works of Professor Röpke and Dr. Burchardt, mentioned above; also Erich Egner, "Zur Lehre vom Zwangssparen" [*Zeitschrift für die gesamte Staatswissenschaft*, vol. 84, no. 3], 1928, p. 537. Occasionally (*Geldzins und Güterpreise*, p. 111 [cf. *Interest and Prices*, p. 120—Ed.]) Wicksell also uses the expression 'normal rate'.

[19] Cf. especially "Appreciation and Interest", *Publications of the American Economic Association*, vol. 11, July 1896 [reprinted in *The Works of Irving Fisher*, ed. Barber, vol. 1: *The Early Professional Works*, pp. 189–298; Hayek's citation is inaccurate, referring erroneously to vol. 11 of the "3rd series".—Ed.]

[20] *Vorlesungen*, vol. 2, p. 220 [cf. *Lectures*, vol. 2, p. 193—Ed.].

"if there were no money transactions and real capital were lent *in natura*".[21] If this last definition were correct, Dr. G. Halm[22] would be right in raising, against the conception of a 'natural rate', the objection that a uniform rate of interest could develop only in a money economy, so that the whole analysis is irrelevant. If Dr. Halm, instead of clinging to this unfortunate formula, had based his reasoning on the correct definition which is also to be found in Wicksell, he would have reached the same conclusion as Professor Adolf Weber—the distinguished head of the school of which he is a member;[23] that is, that the natural rate is a conception "which is evolved automatically from any clear study of economic interconnections".[24] In accordance with this view, Wicksell's conception must be credited with fundamental significance in the study of monetary influences on the economic system; especially if one realises the practical importance of a money rate of interest depressed below the natural rate by a constantly increasing volume of circulating media. Unfortunately, although Wicksell's solution cannot be regarded as adequate at all points, the attention which it has received since he propounded it has borne no relation to its importance. Apart from the works of Professor Mises, mentioned above,[25] the theory has made no progress at all, although many questions concerning it still await solution.[26] This may be due to the fact (on which

---

[21] *Geldzins und Güterpreise*, p. 93. [The Latin phrase *in natura* is taken from the German original. Cf. the translation in *Interest and Prices*, p. 102: "if no use were made of money and all lending were effected in the form of real capital goods".—Ed.]

[22] "Das Zinsproblem", p. 7n.

[23] [In *Geldtheorie*, p. 126, Hayek refers to Weber simply as "his [Halm's] teacher". Georg Nikolaus Halm's (1901–84) article was the published version of his doctoral thesis written under the supervision of Weber at the University of Munich. Thereafter Halm was appointed professor at the University of Würzburg; in 1936 he left Germany for the United States, where he taught as professor of international economic relations at Tufts University. In his contribution, "Further Considerations on the Possibility of Adequate Calculation in a Socialist Community", to *Collectivist Economic Planning*, ed. Hayek, pp. 131–200, he seconded the Austrian point of view.—Ed.]

[24] *Depositenbanken und Spekulationsbanken*, 3rd ed., p. 171. [Literally the quoted passage reads, "which must necessarily result from clearly thinking through these economic interrelationships" (my translation).—Ed.]

[25] [That is, *Theorie des Geldes und der Umlaufsmittel* and *Geldwertstabilisierung*.—Ed.]

[26] Another attempt to develop Wicksell's theory—of which I have learnt only since the above was written—was made, at roughly the time when Mises' work was published, by Prof. Marco Fanno of Padua in a work entitled *Le banche e il mercato monetario* (Rome: Athenaeum, 1912) [the second part translated as *The Money Market*, trans. Cyprian P. Blamires (New York: St. Martin's Press, 1995)—Ed.]. An abridged restatement of Prof. Fanno's theory will shortly appear, in German, in a volume of essays on monetary theory by a number of Dutch, Italian, and Swedish authors, edited by the author of the present essay. [Cf. Marco Fanno, "Die reine Theorie des Geldmarktes", in *Beiträge zur Geldtheorie*, ed. Hayek, pp. 1–113. The other contributors to this volume have been Marius W. Holtrop, Johan G. Koopmans, Gunnar Myrdal, and the late Knut Wicksell.—Ed.]

we have touched already) that the problem had become entangled with that of fluctuations in the general price level. We have already stated our views on this point,[27] and indicated what is necessary for the further development of the theory. Here, we shall try to restate the problem in its correct form, freed from any reference to movements in the price level.

5. The relation between the equilibrium rate and the actual (money) rate of interest

Every given structure of production, i.e., every given allocation of goods as between different branches and stages of production, requires a certain definite relationship between the prices of the finished products and those of the means of production. In a state of equilibrium, the difference necessarily existing between these two sets of prices must correspond to the rate of interest, and at this rate, just as much must be saved from current consumption and made available for investment[28] as is necessary for the maintenance of that structure of production. The latter condition necessarily follows from the fulfilment of the former, since the prices paid for the means of production, plus interest, can only correspond to the prices of the resulting products when, at the given prices and rate of interest, the supply of producers' goods is exactly adequate to maintain production on the existing scale. The price margins between means of production and products, therefore, can only remain constant and in correspondence with the rate of interest so long as the proportion of current income, which at the given rate of interest is not consumed but reinvested in production, remains exactly equal to the necessary capital required to carry on production. Every change in this proportion must begin by impairing the correspondence of price margins and the interest rate; for it influences both in opposite directions, and so leads to further shifts in the whole structure of production, representing an adjustment to altered price-relationships. These resulting changes in the structure of production will not always be the same; they will vary according to whether the change in the proportions of the social income going respectively to consumption goods and investment goods corresponds to real changes in the decisions of individuals as to spending and saving, or whether it was brought about artificially, without any corresponding changes in individual saving activity.

Apart from individual saving activity (which includes, of course, the savings of corporations, of the State and of other bodies entitled to raise compul-

---

[27] See above, p. 145.

[28] [In *Geldtheorie*, p. 127, Hayek does not use the exact equivalents of "saved" and "investment", but writes: "just as much must be stinted of current consumption and made available for capitalistic production . . ."—Ed.]

sory contributions) the proportions between consumption and capital creation can only change as a result of alterations in the effective quantity of money.[29] When changes in the division of the total social dividend,[30] in favour of capital creation, result from changes in the saving activity of individuals, they are self-perpetuating. This is not true of such variations between 'consumption and accumulation' (if we may use for once the terminology of Marxian literature) as are due to additional credits granted to the entrepreneurs; these can be assumed to persist only so long as the proportion is kept artificially high by a progressively increasing rate of credit creation. Such an injection of money into circulation acts only temporarily—*until the additional money becomes income. At that moment, the proportion of capital creation must relapse to the level of voluntary saving activity*, unless *new* credits are granted bearing the same relation to the new total of money incomes as the first injection bore to the former total.[31]

It is clear that such a process of progressive increase in the supply of money cannot be maintained under our existing credit system, especially since, as it proceeds, more extensive use will be made of cash. On the other hand, a mere cessation of further increases—not, therefore, a reversal of credit policy, towards deflation—is sufficient to bring back the proportion of total income available for capital formation to the extent of voluntary savings.

The differences in the effects of these two kinds of variation between consumption and capital formation manifest themselves first of all on the price system, and thus on the natural or equilibrium rate of interest. The first effect of a *diminution of the rate on loans arising from increased saving activity*—so long as the structure of production remains unchanged—is to bring that rate below the margin between the prices of means of production and of products. The increased saving activity, however, must soon cause on the one hand a fall-

---

[29] Very instructive investigations of the problems considered here were carried out by Lampe, *Zur Theorie des Sparprozesses*.

[30] [The 'social' or 'national dividend' is a notion, largely corresponding to net income or net product, introduced by Arthur C. Pigou as a rough measure of economic welfare; cf. his *Wealth and Welfare* (London: Macmillan, 1912), reprinted as vol. 2 of *Collected Economic Writings*, especially pp. 14–16. In *Geldtheorie*, p. 128, Hayek speaks simply of the "total product".—Ed.]

[31] The argument presented in the text (and put in this form for brevity's sake) is imperfect in two respects. Firstly, the flow of voluntary saving can itself vary as a result of a single change in the proportion of capital formation. This factor, however, is unlikely to become important enough for its omission to affect the exposition given in the text. Secondly, the way in which the additional money, which was given in the first instance to entrepreneurs and used by them to lengthen the period of production, will always swell incomes in the long run, needs further elaboration. As a general proposition, however, it is obvious that whoever uses the additional credits to make additional investment goods can do so only by employing additional factors of production; and therefore, since there is in our case no compensating decrease in the demand for factors elsewhere, the total incomes of the factors must increase.

ing off in the demand for consumption goods, and hence a tendency for their prices to fall (a tendency which may merely find expression in decreasing sales at existing prices) and, on the other hand, an increase in the demand for investment goods[32] and thus a rise in their prices. The extension of production will have a further depressing effect on the prices of consumption goods, as the new products come on the market, until, finally, the difference between the respective prices has shrunk to a magnitude corresponding to the new, lower, interest rate. If, however, the fall in the rate of interest is due to an *increase in the circulating media*, it can never lead to a corresponding diminution in the price margin, or to a readjustment of the two sets of prices to the level of an equilibrium rate of interest which will endure. In this case, moreover, the increased demand for investment goods will bring about a net increase in the demand for consumption goods; and therefore the price margin cannot be narrowed more than is permitted by the time-lag in the rise of consumption goods prices—a lag existing only as long as the process of inflation[33] continues. As soon as the cessation of credit inflation puts a stop to the rise in the prices of investment goods, the difference between these and the prices of consumption goods will increase again, not only to its previous level but beyond, since, in the course of inflation, the structure of production has been so shifted that in comparison with the division of the social income between expenditure and saving the supply of consumption goods will be relatively less, and that of production goods relatively greater, than before the inflation began.[34]

6. Forced saving *as a cause of economic crises*

There have recently been increasingly frequent objections to this account of the effects of an increased volume of currency, and the artificial lowering of interest rates conditioned by it, on the grounds that it disregards certain supposedly beneficial effects which are closely connected with this phenomenon. What the objectors have in mind is the phenomenon of so-called 'forced sav-

[32] [Here and in the following, *Produktivgüter* (*Geldtheorie*, p. 129), that is, "producers' goods" or "means of production" (in the terminology used in *Prices and Production*, p. 220), is translated as "investment goods".—Ed.]

[33] [It should be noted that Hayek uses 'inflation' (and conversely, 'deflation') always in the broader sense of an increase in the circulation of money (and not of the price level). In this respect, Gottfried Haberler had coined the term 'relative inflation' for the case of an economy experiencing credit inflation, yet with a stable price level; cf. "Money and the Business Cycle", in *Gold and Monetary Stabilization: Lectures on the Harris Foundation 1932*, ed. Quincy Wright (Chicago: University of Chicago Press, 1932), p. 56, reprinted in *Business Cycle Theory: Selected Texts 1860–1939*, vol. 3, ed. Hagemann, p. 272.—Ed.]

[34] Cf. my article on "The 'Paradox' of Saving", p. 160 [reprinted, pp. 110–11—Ed.].

ing' which has received great attention in recent literature.[35] This phenomenon, we are to understand, consists in an increase in capital creation at the cost of consumption, through the granting of additional credit, *without* voluntary action on the part of the individuals who forgo consumption, and without their deriving any immediate benefit. According to the usual presentation of the theory of forced saving, this occurs through a fall in the general value of money, which diminishes the consumers' purchasing power; the volume of goods thus freed can be used by the producers who obtained additional credits. We must, however, raise the same objection to this theory which we raised against the usual account of the effects of an artificial lowering of the money rate of interest, i.e., that, in principle, forced saving takes place whenever the volume of money is increased, and does not need to manifest itself in changes in the value of money.[36]

The 'depreciation' of money in the hands of the consumer can be, and frequently will be, only relative, in the sense that those diminutions in price which would otherwise have occurred are prevented from occurring. Even this causes a part of the social dividend to be distributed to individuals who have not acquired legitimate claim to it through previous services, nor taken them over from others legitimately entitled to them. It is thus taken away from this part of the community against its will. After what has been said above, this process needs no further illumination.

Nor do we need to adduce further proof that every grant of additional credit induces 'forced saving'—even if we have avoided using this rather unfortunate expression in the course of our argument. There is only one further point— the effect of this artificially induced capital accumulation—on which a few remarks should be added. It has often been argued that the forced saving arising from an artificially lowered interest rate would improve the capital supply

[35] Besides Léon Walras—the originator of this theory (cf. his *Études d'économie politique appliquée* (Lausanne: Rouge; Paris: Pichon, 1898 [2nd ed., 1936]), pp. 348–56), Wicksell, and the well-known works of Professors Mises and Schumpeter, one must mention the recent works of Professor Röpke, Dr. Egner, and Dr. Neisser; and in Anglo-Saxon literature, Mr. D. H. Robertson's *Banking Policy and the Price Level*. As I have pointed out, however, in lecture 1 of *Prices and Production* and—at somewhat greater length—in "A Note on the Development of the Theory [Doctrine] of 'Forced Saving'", *Quarterly Journal of Economics*, vol. 47, November 1932, pp. 123–33 [reprinted as chapter 3 in F. A. Hayek, *Business Cycles, Part II*—Ed.], the concept of 'forced saving' was already known to J. Bentham, H. Thornton, T. R. Malthus, and a number of other writers in the early 19th century, down to J. S. Mill. [Hayek more thoroughly discusses the Walrasian origin in "A Note on the Development of the Doctrine of 'Forced Saving'", reprinted, pp. 167–69. The source quoted above is Walras's "Théorie mathématique du billet de banque" [1879], reprinted in vol. 10 of Auguste et Léon Walras, *Oeuvres économiques complètes* (Paris: Economica, 1992), pp. 318–26, translated by Jan van Daal as "Mathematical Theory of Banknotes", in *Studies in Applied Economics*, vol. 2 (London: Routledge, 2005), pp. 280–85.—Ed.]

[36] Cf. Robertson, *Money*, p. 99; and Pigou, *Industrial Fluctuations*, pp. 251–57.

of the economy to such an extent that the natural rate of interest would have to fall finally to the level of the money rate of interest, and thus a new state of equilibrium would be created—that is, the crisis could be avoided altogether.[37] This view is closely connected with the thesis, which we have already rejected, that the level of the natural rate of interest depends directly upon the whole existing stock of real capital. Forced saving increases only the existing stock of real capital goods, but not necessarily the current supply of free capital disposable for investment—that portion of total income[38] which is not consumed but used as a provision for the upkeep and depreciation of fixed plant. But any addition to the supply of free capital available for new investment or reinvestment must come from those of the investments induced by forced savings which already yield a return; a return large enough to leave over, after providing for supplementary costs connected with the new means of production, a surplus for depreciation and for interest payments on the capital. If the capital supply from this source is to lower the natural rate of interest, it must not, of course, be offset by a diminution elsewhere—resulting from the decline of other undertakings confronted with the reinforced competition of those newly supplied with capital.

The assumption that an artificial increase of fixed capital (i.e., one caused by additional credits) tends to diminish the natural rate of interest in the same way as one effected through voluntary savings activity presupposes, therefore, that the new capital must be incorporated into the economic system in such a way that the prices of the products imputed to it shall cover interest and depreciation. Now a given stock of capital goods is not a factor which will maintain and renew itself automatically, irrespective of whether it is in accordance with the current supply of savings or not. The fact that investments have been undertaken which cannot be 'undone' offers no guarantee whatever that this is the case. Whether capital can be created beyond the limits set by voluntary saving depends—and this is just as true for its renewal as for the creation of new plant—on whether the process of credit creation continues in a steadily increasing ratio. If the new processes of production are to be completed, and if those already in existence are to continue in employment, it is essential that additional credits should be continually injected at a rate which increases fast enough to keep ahead, by a constant proportion, of the expanding purchasing power of the consumer.[39] If a new process of roundabout production can be

[37] [This argument can be found, for example, in Cassel, *The Theory of Social Economy*, new rev. ed., pp. 437–38.—Ed.]

[38] [Here "total income" stands for *Bruttoeinkommen* (*Geldtheorie*, p. 132), that is, gross income inclusive of depreciation allowances.—Ed.]

[39] [As formulated by Hayek, this requires only a constant—not an accelerating—rate of credit inflation; cf. on this David Laidler, *Fabricating the Keynesian Revolution: Studies of the Inter-war Literature on Money, the Cycle, and Unemployment* (Cambridge: Cambridge University Press, 1999),

completed while these conditions still hold good, it can contribute temporarily to a lowering of the natural rate of interest; but this provides no final solution of the difficulty.

For, eventually, a moment must inevitably arrive when the banks are unable any longer to keep up the rate of inflation required, and at that moment there must always be some processes of production, newly undertaken and not yet completed,[40] which were only ventured because the rate of interest was kept artificially low. It does not follow, of course, that these processes in particular will be left unfinished because of the subsequent rise in that rate; on the other hand, their existence does cause the rate of interest to be higher than it would be in their absence, when capital would be required only by processes made possible by voluntary saving without any competing demand arising from processes which were only enabled to start by 'forced saving'. The capital invested in new and not yet completed processes of production will thus merely intensify the demand for further supplies by calling for the capital necessary to complete them—an effect which will be the more pronounced the greater the ratio of capital invested to capital still required. It may therefore quite easily come about that, in order to complete these newly initiated processes, capital may be diverted from the maintenance of complete and old-established undertakings, so that new plant is put into operation and old plant closed down, although the latter would have been kept up, and the former never put in hand, if it had been a question of building up the whole capital equipment of the economy from the start. This does not merely mean that the total return comes to less than it otherwise would; it also means, pri-

---

pp. 43–44. An accelerating rate of credit (and price) inflation would however result as soon as the effect of inflationary expectations were taken into account—an effect of which Hayek must have been aware from his experience with the hyperinflations in Central Europe during the 1920s. See also Hayek's reference to expectations in "Three Elucidations of the Ricardo Effect", *Journal of Political Economy*, vol. 77, March/April 1969, reprinted in F. A. Hayek, *Business Cycles, Part II*, p. 325.—Ed.]

[40] The existence of new long processes, which have not yet been completed, is not a necessary condition in order that the relative increase in the demand for consumers' goods may lead to the abandonment of such processes and, therefore, to the destruction of part of the capital employed there; but it is the case which will always be given in practice and where this effect is most easily seen. In this connection it should, however, be noted that the introduction of a longer roundabout process of production will, in almost all cases, affect not only a single enterprise but a series of enterprises representing successive stages of production. Even a completed plant may, in this sense, represent part of an incomplete process—if the capital is lacking which would have to be invested in the machines or other capital goods to be produced by this plant. Plant equipped to satisfy a demand for machinery which cannot be permanently maintained is, in this sense, part of a roundabout process which cannot be continued. For a fuller description, see *Prices and Production*, lecture 3, and, especially, my article "Kapitalaufzehrung" [cf. "Capital Consumption"—Ed.].

marily, that production is forced into channels to which it will only keep for as long as the new and spuriously produced stock of fixed capital can remain in use. The value of capital invested in processes which can be continued, and, still more, that in processes where continuance is impracticable, will shrink rapidly in value—this shrinkage being accompanied by the phenomena of a crisis. Thus on purely technical grounds it will become uneconomic to maintain them.[41] It should be particularly remarked that, from the point of view of the fate of individual enterprises, capital invested in fixed plant, but raised by borrowing, is of precisely the same importance as working capital, i.e., the loss of value does not merely necessitate writing down, it generally makes it impossible to carry on at all.

The cause of this development is, evidently, that an unwarranted accumulation of capital has been taking place; though people may regard it (under the alluring name of 'forced saving') as a thoroughly desirable phenomenon. After what has been said above *it is probably more proper to regard forced saving as the cause of economic crises than to expect it to restore a balanced structure of production.*

7. Interest rates in the money *and* capital *markets respectively*

There remains one problem of interest theory, in the wider sense of the word, which we need to examine more closely than we have yet done—in order to exhibit a problem of first-class importance to the progress of Trade Cycle theory. This is the problem of the varying height and independent movements of rates of interest ruling at the same place and at the same time. We are not thinking, of course, of differences conditioned either by the unequal standing of borrowers or by the fact that under the name of interest payments are also made for the services or costs connected with the granting of credit. We are interested only in the problem of variations arising *within* the pure or net rate of interest, as they can be observed between credits of varying duration—the problem usually known in economic literature as the problem of interest rates, in the *money*, and in the *capital* (investment) market, respectively.

In this respect we may repeat what we have already said at the beginning of this chapter—that the theoretical investigations of interest have been broken off at far too early a stage to afford much understanding of the rates actually ruling at any given moment. It is very remarkable that none of the great theorists to whom we owe our insight into the fundamental factors determining the equilibrium rate of interest made the slightest attempt to explain these differences between interest rates. Systematic investigation of this problem came

---

[41] [That is, "to maintain the processes in question".—Ed.]

much later and then characteristically the investigation related chiefly to the question of the "external order of the capital or money market"; and it is only recently that Dr. G. Halm[42] has treated the simultaneous existence of varying interest rates "as a problem of interest theory".[43] Although Dr. Halm deserves full credit for the undeniable service he has rendered in putting the problem in the proper form for discussion, his attempt at solution can hardly be regarded as fully successful. Thus we still stand at the beginning of a crucially important development of a special theory of money rates of interest.

The clearing up of these interconnections is of primary importance to Trade Cycle theory, since the discrepancies between the expected yields of existing means of production and the actual yield obtainable from the available liquid capital must necessarily arise in the course of the cycle. Given a sufficient insight into the influences determining the yields of both types of investment, the simultaneous changes in the height of both kinds of interest rates should afford extraordinarily valuable material for the diagnosis of any actual situation, and thus the growth of this part of interest theory would provide an important basis for the development of empirical research and forecasting.[44] A particularly promising approach might consist in an examination of the ques-

[42] "Das Zinsproblem". Of the comprehensive bibliography given by Halm, the following, together with some more recent additions, are worth mention: Arthur Spiethoff: (1) "Die äußere Ordnung des Kapital- und Geldmarktes" [that is, "The External Order of the Capital and Money Market", as quoted in the text—Ed.]; (2) "Das Verhältnis von Kapital, Geld und Güterwelt"; (3) "Der Kapitalmangel in seinem Verhältnis[se] zur Güterwelt", all in Schmoller's *Jahrbuch für Gesetzgebung, Verwaltung und Volkswirtschaft im Deutschen Reiche*, vol. 33, 1909, no. 2, pp. 17–39, no. 3, pp. 65–89, and no. 4, pp. 43–63, respectively. Also, by the same author: "Der Begriff des Kapital- und Geldmarktes", *Schmollers Jahrbuch für Gesetzgebung, Verwaltung und Volkswirtschaft im Deutschen Reiche*, vol. 44, no. 4, 1920, pp. 33–52, [which is a critical review of] Herbert von Beckerath, *Kapital[markt] und Geldmarkt* (Jena: Fischer, 1916).

Professor Schumpeter's, Dr. Neisser's, and Professor Fetter's works already mentioned; Albert Hahn, "Zur Theorie des Geldmarktes", *Archiv für Sozialwissenschaft und Sozialpolitik*, vol. 51, no. 2, 1924, pp. 289–321; Karin Kock, *A Study of Interest Rates*, Stockholm Economic Studies, no. 1 (London: King, 1929).

Winfield W. Riefler, *Money Rates and [Money] Markets in the United States* (New York and London: Harper, 1930).

The problems arising out of empirical research are well summarised by Otto Donner and Arthur Hanau, "Untersuchungen zur Frage der Marktzusammenhänge", *Vierteljahrshefte zur Konjunkturforschung*, 3rd year, no. 3A [that is, series A, vol. 3, no. 2] (Berlin: Institut für Konjunkturforschung, 1928), an investigation which is a model of its kind. [The article in question was published anonymously. Arthur Hanau (1902–85) became famous for his work on the hog cycle; cf. his "Die Prognose der Schweinepreise", *Vierteljahrshefte zur Konjunkturforschung*, Sonderheft 2 (Berlin: Hobbing, 1927).—Ed.]

[43] [Cf. Halm, "Das Zinsproblem", p. 2, where he refers to "the simultaneous existence of varying yield curves [*Zinskurven*] as an essential problem of interest theory" (my translation).—Ed.]

[44] [*Geldtheorie*, p. 138, less specifically, refers to "the development of practical business cycle research".—Ed.]

tion from the point of view of an equalisation of the time-differences between the rates of interest which would prevail if the whole supply of capital, at any time, had to be invested for a longer period.[45] Such an equalisation would be brought about by a kind of *arbitrage* for which, naturally, only money lent at call or at short notice could be considered.

In this field, too, the extension of equilibrium analysis to successively occurring phenomena, which I have attempted in another work,[46] may prove fruitful. At any rate, an explanation of this arbitrage could also explain why the rates on short-term credits can be temporarily lower, or on the other hand higher, than the long-term rate, since both borrower and lender would find such an arbitrage to their advantage. This view cannot be refuted by the objection that the rates on short-term credits not only change earlier but also change to a greater degree than those in the capital market; for it may be economically entirely justifiable to pay higher rates or obtain lower ones, for a short term, than one expects for a long term, since the expectation of getting better terms at a later period, under more favourable conditions, may compensate for the relative disadvantages suffered in the short run.

8. *Problems for statistical investigation*

Finally, we should like to point out quite briefly certain tasks in the field of statistical research which according to our theoretical analysis seem likely to be particularly fruitful. In connection with the last question dealt with, we should draw attention to the statistics of the money market, which are still, unfortunately, in a very elementary stage, partly for technical reasons but mainly because of difficulties of interpretation. These latter arise largely from the fact that the statistical determination of the absolute height of the interest rate, or even of its movements, discloses almost nothing as to its bearing on the economic system.[47] The same rate of interest which at one moment may be too low in relation to the whole economic situation may be too high at the next, or vice versa. Misunderstandings on this point may be responsible for certain erroneous views, concerning the alleged insignificance of the height of interest rates, which are often held by statistical economists. The innumerable attempts to minimise the significance of interest rates by means of statistical

---

[45] [More accurately, "for the same longer period" (cf. *Geldtheorie*, p. 138).—Ed.]

[46] Cf. "Das intertemporale Gleichgewichtssystem der Preise" ["Intertemporal Price Equilibrium"—Ed.], already quoted.

[47] The statistical determination of nominal changes in the interest rate is also rendered very difficult by the fact that changes can take place in the form of changes in stipulations as to the quality of the bills discounted at a given rate, and so on. The same rate may be merely applied to a better class of borrowers, or the same borrowers may be required to pay a higher rate.

investigations, which abound in the United States[48] (where they do not even shrink from such absurdities as an attempt to find an explanation (!) of interest by way of statistical investigation), would be impossible but for the complete confusion persisting as to the limits of statistical research. Here again we have to repeat what was asserted at the beginning of this book: statistics can never prove or disprove a theoretical explanation, they can only present problems or offer fields for theoretical research.

For precisely this reason—viz. that the absolute height of interest rates tells us nothing of their significance—an examination of the extent and regularity of *shifts* between various interest rates offers a promising field for statistical technique. An interesting first attempt in this direction is the famous 'Three Market Barometer' of the Harvard Economic Service,[49] which uses the trend of the long-term interest rate as a base-line in plotting the curve of the money market rates. Such an empirical consideration of the differences between interest rates does not, of course, exhaust the lines of approach which a complete theoretical explanation of these rates might indicate as suitable for empirical research. The fact that theoretical research itself can be stimulated and awakened to new problems to an important degree from the application of our sketchy knowledge to statistical investigations is amply demonstrated by the investigations of Donner and Hanau, which we have already mentioned.

It is in the statistics of private banking, however, that the heaviest task presents itself. In Europe we are still worse supplied with these than with those of the money market proper. In the United States, on the other hand, some pioneer work has been done in this field,[50] since the ample statistical material available there provided is itself a sufficient incentive for such investigations.

---

[48] Cf., e.g., Carl Snyder, "The Influence of the Interest Rate on the Business Cycle", *American Economic Review*, vol. 15, December 1925, pp. 684–99, reprinted [in a revised version, "The Interest Rate and the Business Cycle"—Ed.] in *Business Cycles and Business Measurements* (New York: Macmillan, 1927), pp. 205–29.

[49] [Cf. the editor's note, p. 73, above.—Ed.]

[50] Cf. first of all Allyn Abbott Young, *An Analysis of Bank Statistics for the United States* (Cambridge, MA: Harvard University Press, 1928), reprinted from *Review of Economic Statistics*, vol. 6, October 1924, pp. 284–96, vol. 7, January 1925, pp. 19–37 and April 1925, pp. 86–104, and vol. 9, July 1927, pp. 121–41; Holbrook Working, "Prices and the Quantity of the Circulating Medium [of Circulating Medium], 1890–1921", *Quarterly Journal of Economics*, vol. 37, February 1923, pp. 228–56, and "Bank Deposits as a Forecaster of the General Wholesale Price Level", *Review of Economic Statistics*, vol. 8, July 1926, pp. 120–33, of the same author; Carl Snyder, "Deposits Activity as a Measure of Business Activity", *Review of Economic Statistics*, vol. 6, October 1924, pp. 253–59, reprinted in *Business Cycles and Business Measurements* [chapter 7 is a summary of some of his papers on the same issue—Ed.]; Warren M. Persons, "Cyclical Fluctuations of the Ratio of Bank Loans to Deposits", *Review of Economic Statistics*, vol. 6, October 1924, pp. 260–83; L. Albert Hahn, "Zur Frage des volkswirtschaftlichen Erkenntnisinhalts der Bankbilanzziffern", *Vierteljahrshefte zur Konjunkturforschung*, vol. 1, 1926, Ergänzungsheft 4 (Berlin, Hobbing, 1927), pp. 49–70.

In Europe the lack of any kind of material makes even a first step in this direction impossible.

In many respects the most remarkable of these enquiries are those of Mr. Holbrook Working. Using the data concerning the state of deposits in the 'National Banks',[51] which are available for many years past and at intervals of only a few months, he succeeds in establishing a far-reaching parallelism between the movements of deposits and the fluctuations of the wholesale price level. Like most theoretical investigations in the same field, however, his results are distorted by the superficial assumption that monetary influences can only manifest themselves in movements of the price level, while those changes in the volume of bank credits which are just sufficient to prevent changes in the price level are supposed, on this assumption, to exercise no active influence on the Trade Cycle. It should be mentioned—as having particular bearing upon the views developed in this essay—that, according to Mr. Working's calculations, before the War[52] a yearly increase in deposits of more than 5 per cent would have been necessary in order to keep the price level steady; that is to say, additional credits would have had to be created to an extent which must have caused considerable changes in the structure of production.

If the results of our theoretical analysis were to be subjected to statistical investigation, it is not the connection between changes in the volume of bank credit and movements in the price level which would have to be explored. Investigation would have to start on the one hand from alterations in the rate of increase and decrease in the volume and turnover of bank deposits and, on the other, from the extent of production in those industries which as a rule expand excessively as a result of credit injection.[53] Every increase in the circulating media brings about the same effect, so long as each *stands in the same proportion* to the existing volume; and only an increase in this proportion makes possible a further increase in investment activity. On the other hand, every diminution of the *rate of increase* in itself causes some portion of existing investment, made possible through credit creation, to become unprofitable. It follows that a curve exhibiting the monetary influences on the course of the cycle ought to show not the movements in the total volume of circulating media, but the alteration in the rate of change of this volume.[54] Every up-turn of this

[51] [National banks are U.S. commercial banks established by federal charter; they are compelled to join the Federal Reserve System (in contrast to state banks, which are state chartered and need not be members of the Federal Reserve System).—Ed.]

[52] [That is, World War I.—Ed.]

[53] Cf. the instructive graphs given by Harold L. Reed in his *Federal Reserve Policy 1921–1930* (New York and London: McGraw Hill, 1930), pp. 181 et seq. [pp. 181–82].

[54] Mathematically speaking, the question is one of the graphical presentation, in place of the curve showing the original movements at any moment, of the first differential of this function. On the subject of this method, which has been frequently used of late, cf. Irving Fisher, "The

curve would show that an artificial lowering of the money rate of interest or, if the curve was already rising, a further lowering of the money rates, was making possible additional investments for which voluntary savings would not suffice; and every down-turn would show that current credit creation was no longer sufficient to ensure the continuance of all the enterprises which it originally called into existence. It would be of great interest to correlate this presentation of the influence causing an excessive production of capital goods with actual changes in the production of these goods, on the basis of available data.[55]

The possible contributions of banking statistics to Trade Cycle research are by no means exhausted by the chance they offer of observing the immediate connection between the granting of credit and the movements of production, though these may some day constitute the most important basis of business forecasting. No less important would be an investigation into the volume, at any given moment, of those factors which determine credit expansion, under the other headings of bank balance sheets, and, in particular, an examination of the relation between the total amount of earning assets and the current accounts, the relation between these and the cash-circulation, and so on. Such an investigation, if it were not merely to exhibit their movements in time but also to analyse the deeper connections between them, and most especially if it were to clear up the relationship between interest rates, profits, and the liquidity of the banks, would further our insight into the factors determining credit expansion as well as our knowledge of their limits, and thus make it possible to forecast movements in the factors determining the total development of the economic situation.

It is very unfortunate that such inquiries, especially on the continent of Europe, are almost impossible owing to the lack of necessary data in the form of returns showing the state of the banks, and published at short intervals; in so far as they are possible at all it is only in a few countries and for a very short period.[56] As soon as it is realised that, owing to the existence of banks,

---

Business Cycle Largely a 'Dance of the Dollar'", *Quarterly Publication of the American Statistical Association* [*Journal of the American Statistical Association*—Ed.], vol. 18, December 1923, pp. 1024–28 [reprinted in *The Works of Irving Fisher*, ed. Barber, vol. 8: *The Money Illusion*, pp. 8–12.—Ed.].

[55] [Hayek's opinion on the most promising path for future empirical work may be gauged from a letter to Gottfried Haberler (September 9, 1934, in the Gottfried Haberler Papers, box 66, Hoover Institution Archives, Stanford University). With regard to an empirical supplement to Haberler's League of Nations study (which eventually turned into *Prosperity and Depression*) Hayek suggested an investigation into the relative movements of profits in the various branches of production typical for producers' and consumers' goods.—Ed.]

[56] [In 1929 the text of *Geldtheorie*, pp. 144–45, contained the following sentence: "The great progress witnessed in the United States not only with regard to the insight into the causes of cyclical fluctuations, but also to the methods of business cycle policy, can be attributed to the fact that legislation has enforced on the banks a far-reaching and still increasing duty of publicity" (my translation).—Ed.]

the equilibrating forces of the economic system cannot bring about that automatic adjustment of all its branches to the actual situation, which is described by classical economic theory, it is justifiable even from a liberal point of view that the banks should be subjected to degrees of publicity as to the state of their business which is not necessary in the case of other undertakings; and this would by no means imply a violation of the principle of business secrecy, since it would be quite sufficient for this purpose if the authorities were to adopt the United States' plan of publishing summary returns for all banks at frequent intervals. Our reflections thus yield the conclusion that an alleviation of cyclical fluctuations should be expected pre-eminently from a greater publicity among business enterprises, and particularly among the banks. The example of the United States, which is far ahead in this respect in all the branches of its economic system, will not only silence in time the objections raised against such publicity, but sooner or later will force us to follow in their path.

PRICES AND PRODUCTION

FOREWORD TO THE FIRST EDITION (1931)

The pure theory of economic equilibrium, the great achievement of nineteenth century Economics, provides no explanation of trade depression. It explains the tendencies conducive to stability in the economic system. It explains the forces making for readjustment in the face of external change. But it does not explain the occurrence of periodic disequilibrium. It does not exclude the possibility of fluctuations in the sense of orderly adaptations. But it does not explain the existence within the economic system of tendencies conducive to disproportionate development. It does not explain the existence of tendencies which conduce to movement *away* from the 'ideal' equilibrium.

To explain these tendencies it is therefore necessary to invoke factors not contemplated by this theory. It is necessary to show the existence within the economic system of factors whose operation is not taken into account by the pure theory of equilibrium. Of these factors, the most conspicuous are fluctuations in the volume or the 'efficiency' of the prevailing means of payment—'monetary factors' as it is customary to call them. It is almost axiomatic that fluctuations in the volume or the 'efficiency' of money must complicate the operation of the equilibrating tendencies. In the pure theory of equilibrium, the spending power in the hands of spenders is made available by the general process of production. Money which is free to be spent on commodities has been released by the production of other commodities. Incomes fluctuate with the value of marginal net products. In such circumstances it is difficult to see how general disequilibrium can arise. But if spending power is varied, either by the operation of state printing presses or by the credit-creating manipulations of central banks, a new situation is created. Some spending power is now available which has not been released by the production of other commodities. The forces mirrored in the equations of equilibrium no longer alone determine the money receipts of producers. A guarantee that equilibrium will be preserved is no longer given.

Here, then, is the clue which is the rational basis of all attempts to provide a monetary explanation of cyclical fluctuation. Unfortunately, hitherto, as Dr. Hayek has shown,[1] the majority of such attempts have not been suc-

---

[1] See lecture 1 below, and *Geldtheorie und Konjunkturtheorie*. Beiträge zur Konjunkturforschung, vol. 1, ed. Österreichisches Institut für Konjunkturforschung (Vienna: Springer, 1929 [reprinted,

cessful. Misled by a preoccupation with the *value* of money, they have concentrated only on the causes and effects of changes in the so-called general level of prices, to the exclusion of the more fundamental problem of the effects of changes in the *supply* of money. In so doing, they have failed completely to produce a theory which explains those changes in the 'real' structure of production which are the most characteristic feature of trade fluctuation as we know it. In short, the monetary theories have been too monetary. They have treated fluctuations in monetary factors as merely general and superficial phenomena. They have totally failed to bring the theory of money into harmony with the theory of production.

But there is one group of monetary theories which is immune from these strictures. The School of Vienna, which in recent years, under the leadership of Professor Mayer[2] and Professor Mises, has experienced such a marvellous renaissance, has laid the scientific world under yet another lasting obligation. Working on the basis of the Böhm-Bawerkian theory of capital and the Wicksellian theory of divergences between money and equilibrium rates of interest, Professor Mises and Dr. Hayek have advanced theories which, though they fall into the general category of monetary explanations, yet seem altogether free from those deficiencies which have marked monetary explanations in general. They explain the effects of fluctuations in the supply of money not so much in terms of fluctuations of the general price level as in terms of fluctuations of relative prices and the consequent effects on what may be called the 'time-structure' of production. In this way they succeed in reconciling the facts of the credit system as explained by, say, Mr. R. G. Hawtrey with the 'real' disproportionalities of the trade cycle as observed by such writers as Cassel and Spiethoff.

I do not think that in the past these theories have received sufficient attention in this country. Böhm-Bawerk is translated[3] but seldom read. (It is com-

---

Salzburg: Neugebauer, 1976; translated as *Monetary Theory and the Trade Cycle*, trans. Nicholas Kaldor and Honoria Croome (London: Cape, 1933), reprinted in this volume—Ed.], chapters 2 and 3.

[2] [Hans Mayer (1879–1955) was a student of Friedrich Wieser, whom he succeeded in 1923 as professor of economics at the University of Vienna. From 1929 he edited the *Zeitschrift für Nationalökonomie*, yet in his scientific accomplishments was not able to live up to the expectations of his fellow Austrian economists. On Mises see above, p. 60. See also the editor's introduction to this volume, pp. 1–7.—Ed.]

[3] Unfortunately only in the first edition. The fourth edition, with its new volume of critical excursions, probably the most remarkable feat of dialectics in the whole literature of Economic Theory, is still inaccessible to those English-speaking economists who do not think it worth while learning German. [Robbins refers to Eugen von Böhm-Bawerk's *Kapital und Kapitalzins*, 1st ed., vol. 1: *Geschichte der Kapitalzinstheorien*, and vol. 2: *Positive Theorie des Kapitales* (Innsbruck: Wagner, 1884 and 1889; reprinted, Düsseldorf: Verlag Wirtschaft und Finanzen, 1994 and 1991), and its translation as *Capital and Interest*, vol. 1: *A Critical History of Economical Theory*, and vol. 2: *The Posi-*

monly thought, I believe, that Marshall disposed of him in a footnote.[4]) Wicksell was almost unheard of until the other day; even now, the existence of his magnum opus, the *Vorlesungen über Nationalökonomie* (which is much later in time and much more refined in theory than the suddenly celebrated *Geldzins und Güterpreise*) has yet to be discovered.[5] And, outside the alumni of one institution, I doubt whether half-a-dozen people in the country have read Professor Mises' monumental treatise on Money[6] which, since 1912, has explained to first-year students on the Continent the notions of 'forced saving' and money rates of interest out of harmony with equilibrium rates—not to mention all that is true in the 'purchasing power parity' theory of the foreign exchanges[7] and a host of other good things which have since been rediscovered by others. I hope that the publication of Dr. Hayek's Lectures, which stand in the midstream of this great tradition, will do something to persuade English readers that here is a school of thought which can only be neglected at the cost of los-

---

tive Theory of Capital, trans. William Smart (London: Macmillan, 1890 and 1891; reprinted, New York: Kelley, 1970). The fourth edition in three volumes (Jena: Fischer, 1921) has since been translated as *Capital and Interest*, vol. 1: *History and Critique of Interest Theories*, vol. 2: *Positive Theory of Capital*, and vol. 3: *Further Essays on Capital and Interest*, trans. George D. Huncke and Hans F. Sennholz (South Holland, IL: Libertarian Press, 1959).—Ed.]

[4] I am sure that this belief was not held by Marshall. [In the *Principles of Economics*, 1st ed. (London: Macmillan, 1890), p. 615n., Alfred Marshall asked in a footnote "whether he [Böhm-Bawerk] has not somewhat exaggerated the difference between his own position and that of his predecessors; whether the sharp contrasts which he finds between the doctrines of successive schools really existed; and whether those doctrines were generally as fragmentary and one-sided as he thinks". Cf. the ninth variorum edition with annotations by C. W. Guillebaud (London: Macmillan, 1961), reprinted in 2 vols. in *The Collected Works of Alfred Marshall* (1997), vol. 2, p. 643; the passage in question has been reformulated in the second edition and deleted from all the later editions.—Ed.]

[5] [Cf. Knut Wicksell, *Vorlesungen über Nationalökonomie auf Grundlage des Marginalprinzips*, vol. 1, and vol. 2: *Geld und Kredit* (Jena: Fischer, 1914 and 1922; reprinted, Aalen: Scientia, 1969), and *Geldzins und Güterpreise: Eine Studie über die den Tauschwert des Geldes bestimmenden Ursachen* (Jena: Fischer, 1898; reprinted, Aalen: Scientia, 1968); the respective English translations were soon to appear as *Lectures on Political Economy*, trans. Ernest Classen, vol. 1: *General Theory*, and vol. 2: *Money* (London: Routledge, 1934 and 1935; reprinted, New York: Kelley, 1967; Auburn, AL: Ludwig von Mises Institute, 2007), and *Interest and Prices: A Study of the Causes Regulating the Value of Money*, trans. Richard F. Kahn (London: Macmillan, 1936; reprinted, New York: Kelley, 1965; Auburn, AL: Ludwig von Mises Institute, 2007).—Ed.]

[6] [That is, Ludwig von Mises, *Theorie des Geldes und der Umlaufsmittel* (Munich and Leipzig: Duncker and Humblot, 1912), the 2nd revised edition (1924) translated as *The Theory of Money and Credit*, trans. Harold E. Batson (London: Cape, 1934; reprinted, Indianapolis: Liberty Classics, 1981).—Ed.]

[7] [Cf., e.g., *The Theory of Money and Credit*, chapter 9 on "Interlocal Price Differences". The main 'rediscoverer' and propagator of a simplified version of the purchasing power parity theory was, of course, Gustav Cassel, see, e.g., *Money and Foreign Exchange After 1914* (London: Constable, 1922; reprinted, New York: Arno Press, 1972).—Ed.]

ing contact with what may prove to be one of the most fruitful scientific developments of our age.

On the actual lectures, it would be otiose for me to expatiate. They speak for themselves. Good wine needs no bush, and Dr. Hayek provides a vintage over which all true economists will linger long. I can only say that for profound theoretical insight and power to open up totally new horizons, I know only one work of its kind which has been published in English since the war with which they can be compared—Mr. Dennis Robertson's *Banking Policy and the Price Level*.[8] English-speaking readers will know that one could give no higher praise. I would not urge that Dr. Hayek has solved all the riddles of cyclical fluctuation. I am sure that Dr. Hayek himself would be the first to repudiate such a suggestion. But I do think he has advanced considerations which any future work on this problem will have to take very seriously into account.

As to the practical implications of his theories, Dr. Hayek, in the true scientific spirit, makes very modest claims. He does not claim to provide a cut and dried cure for all the evils of the monetary system. Indeed, he goes out of his way repeatedly to disavow any intention of providing positive recommendations for practice, claiming only that what he has to say may serve to make us more sceptical of the facile proposals for reform which are generally prevalent nowadays. None-the-less, it is difficult to deny all *interpretive* value to his contribution. I am bound to say that it seems to me to fit certain facts of the American slump better than any other explanation I know. And I cannot think that it is altogether an accident that the Austrian Institut für Konjunkturforschung, of which Dr. Hayek is director,[9] was one of the very few bodies of its kind which, in the spring of 1929, predicted a setback in America with injurious repercussions on European conditions.[10] Most monetary theorists seem to have failed utterly to apprehend correctly the nature of the forces operative in America before the coming of depression, thinking apparently

[8] [Cf. Dennis H. Robertson, *Banking Policy and the Price Level: An Essay in the Theory of the Trade Cycle* (London: King, 1926), reprinted as vol. 3 of *The Development of Monetary Theory, 1920s and 1930s*, ed. Forrest Capie and Geoffrey E. Wood (London: Routledge, 2000).—Ed.]

[9] [Hayek had been director of the Austrian Institute for Business Cycle Research since its foundation in 1927; he was granted a leave in October 1931, when he left Vienna for LSE, and eventually was succeeded by Oskar Morgenstern in 1933.—Ed.]

[10] [Robbins's contention has sometimes been interpreted (or possibly misunderstood) as referring to a *concrete* prediction of the American crisis of 1929; yet although this crisis conformed to the pattern elaborated, for example, in Hayek's *Geldtheorie und Konjunkturtheorie* (1929), there is no textual evidence for Hayek forecasting it as a concrete event in time and place. Cf. on this Hansjoerg Klausinger, "Hayek on Practical Business Cycle Research: A Note", in *Austrian Economics in Transition*, ed. Harald Hagemann, Tamotsu Nishizawa, and Yukihiro Ikeda (London: Palgrave Macmillan, 2010), pp. 225–27. It should be noted that a few years later Robbins in his monograph *The Great Depression* (London: Macmillan, 1934; reprinted, Auburn, AL: Ludwig von Mises Institute, 2007) largely followed the Austrian line of explanation.—Ed.]

that the relative stability of the price level indicated a state of affairs necessarily free from injurious monetary influences. The Austrian theory, of which Dr. Hayek is such a distinguished exponent, can claim at least this merit, that no one who really understood its principal tenets could have cherished for a moment such vain delusions.

Lionel Robbins
London School of Economics
June 1931

PREFACE TO THE FIRST EDITION (1931)

While the more naive forms of inflationism[1] are sufficiently discredited today not to do much harm in the near future, contemporary economic thought is so much permeated by an inflationism of a subtler kind that it is to be feared that for some time we shall still have to endure the consequences of a good deal of dangerous tampering with currency and credit. It is my belief that some even of those doctrines which are generally accepted in this field have no other basis than an uncritical application to the problems of society in general of the experience of the individual, that what he needs is more money. In what follows, one of my tasks will be to attempt to demonstrate that the cry for an 'elastic' currency which expands or contracts with every fluctuation of 'demand' is based on a serious error of reasoning.

The following lectures owe their present form to a generous invitation from the Senate of the University of London to deliver four lectures in advanced Economics during the academic year 1930–31. They are partly a restatement and mainly an extension of theories which I have outlined during the last three years in a book and two periodical articles published in German.[2] The selection of the particular problem which is here discussed from the larger field which these publications cover, was dictated by the impression that the Anglo-American literature on this subject is deficient in certain leading notions which on the European Continent and in Scandinavia—probably on account of the greater influence of Böhm-Bawerk in those parts—have been more explored, and whose use has proved very fruitful. I have, accordingly, confined

---

[1] [Mises, *The Theory of Money and Credit*, p. 251, defines "inflationism" as "that monetary policy that seeks to increase the quantity of money".—Ed.]

[2] *Geldtheorie und Konjunkturtheorie*; "Das intertemporale Gleichgewichtssystem der Preise und die Bewegungen des 'Geldwertes'", *Weltwirtschaftliches Archiv*, vol. 28, July 1928, pp. 33–76 [translated as "Intertemporal Price Equilibrium and Movements in the Value of Money" and reprinted as chapter 5 of *Good Money, Part I: The New World*, ed. Stephen Kresge, vol. 5 (1999) of *The Collected Works of F. A. Hayek* (Chicago: University of Chicago Press; London: Routledge)—Ed.]; and "Gibt es einen 'Widersinn des Sparens'?" *Zeitschrift für Nationalökonomie*, vol. 1, 1930 [November 1929], pp. 387–429 [translated as "The 'Paradox' of Saving", *Economica*, no. 32, May 1931, pp. 125–69, reprinted as chapter 2 of *Contra Keynes and Cambridge: Essays, Correspondence*, ed. Bruce Caldwell, vol. 9 (1995) of *The Collected Works of F. A. Hayek*—Ed.].

myself to those topics which I believe to be unduly neglected in most English and American works on the same subject—topics which seem to be neglected even in the most recent work on this subject, Mr. J. M. Keynes's highly stimulating *Treatise on Money*,[3] which came into my hands only when these lectures were almost completed, too late for me to make the frequent references to it which otherwise would have been desirable. I hope that by emphasising these neglected points I have succeeded indirectly in demonstrating the defects of certain theories which have been very prominent in recent years, and in exhibiting some of the dangers of the remedies for various social ills proposed by their protagonists.

In particular, it is my hope that the analysis of the working of the price mechanism during a transition to more or less capitalistic methods of production, which is attempted in the third lecture, will fill a gap, the existence of which in the past has undoubtedly made the whole line of approach here adopted less convincing than otherwise it might have been. I am less confident in regard to the last lecture. The territory into which it makes a few tentative steps is little explored and particularly difficult. I can only repeat here what I insist upon in that lecture, that I am profoundly convinced that we are yet very far from the day when our knowledge of these problems will be sufficient to justify any drastic changes in the traditional monetary policy.

I should like to take this opportunity of expressing my gratitude to Mr. Albert G. Hart,[4] who gave me the benefit of his advice when I was drafting the original English manuscript of these lectures. My chief obligation, however, is to Professor Lionel Robbins, to whom I am indebted for the very considerable labour of putting the manuscript into a form fit for publication, and seeing it finally through the press.

F. A. Hayek

[3] [John Maynard Keynes, *A Treatise on Money*, 2 vols. (London: Macmillan, 1930), reprinted as vols. 5 and 6 (1971) of *The Collected Writings of John Maynard Keynes*, ed. Austin Robinson and Donald Moggridge (London: Macmillan; Cambridge: Cambridge University Press). John Maynard Keynes (1883–1946), whose *Treatise on Money* soon was subjected to heavy criticism by Hayek, later on as the founder of the 'Keynesian Revolution' was to become Hayek's most important adversary in the field of monetary or 'macro'-economics.—Ed.]

[4] [Albert Gailord Hart (1909–97) had spent the winter term 1930–31 as a student at the University of Vienna, where he participated in the Haberler-Hayek-Morgenstern seminar. Cf. his *Anticipations, Uncertainty, and Dynamic Planning* (Chicago: University of Chicago Press, 1940; reprinted, New York: Kelley, 1951 and 1965), pp. v–vi. Later on Hart was to become a professor at Columbia University (1946–78).—Ed.]

PREFACE TO THE SECOND EDITION (1935)

This book owes its existence to an invitation by the University of London to deliver during the session 1930–31 four lectures to advanced students in economics, and in the form in which it was first published it literally reproduced these lectures. This invitation offered to me what might easily have been a unique opportunity to lay before an English audience what contribution I thought I had then to make to current discussions of theoretical economics; and it came at a time when I had arrived at a clear view of the outlines of a theory of industrial fluctuations but before I had elaborated it in full detail or even realised all the difficulties which such an elaboration presented. The exposition, moreover, was limited to what I could say in four lectures, which inevitably led to even greater oversimplification than I would probably have been guilty of in any other case. But although I am now conscious of many more defects of this exposition than I was even at the time of its first publication, I can only feel profoundly grateful to the circumstances which were such an irresistible temptation to publish these ideas at an earlier date than I should otherwise have done. From the criticisms and discussions that publication has caused I hope to have profited more for a later more complete exposition[1] than I could possibly have done if I had simply continued to work on these problems for myself. But the time for that more exhaustive treatment of these problems has not yet come. It is perhaps the main gain which I derived from the early publication that it made it clear to me that before I could hope to get much further with the elucidation of the main problems discussed in this book it would be necessary considerably to elaborate the foundations on which I have tried to build. Contact with scientific circles which were less inclined than I was to take for granted the main propositions of the 'Austrian' theory of capital on which I have drawn so freely in this book has shown—not that these propositions were wrong or that they were less important than I had thought for the task for which I had used them—but that they would have to be developed

---

[1] [Here Hayek referred to his ongoing project on capital theory, which culminated in *The Pure Theory of Capital* (London: Macmillan, 1941), reprinted, ed. Lawrence White, as vol. 12 (2007) of *The Collected Works of F. A. Hayek.*—Ed.]

in far greater detail and have to be adapted much more closely to the complicated conditions of real life before they could provide a completely satisfactory instrument for the explanation of the particularly complicated phenomena to which I have applied them. This is a task which has to be undertaken before the theses expounded in the present book can be developed further with advantage.

Under these circumstances, when a new edition of this book was called for, I felt neither prepared to rewrite and enlarge it to the extent that a completely adequate treatment of the problems taken up would make necessary, nor to see it reappear in an altogether unchanged form. The compression of the original exposition has given rise to so many unnecessary misunderstandings which a somewhat fuller treatment would have prevented that certain additions seemed urgently necessary. I have accordingly chosen the middle course of inserting into the, on the whole unchanged, original text further elucidations and elaborations where they seemed most necessary. Many of these additions were already included in the German edition[2] which appeared a few months after the first English edition. Others are taken over from a number of articles in which in the course of the last three years I have tried to develop or to defend the main thesis of this book. It has, however, been by no means possible to incorporate all the further elaborations attempted in these articles in the present volume and the reader who may wish to refer to them will find them listed in the footnote below.[3]

---

[2] [F. A. Hayek, *Preise und Produktion* (Vienna: Springer, 1931; reprinted, 1976; Düsseldorf: Verlag Wirtschaft und Finanzen, 1995). In the following all translations from *Preise und Produktion* are mine.—Ed.]

[3] "The Pure Theory of Money. A Rejoinder to Mr. Keynes", *Economica*, no. 34, November 1931, pp. 398–403; "Money and Capital. A Reply to Mr. Sraffa", *Economic Journal*, vol. 42, June 1932, pp. 237–49 [both reprinted, respectively, as chapters 5 and 8 of F. A. Hayek, *Contra Keynes and Cambridge*; Hayek's citation of the second article is incorrect insofar as he added "to Mr. Sraffa" to the title—Ed.]; "Kapitalaufzehrung", *Weltwirtschaftliches Archiv*, vol. 36, July 1932, pp. 86–108 [translated as "Capital Consumption" and reprinted as chapter 6 of F. A. Hayek, *Money, Capital and Fluctuations: Early Essays*, ed. Roy McCloughry (Chicago: University of Chicago Press; London: Routledge and Kegan Paul, 1984); to be included in *Capital and Interest*, ed. Lawrence White, vol. 11 (forthcoming) of *The Collected Works of F. A. Hayek*—Ed.]; "A Note on the Development of the Doctrine of 'Forced Saving'", *Quarterly Journal of Economics*, vol. 47, November 1932, pp. 123–33 [reprinted as chapter 3 of *Business Cycles, Part II*, ed. Hansjoerg Klausinger, vol. 8 (2012) of *The Collected Works of F. A. Hayek*—Ed.]; "Der Stand und die nächste Zukunft der Konjunkturforschung", in *Festschrift für Arthur Spiethoff*, ed. Gustav Clausing (Munich: Duncker and Humblot, 1933), pp. 110–17 [translated as "The Present State and Immediate Prospects of the Study of Industrial Fluctuations", chapter 6 of *Profits, Interest and Investment. And Other Essays on the Theory of Industrial Fluctuations* (London: Routledge, 1939), reprinted as chapter 4 of F. A. Hayek, *Business Cycles, Part II*—Ed.]; "Über 'neutrales Geld'", *Zeitschrift für Nationalökonomie*, vol. 4, October 1933, pp. 659–61 [translated as "On Neutral Money" and reprinted as chapter 6 of F. A. Hayek, *Good Money, Part I: The New World*—Ed.]; "Capital and Industrial Fluctuations", *Econometrica*, vol. 2, April 1934, pp 152–67 [reprinted as chapter 6 of F. A. Hayek, *Business Cycles,*

By these modifications I hope to have removed at least some of the difficulties which the book seems to have presented in its original form. Others were due to the fact that the book was in some ways a continuation of an argument which I had begun in other publications that at the time of its first appearance were available only in German. In the meantime English translations have, however, been published[4] and in those the reader will find explained some of the assumptions which are implicit rather than explicitly stated in the following discussion.

Some of the real difficulties which I fully realise this book must present to most readers will, however, not be removed by either of these changes because they are inherent in the mode of exposition adopted. All I can do in this respect short of replacing this book by an entirely new one is to draw the attention of the reader in advance to this particular difficulty and to explain why the mode of exposition which causes it had to be adopted. This is all the more necessary since this irremediable defect of the exposition has caused more misunderstandings than any other single problem.

The point in question is shortly this. Considerations of time made it necessary for me in these lectures to treat at one and the same time the real changes of the structure of production which accompany changes in the amount of capital and the monetary mechanism which brings this change about. This was possible only under highly simplified assumptions which made any change in the monetary demand for capital goods proportional to the change in the total demand for capital goods which it brought about. Now 'demand' for capital goods, in the sense in which it can be said that demand determines their value, of course does not consist exclusively or even primarily in a demand exercised on any market, but to a perhaps even greater degree in a demand or willingness to continue to hold capital goods for a further period of time. On the relationship between this total demand and the monetary demand for capital goods which manifests itself on the markets during any period of time, no general statements can be made; nor is it particularly relevant for my problems what this quantitative relationship actually is. What was, however, of prime importance for my purpose was to emphasise that any change in the monetary demand for capital goods could not be treated as something which made itself felt only on some isolated market for new capital goods, but that it could be only understood as a change affecting the general demand for capital goods which is an essential aspect of the process of maintaining a given structure of production. The simplest assumption of this kind which I could make was to assume a fixed relationship between the monetary and the total demand

---

Part II—Ed.]; "On the Relationship between Investment and Output", *Economic Journal*, vol. 44, June 1934, pp. 207–31.

[4] *Monetary Theory and the Trade Cycle*; "The 'Paradox' of Saving".

for capital goods so as to make the amount of money spent on capital goods during a unit period of time equal to the value of the stock of capital goods in existence.

This assumption, which I still think is very useful for my main purpose, proved however to be somewhat misleading in two other, not unimportant, respects. In the first instance it made it impossible to treat adequately the case of durable goods. It is impossible to assume that the potential services, embodied in a durable good and waiting for the moment when they will be utilised, change hands at regular intervals of time. This meant that so far as that particular illustration of the monetary mechanism was concerned I had to leave durable goods simply out of account. I did not feel that this was too serious a defect, particularly as I was under the—I think not unjustified—impression that the rôle which circulating capital played was rather neglected and accordingly wanted to stress it as compared with that of fixed capital. But I realise now that I should have given proper warning of the exact reason why I introduced this assumption and what function it performed, and I am afraid that the footnote which I inserted in the first edition at the last moment,[5] when my attention was drawn to the difficulty which my argument might present, has served rather to confuse than to clear up the point.

The second effect of this assumption of separate 'stages' of production of equal length was that it imposed upon me a somewhat one-sided treatment of the problem of the velocity of circulation of money. It implied more or less that money passed through the successive stages at a constant rate which corresponded to the rate at which the goods advanced through the process of production, and in any case excluded considerations of changes in the velocity of circulation or the cash balances held in the different stages. The impossibility of dealing expressly with changes in the velocity of circulation so long as this assumption was maintained served to strengthen the misleading impression that the phenomena I was discussing would be caused only by actual changes in the quality of money[6] and not by every change in the money stream, which in the real world are probably caused at least as frequently, if not more frequently, by changes in the velocity of circulation than by changes in the actual quantity. It has been put to me that any treatment of monetary problems which neglected in this way the phenomenon of changes in the desire to hold money balances could not possibly say anything worthwhile. While in my opinion this is a somewhat exaggerated view, I should like to emphasise in this connection how small a section of the whole field of monetary theory is actually treated in this book. All that I claim for it is that it deals with an aspect which has been more neglected and misunderstood than perhaps any other and the

[5] Cf. *Prices and Production*, 1st ed., p. 37n.2 [this volume, p. 223 ("first footnote")—Ed.].
[6] [Apparently, "quality of money" is a misprint for "quantity of money".—Ed.]

insufficient understanding of which has led to particularly serious mistakes. To incorporate this argument into the body of monetary theory is a task which has yet to be undertaken and which I could not and did not try to undertake here. But I may perhaps add that so far as the general theory of money (as distinguished from the pure theory of capital) is concerned, it is the work of Professor Mises[7] much more than that of Knut Wicksell which provides the framework inside which I have tried to elaborate a special point.

In addition to this acknowledgment of a great intellectual obligation I should like to repeat from the Preface to the first edition not only the acknowledgment of what I owe to the great tradition in the field of the theory of capital which is connected with the names of W. S. Jevons,[8] E. v. Böhm-Bawerk, and K. Wicksell, but also of the more specific debt to those who have helped me in the preparation of these lectures: to Mr. Albert G. Hart, now of the University of Chicago, who gave me the benefit of his advice when I was drafting the original English manuscript of these lectures, and particularly to Professor Lionel Robbins, who, when the first edition was published, undertook the considerable labour of putting the manuscript into a form fit for publication and seeing it through the press, and who ever since has most generously given me his help with all my English publications, including the present second edition of this book.

F. A. v. Hayek
The London School of Economics and Political Science
August 1934

[7] See particularly his *Theorie des Geldes und der Umlaufsmittel*, first published in 1912 and now fortunately available in an English translation: Mises, *The Theory of Money and Credit* (1934). Cf. also my *Monetary Theory and the Trade Cycle*, which is concerned more with the monetary factors which *cause* the trade cycle than the present book which is mainly devoted to the real phenomena which constitute it.

[8] [William Stanley Jevons (1835–82), British economist and, with Carl Menger and Léon Walras, one of the great figures of the Marginal Revolution. Similarly to the Austrian capital theory, put forward later on by Böhm-Bawerk and developed by Wicksell, he emphasised the time dimension of production.—Ed.]

PREFACE TO THE GERMAN EDITION, *PREISE UND PRODUKTION* (1931)[1]

While the more naive forms of inflationism are sufficiently discredited today not to do much harm in the near future, contemporary economic thought is so much permeated by an inflationism of a subtler kind that it is to be feared that for some time we shall still have to endure the consequences of a good deal of dangerous tampering with currency and credit. It is my belief that some even of those doctrines which are generally accepted in this field have no other basis than an uncritical application to the problems of society in general of the experience of the individual, that what he needs is more money. In what follows, one of my tasks will be to attempt to demonstrate that the cry for an 'elastic' currency which expands or contracts with every fluctuation of 'demand' is based on a serious error of reasoning.

Ever since I wrote those sentences, about nine months ago, for the English edition[2] of this work, unfolding developments have conferred on them an unexpectedly rapid confirmation. No one would have expected a resurrection of proposals favourable to inflation to emerge so soon after the last major experience with inflation, as can be witnessed not only among the broad general public in the past few months, but also in scientific circles. That it was nevertheless possible for inflationist policies to celebrate such a sudden resurrection, in spite of the conviction that they had been banished for decades to come, can be attributed to the fact that science, with the slogan 'price stabilisation', provided a new banner which served to rally the supporters of those policies, both those who were aware of what was happening and those who were not.

And although further insight will probably show that the attempts to stabilise the price level have been one of the chief causes of the current crisis, and thereby of the current and continuing collapse in prices, it is still to be feared that current experiences will further strengthen demands for price stabilisation. One of the principal objectives of this work is to show the risks which

---

[1] [Translated by Ciaran Cassidy.—Ed.]

[2] It appeared under the title *Prices and Production* [cf. 1st ed., p. xiii; this volume, p. 174—Ed.].

such stabilisation attempts involve and how they must lead to a misdirection of production, which ultimately and inevitably leads to a collapse of the stabilisation policy itself.

The specific form of the presentation is attributable to an invitation extended by the University of London, on the occasion of which I held four lectures at the London School of Economics and Political Science in January of this year.[3] The four chapters of this work correspond, by and large, to these lectures. The study represents, in part, a summary, but above all an extension, of the ideas which I have developed over the past six years in a series of essays.[4] The selection of topics dealt with here from the broad problem areas covered by those publications was determined on the one hand by the public to whom the lectures were addressed. On the other hand, it seemed highly desirable to me to shift the emphasis somewhat, relative to that in my presentation in *Geldtheorie und Konjunkturtheorie*, in order to reflect the development of theoretical ideas in Germany in recent times. Whereas in the above-mentioned work I placed the emphasis on the *monetary causes* which *trigger* the trade cycle, in the current presentation I stress the *real adjustments* in the structure of production which constitute those fluctuations. This seems to me to be all the more necessary in view of the growing proliferation of oversimplified monetary explanations, which associate cyclical fluctuations with changes in the general price level, which view every change in the price level as caused by monetary factors, and thus, in particular, regard the depression as the consequence of a deflation.

In contrast to the English edition of this work, I have not adhered to the structure of the lectures and I have sought to avoid superfluous repetition of ideas expounded in my earlier works. In addition, I have expanded significantly on the rather skimpy references to the literature to be found in the English edition, which is typical of published lectures. In the first chapter dealing with the history of economic thought, I have been able to take account of work which has come to my attention in the intervening period.[5] On the other hand, my intention for the German edition of incorporating an analysis of J. M. Keynes's *Treatise on Money* could not be realised. When this work

---

[3] [That is, 1931.—Ed.]

[4] "Die Währungspolitik der Vereinigten Staaten seit der Überwindung der Krise von 1920", *Zeitschrift für Volkswirtschaft und Sozialpolitik*, n.s., vol. 5, nos. 1 and 2, 1925, pp. 25–63 and 254–317 [translated as "Monetary Policy in the United States after the Recovery from the Crisis of 1920" and reprinted as chapter 2 of F. A. Hayek, *Good Money, Part I: The New World*—Ed.]; "Das intertemporale Gleichgewichtssystem der Preise"; *Geldtheorie und Konjunkturtheorie*; and "Gibt es einen 'Widersinn des Sparens'?", revised and extended offprint (Vienna: Springer, 1931). [The offprint was produced in April 1931, possibly during the course of the translation of the original article of 1929, yet these revisions are not completely identical to those in "The 'Paradox' of Saving".—Ed.]

[5] [Hayek included these additional sources in the second edition of *Prices and Production*, cf. this volume, pp. 206–9.—Ed.]

first appeared, the original English manuscript of the present work was all but complete. Moreover, as such an analysis would require much more space than it is possible to dedicate to it in this current work, I was obliged to reserve it for a special essay, the first part of which has already been published.[6] In spite of all the effort expended on the German edition, I can scarcely hope that I succeeded in eliminating all traces of the circumstance that what we are dealing with here originated as prepared lectures in the English language.

With reference to the content of the present work I would just like to mention my special hope that the analysis of the working of the price mechanism over the trade cycle, contained in the third chapter, will close a gap. The existence of this gap has, until now, diminished the persuasive power of all analytical efforts, from which the present theory stems. I am far less confident with regard to the subject matter dealt with in the fourth chapter. That subject area, into which some steps are attempted, has hardly been researched and is particularly difficult. I can only repeat here, what I emphasise in that chapter, my total conviction that we are still far removed from that point in time in which our understanding of those problems will be adequate to justify decisive changes in traditional monetary policy.

Although most of the questions dealt with in the following pages are currently of the greatest topicality, still I have considered it the correct approach not to confuse the theoretical problem with factual questions, to restrict myself to the presentation of the theoretical argument, and to make no attempt to enter into the problems of the day. It is, therefore, all the more appropriate to comment here on the application of these theoretical arguments to the problems of the current crisis.

The most widely disseminated explanations of the crisis at present can be most starkly contrasted with each other on the basis of two points: On the one hand, it is actually maintained that the origin of the crisis arises from an insufficient level of world consumption, a view which stands in contrast to the polar opposite, logically incompatible, belief, to which I subscribe, that the cause of the crisis is to be found in a shortage of capital. On the other hand, we have a group of theorists who assert that the cause of the crisis is to be sought in a currently ongoing deflation (caused either by a shortage of gold or by a restrictive policy of the central banks), while another group of theorists seeks the cause in an inflation which mainly occurred in the years 1927 to 1929 and a consequent misdirection of production.

For closely-related theoretical reasons, we find that the same persons support either the theories of insufficient demand and deflation or the theories

---

[6] It appeared under the title, "Reflections on the Pure Theory of Money of Mr. J. M. Keynes", *Economica*, no. 33, August 1931, pp. 270–95 [reprinted as chapter 3 of F. A. Hayek, *Contra Keynes and Cambridge*—Ed.].

of capital shortage and past inflation, as causes of the crisis. I have nothing to add to what I have already said in the text of this work, as well as in my earlier publications, concerning the reasons why I believe I must reject the purchasing power theory with all its conclusions, even in its most refined forms. I hope to show in the near future, in a special work, that an acute capital shortage has emerged not only in periodic economic crises and more especially in the current crisis, but over and above that certain European countries in recent years have been subject to a chronic process of capital consumption.[7]

However, a short remark should be added about the various interpretations of the monetary forces which are at work. The dispute here centres on the question whether the tremendous drop in prices in the past two years was caused by concurrent deflationary processes, or whether it represented an unavoidable consequence of a previous inflation. This earlier inflationary episode had transpired not as an increase in prices, but rather in a retardation of the general fall in prices, which would otherwise have occurred as a consequence of the increase in output. According to this viewpoint, with which I believe I must concur, this retardation of the natural decline in prices, engineered through an expansion of credit, was essential in keeping the prices of individual goods, in particular of raw materials, at a high level so that it led to a misdirection of production. Ultimately, as a consequence of this misdirection, the dramatic decline in prices was not only much more rapid, but prices dropped to a level far below that which would otherwise have occurred.[8]

The extent to which the crisis, once it had commenced, triggered a secondary deflationary process which still further reinforced the fall in prices, is an important question which requires urgent and thorough investigation. Very little evidence has been produced to date which would support this suggestion. The bare fact that prices fall does not, of itself, constitute proof that this fall could only have been brought about by currently working monetary causes,

[7] [The essay in question, "Kapitalaufzehrung" (cf. "Capital Consumption"), appeared in 1932.—Ed.]

[8] It is slowly being acknowledged that in the years prior to 1929 the United States experienced a massive expansion of credit, which was not reflected in an increase in prices. In recent times, a number of articles which have appeared in American journals are especially informative in this regard, in particular C. J. [Charles E.] Persons, "Credit Expansion, 1920 to 1929, and Its Lessons", *Quarterly Journal of Economics*, vol. 45, November 1930, pp. 94–130; C. Reinold Noyes, "The Gold Inflation in the United States 1921 to 1929", *American Economic Review*, vol. 20, June 1930, pp. 181–98; and A. Ross Eckler, "Recent Expansion of Bank Credit", *Review of Economic Statistics*, vol. 11, February 1921 [1929], pp. 46–51. In this context I would like to point out that in my 1925 article, mentioned above, "Die Währungspolitik der Vereinigten Staaten", in particular pp. 260, 271, and 275–76 [cf. "Monetary Policy in the United States", pp. 105, 114 and 118—Ed.], I drew attention to the immense possibilities for credit expansion created by the Federal Reserve System, as well as the inherent dangers of a policy geared towards the stabilisation of the price level.

as the supporters of the mechanistic quantity theory believe. Nor is it by any means obvious that an expansion of credit could eliminate the more fundamental causes of a fall in prices, but rather produce a temporary standstill from which prices must continue their downward path as soon as the credit expansion ceases.

It is a curious fact that the general reluctance to ascribe the causes of the boom to monetary factors would be replaced within a short space of time by an even greater readiness to attribute the blame for the depression to the mistakes of our monetary institutions. And so it happens that, in a little over two years after I dedicated a study[9] exclusively to a justification of monetary explanations, I feel obliged to come out so decisively against the over-simplistic monetary explanation of the crisis which are so widespread today. This rejection actually applies only to the superficial monetary theories, as am inclined to call them, and does not apply to that type of monetary explanations which I defended in my earlier book and to whose development this current book serves.

F. A. Hayek
Vienna, September 1931

[9] [That is, *Geldtheorie und Konjunkturtheorie.*—Ed.]

PREFACE TO THE REPRINT OF THE
GERMAN EDITION (1976)[1]

It is a very special pleasure for me to witness the reappearance of that small monograph, the most influential of all my theoretical works, in its original German form following an absence of forty-five years. The first German edition was quickly sold out, so that for more than four decades it has been almost impossible to get hold of a copy. By contrast, the original English edition enjoyed unusual success for a specialised investigation of this sort, so that the publisher kept it in print for the entire forty-five-year period with only very short intermissions. For this reason, it is perhaps appropriate to explain in greater detail the circumstances of the appearance of the original English edition; what started off as a rather fortuitous publication was to become the only available source in which my explanation of cyclical fluctuations was systematically presented.

On my return to Vienna in 1924 from a study visit to the United States, I commenced writing a critical evaluation of the monetary-theoretic ideas which were dominant over there, and which was to appear under the title "Geldtheoretische Untersuchungen".[2] Of the drafts which I wrote at that time, only two articles have appeared in print—"Die Währungspolitik der Vereinigten Staaten seit der Überwindung der Krise von 1920", published in the *Zeitschrift für Volkswirtschaft und Sozialpolitik* in 1925, and "Das intertemporale Gleichgewichtssystem der Preise und die Bewegungen des 'Geldwertes'" in *Weltwirtschaftliches Archiv*, 1928. The first of these articles, which by all appearances almost no one has read (and as even I discovered only years later, the type-setter had managed to jumble-up the pages after I had sent him the corrected final draft, so that the presentation was pretty incomprehensible), contains a compressed outline of the theory of the trade cycle in a lengthy footnote,[3] which I had developed

---

[1] [In 1976 a reprint of the German edition was published, on which occasion Hayek added a new preface. The translation is by Ciaran Cassidy.—Ed.]

[2] [The typescript of "Geldtheoretische Untersuchungen" has been preserved in the Friedrich A. von Hayek Papers, box 105, folders 1–4, Hoover Institution Archives, Stanford University. A translation, titled "Investigations into Monetary Theory", appears as chapter 1 of F. A. Hayek, *Business Cycles, Part II*.—Ed.]

[3] Cf. "Die Währungspolitik der Vereinigten Staaten", p. 261 [pp. 261–62n.1; cf. "Monetary Policy in the United States", pp. 105–6n.28—Ed.].

from approaches I owed to Knut Wicksell and Ludwig von Mises. Although my Viennese friends pressed me, even then, to develop this outline, I would certainly have postponed it as part of my planned larger work on monetary theory, had not a special opportunity arisen. At that time, work on this latter project was once more interrupted as I undertook the task to write the (still today) missing volume on "Geldtheorie" for the compendium *Grundriß der Sozialökonomik*.[4]

I began this task with a very detailed study of the history of monetary theory, whereby I could not resist devoting an inordinate amount of time to the extremely interesting developments in English monetary theory in the first half of the nineteenth century. This project, too, was never carried through to completion;[5] at first it was interrupted by my taking up a professorship in London in 1931, and was finally abandoned when the publisher pleaded to be released from the contract after Hitler had seized power.

In the meantime, some ideas originally intended for my planned study on monetary theory had been used for my habilitation (*Geldtheorie und Konjunkturtheorie*), as well as for my habilitation lecture "Gibt es einen 'Widersinn des Sparens'?" It was this lecture which attracted the attention of Lionel C. Robbins (now Lord Robbins), recently appointed professor at London University, who was my contemporary, even if completely unknown to me at the time. This led him to invite me in January 1931 to hold four lectures at the London School of Economics.

This invitation could not have come at a more opportune moment as far as the impact of the lectures was concerned. I had a very clear grasp of the theory concerning the influence of changes in the quantity of money on the structure of the economy, something which was only hinted at in the literature, by von Mises in particular. In the normal course of events, it would probably have taken me years to develop this theory in all its detail. Apart from that, I had immersed myself intensively in the older English theoretical tradition, which lent itself more readily to these developments. Thus, I was intellectually prepared to present the larger relationship, without being overly concerned with the many difficulties which would have arisen in a more detailed elaboration of the theory. It might have been scientifically more satisfactory, but certainly not a more stimulating or impressive presentation, had I waited until I had completed the publication and solved all the weak points in the analysis. My earlier stay in the United States made it possible for me to draft the lectures in English, and to deliver them in English at a level which was just about adequate.

---

[4] [That is, the volume on money and credit; cf. also the editor's introduction to this volume, p. 9.—Ed.]

[5] [Four chapters of this history have been translated and reprinted in part 3 of *The Trend of Economic Thinking: Essays on Political Economists and Economic History*, ed. W. W. Bartley III and Stephen Kresge, vol. 3 (1991) of *The Collected Works of F. A. Hayek.*—Ed.]

It was thanks to this concurrence of circumstances that the lectures proved such an unusual success, I would say to an undeserved extent, and that the problems they identified were to be one of the main topics of discussion in monetary theory in the English-speaking world throughout the following years. The tremendous success these lectures enjoyed when they appeared in book form in England, can be attributed, above all, to the efforts Lionel Robbins devoted to the task of transforming my texts into really good English.

The lectures then led to an offer of a professorship at London University, a post I took up in the following autumn. In the meantime, I returned to the Austrian Institute for Business Cycle Research, which I had led for more than four years. I set about personally to translate the original text of the lectures into German, with a view to having them appear in the Institute's own series, Beiträge zur Konjunkturforschung, just as *Geldtheorie und Konjunkturtheorie*[6] had appeared previously. Given that Robbins had so greatly improved the style of the English version, it is possible that the wording of the German edition of the lectures corresponds more closely, in certain respects, to the English version than to the book *Prices and Production*. On the other hand, I can see from the preface to the second edition of the English version, that I had incorporated some further elaborations into the German edition, which were only to appear in the second edition of the English version. In the course of time, this book was to appear, along with translations into Japanese and Chinese; most recently, it has appeared in French with an introduction by Christian Schmidt.[7]

The preface to the second English edition, which appeared in 1935, contained a few sentences which reflected the next stage in the development of my theoretical ideas. I would like to reproduce them here:

Contact with scientific circles which were less inclined than I was to take for granted the main propositions of the 'Austrian' theory of capital on which I have drawn so freely in this book has shown—not that these propositions were wrong or that they were less important than I had thought for the task for which I had used them—but that they would have to be developed in far greater detail and have to be adapted much more closely to the complicated conditions of real life before they could provide a completely satisfactory instrument for the explanation of the particularly complicated phenomena to which I have applied them. This is a task which has to be undertaken before the theses expounded in the present book can be developed further with advantage.[8]

---

[6] [As the first volume of the series; *Preise und Produktion* followed as volume 3.—Ed.]
[7] [Cf. *Prix et production* (Paris: Calmann-Levy, 1975).—Ed.]
[8] [*Prices and Production*, 2nd ed., p. viii, this volume, pp. 176–77.—Ed.]

The second English edition was nonetheless extended significantly (by up to a half), partly due to various extensions to the original text, partly due to the addition of appendices to the third and fourth lectures (dealing with precursors, as well as the concept of 'neutral money'), and finally due to a reply to an understanding review of the book which Professor Alvin Hansen and Dr. Herbert Tout had published in the first volume of *Econometrica*.[9] These extensions as well as the references to contemporary writers, which appeared in the second English edition, are part of the ongoing effort at that time to clear up misunderstandings concerning the intellectual background to my theories. They were mainly directed at the English readership, which was unfamiliar with this background. For this reason, an adequate knowledge of the English language is an indispensable requirement, for the specialist in the theory of the cycle who is interested in all the detailed discussions of those years, just as it is for anyone today who wants to work in the realm of economic theory. Only thus can one really follow the debate. The more precise German version, which is now being reissued, is probably more useful for the more general reader as well as for students, who are more interested in the broad outline of the development of the theory. This short version is available only in German, so that the photomechanical reproduction of the text appeared to be the most useful procedure.

Even at the time that I wrote them, I regarded the various extensions from those years as purely temporary. For reasons that I referred to in the last paragraph, I devoted the scientific research of the first eight years of my London stay predominantly to a study of capital theory; the most important result of this work appeared finally in 1941 under the title *The Pure Theory of Capital*. I had originally hoped for this work to go beyond equilibrium theory, and to address the problems of dynamics as well as the links to monetary theory. But *The Pure Theory of Capital* proved to be so difficult that after eight years of working on the project, I felt rather 'tired'. I would almost say that I used the outbreak of war as an excuse to publish as a complete work, what had really been intended as no more than a first part. The application of these theoretical ideas to the theory of the cycle was therefore only to make progress in my various publications about the 'Ricardo Effect', at first in "Profits, Interest and Investment" (1939) and in later essays.[10] In my opinion, this application represented an improved and more general representation of the relationships which are dealt with in *Prices and Production*, in that the theory does not depend

---

[9] [Cf. Hayek, "Capital and Industrial Fluctuations". The reply is to Alvin H. Hansen and Herbert Tout, "Annual Survey of Business Cycle Theory: Investment and Saving in Business Cycle Theory", *Econometrica*, vol. 1, April 1933, pp. 119–47.—Ed.]

[10] [Cf. Hayek, "Profits, Interest and Investment", chapter 1 of *Profits, Interest and Investment*, and "The Ricardo Effect", *Economica*, n.s. vol. 9, May 1942, pp. 127–52, reprinted as chapters 8 and 9, respectively, of F. A. Hayek, *Business Cycles, Part II*.—Ed.]

on a number of excessively simplified assumptions. This is the starting point from which I would now have attempted to continue, had not my attention been increasingly distracted by completely different problems.

Unfortunately, the task of refining those ideas, which I have always held as being basically correct and full of promise, was generally disrupted by the Keynesian deluge, which has swamped the study of economics during the past generation and strangled many fertile ideas. When I look back on the first appearance of this book, when researchers such as D. H. Robertson, R. G. Hawtrey, Erik Lindahl, A. W. Marget, or Marco Fanno[11] were the most important contemporaries in discussing problems of monetary theory, only to realise that these names are all but unknown to the current generation of economists, I cannot help but feel that this area of science has suffered a severe setback. And it appears to me that the main reason for this regression of knowledge arose from the influence of Lord Keynes and the econometricians. Their concern was to build a macro-theory based on statistical variables, and they dispensed with any effort to integrate the theory of money into a microeconomic theory based on methodological individualism. As long as forty-five years ago, this book had opposed those ideas and the resulting theories concerning the relationship between aggregate demand and employment, as well as the consequential inflationism. At that time we were confronted with a rather curious situation. Economists in the English-speaking world tended to favour an exclusively monetary explanation of cyclical fluctuations, based on an oversimplified version of the quantity theory, whereas in the German-speaking world one would have to plead, in this context, for attributing monetary influences any significance at all. Since then, a monetary theory of 'the circular flow' has totally dominated the discussion, throughout the world and for a generation.

In order to overcome the errors of this era, it will be necessary to return to an analysis of the effects of monetary changes on the real structure of the economy. In this pursuit, the investigations to a large extent will have to take

---

[11] [On Robertson and Hawtrey, see above pp. 84 and 126. Erik Robert Lindahl (1891–1960), professor at Lund University, was—jointly with Nobel Prize winners Gunnar Myrdal and Bertil Ohlin—a member of the Stockholm school of economics, which built on the theories of Wicksell. Apparently in 1929 Lindahl had introduced the notion of 'intertemporal equilibrium' independently of Hayek. Arthur William Marget (1899–1962), American economist, professor at the University of Minnesota, 1927–48, staunchly defended orthodoxy in monetary theory against the Keynesian onslaught, cf. his monumental *The Theory of Prices: A Re-examination of the Central Problems of Monetary Theory*, 2 vols. (New York: Prentice-Hall, 1938 and 1942). Marco Fanno (1878–1965) was an important Italian economist of the interwar period, professor of Political Economy at Padua. Hayek highly esteemed Fanno's contributions to the theory of money and the cycle; see also Fanno's article "Irrtümer in der Zeit als Ursachen wirtschaftlicher Schwankungen", *Zeitschrift für Nationalökonomie*, vol. 4, no. 1, 1932, pp. 25–51, for his emphasis on errors in expectations as causes of the cycle.—Ed.]

as a point of departure the literature of the 1930s. And one of the works to which researchers will have to turn is, in my opinion, this book before us. It can offer little more than a starting point, and the theories which I have sketched within this book will require much more development before they can be regarded as a satisfactory theory of cyclical fluctuations, or meet the demands which are rightly made of such a theory.

The reader will certainly find very helpful the bibliography of my most relevant work,[12] which has been compiled by Mr. Kurt Leube, my long-serving assistant at the Department of Economics at the University of Salzburg. I am also particularly indebted to Mr. Leube in that he arranged that the Springer Verlag in Vienna, which originally published the book, should reissue it again after so many years.

F. A. Hayek
Salzburg, November 1975

[12] [The bibliography has not been reproduced in this volume.—Ed.]

THEORIES OF THE INFLUENCE
OF MONEY ON PRICES

"He realised well that the abundance of money makes everything dear, but he did not analyse how that takes place. The great difficulty of this analysis consists in discovering by what path and in what proportion the increase of money raises the price of things."

Richard Cantillon (died 1734), *Essai sur la nature du commerce en général*, II, 6[1]

1.

That monetary influences play a dominant rôle in determining both the volume and direction of production is a truth which is probably more familiar to the present generation than to any which have gone before. The experiences of the war- and post-war-inflation, and of the return to the gold standard, particularly where, as in Great Britain, it was accomplished by a contraction of the circulation, have given abundant evidence of the dependence on money of every productive activity. The widespread discussions of recent years concerning the desirability and practicability of stabilising the value of

---

[1] [This is Hayek's own translation from the French edition of the *Essai* of 1755 (Traduit de l'Anglois, London: Fletcher Gyles, 2eme partie, chapitre 6, p. 213). Cf. the *Essai* as edited, with an English translation, by Henry Higgs, *Essay on the Nature of Trade in General* (London: Royal Economic Society, Macmillan, 1931; reprinted, New York: Kelley, 1964), p. 161; the English translation reprinted, with a new introduction by Anthony Brewer (New Brunswick: Transaction Publishers, 2001), p. 67: "He [that is, John Locke] has clearly seen that the abundance of money makes everything dear, but he has not considered how it does so. The great difficulty of this question consists in knowing in what way and in what proportion the increase of money raises prices." Hayek also edited a German version of the *Essai*, translated by Hella Hayek as *Abhandlung über die Natur des Handels im allgemeinen* (Jena: Fischer, 1931); for Hayek's introduction and a review of the Higgs edition see chapter 13 of F. A. Hayek, *The Trend of Economic Thinking*. Richard Cantillon (1680?–1734) was a banker with a somewhat mysterious biography; the *Essai* being his one great achievement in political economy. It was published posthumously and, indeed, the alleged translation from the English was a mystification for the sake of circumventing French censorship. The structural effects of monetary changes, which he emphasised in the *Essai*, have since been christened 'Cantillon effects'.—Ed.]

money are due mainly to a general recognition of this fact. At the present moment many of the best minds believe the cause of the existing world-wide depression to be a scarcity of gold and seek accordingly for monetary means to overcome it.

And yet, if it were asked whether understanding of the connection between money and prices has made great progress during these years, at any rate until very recently, or whether the generally accepted doctrines on this point have progressed far beyond what was generally known a hundred years ago, I should be inclined to answer in the negative. This may seem paradoxical, but I think anyone who has studied the monetary literature of the first half of the nineteenth century[2] will agree that there is hardly any idea in contemporary monetary theory which was not known to one or more writers of that period. Probably the majority of present-day economists would contend that the reason why progress has been so slight is that monetary theory has already reached such a state of perfection that further progress must of necessity be slow. But I confess that to me it still seems that some of the most fundamental problems in this field remain unsolved, that some of the accepted doctrines are of a very doubtful validity, and that we have even failed to develop the suggestions for improvement which can be found in the works of these early writers.

If that be true, and I hope to convince you that it is, it is surely somewhat astonishing that the experiences of the last fifteen years have not proved more fruitful. In the past, periods of monetary disturbance have always been periods of great progress in this branch of Economics. The Italy of the sixteenth century has been called the country of the worst money and the best monetary theory. If recently that has not been true to the same extent, the reason seems to me to lie in a certain change of attitude on the part of most economists in regard to the appropriate methodology of economics, a change which in many quarters is hailed as a great progress: I mean the attempt to substitute quantitative for qualitative methods of investigation. In the field of monetary theory, this change has been made even by economists who in general reject the 'new' point of view, and indeed several had made it some years before the quantitative method had become fashionable elsewhere.

2.

The best known instance, and the most relevant case in point, is the resuscitation by Irving Fisher some twenty years ago of the more mechanistic forms

---

[2] [Here Hayek refers to the Bullionist and the Currency-Banking controversies; see below, pp. 209n.35 and 271n.13.—Ed.]

of the quantity theory of the value of money in his well-known 'equation of exchange'.[3] That this theory, with its apparatus of mathematical formulae constructed to admit of statistical verification, is a typical instance of 'quantitative' economics, and that it indeed probably contributed a good deal to influence the methodology of the present representatives of this school, are propositions which are not likely to be denied. I do not propose to quarrel with the positive content of this theory: I am even ready to concede that so far as it goes it is true, and that, from a practical point of view, it would be one of the worst things which would befall us if the general public should ever again cease to believe in the elementary propositions of the quantity theory. What I complain of is not only that this theory in its various forms has unduly usurped the central place in monetary theory, but that the point of view from which it springs is a positive hindrance to further progress. Not the least harmful effect of this particular theory is the present isolation of the theory of money from the main body of general economic theory.[4]

For so long as we use different methods for the explanation of values as they are supposed to exist irrespective of any influence of money, and for the explanation of that influence of money on prices, it can never be otherwise. Yet we are doing nothing less than this if we try to establish *direct* causal connections between the *total* quantity of money, the *general level* of all prices and, perhaps, also the *total* amount of production. For none of these magnitudes *as such* ever exerts an influence on the decisions of individuals; yet it is on the assumption of a knowledge of the decisions of individuals that the main propositions of non-monetary economic theory are based.[5] It is to this 'individualistic' method that we owe whatever understanding of economic phenomena we possess; that the modern 'subjective' theory has advanced beyond the classical school in its consistent use is probably its main advantage over their teaching.

If, therefore, monetary theory still attempts to establish causal relations between aggregates or general averages, this means that monetary theory lags behind the development of economics in general. In fact, neither aggregates nor averages do act upon one another, and it will never be possible to establish necessary connections of cause and effect between them as we can between

---

[3] [Cf. Irving Fisher's *The Purchasing Power of Money* (New York: Macmillan, 1911), the 2nd revised edition (1913) reprinted as vol. 4 of *The Works of Irving Fisher*, ed. William Barber (London: Pickering and Chatto, 1997).—Ed.]

[4] [Drawing on the German version (*Preise und Produktion*, pp. 4, 8, and 34) it is evident that here and in the following Hayek used 'general economic theory' synonymously with 'pure economic theory' or 'static theory'.—Ed.]

[5] [In *Preise und Produktion* Hayek formulates his adherence to the individualistic method somewhat differently: "yet it is the knowledge of how individuals react to changes in their environment that enables us to foresee the economic consequences of any such event" (p. 4).—Ed.]

individual phenomena, individual prices, etc. I would even go so far as to assert that, from the very nature of economic theory, averages can never form a link in its reasoning; but to prove this contention would go far beyond the subject of these lectures. I shall here confine myself to an attempt to show in a special field the differences between explanations which do and explanations which do not have recourse to such concepts.

3.

As I have said already, I do not want to criticise the doctrines of these theories so far as they go; I indicate their characteristics only in order to be able to show later on how much more another type of theory may accomplish. The central preoccupation of these theories is changes in the general price level. Now everybody agrees that a change of prices would be of no consequence whatever if all prices in the widest sense of the term were affected equally and simultaneously. But the main concern of this type of theory is avowedly with certain suppositious[6] "tendencies, which affect *all* prices equally, or at any rate impartially, at the same time and in the same direction".[7] And it is only after the alleged causal relation between changes in the quantity of money and average prices has thus been established that effects on relative prices are considered. But as the assumption generally is that changes in the quantity of money affect only the general price level, and that changes of relative prices are due to 'disturbing factors' or 'frictions', changes in relative prices are not part of this explanation of the changes in the price level. They are mere accompanying circumstances which experience has taught us to be regularly connected with changes of the price level, not, as might be thought, necessary consequences of the same causes. This is very clear from the form of exposition and the concepts it employs. Certain 'lags' are found to exist between the changes of different prices. The prices of different goods are said generally to be affected in a definite sequence, and it is always implied that all this would never take place if the general price level did not change.

When we come to the way in which the influence of prices on production is conceived by this theory, the same general characteristics are to be discovered. It is the price level, the changes of which are supposed to influence production; and the effect considered is not the effect upon particular branches of production, but the effect upon the volume of production in general. In most cases, no attempt is made to show why this must be so; we are referred to statistics which show that in the past a high correlation of general prices

---

[6] [The second edition erroneously corrected this word to "suppositions".—Ed.]

[7] This is the formulation of Ralph G. Hawtrey. Cf. his lecture on "Money and Index Numbers" in the *Journal of the Royal Statistical Society*, vol. 93, part 1, 1930, p. 65.

and the total volume of production has been present. If an explanation of this correlation is attempted, it is generally simply to the effect that the expectation of selling at higher prices than present costs will induce everybody to expand production, while in the opposite case the fear of being compelled to sell below costs will prove a strong deterrent. That is to say, it is only the general or average movement of prices which counts.

Now this idea that changes of relative prices and changes in the volume of production are consequent upon changes in the price level, and that money affects individual prices only by means of its influence on the general price level, seems to me to be at the root of at least three very erroneous opinions: *Firstly*, that money acts upon prices and production only if the general price level changes, and, therefore, that prices and production are always unaffected by money—that they are at their 'natural' level—if the price level remains stable. *Secondly*, that a rising price level tends always to cause an increase of production, and a falling price level always a decrease of production; and *thirdly*, that "monetary theory might even be described as nothing more than the theory of how the value of money is determined".[8] It is such delusions, as we shall see, which make it possible to assume that we can neglect the influence of money so long as the value of money is assumed to be stable, and apply without further qualification the reasonings of a general economic theory which pays attention to 'real causes' only, and that we have only to add to this theory a separate theory of the value of money and of the consequences of its changes in order to get a complete explanation of the modern economic process.

Further details are unnecessary. You are all sufficiently familiar with this type of theory to supply these for yourselves and to correct any exaggerations which I may have committed in my endeavour to make the contrast with the other types of theory as strong as possible. Any further strengthening of the contrast can best be carried out by my proceeding forthwith to the second of the major stages in the development of monetary theory. I wish only to emphasise, before I pass on to that, that henceforward when I speak of stages of development, I do not mean that each of these stages has in turn taken the place of the foregoing as the recognised doctrine. Quite on the contrary, each of these stages is still represented among contemporary monetary theorists and indeed in all probability the first has still the greatest number of adherents.

4.

As might be expected, the second stage arises by way of dissatisfaction with the first. This dissatisfaction makes its appearance quite early. Locke and Mon-

[8] Ibid., p. 64.

tanari,[9] at the end of the seventeenth century, had stated quite clearly the theory I have been discussing.[10] Richard Cantillon, whose criticism of Locke I have taken as the motto of this lecture, realised its inadequacy, and in his famous *Essai sur le Commerce* (published 1755),[11] he provides the first attempt known to me to trace the actual chain of cause and effect between the amount of money and prices. In a brilliant chapter, which W. S. Jevons called "one of the most marvellous things in the book",[12] he attempts to show "by what path and in what proportion the increase of money raises the price of things".[13] Starting from the assumption of the discovery of new gold or silver mines, he proceeds to show how this additional supply of the precious metals first increases the incomes of all persons connected with their production, how the increase of the expenditure of these persons next increases the prices of things which they buy in increased quantities, how the rise in the prices of these goods increases the incomes of the sellers of these goods, how they, in their turn, increase their expenditure, and so on. He concludes that only those persons are benefited by the increase of money whose incomes rise early, while to persons whose incomes rise later the increase of the quantity of money is harmful.

Better known is the somewhat shorter exposition of the same idea which David Hume gave a little later in a famous passage of his *Political Discourses*,[14]

---

[9] [John Locke (1632–1704), English philosopher of the Enlightenment; for his contribution to monetary theory cf. *Some Considerations of the Consequences of the Lowering of Interest, and Raising the Value of Money* (1692), reprinted in *Locke on Money*, 2 vols., ed. Patrick Hyde Kelly (Oxford: Clarendon Press; New York: Oxford University Press, 1991), vol. 1, pp. 203–342 (which is part of the *Clarendon Edition of the Works of John Locke*). Geminiano Montanari (1633–87), professor of mathematics and astronomy at the Universities of Bologna and Padua, developed the quantity theory of money in his *Della moneta trattato mercantile* (1683), reprinted in *Scrittori classici italiani di economia politica* (Milan: Destefanis, 1804; reprinted, Rome: Bizzari, 1965). See also the discussion of Locke and Montanari in chapter 9 of F. A. Hayek, *The Trend of Economic Thinking*, pp. 137–43.—Ed.]

[10] [In the first edition the word is "stating" instead of "discussing".—Ed.]

[11] [That is, his *Essai sur la nature du commerce en général*. The word "published" has been inserted in the second edition, perhaps to indicate that the *Essai* had been written earlier, around 1730.—Ed.]

[12] [William Stanley Jevons, "Richard Cantillon and the Nationality of Political Economy" (1881), reprinted in *The Principles of Economics* (London: Macmillan, 1905), which is reprinted as vol. 8 of Jevons, *Writings on Economics* (Basingstoke: Palgrave, 2001), p. 171; cf. also Cantillon, *Essay*, ed. Higgs, pp. 333–60; ed. Brewer, pp. 133–57.—Ed.]

[13] [See above, the motto from Cantillon preceding lecture 1.—Ed.]

[14] Published 1752, republished as part of his *Essays. Moral, Political and Literary* (part 2, essay 4 [essay 3], "Of Money") which originally appeared in 1742, and therefore are often wrongly quoted with that date. [David Hume (1711–76), philosopher of the Scottish Enlightenment, significantly contributed to monetary theory, e.g., by sketching what later became known as the specie-flow mechanism, that is, the equilibrating mechanism working within an international gold standard.—Ed.]

which so closely resembles the words of Cantillon that it is hard to believe that he had not seen one of those manuscripts of the *Essai* which are known to have been in private circulation at the time when the *Discourses* were written. Hume, however, makes it clear that, in his opinion, "it is only in this interval or intermediate situation, between the acquisition of money and the rise of prices, that the increasing quantity of gold and silver is favourable to industry".[15]

To the Classics, this line of reasoning did not seem susceptible of improvement. While Hume is often quoted, his method of approach was not amplified for more than a century. It was not until the increase of the supply of gold consequent upon the Californian and Australian discoveries that there was any new impetus to this type of analysis. J. E. Cairnes's *Essay on the Australian Gold Discoveries*[16] contains probably the most noteworthy refinement of the argument of Cantillon and Hume before it was finally incorporated into more modern explanations based upon the subjective theories of value.

It was inevitable that modern theory should be sympathetic towards a point of view which traces the effects of an increase of money to its influence on individual decisions. But a generation passed before serious attempts were made to base the explanation of the value of money and the effects of changes in the amount of money upon the fundamental concepts of marginal utility

---

[15] [David Hume, *Political Discourses* (Edinburgh: Kincaid and Donaldson, 1752), p. 47; reprinted in *Essays. Moral, Political and Literary*, ed. T. H. Green and T. H. Grose, 2 vols. (London: Longmans, 1875), vol. 1, p. 313; ed. Eugene F. Miller (Indianapolis: Liberty Classics, 1985), p. 286. Hayek's quotation is slightly inaccurate; it should read, "and rise of prices".—Ed.]

[16] John Elliot Cairnes, "Essays towards a Solution of the Gold Question", in *Essays in Political Economy, Theoretical and Applied* (London: Macmillan, 1873 [reprinted, New York: Kelley, 1965]), particularly essay 2: "The Course of Depreciation". These *Essays* were originally published in 1855–60 in *Frazers Magazine* and the *Edinburgh Review*. [Hayek's identification is not wholly accurate. The four essays in question were published in *Fraser's Magazine* in September 1859 and January 1860, and in the *Edinburgh Review* in July 1860; the essay "The Course of Depreciation" had been read before the British Association in September 1858. None of the essays is titled "Essay on the Australian Gold Discoveries", so that the italicisation in the text is misleading. Cf. also the reprint of the *Essays* as vol. 4 of *The Collected Works of John Elliot Cairnes*, ed. Tom Boylan and Tadhg Foley (London: Routledge, 2004). John Elliot Cairnes (1823–75), a disciple of John Stuart Mill, has often been regarded as the last of the classical economists. The gold discoveries in California and Australia resulted in a fall in the costs of producing gold, and within an international monetary system based on gold (and partly on silver) led to rising prices in the rest of the world by means of balance of payments surpluses against gold producing countries and the subsequent inflow of gold. Cairnes's essays documented this process.—Ed.] It may be of interest to mention here that Carl Menger, who has decisively influenced modern development in this field, was well acquainted with Cairnes's exposition. Cf. on this point my "Introduction" to vol. 1 of *The Collected Works of Carl Menger* in the Series of Reprints of Scarce Tracts in Economics, vol. 17 (London: London School of Economics, 1934) [reprinted in an augmented version as chapter 2 of *The Fortunes of Liberalism: Essays on Austrian Economics and the Ideal of Freedom*, ed. Peter G. Klein, vol. 4 (1992) of *The Collected Works of F. A. Hayek*; see in particular p. 88. The last two sentences referring to Menger do not appear in the first edition.—Ed.]

theory. I shall not dwell here at any length on the variety of forms this assumes in the different modern theories which base the explanation of the value of money on the subjective elements determining the demand for money on the part of the individual.[17] In the form this theory[18] has received at the hands of Professor Mises, it belongs already to the third and fourth of our main stages of development, and I shall have occasion to refer to it later. It is worth noticing, however, that, in so far as these theories are confined to an explanation of the manner in which the effects of an increase[19] in the amount of money are distributed through the various channels of trade, they still suffer from a not unimportant defect. While they succeed in providing a general scheme for the deduction of the successive effects of an increase or decrease of the amount of money, provided that we know where the additional money enters into circulation, they do not help us to make any *general* statements about the effects which any change in the amount of money must have. For, as I shall show later, everything depends on the point where the additional money is injected into circulation (or where money is withdrawn from circulation), and the effects may be quite opposite according as the additional money comes first into the hands of traders and manufacturers or directly into the hands of salaried people employed by the State.[20]

5.

Very early, and, in the beginning, with only little relation to the problem of the value of money, there had, however, sprung up a doctrine, or rather a number of closely related doctrines, the importance of which was not appreciated at the time, although in the end they were to be combined to fill the gap I have been discussing. I refer to the doctrines of the influence of the quantity of money on the rate of interest, and through it on the relative demand for consumers' goods on the one hand and producers' or capital goods on the other.[21] These form the third stage in the development of monetary theory. These doctrines have had to surmount unusual obstacles and prejudices, and until recently they received very little attention. It almost seems as if econo-

---

[17] [In the first edition, the previous sentence reads, "I shall not dwell here at any length on the variety of forms this assumes in the 'income theories' of the value of money by Wieser, Professor Aftalion and Professor Mises."—Ed.]

[18] [The first edition reads, "it", instead of "this theory".—Ed.]

[19] [In the second edition, possibly due to a misprint, this reads, "of increase".—Ed.]

[20] [As Hayek notes in *Preise und Produktion*, p. 12, in the latter case the additional money "will at first be used for the purchase of consumers' goods".—Ed.]

[21] [According to the definitions given below (see p. 200), producers' goods include not only capital goods but also the original means of production.—Ed.]

mists had for so long a time struggled against the popular confusions between the value of money proper and the price for a money loan that in the end they had become almost incapable of seeing that there was any relation at all between the rate of interest and the value of money. It is therefore worth while attempting to trace their development in rather greater detail.

While the existence of some relation between the quantity of money and the rate of interest was clearly recognised very early—traces of an understanding could certainly be found in the writings of Locke and Dutot[22]—the first author known to me to enunciate a clear doctrine on this point was Henry Thornton. In his *Paper Credit of Great Britain*, published in 1802 at the beginning of the discussion on Bank Restriction[23]—a really remarkable performance, the true importance of which is only now beginning to be recognised—he struck for the first time one of the leading notes of the new doctrine. The occasion for his statement was an inquiry into the question whether there existed a natural tendency to keep the circulation of the Bank of England within the limits which would prevent a dangerous depreciation. Thornton denied that such a natural tendency existed and held that, on the contrary, the circulation might expand beyond all assignable limits if the Bank would only keep its rate of interest low enough. He based his opinion on considerations so weighty that I cannot resist quoting them at some length:

> In order to ascertain how far the desire of obtaining loans at the Bank may be expected at any time to be carried, we must enquire into the subject of the quantum of profit likely to be derived from borrowing there under the existing circumstances. This is to be judged of by considering two points: the amount, first, of interest to be paid on the sum borrowed; and, secondly, of the mercantile or other gain to be obtained by the employment of the borrowed capital. The gain which can be acquired by the means of commerce

[22] [Dutot (or Du Tot) (ca. 1670–after 1740), French economist, of whom neither dates of birth and death nor surname are known, author of *Réflexions politiques sur les finances et le commerce*, 2 vols. (The Hague, 1738), translated as *Political Reflections upon the Finances and Commerce of France* (London: Millar, 1739; reprinted, Clifton: Kelley, 1974). He occupied an important position in John Law's system, which ended in financial collapse.—Ed.]

[23] [Henry Thornton, *An Enquiry into the Nature and Effects of the Paper Credit of Great Britain* (London: J. Hatchard, F. and C. Rivington, 1802). The American edition (Philadelphia: J. Humphreys, 1807) has been reprinted in *A Select Collection of Scarce and Valuable Tracts and Other Publications on Paper Currency and Banking*, ed. James Ramsey McCulloch (London: Murray, 1857), which is reprinted as vol. 3 of *Classical Writings on Economics* (London: Pickering and Chatto, 1995); cf. also the reprint *An Enquiry into the Nature and Effects of the Paper Credit of Great Britain together with His Evidence given before the Committee of Secrecy of the Two Houses of Parliament in the Bank of England, March and April 1797, Some Manuscript Notes, and his Speeches on the Bullion Report, May 1811*, ed. F. A. Hayek (London: Allen and Unwin, 1939; reprinted, New York: Kelley, 1991). On Thornton, see above p. 105.—Ed.]

is commonly the highest which can be had; and it also regulates, in a great measure, the rate in all other cases. We may, therefore, consider this question as turning principally on a comparison of the rate of interest taken at the bank with the current rate of mercantile profit.[24, 25]

Thornton restated these doctrines in the first of his two speeches on the Bullion Report, which were also published as a booklet[26] and would deserve being recovered from oblivion. In this speech he attempts to call the attention of the House to the subject of the rate of interest as "a very great and turning point", and, after restating his theory in a shorter form, adds a new and different theory on the relations between prices and interest (which must on no account be confused with his other theory), namely a theory of the influence of an expectation of a rise of prices on the money rate of interest, a theory which later on was to be re-discovered by A. Marshall and Irving Fisher.[27] This theory, however, does not concern us here.[28]

Thornton's theory seems to have been generally accepted among the 'bullionists', though it appears to have been forgotten[29] by the time that the doctrine of this school became the target of those attacks of the Banking School[30]

---

[24] Thornton, *Paper Credit*, p. 287 [cf. the American edition (1807), p. 183; *Scarce Tracts on Paper Currency*, ed. McCulloch, p. 319; *Paper Credit*, ed. Hayek, pp. 253–54. Hayek listed in the first edition the page number incorrectly as 267. In the original "bank" is not capitalised in the first sentence of the quotation.—Ed.]

[25] In order to appreciate the importance of this statement, another passage occurring a little earlier in the same chapter (*Paper Credit*, p. 261 [pp. 261–62; cf. the American edition, p. 169; *Scarce Tracts on Paper Currency*, ed. McCulloch, p. 305; *Paper Credit*, ed. Hayek, p. 238—Ed.]) should be consulted. In the course of this passage, Thornton writes: "As soon, however, as the circulating medium *ceases to increase* [*encrease*], the extra profit is at an end." (Italics mine.)

[26] *Substance of two speeches by Henry Thornton, Esq., in the debate in the House of Commons on the report of the Bullion Committee on the 7th and 14th May, 1811* (London: J. Hatchard, 1811). Cf. particularly pp. 19 et seq. [The quotation is from p. 19; cf. also *Paper Credit*, ed. Hayek, p. 335. On the Bullion Report see note 35 below.—Ed.]

[27] [Cf. Marshall, *Principles of Economics*, 9th variorum ed., vol. 1, pp. 593–95, and Irving Fisher, "Appreciation and Interest", *Publications of the American Economic Association*, vol. 11, July 1896, reprinted in *The Works of Irving Fisher*, ed. Barber, vol. 1: *The Early Professional Works*, pp. 189–298. For a more detailed recent account of the nominal-real interest rate distinction cf. David Laidler, *The Golden Age of the Quantity Theory* (New York: Philip Alan, 1991), pp. 90–95.—Ed.]

[28] Cf. T. E. Gregory, "Introduction" to Tooke and Newmarch's *A History of Prices and of the State of the Circulation from 1792 to 1876*, in 6 vols. (London: King; New York: Adelphi, 1928 [reprinted, London: London School of Economics and Political Science, 1962]), p. 23. Professor Gregory does not, however, clearly distinguish between the two theories. [Theodore E. Gregory (1890–1970), British economist and as Cassel Professor of Economics, 1927–37, Hayek's colleague at LSE.—Ed.]

[29] [In the first edition, the passage reads, "it was forgotten".—Ed.]

[30] [Namely, the Banking school's doctrine that the demand for credit is virtually independent of the rate of interest. See below.—Ed.]

to which it would have been a sufficient answer. Within the next two years it had been restated by Lord King[31] and J. L. Foster,[32] and, what is much more important, it was accepted by David Ricardo, in his pamphlet of 1809, who gave it a still more modern ring by speaking of the rate of interest falling below its *natural level* in the interval between the issues of the Bank and their effects on prices.[33] He repeated this also in his *Principles*,[34] which should have been sufficient to make it generally known. The doctrine makes its appearance in the Bullion Report,[35] and it remained familiar to economists for some time after the restriction period.

In 1823, Thomas Joplin, the inventor of the currency doctrine, enunciates the same principle which a few years later he elaborated into a peculiar but very interesting theory of the "pressure and anti-pressure of capital upon cur-

[31] *Thoughts on the Effects of the Bank Restriction* (London: Cadell and Davies, and Debrett, 1803), p. 20. [The reference is inaccurate: *Thoughts on the Effects of the Bank Restrictions* (not *Restriction*) appeared in 1804 as the second and enlarged edition of *Thoughts on the Restriction of Payments in Specie at the Banks of England and Ireland* (1803); the quotation is from pp. 19–20 of the first edition and from p. 22 of the second edition, respectively. Lord Peter King (1776–1833), English politician and pamphleteer, sided with the bullionists during the restriction period. He suggested to use the market price of gold and the state of the exchanges as tests for depreciation.—Ed.]

[32] *An Essay on the Principles of Commercial Exchanges, and More Particularly of the Exchange between Great Britain and Ireland: with an Inquiry into the Practical Effects of the Bank Restrictions* (London: Hatchard, 1804), p. 113. [John Lesley Foster (1781?–1842), Irish politician and another bullionist.—Ed.]

[33] *The High Price of Bullion: A Proof of the Depreciation of Banknotes*, 3rd ed. (London: Murray,1810), p. 47, reprinted in *Economic Essays*, ed. Edward C. K. Gonner (London: Bell, 1923), p. 35 [cf. *The Works and Correspondence of David Ricardo*, ed. Piero Sraffa, vol. 3: *Pamphlets and Papers, 1809–1811* (Cambridge: Cambridge University Press, 1951; reprinted, Indianapolis: Liberty Press, 2004), p. 91—Ed.].

[34] *On the Principles of Political Economy and Taxation* [1817; 3rd ed., 1821], reprinted in *The Works of David Ricardo*, ed. John Ramsey McCulloch (London: Murray, 1846), p. 220 [cf. *Works and Correspondence*, ed. Sraffa, vol. 1, pp. 363–64—Ed.].

[35] *Bullion Report*, etc. [*Report, together with Minutes of Evidence, and Accounts, from the Select Committee on the High Price of Gold Bullion*—Ed.], octavo edition, 1810, p. 56; *The Paper Pound of 1797–1821: A Reprint of the Bullion Report*, ed. Edwin Cannan, 2nd ed. (London: King, 1925 [reprinted, New York: Kelley, 1969]), p. 51 [p. 56; the pagination of the octavo and the Cannan edition is identical. The Bullion Report addressed the question of the causes of the high price of bullion (that is, of unminted gold in terms of Bank of England notes, which were at a par with minted gold), and thereby also of foreign exchange. This divergence in price had been made possible by the 1797 Restriction Act, by which, during the Napoleonic wars and in the face of a severe external drain, the Bank of England had been prohibited to redeem its notes into gold. Under these circumstances the 'bullionists', most notably Thornton and Ricardo, identified the over-issue of notes as the cause of the price rise, and recommended the resumption of cash payments by the Bank. In contrast, the 'anti-bullionists' sided with the Bank of England in maintaining that over-issue was impossible as long as only solid 'real bills' were accepted for discounting. The report argued along the lines of the bullionists, yet failed to win the support of Parliament in 1811. For a more detailed account cf. F. A. Hayek, "The Period of Restrictions, 1797–1821, and the Bullion Debate in England", chapter 11 of F. A. Hayek, *The Trend of Economic Thinking*.—Ed.]

rency" and propounds it as a new discovery.[36] Though his theory is interwoven with some quite erroneous opinions, which probably prevented his contemporaries from recognising the real contributions contained in his writings, yet, nevertheless, he succeeds in providing the clearest explanation of the relations between the rate of interest and the fluctuations of the note circulation which had been given up to that time. The principle which, in Joplin's opinion, neither Thornton nor those who adopted his opinions discovered, and which probably was responsible for "every great fluctuation in prices that has occurred since the first establishment of our banking system", is that when the supply of capital exceeds the demand, it has the effect of compressing the country circulation: when the demand is greater than the supply, it has the effect of expanding it again.[37] He devotes some pages to an exposition of how the rate of interest operates to equalise the demand for and the supply of capital, and how any change of that rate affects productive activity, and then proceeds: "But, with our currency, or rather the currency of the country

---

[36] In a work entitled *Outlines of a System of Political Economy; written with a view to prove to Government and the Country that the cause of the present agricultural distress is entirely artificial, and to suggest a plan for the management of currency by which it may be remedied now and any recurrence of similar evils be prevented in the future* [*in future*] (London: Baldwin, Craddock, and Joy, 1823 [reprinted, New York: Kelley, 1970]), pp. 62 and 198 et seq. [pp. 198–201]. This work probably contains also the first exposition of the programme later advocated and put into practice by the members of the 'Currency School'. Joplin's second work referred to in the text is *An Analysis and History of the Currency Question* [*together with an account of the origin and growth of joint stock banking in England; comprised in a brief memoir of the writer's connexion with these subjects*—Ed.] (London: Ridgway, 1832). [The quotation referring to "pressure and anti-pressure" is from *Analysis and History*, p. 101. In the first edition, the corresponding footnote is placed directly after "Thomas Joplin" and reads, "In a work entitled *Outlines of a System of Political Economy; written with a view to prove . . . that the cause of the present agricultural distress is entirely artificial, and to suggest a plan for the management of currency*, London, 1823. I have not been able to obtain a copy of the original work. The exposition of Joplin's doctrines given in the text is based on a later book by the author, entitled *An Analysis and History of the Currency Question*, London, 1832, in which he repeats the doctrines expounded in the former book, which, as he says, was a failure and not noticed by more than two reviews which both abused it. The references in the text are to the *Analysis and History*." Thomas Joplin (ca. 1790–1847), banker, is best known for his advocacy of joint-stock banks and criticism of the monopoly of the Bank of England; his contributions to contemporary monetary debate although original, e.g., in his emphasis on the money supply of country banks, were largely neglected.—Ed.]
[In the first edition, the sentence to which this footnote is attached reads, "In 1823, Thomas Joplin, the inventor of the currency doctrine, enumerates the same principle in his peculiar but very interesting theory of the 'pressure and anti-pressure' of capital upon currency' and propounds it as a new discovery." The footnote immediately followed Joplin's name rather than being placed at the end of the sentence.—Ed.]
[37] Joplin, *Analysis and History*, p. 101. [In the original "banking" is capitalised. In the first edition the reference is placed directly in the text as "(p. 101)". Note that British banking could then be described as a three-tiered system consisting of the Bank of England as the central bank, London banks, and country banks, where the banks hold fractional reserves, consisting of gold or central bank notes.—Ed.]

banks . . . the effects are different. The interest of money, when it is abundant, is not reduced, but the circulation . . . is diminished; and on the contrary, when money is scarce, an enlargement of issues takes place, instead of a rise in the rate of interest. The Country Bankers never vary the interest they charge . . . He must, of necessity, have one fixed charge, whatever it may be: for he never can know what the true rate is. With a metallic currency, on the contrary, the Banker would always know the state of the market. In the first place, he could not lend money until it had been saved and placed in his hands, and he would have a particular amount to lend. On the other hand, he would have more or fewer persons wanting to borrow, and in proportion as the demand would exceed or fall short of the amount he had to lend, he would raise or lower his terms: . . . But, in consequence of the Country Banks being not only dealers in incipient capital, but issuers of currency, the demand for currency and the demand for capital are so mingled together that all knowledge of either is totally confounded."[38]

For the next seventy-five years there was hardly any progress in this connection. Three years after Joplin, in 1826, Thomas Tooke (who eighteen years later was to enlarge upon the erroneousness of what he then could already call the commonly received doctrine that a low rate of interest is calculated to raise prices and a high rate to depress them)[39] accepted Thornton's doctrine, and developed it in some minor points.[40] In 1832 J. Horsley Palmer reproduced it before the parliamentary committee on the Renewal of the Bank Charter,[41] and as late as 1840 the doctrine that the "demand for loans and dis-

---

[38] *Analysis and History*, pp. 108–9. Cf. also pp. 111–13. [Apart from punctuation, the quotation is slightly inaccurate. In the fourth sentence it should read, "the true rate of interest", and the last sentence start as, "But, in consequence of our Country Banks being not only dealers in incipient capital, but issuers of the currency . . ." In the first edition the reference is placed directly in the text as "(pp. 108–9. Cf. also pp. 111–13)".—Ed.]

[39] Thomas Tooke, *An Inquiry into the Currency Principle* [*the connection of the currency with prices, and the expediency of a separation of issue from banking*] (London: Longmans, 1844 [reprinted, London: Routledge and Thoemmes Press, 1996]), p. 77. [The passage starting with "the commonly received doctrine . . ." is indeed a literal quotation. Thomas Tooke (1774–1858) was an English merchant and the preeminent member of the Banking school, and thus a critic of the currency principle and the quantity theory on which it was based. Note that at LSE Hayek occupied the Tooke chair for economics and statistics.—Ed.]

[40] Thomas Tooke, *Considerations on the State of the Currency* (London: Murray, 1826 [reprinted, New York: Garland, 1983]), p. 22 [pp. 22–23], footnote. As late as 1840 he still reprinted this note in the appendix to the first volume of his *History of Prices* [cf. 1st ed. (London: Longmans, 1838)—Ed.] though not without omitting some important sentences. Cf. Gregory, "Introduction", p. 25.

[41] *Report on* [*from*] *the Committee of Secrecy on the Bank of England Charter* (London: Hansard, 1833 [1832; reprinted, Shannon: Irish University Press, 1968]), p. 18. Q. 191–97. [The phrase that begins the sentence, "In 1832 J. Horsley Palmer reproduced it before the parliamentary committee on the Renewal of the Bank Charter, and . . ." as well as the present footnote is added in

---

counts at a rate below the usual rate is insatiable" was treated almost as a matter of course by N. W. Senior,[42] and it even entered, though in a somewhat emasculated form, into J. S. Mill's *Principles of Political Economy*.[43]

6.

Before following the more modern development of this theory, I must, however, trace the origins of the second strand of thought which in the end became interwoven with the one just considered to constitute modern doctrine in this matter. While the line of thought we have already considered pays attention only to the relation between the rate of interest, the amount of money in circulation and, as a necessary consequence of the latter, the general price level, the second pays attention to the influence which an increase in the amount of money exercises upon the production of capital, either directly or through the rate of interest. The theory that an increase of money brings about an increase of capital, which has recently become very popular under the name of 'forced saving', is even older than the one we have just been considering.[44]

The first author clearly to state this doctrine and the one who elaborated it in greater detail than any of his successors up to very recent times was J. Ben-

---

the second edition, with the surname misspelled as "Horlsey". In the first edition the sentence begins, "As late as 1840 . . ." On Palmer see below, p. 271n.13—Ed.]

[42] In an anonymous article entitled "Lord King" in the *Edinburgh Review*, vol. 84, October 1846, later reprinted in N. W. Senior's *Biographical Sketches* (London: Longman, Green, 1863). The relevant parts of this article are now also reproduced in N. W. Senior's *Industrial Efficiency and Social Economy*, ed. S. Leon Levy (New York: Holt, 1928), vol. 2, pp. 117–18. [Indeed, Senior's article in question is a book review of Earl Fortescue's *A Selection from the Speeches and Writings of the Late Lord King* (London, 1844) and is now reprinted in *Money*, vol. 2 of *The Collected Works of Nassau William Senior*, ed. Donald Rutherford (Bristol: Thoemmes Press, 1998). The passage (on p. 321 of the *Edinburgh Review*) is quoted inaccurately; it should read, "demands of commerce for loans and discounts at a rate below the usual rate are insatiable". —In the first edition, in the text preceding this note Senior is referred to as "another great genius, N. W. Senior". Nassau William Senior (1790–1864), economist and policy advisor in the era between Ricardo and John Stuart Mill, was the first Drummond Professor of Political Economy at Oxford.—Ed.]

[43] Book 3, chapter 23, paragraph 4, ed. William James Ashley (London: Longmans, Green, 1909; new ed., 1921 [the 1909 edition reprinted, New York: Kelley, 1976]), pp. 646 et seq. [pp. 646–49. Cf. *Principles of Political Economy, Part 2*, ed. John M. Robson, vol. 3 (1965) of the *Collected Works of John Stuart Mill* (Toronto: University of Toronto Press; London: Routledge and Kegan Paul; reprinted, Indianapolis: Liberty Fund, 2006), pp. 653–58. John Stuart Mill (1806–73), British classical economist and moral philosopher, whose *Principles of Political Economy* was the leading textbook before the advent of Marshall's *Principles* and of neoclassical economics.—Ed.]

[44] [In the first edition this sentence reads, "The theory that an increase of money brings about an increase of capital, which has recently become very popular under the new-fangled name of 'forced saving', is almost as old as the one we have just been considering."—Ed.]

tham.[45] In a passage of his *Manual of Political Economy* written in 1804 but not published until 1843,[46] he deals in some detail with the phenomenon which he calls "Forced Frugality". By this he means the increased "addition to the mass of future wealth" which a government can bring about by applying funds raised by taxation or the creation of paper money to the production of capital goods. But interesting and important as this discussion by Bentham is, and although it is more than probable that it was known to some of the economists of this circle, the fact that it appeared in print only so many years later reduces its importance for the development of the doctrine very much.[47]

The honour of first having discussed the problem in some detail in print is apparently due to T. R. Malthus, who, in 1811, in an unsigned review[48] of Ricardo's first pamphlet, introduces his remarks with the complaint that no writer he is acquainted with "has ever seemed sufficiently aware of the influence which a different distribution of the circulating medium of the country must have on those accumulations which are destined to facilitate future production".[49] He then demonstrates on an assumed 'strong case' that a change of the proportion between capital and revenue to the advantage of capital so "as to throw the produce of the country chiefly in the hands of the

---

[45] [Jeremy Bentham (1748–1832), philosopher and legal reformer, was a major propagator of the idea of utilitarianism.—Ed.]

[46] [Cf. Jeremy Bentham, *A Manual of Political Economy, now first edited from the mss*, in *The Works of Jeremy Bentham*, published under the superintendence of his executor, John Bowring, vol. 3 (Edinburgh: William Tait, 1843; reprinted, Bristol: Thoemmes Press, 1995), p. 44; cf. also "Institute of Political Economy", in *Jeremy Bentham's Economic Writings*, ed. Werner Stark, vol. 3 (London: Allen and Unwin, 1954; reprinted, London: Routledge, 2004), p. 342. The second quotation reads in full: "By a proportionate sacrifice of present comfort, it [government] may make any addition that it pleases to the mass of future wealth."—Ed.]

[47] Bentham's contribution to this problem is discussed in somewhat greater detail in a note by the present author on "The Development of the Doctrine of 'Forced Saving'" where also an even earlier reference to the problem by H. Thornton and a number of later contributions to the discussion on it are mentioned, which are omitted in the present sketch. [Neither this footnote, nor the paragraph to which it attaches, which begins with the phrase "The first author clearly to state . . .", appear in the first edition. There is no paragraph break, and the next sentence in the first edition reads, "The honour of having drawn attention to this problem is probably due to T. R. Malthus, who, in 1811 . . .". The sentence then continues as in the second edition.—Ed.]

[48] [That is, "Review of Ricardo, *The High Price of Bullion*"—Ed.] *Edinburgh Review*, vol. 17, February 1811, pp. 363 et seq. [pp. 363–64; reprinted in *The Works of Thomas Robert Malthus*, ed. E. A. Wrigley and David Souden, vol. 7: *Essays on Political Economy* (London: Pickering, 1986), pp. 46–48. Thomas Robert Malthus (1766–1834), important classical economist, is best known for his views on population and his debate with Ricardo on the possibility of general gluts.—Ed.]. Cf. also the reply of Ricardo in the appendix to the fourth edition of his pamphlet on *High Price of Bullion* [1811; cf. *Works and Correspondence*, ed. Sraffa, vol. 3, pp. 99–127—Ed.].

[49] [Malthus, "Review of Ricardo", p. 363; reprinted, *The Works of Thomas Robert Malthus*, ed. Wrigley and Souden, vol. 7, p. 46. Hayek's quotation is inaccurate: it should read, "the circulating medium of a country" and "future productions".—Ed.]

productive classes" would have the effect that "in a short time, the produce of the country would be greatly augmented".[50] The next paragraph must be quoted in full. He writes:

> Whenever, in the actual state of things, a fresh issue of notes comes into the hands of those who mean to employ them in the prosecution and extension of profitable business, a difference in the distribution of the circulating medium takes place, similar in kind to that which has been last supposed; and produces similar, though of course comparatively inconsiderable effects, in altering the proportion between capital and revenue in favour of the former. The new notes go into the market as so much additional capital, to purchase what is necessary for the conduct of the concern. But, before the produce of the country has been increased, it is impossible for one person to have more of it, without diminishing the shares of some others. This diminution is affected by the rise of prices, occasioned by the competition of the new notes, which puts it out of the power of those who are only buyers, and not sellers, to purchase as much of the annual produce as before: While all the industrious classes—all those who sell as well as buy—are, during the progressive rise of prices, making unusual profits; and, even when this progression stops, are left with the command of a greater portion of the annual produce than they possessed previous to the new issues.[51]

The recognition of this tendency of an increased issue of notes to increase the national capital does not blind Malthus to the dangers and manifest injustice connected with it. He simply offers it, he says, as a rational explanation of the fact that a rise of prices is generally found conjoined with public prosperity.

With a single exception this suggestion of Malthus does not seem to have been appreciated at the time—though the mere fact that Ricardo replied to it at length should have made it familiar to economists.[52] The exception is a

[50] [Ibid., p. 364; reprinted, ibid., p. 47.—Ed.]

[51] [Ibid., p. 364; reprinted, ibid., pp. 47–48. There are some inaccuracies in Hayek's quotation: the first sentence refers to the "extension of a profitable business", in the fourth sentence "effected" is correct instead of "affected", and in the last sentence the passage between dashes reads, "all those that sell as well as buy".—Ed.]

[52] [There are numerous differences between the first and second editions at this juncture. In the first edition, this sentence begins a new section (section 7) and reads, "This suggestion of Malthus was not appreciated at the time—though the mere fact that Ricardo replied to it at length should have made it familiar to economists—and I have also not succeeded in tracing any direct influence on other writers of the first half of the nineteenth century, though this might very likely be possible." The next sentence reads, "Even in the period after the publication of J. S. Mills' *Principles* . . .", which appears in a slightly modified form as the first sentence of section 7 in the second edition. Three new paragraphs and two new footnotes are added in the sec-

series of memoranda on the Bullion Report which Dugald Stewart prepared in 1811 for Lord Lauderdale and which were later reprinted as an appendix to his *Lectures on Political Economy*.[53] Objecting to the oversimplified version of the quantity theory employed in the reasoning of the Bullion Report he attempts to explain the more "indirect connection between the high prices and an increased circulating medium".[54] In the course of this discussion he comes very near to the argument employed by Malthus and in one of the later memoranda actually refers to the article which in the meantime had come to his notice, and reproduces the paragraph quoted above.

There are further allusions to the problem by other authors of the early nineteenth century, notably by T. Joplin and R. Torrens,[55] and John Stuart Mill in the fourth of his *Essays on Some Unsettled Questions of Political Economy*— "On Profits and Interest"—(written in 1829 or 1830) goes at least so far as to mention that, as the result of the activity of bankers, "revenue" may be "converted into capital; and thus, strange as it may appear, the depreciation of the currency, when effected in this way, operates to a certain extent as a forced accumulation".[56]

But he believed then that this phenomenon belonged to the "further anomalies of the rate of interest which have not, so far as we are aware, been hitherto brought within the pale of exact science".[57] The first edition of his *Principles*

---

ond edition: The paragraph beginning with the phrase "With a single exception . . ." and the two that follow it, as well as the footnotes on Dugald Stewart and on Mill's *Essays on Some Unsettled Questions*, are all new. Between editions Hayek had evidently succeeded in tracing influences "on other writers of the first half of the nineteenth century", as he alluded was likely possible in the first edition.—Ed.]

[53] Cf. *The Collected Works of Dugald Stewart*, ed. Sir William Hamilton, vol. 8 [i.e., *Lectures on Political Economy*, vol. 1—Ed.] (London: Hamilton, Adams, and Edinburgh: Constable, 1855 [reprinted, London: Thoemmes Press, 1994]), pp. 440–49. A fuller discussion of D. Stewart's views on the subject will be found in the note on "The Development of the Doctrine of 'Forced Saving'", quoted before. [Dugald Stewart (1753–1828), Scottish philosopher, succeeded Adam Ferguson at the University of Edinburgh in the chair of moral philosophy, which he occupied 1785–1810. James Maitland, 8th Earl of Lauderdale (1759–1839), English politician, a strong defender of the Bullion Report and author of *An Inquiry into the Nature and Origin of Public Wealth: and into the means and causes of its increase* (Edinburgh: Constable, 1804; 2nd ed., 1819, reprinted, New York: Kelley, 1962).—Ed.]

[54] [Stewart, *Lectures on Political Economy*, vol. 1, p. 440; indeed, this is Lauderdale quoted by Stewart. The quotation is slightly inaccurate. It should read, "indirect connexion between high prices and an increased circulating medium".—Ed.]

[55] [Robert Torrens (1780–1864), a retired army officer and journalist, best known as the author of a classic defence of the currency principle.—Ed.]

[56] *Essays on Some Unsettled Questions of Political Economy* (London: Parker, 1844), p. 118. [Cf. also the reprint in *Essays on Economics and Society, Part 1*, ed. John M. Robson, vol. 4 (1967) of the *Collected Works of John Stuart Mill*, p. 307.—Ed.]

[57] [Ibid., p. 114; cf. reprinted, ed. Robson, p. 305. Hayek's quotation is inaccurate. It should read, "further anomalies in the rate of interest".—Ed.]

seems to contain nothing on this point. But in 1865, in the sixth edition, he added to his chapter on "Credit as a Substitute for Money" a footnote which so closely resembles the statement by Malthus that it seems very probable that something—perhaps the publications of D. Stewart's *Collected Works*—had directed his attention to the earlier discussion of the point.[58]

7.

In the period after the publication of J. S. Mill's *Principles* for a long time attention was paid only to the first of the two related ideas we have been analysing. For many years there was very little progress at all. Occasional restatements of the views of the earlier authors occurred, but added nothing and received little attention.[59] The doctrine of the "indirect chain of effects connecting money and prices", as developed by Sidgwick, Giffen, Nicholson, and even Marshall,[60] adds hardly anything to what had been evolved from Thornton to Tooke. More significant is the further development and perhaps independent re-discovery of the forced saving doctrine by Léon Walras in 1879.[61] Although his contribution had been practically forgotten and has only recently been recovered from oblivion by Professor Marget,[62] it is of special interest because it is probably through Walras that this doctrine reached Knut Wicksell. And it was only this great Swedish economist who at the end of the century finally succeeded in definitely welding the two, up to then, separate strands of thoughts into one.[63]

[58] Mill, *Principles of Political Economy*, ed. Ashley, p. 512. [Cf. reprinted, ed. Robson, *Part 2*, p. 528n.65. Hayek quotes the footnote in full in his "A Note on the Development of the Doctrine of 'Forced Saving'", reprinted, p. 167.—Ed.].

[59] An instance of such restatement of earlier doctrine which is somewhat surprising in view of the later opinions of this author, occurs in Adolf Wagner's early *Beiträge zur Lehre von den Banken* (Leipzig: Voss, 1857 [reprinted, Vaduz: Topos, 1977]), pp. 236–39. [Adolph Wagner (1835–1917), a founding member of the Verein für Sozialpolitik, taught from 1870 at the University of Berlin; in his 'later opinions' he became a strict advocate of state socialism. This note and the sentence to which it is attached are new to the second edition.—Ed.]

[60] Cf. James W. Angell, *Theory of International Prices: History, Criticism and Restatement* (Cambridge, MA: Harvard University Press, 1926 [reprinted, New York: Kelley, 1965]), pp. 117 et seq. [pp. 117–25].

[61] Léon Walras, "Théorie mathématique du billet de banque" [1879], reprinted in *Études d'économie politique appliqué[e]* (Lausanne: Rouge, and Paris: Pichon, 1898 [2nd ed., 1936]), pp. 348–56 [reprinted as vol. 10 of Auguste et Léon Walras, *Oeuvres économiques complètes* (Paris: Economica, 1992), pp. 318–26; translated as "Mathematical Theory of Banknotes", by Jan van Daal in *Studies in Applied Economics*, vol. 2 (London: Routledge, 2005), pp. 280–85—Ed.].

[62] [Cf. Arthur W. Marget, "Léon Walras and the 'Cash Balance Approach' to the Problem of the Value of Money", *Journal of Political Economy*, vol. 39, October 1931, pp. 569–600.—Ed.]

[63] [The paragraph that begins section 7 picks up the second sentence in section 7 of the first edition. The sentences in the first edition read as follows: "Even in the period after the publica-

His success in this regard is explained by the fact that his attempt was based on a modern and highly developed theory of interest, that of Böhm-Bawerk. But by a curious irony of fate, Wicksell[64] has become famous, not for his real improvements on the old doctrine, but for the one point in his exposition in which he definitely erred: namely, for his attempt to establish a rigid connection between the rate of interest and the changes in the general price level.

Put concisely, Wicksell's theory is as follows: If it were not for monetary disturbances, the rate of interest would be determined so as to equalise the demand for and the supply of savings.[65] This equilibrium rate, as I prefer to call it, he christens the natural[66] rate of interest. In a money economy, the actual or money rate of interest ('*Geldzins*') may differ from the equilibrium or natural rate, because the demand for and the supply of capital do not meet in their natural form but in the form of money, the quantity of which available for capital purposes may be arbitrarily changed by the banks.

Now, so long as the money rate of interest coincides with the equilibrium rate, the rate of interest remains 'neutral' in its effects on the prices of goods, tending neither to raise nor to lower them. When the banks, however, lower the money rate of interest below the equilibrium rate, which they can do by lending more than has been entrusted to them, i.e., by adding to the circulation, this must tend to raise prices; if they raise the money rate above the equilibrium rate—a case of less practical importance—they exert a depressing influence on prices. From this correct statement, however, which does not imply

---

tion of J. S. Mill's *Principles*, for a long time attention was paid only to the first of the two related ideas we have been analysing. For a long time there was very little progress at all. The doctrine of the indirect chain of effects connecting money and prices, as developed by Sidgwick, Giffen, Nicholson, and even Marshall adds hardly anything to what had been evolved from Thornton to Tooke. It is only quite at the end of the century that the Swede, Knut Wicksell, made a contribution of signal importance by a rediscovery of the doctrine which had been enunciated by Thornton, combined with a theory of the influence of changing money supplies on the formation of capital." The footnotes to Mill's *Principles*, to Wagner's *Beiträge zur Lehre von den Banken*, and to Walras's "Théorie mathématique du billet de banque" do not appear in the first edition. The rest of the paragraph from this point is identical in the two editions.—Ed.]

[64] Wicksell's first and most important exposition of this doctrine is in his *Geldzins und Güterpreise* (published in German) which should be consulted together with Wicksell's later restatement in the second volume of his *Vorlesungen über Nationalökonomie* [cf. *Interest and Prices* and *Lectures on Political Economy*, vol. 2—Ed.].

[65] [In the first edition this sentence reads, "If it were not for monetary disturbances, the rate of interest would be determined so as to equalise the demand for real capital and the supply of savings."—Ed.]

[66] Sometimes also the "normal" (*Geldzins und Güterpreise*, p. 111 [cf. *Interest and Prices*, p. 120—Ed.]) or "real" rate of interest. This latter form of expression has given rise to a confusion with a different theory concerning the influence of an expectation of price changes on the rate, which is commonly associated with the name of Fisher, but which, as mentioned before, was already known to Thornton, Ricardo, and Marshall.

that the price level would remain unchanged if the money rate corresponds to the equilibrium rate, but only that, in such conditions, there are no *monetary* causes tending to produce a change in the price level, Wicksell jumps to the conclusion that, so long as the two rates agree, the price level must always remain steady. There will be more to say about this later. For the moment, it is worth observing a further development of the theory. The rise of the price level which is supposed to be the necessary effect of the money rate remaining below the equilibrium rate, is in the first instance brought about by the entrepreneurs spending on production the increased amount of money loaned by the banks. This process, as Malthus had already shown, involves what Wicksell now called enforced or compulsory saving.[67] That is all I need to say here in explanation of the Wicksellian theory. Nor shall I here discuss the important development of this theory added by the Austrian economist, Professor Mises.[68] An exposition of the present form of this theory will form the main

---

[67] *Geldzins und Güterpreise*, pp. 102, 143 [cf. *Interest and Prices*, pp. 111, 155—Ed.]. [In the first edition this sentence reads, "This process, as Malthus had already shown, involves what Wicksell now for the first time called enforced or compulsory saving."—Ed.]

[68] *Theorie des Geldes und der Umlaufsmittel* (1912). Simultaneously with Professor Mises a distinguished Italian economist, Professor Marco Fanno, made in an exceedingly interesting and now very rare book on *Le banche e il mercato monetario* (Rome: Athenaeum, 1912) [the second part translated as *The Money Market*, trans. Cyprian P. Blamires (New York: St. Martin's Press, 1995)—Ed.], an independent attempt to develop Wicksell's theory further. A revised shorter German version of the views of this author is now available in his contribution ["Die reine Theorie des Geldmarktes"—Ed.] to the *Beiträge zur Geldtheorie*, ed. F. A. Hayek (Vienna: Springer, 1933 [reprinted, Berlin, Heidelberg, and New York: Springer, 2007), pp. 1–113—Ed.].

Considerable elements of Professor Mises' theory and particularly the doctrine of 'Forced Saving' seem to have been introduced into America through Professor Schumpeter's *Theorie der wirtschaftlichen Entwicklung*, 2nd ed. (Munich and Leipzig: Duncker and Humblot, 1926) [translated as *The Theory of Economic Development*, trans. Redvers Opie (Cambridge, MA: Harvard University Press, 1934)—Ed.] and Dr. Benjamin M. Anderson's *The Value of Money* (New York: Macmillan, 1917 [reprinted, Grove City, PA: Libertarian Press, 2005]) and gained considerable vogue since. In any case since the publication of this book in 1917 'Forced Saving' has been discussed by Professors Frank W. Taussig, *Principles of Economics*, 3rd ed. (New York: Macmillan, 1923), vol. 1, pp. 351, 359 [pp. 351, 398–99]; Frank H. Knight, *Risk, Uncertainty and Profit* (Boston: Houghton and Mifflin, 1921 [reprinted, New York: Kelley, 1964; Chicago: University of Chicago Press, 1985—Ed.]), p. 166n. [p. 165n.2] and Index [p. 379]; David Friday, *Profit, Wages and Prices* (New York: Harcourt, Brace, and Co., 1921), pp. 216–17; and Alvin H. Hansen, *Cycles of Prosperity and Depression in the United States, Great Britain and Germany*, University of Wisconsin Studies in the Social Sciences and History, vol. 5 (Madison: University of Wisconsin, 1921), pp. 104–6. Whether the American author whose views on these problems comes nearest to those expressed in the present book, Mr. Myron W. Watkins, whose exceedingly interesting article [jointly with H. W. Moulton—Ed.] on "Commercial Banking and the Formation of Capital: A Criticism", *Journal of Political Economy*, vol. 27, July 1919, pp. 578–605, I have only recently become acquainted with, is indebted to the same source I do not know.

In England similar ideas seem to have been developed independently, first by Professor Pigou ([titled "Correctives of the Trade Cycle"—Ed.] in *Is Unemployment Inevitable? An Analysis and a*

subject of my next two lectures. Here it is only necessary to point out that Professor Mises has improved the Wicksellian theory by an analysis of the different influences which a money rate of interest different from the equilibrium rate exercises on the prices of consumers' goods on the one hand, and the prices of producers' goods on the other. In this way, he has succeeded in transforming the Wicksellian theory into an explanation of the credit cycle which is logically satisfactory.

8.

But this brings me to the next part of my discussion. For it is partly upon the foundations laid by Wicksell and partly upon criticism of his doctrine that what seems to me the fourth of the great stages of the progress of monetary theory is being built. (I ought, perhaps, expressly to warn you that while up to this point of our survey I have been describing developments which have already taken place, what I am about to say about the fourth stage concerns rather what I think it should be than what has already taken definite shape.)

It would take too much time to trace chronologically the steps by which, by degrees, the Wicksellian theory has been transformed into something new. You will be better able to appreciate this change if I turn immediately to the discussion of those deficiencies of his doctrine which eventually made it necessary definitely to break away from certain of the fundamental concepts in the theory which had been taken over by him from his predecessors.

I have mentioned already that, according to Wicksell, the equilibrium rate of interest was a rate which simultaneously restricted the demand for real capital to the amount of savings available *and* secured stability of the price level. His idea was obviously one which is very generally held even at the present time, namely, that as, at an equilibrium rate of interest, money would remain neutral towards prices, therefore in such circumstances there could be no reason at all for a change of the price level.

Nevertheless, it is perfectly clear that, in order that the supply and demand for real capital should be equalised, the banks must not lend more or less than has been deposited with them as savings (and such additional amounts as may have been saved and hoarded). And this means naturally that (always excepting the case just mentioned) they must never allow the effective amount of

---

Forecast. A Continuation of the Investigations Embodied in "The Third Winter of Unemployment" (London: Macmillan, 1925), pp. 100–111 [reprinted in *Business Cycle Theory: Selected Texts 1860–1939*, vol. 3: *Monetary Theories of the Business Cycle*, ed. Harald Hagemann (London: Pickering and Chatto, 2002), pp. 128–39—Ed.]) and then in much greater detail by Mr. D. H. Robertson (*Banking Policy and the Price Level*, passim). [In the first edition, this footnote contains only the reference to Mises's work that makes up the first sentence of the present footnote.—Ed.]

money in circulation to change.[69] At the same time, it is no less clear that, in order that the price level may remain unchanged, the amount of money in circulation must change as the volume of production increases or decreases. The banks could *either* keep the demand for real capital within the limits set by the supply of savings, *or* keep the price level steady; but they cannot perform both functions at once. Save in a society in which there were no additions to the supply of savings, i.e., a stationary society, to keep the money rate of interest at the level of the equilibrium rate would mean that in times of expansion of production the price level would fall. To keep the general price level steady would mean, in similar circumstances, that the loan rate of interest would have to be lowered below the equilibrium rate. The consequences would be what they always are when the rate of investment exceeds the rate of saving.

It would be possible to cite other cases where the influence of money on prices and production is quite independent of the effects on the general price level. But it seems obvious as soon as one once begins to think about it that almost any change in the amount of money, whether it does influence the price level or not, must *always* influence relative prices. And, as there can be no doubt that it is relative prices which determine the amount and the direction of production, almost any change in the amount of money must necessarily also influence production.

But if we have to recognise that, on the one hand, under a stable price level, relative prices may be changed by monetary influences, and, on the other, that relative prices may remain undisturbed only when the price level changes, we have to give up the generally received opinion that if the general price level remains the same, the tendencies towards economic equilibrium are not disturbed by monetary influences, and that disturbing influences from the side of money cannot make themselves felt otherwise than by causing a change of the general price level.

This doctrine, which has been accepted dogmatically by almost all monetary theorists, seems to me to lie at the root of most of the shortcomings of present-day monetary theory and to be a bar to almost all further progress. Its bearing on various proposals for stabilisation is obvious. In these lectures,[70]

---

[69] From now onward the term 'amount of money in circulation' or even shortly 'the quantity of money' will be used for what should more exactly be described as the effective money stream or the amount of money payments made during a unit period of time. The problems arising out of possible divergences between these two magnitudes will only be taken up in lecture 4. [In the first edition, this footnote does not appear, and the two sentences in the text read as follows: "Nevertheless, it is perfectly clear that, in order that the supply and demand for real capital should be equalised, the banks must not lend more or less than has been deposited with them as savings. And this means naturally that they must never change the amount of their circulation."—Ed.]

[70] [In the first edition, the sentence begins with "For the moment".—Ed.]

however, it is in the theoretical foundations of these schemes rather than in the formulation of alternative practical proposals that we are interested. And here, it may be suggested, it is possible very greatly to underestimate the changes in economic theory which are implied if once we drop these unjustified assumptions. For when we investigate into all the influences of money on individual prices, quite irrespective of whether they are or are not accompanied by a change of the price level, it is not long before we begin to realise the superfluity of the concept of a general value of money, conceived as the reverse of some price level. And, indeed, I am of the opinion that, in the near future, monetary theory will not only reject the explanation in terms of a direct relation between money and the price level, but will even throw overboard the concept of a general price level and substitute for it investigations into the causes of the changes of relative prices and their effects on production. Such a theory of money, which will be no longer a theory of the value of money in general, but a theory of the influence of money on the different ratios of exchange between goods of all kinds, seems to me the probable fourth stage in the development of monetary theory.

This view of the probable future of the theory of money becomes less startling if we consider that the concept of relative prices includes the prices of goods of the same kind at different moments, and that here, as in the case of interspatial price relationships, only one relation between the two prices can correspond to a condition of 'intertemporal' equilibrium, and that this need not, a priori, be a relation of identity or the one which would exist under a stable price level. (This has a particular bearing on the problem of money as a standard of deferred payments, because in this function money is to be conceived simply as the medium which effects an intertemporal exchange.) If this view is correct, the question which in my opinion will take the place of the question whether the value of money has increased or decreased will be the question whether the state of equilibrium of the rates of intertemporal exchange is disturbed by monetary influences in favour of future or in favour of present goods.[71]

9.

It will be the object of the following lectures to show how it is possible to solve at least some of the most important problems of monetary theory without recourse to the concept of a value of money in general. It will then remain for you to make up your mind whether we can conceivably entirely dispense

[71] I have dealt more fully with the difficult question of the conditions of intertemporal equilibrium of exchange in an article "Das intertemporale Gleichgewichtssystem der Preise".

with it. For the moment, I wish only to remind you of one further reason why it seems that, in the case of money, in contrast to any other good, the question of its value in general is of no consequence.[72]

We are interested in the prices of individual goods because these prices show us how far the demand for any particular good can be satisfied. To discover the causes why certain needs, and the needs of certain persons, can be satisfied to a greater degree than others is the ultimate object of economics. There is, however, no *need* for money in this sense—the absolute amount of money in existence is of no consequence to the well-being of mankind—and there is, therefore, no objective value of money in the sense in which we speak of the objective value of goods. *What we are interested in is only how the relative values of goods as sources of income or as means of satisfaction of wants are affected by money.*

The problem is never to explain any 'general value' of money but only how and when money influences the relative values of goods and under what conditions it leaves these relative values undisturbed, or, to use a happy phrase of Wicksell, when money remains *neutral* relatively to goods.[73] Not a money which is *stable* in value but a *neutral* money must therefore form the starting point for the theoretical analysis of monetary influences on production, and the first object of monetary theory should be to clear up the conditions under which money might be considered to be neutral in this sense. We stand as yet at the very beginning of this kind of investigation. And, though I hope that what I say in the next lectures may help a little, I am fully conscious that all results we obtain at this stage should only be regarded as tentative. So far as I am concerned, it is the method of approach more than the details of the results which is of importance in what follows.

[72] [In the first edition this sentence reads, "For the moment, I wish only to give one further reason why it seems to me that, in the case of money, in contrast to any other good, the question of its value in general is of no consequence."—Ed.]

[73] Cf. the appendix to lecture 4. [The appendix and thus the footnote does not appear in the first edition.—Ed.]

THE CONDITIONS OF EQUILIBRIUM BETWEEN THE PRODUCTION OF CONSUMERS' GOODS AND THE PRODUCTION OF PRODUCERS' GOODS

"The question of how far, and in what manner, an increase of currency tends to increase capital appears to us so very important, as fully to warrant our attempt to explain it . . . It is not the *quantity* of the circulating medium which produces the effects here described, but the *different distribution* of it . . . on every fresh issue of notes . . . a larger proportion falls into the hands of those who consume and produce, and a smaller proportion into the hands of those who only consume."
—T. R. Malthus, *Edinburgh Review*, vol. 17, 1811, pp. 363 et seq.[1]

1.

Before we can attempt to understand the influence of prices on the amount of goods produced, we must know the nature of the immediate causes of a variation of industrial output.[2] Simple as this question may at first appear, contemporary theory offers at least three explanations.

2.

First of these, we may take the view that the main causes of variations of industrial output are to be found in changes of the willingness of individuals to expand effort.[3] I mention this first, because it is probably the theory which has at present the greatest number of adherents in this country. That this point of view is so widely accepted in England is probably due to the fact that a comparatively great number of economists here are still under the influ-

---

[1] [Malthus, "Review of Ricardo", pp. 363–64; reprinted, *The Works of Thomas Robert Malthus*, ed. Wrigley and Souden, vol. 7, pp. 46–48.—Ed.]

[2] [In the corresponding passage of *Preise und Produktion* Hayek speaks of "the net product of the economy" (p. 32).—Ed.]

[3] [In the first edition, "to expend effort".—Ed.]

ence of 'real cost' theories of value[4] which make this type of explanation of any change in the total value of output the natural one. Mr. D. H. Robertson's stimulating book on *Banking Policy and the Price Level* provides, perhaps, the best example of reasoning based on this assumption. Yet I do not think that this assumption is at all justified by our common experience; it is a highly artificial assumption to which I would only be willing to resort when all other explanations had failed. But its correctness is a question of fact, and I shall make no attempt to refute it directly. I shall only try to show that there are other ways of accounting for changes in industrial output which seem less artificial.

3.

The second type of explanation is the one which 'explains' variations of production simply by the changes of the amount of factors of production used. In my opinion this is no explanation at all. It depends essentially upon a specious appeal to facts. Starting from the existence of unused resources of all kinds, known to us in daily experience, it regards any increase of output simply as the consequence of bringing more unused factors into use, and any diminution of output as the consequence of more resources becoming idle. Now, that any such change in the amount of resources employed implies a corresponding change in output is, of course, beyond question. But it is not true that the existence of unused resource is a *necessary* condition for an increase of output, nor are we entitled to take such a situation as a starting point for theoretical analysis. If we want to explain fluctuations of production, we have to give a complete explanation. Of course this does not mean that we have to start for that purpose ab ovo with an explanation of the whole economic process. But it does mean that we have to start where general economic theory stops; that is to say at a condition of equilibrium when no unused resources exist. The existence of such unused resources is itself a fact which needs explanation. It is not explained by static analysis and, accordingly, we are not entitled to take it for granted. For this reason I cannot agree that Professor Wesley Mitchell is justified when he states that he considers it no part of his task "to determine how the fact of cyclical oscillations in economic activity can be reconciled with the general theory of equilibrium, or how that theory can be reconciled

---

[4] [The 'real cost' theories of the classical economists, which Marshall had integrated into the framework of his *Principles* by way of the supply schedule, maintained that the prices of consumers' goods derive from the quantity of the means of production used up in manufacturing them. In contrast, from Menger onwards, Austrian economists emphasised the role of opportunity costs so that the price of consumers' goods reflects the utility foregone in choosing a specific good among a set of alternatives.—Ed.]

with facts".[5] On the contrary, it is my conviction that if we want to explain economic phenomena at all, we have no means available but to build on the foundations given by the concept of a tendency towards an equilibrium. For it is this concept alone which permits us to explain fundamental phenomena like the determination of prices or incomes, an understanding of which is essential to any explanation of fluctuation[6] of production. If we are to proceed systematically, therefore, we must start with a situation which is already sufficiently explained by the general body of economic theory. And the only situation which satisfies this criterion is the situation in which all available resources are employed. The existence of unused resources must be one of the main objects of our explanation.[7]

4.

To start from the assumption of equilibrium has a further advantage. For in this way we are compelled to pay more attention to causes of changes in the industrial output whose importance might otherwise be underestimated. I refer to changes in the methods of using the existing resources. Changes in the direction given to the existing productive forces are not only the main cause of fluctuations of the output of individual industries; the output of industry as a whole may also be increased or decreased to an enormous extent by changes in the use made of existing resources. Here we have the third of the contemporary explanations of fluctuations which I referred to at the beginning of the lecture. What I have here in mind are *not* changes in the methods of production made possible by the progress of technical knowledge, but the increase of output made possible by a transition to more capitalistic methods of production, or, what is the same thing, by organising production so that, at any given moment, the available resources are employed for the satisfaction of the needs of a future more distant than before. It is to this effect of a transition to more or less 'roundabout'[8] methods of production that I wish particularly to direct your attention. For, in my opinion, it is only by an analysis of

---

[5] Wesley C. Mitchell, *Business Cycles: The Problem and Its Setting* (New York: National Bureau of Economic Research, 1927), p. 462.

[6] [In the first edition, "fluctuations".—Ed.]

[7] I have dealt more fully with the relation between pure economic theory and the explanation of business fluctuations in my book *Monetary Theory and the Trade Cycle*, chapters 1 and 2. [In the first edition Hayek cites the German edition of the book, *Geldtheorie und Konjunkturtheorie*.—Ed.]

[8] [In the first edition, this word is hyphenated, "round-about". The notion of 'roundabout methods of production' refers to Böhm-Bawerk's idea of the productivity of time, that is, the superiority of more time-consuming production processes. Cf. also the editor's introduction to this volume, pp. 25–26.—Ed.]

this phenomenon that in the end we can show how a situation can be created in which it is temporarily impossible to employ all available resources.

The processes involved in any such transition from a less to a more capitalistic form of production are of such a complicated nature that it is only possible to visualise them clearly if we start from highly simplified assumptions and work through gradually to a situation more like reality. For the purpose of these lectures, I shall divide this investigation into two parts. Today I shall confine myself to a consideration of the conditions under which an equilibrium between the production of producers' goods and the production of consumers' goods is established, and the relation of this equilibrium to the flow of money; I reserve for the next lecture a more detailed explanation of the working of the price mechanism during the period of transition, and of the relations between changes in the price system and the rate of interest.

5.

My first task is to define the precise meaning of certain terms. The term *production* I shall always use in its widest possible sense, that is to say, all processes necessary to bring goods into the hands[9] of the consumer. When I mean land and labour, I shall speak of *original means of production*. When I use the phrase *factors of production* without further qualification this will cover capital also, that is to say this term will include all factors from which we derive *income* in the form of wages, rent, and interest. When I use the expression *producers' goods*, I shall be designating all goods existing at any moment which are not consumers' goods, that is to say, *all* goods which are directly or indirectly used in the production of consumers' goods, *including* therefore the original means of production, as well as instrumental goods and all kinds of unfinished goods. Producers' goods which are not original means of production, but which come between the original means of production and consumers' goods, I shall call *intermediate products*. None of these distinctions coincides with the customary distinction between durable and non-durable goods, which I do not need for my present purpose. I shall, however, have to use this distinction and to add a new one, which stands in some relation to it, in my next lecture.

6.

I have already pointed out that it is an essential feature of our modern, 'capitalistic', system of production that at any moment a far larger proportion of

---

[9] [In the first edition, "hand".—Ed.]

the available original means of production is employed to provide consumers' goods for some more or less distant future than is used for the satisfaction of immediate needs. The raison d'être of this way of organising production is, of course, that by lengthening the production process we are able to obtain a greater quantity of consumers' goods out of a given quantity of original means of production. It is not necessary for my present purpose to enter at any length into an explanation of this increase of productivity by roundabout methods of production. It is enough to state that within practical limits we may increase the output of consumers' goods from a given quantity of original means of production indefinitely, provided we are willing to wait long enough for the product. The thing which is of main interest for us is that any such change from a method of production of any given duration to a method which takes more or less time implies quite definite changes in the organisation of production, or, as I shall call this particular aspect of organisation, to distinguish it from other more familiar aspects, changes in the *structure of production*.

In order to get a clear view of what is actually implied by these changes in the structure of production it is useful to employ a schematic representation.[10] For this purpose, I find it convenient to represent the successive applications of the original means of production which are needed to bring forth the output of consumers' goods accruing at any moment of time, by the hypotenuse of a right-angled triangle, such as the triangle in fig. 1.

The value of these original means of production is expressed by the horizontal projection of the hypotenuse, while the vertical dimension, measured in arbitrary periods from the top to the bottom, expresses the progress of time, so that the inclination of the line representing the amount of original means of production used means that these original means of production are expended continuously during the whole process of production. The bottom of the triangle represents the value of the current output of consumers' goods. The area of the triangle thus shows the totality of the successive stages through which the several units of original means of production pass before

[10] The following diagrams were originally the result of an attempt to replace the somewhat clumsy tables of figures, used for the same purpose in my "'Paradox' of Saving", by a more easily grasped form of representation. Later I noticed that similar triangular figures had been used as representations of the capitalistic process of production not only by William Stanley Jevons, *The Theory of Political Economy*, 4th ed. (London: Macmillan, 1911) [reprinted as vol. 3 of Jevons, *Writings on Economics*—Ed.], pp. 230–37, but particularly also by Wicksell, *Lectures*, vol. 1, pp. 152 et seq. [cf. pp. 152 and 159–60—Ed.], and, following him, Gustaf Åckerman [Åkerman], *Realkapital und Kapitalzins, Part I* (Stockholm: Centraltryckeriet, 1923) [cf. chapter 6—Ed.]. Dr. Marschak has recently made the very appropriate suggestion to designate these triangular figures as the "Jevonian Investment Figures". [Cf. Jacob Marschak, "Volksvermögen und Kassenbedarf", *Archiv für Sozialwissenschaft und Sozialpolitik*, vol. 68, no. 4, 1933, p. 395n.13. This footnote does not appear in the first edition.—Ed.]

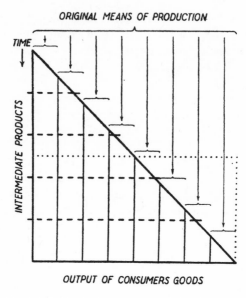

Figure 1

they become ripe for consumption. It also shows the total amount of intermediate products which must exist at any moment of time in order to secure a continuous output of consumers' goods. For this reason we may conceive of this diagram not only as representing the successive stages of the production of the output of any given moment of time, but also as representing the processes of production going on simultaneously in a stationary society. To use a happy phrase of J. B. Clark's, it gives a picture of the 'synchronised process of production'.[11, 12]

---

[11] The methodological bearing of the concept of a synchronised production is particularly well brought out by Hans Mayer in his article "Produktion", in the *Handwörterbuch der Staatswissenschaften*, 4th ed. rev., ed. Ludwig Elster, Adolf Weber, and Friedrich Wieser, vol. 6 (Jena: Fischer, 1925), pp. 1115 et seq. [pp. 1115–16]. [In the first edition, the reference reads, "by Hans Mayer in his brilliant article".—Ed.]

[Cf. for example John Bates Clark, *The Distribution of Wealth: A Theory of Wages, Interest and Profits* (New York: Macmillan, 1899; reprinted, Kelley, 1975), chapter 20: "Production and Consumption Synchronized by Rightly Apportioned Capital". John Bates Clark (1847–1938), professor of economics at Columbia University, 1895–1923, energetically propagated a marginal productivity theory of distribution.—Ed.]

[12] So long as we confine ourselves to the real aspects of the capital structure the triangular figures may be taken to represent not only the stock of goods in process but also the stock of durable instruments existing at any moment of time. The different instalments of future services which such goods are expected to render will in that case have to be imagined to belong to different 'stages' of production corresponding to the time interval which will elapse before these

Now it should be clear without further explanation that the proportion between the amount of intermediate products (represented by the area of the triangle) which is necessary at any moment of time to secure a continuous output of a given quantity of consumers' goods, and the amount of that output,[13] must grow with the length of the roundabout process of production. As the average time interval between the application of the original means of production and the completion of the consumers' goods increases, production becomes more capitalistic, and vice versa. In the case we are contemplating in which the original means of production are applied at a constant rate throughout the whole process of production, this average time is exactly half as long as the time which elapses between the application of the first unit of original means of production and the completion of the process. Accord-

---

services mature. (For a more detailed discussion of the problems arising out of the two different aspects, of actual duration of production and the durability of goods, in which time enters in the productive process, cf. my article "On the Relationship between Investment and Output"). But as soon as it is tried to use the diagrammatic representations to show the successive transfers of the intermediate products from stage to stage in exchange for money it becomes evidently impossible to treat durable goods in the same way as goods in process since it is impossible to assume that the individual services embodied in any durable goods will regularly change hands as they approach a stage nearer to the moment when they will actually be consumed. For this reason it has been necessary, as has been pointed out in the preface, to abstract from the existence of durable goods so long as the assumption is made that the total stock of intermediate products as it gradually proceeds towards the end of the process of production is exchanged against money at regular intervals.

[This footnote is new in the second edition, and replaces two footnotes from the first. The deleted footnotes read as follows:

First footnote: "There is some difficulty in regard to the way in which durable goods, particularly instrumental goods, rendering services continuously throughout their working life, are to be taken account of in our schematic representation. While, for purposes of general theory, their period of life is to be considered as equivalent to a roundabout production of corresponding length, for our purpose, it is more convenient to regard only that part of these durable goods which is currently used up and renewed as entering into the total of intermediate products existing at any moment."

Second footnote: "It is perhaps worth observing that a substantially similar diagram was used by Jevons to illustrate his theory of capital. See *The Theory of Political Economy*, 2nd ed. (London: Macmillan, 1879) [reprinted as vol. 2 of *Writings on Economics*—Ed.], pp. 241–87."—Ed.]

[13] It would be more exact to compare the stock of intermediate products existing *at a moment* of time not with the output of consumers' goods *during a period* of time, but rather with the rate at which consumers' goods mature at the same moment of time. Since, however, this output at a moment of time would be infinitely small, that proportion could only be expressed as a differential quotient of a function which represents the flow of intermediate products at the point where this flow ends, i.e., where the intermediate products become consumers' goods. This relationship is essentially the same as that between the total quantity of water in a stream and the rate at which this water passes the mouth of this stream. (This simile seems to be more appropriate than the more familiar one which considers capital as a 'stock' and only income as a 'flow'. Cf. on this point Nico Jacob Polak, *Grundzüge der Finanzierung mit Rücksicht auf die Kreditdauer* (Ber-

ingly, the total amount of intermediate products may also be represented by a rectangle half as high as the triangle, as indicated by the dotted line in the diagram. The areas of the two figures are necessarily equal, and it sometimes assists the eye to have a rectangle instead of a triangle when we have to judge the relative magnitude represented by the area of the figure. Furthermore, it should be noticed that, as the figure represents values and not physical production, the surplus return obtained by the roundabout methods of production is not represented in the diagram. In this lecture I have intentionally neglected interest. We shall have to take that into consideration next time. Until then we may assume that the intermediate products remain the property of the owners of the original means of production until they have matured into consumers' goods and are sold to consumers. Interest is then received by the owners of the original means of production together with wages and rent.

7.

A perfectly continuous process of this sort is somewhat unwieldy for theoretical purposes: moreover such an assumption is not perhaps sufficiently realistic. It would be open to us to deal with the difficulties by the aid of higher mathematics. But I, personally, prefer to make it amenable to a simpler method by dividing the continuous process into distinct periods, and by substituting for the concept of a continuous flow the assumption that goods move intermittently in equal intervals from one stage of production to the next. In this way, in my view, the loss in precision is more than compensated by the gain in lucidity.

Probably the simplest method of transforming the picture of the continuous process into a picture of what happens in a given period is to make cross sections through our first figure at intervals corresponding to the periods chosen, and to imagine observers being posted at each of these cross cuts who watch and note down the amount of goods flowing by. If we put these cross sections, as indicated by the broken lines in fig. 1, at the end of each period, and represent the amount of goods passing these lines of division in a period

---

lin: Spaeth and Linde, 1926), p. 13.) It is convenient to treat the quantity of intermediate products at any point of this stream as a function of time $f(t)$ and accordingly the total quantity of intermediate products in the stream, as an integral of this function over a period r equal to the total length of the process of production. If we apply this to any process of production beginning at the moment x, the total quantity of intermediate products in the stream will be expressed by $\int_x^{x+r} f(t)dt$, and the output of consumers' goods at a moment of time by $f(x+r)$. In the diagrams used in the text the function $f(t)$ is represented by the hypotenuse, its concrete value $f(x+r)$ by the horizontal side and the integral by the area of the triangle. There is of course no reason to assume that the function $f(t)$ will be linear, i.e., that the amount of original factors applied during successive stages of the process is constant, as is assumed in the diagrams. On these and some connected points see the article "On the Relationship between Investment and Output", quoted in the preceding footnote. [This footnote does not appear in the first edition.—Ed.]

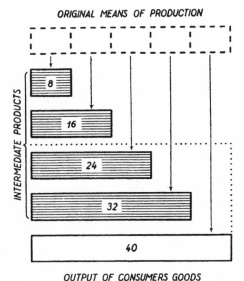

ORIGINAL MEANS OF PRODUCTION

INTERMEDIATE PRODUCTS

8

16

24

32

40

OUTPUT OF CONSUMERS GOODS

Figure 2

by a rectangle of corresponding size, we get the new illustration of the same process given in fig. 2.

It is convenient for the purposes of exposition to count only that part of the total process of production which is completed during one of these periods, as a separate stage of production. Each of the successive shaded blocks in the diagram will then represent the product of the corresponding stage of production as it is passed on to the next while the differences in the length of the successive blocks correspond to the amount of original means of production used in the succeeding stage. The white block at the bottom represents the output of consumers' goods during the period. In a stationary state, which is still the only state I am considering, this output of consumers' goods is necessarily equal to the total income from the factors of production used, and is exchanged for this income. The proportion of the white area to the shaded area, in this diagram 40:80 or 1:2, expresses the proportion between the output of consumers' goods and the output of intermediate products (or between the amount of consumption and the amount of new and renewed investment during any period of time).

So far, I have used this schematic illustration of the process of production only to represent the movements of goods. It is just as legitimate to use it as an illustration of the movement of money. While goods move downwards from the top to the bottom of our diagram, we have to conceive of money moving in the opposite direction, being paid first for consumers' goods and thence moving upwards until, after a varying number of intermediary movements, it

225

is paid out as income to the owners of the factors of production, who in turn use it to buy consumers' goods. But in order to trace the relation between actual money payments, or the proportional quantities of money used in the different stages[14] of production, and the movements of goods, we need a definite assumption in regard to the division of the total process among different firms, which alone makes an exchange of goods against money necessary. For this does not by any means necessarily coincide with our division into separate stages of production of equal length. I shall begin with the simplest assumption, that these two divisions do coincide, that is to say that goods moving towards consumption do change hands against money in equal intervals which correspond to our unit production periods.

In such a case, the proportion of money spent for consumers' goods and money spent for intermediate products is equal to the proportion between the total demand for consumers' goods and the total demand for the intermediate products necessary for their continuous production; and this, in turn, must correspond, in a state of equilibrium, to the proportion between the output of consumers' goods during a period of time and the output of intermediate products of all earlier stages during the same period. Given the assumptions we are making, all these proportions are accordingly equally expressed by the proportion between the area of the white rectangle and the total shaded area. It will be noticed that the same device of the dotted line as was used in the earlier figure is employed to facilitate the comparison of the two areas. The dotted rectangle shows that, in the kind of production represented by fig. 2, which actually takes four successive stages, the average length of the roundabout process is only two stages, and the amount of intermediate products is therefore twice as great as the output of consumers' goods.

8.

Now if we adopt this method of approach, certain fundamental facts at once become clear. The first fact which emerges is that the amount of money spent on producers' goods during any period of time may be far greater than the amount spent for consumers' goods during the same period. It has been computed, indeed, that in the United States, payments for consumers' goods amount only to about one-twelfth of the payments made for producers' goods of all kinds.[15] Nevertheless, this fact has not only very often been overlooked, it was even expressly denied by no less an authority than Adam Smith. Accord-

---

[14] [In the first edition, misprinted as "stage".—Ed.]

[15] Cf. Marius W. Holtrop, *De Omloopssnelheid van het Geld* (Amsterdam: Paris, 1928), p. 181 [cf. the abridged version translated into German by Erich Schiff as "Die Umlaufsgeschwindigkeit des Geldes" and reprinted in *Beiträge zur Geldtheorie*, ed. Hayek, p. 186—Ed.].

ing to Smith:[16] "The value of goods circulated between the different dealers never can exceed the value of those circulated between dealers and consumers; whatever is bought by the dealer being ultimately destined to be sold to the consumers." This proposition clearly rests upon a mistaken inference from the fact that the total expenditure made in production must be covered by the return from the sale of the ultimate products; but it remained unrefuted, and quite recently in our own day it has formed the foundation of some very erroneous doctrines.[17] The solution of the difficulty is, of course, that most goods are exchanged several times against money before they are sold to the consumer, and on the average exactly as many times as often as the total amount spent for producers' goods is larger than the amount spent for consumers' goods.

Another point which is of great importance for what follows, and which, while often overlooked in current discussion,[18] is quite obvious if we look at our diagram, is the fact that what is generally called the capital equipment of society—the total of intermediate products in our diagram—is not a magni-

---

[16] Adam Smith, *An Inquiry into the Nature and Causes of the Wealth of Nations* (1776), book 2, chapter 1 [chapter 2, paragraph 88], ed. Edwin Cannan, 5th ed. (London: Methuen, 1930), vol. 1, p. 305. [Cf. *The Glasgow Edition of the Works and Correspondence of Adam Smith*, vol. 1, ed. R. H. Campbell and A. S. Skinner (Oxford: Oxford University Press, 1976; reprinted, Indianapolis: Liberty Press, 1981), p. 322. The quotation is slightly inaccurate. It should read, "The value of the goods circulated between the different dealers, never can exceed the value of those circulated between the dealers and the consumers; whatever is bought by the dealers, being ultimately destined to be sold to the consumers."—Ed.] It is interesting to note that this statement of Adam Smith is referred to by Thomas Tooke as a justification of the erroneous doctrines of the Banking School. (Cf. *An Inquiry into the Currency Principle*, p. 71.)

[17] Cf. William Truffant Foster and Wadill Catchings, *Profits*, Publications of the Pollak Foundation, no. 8 (Boston and New York: Houghton Mifflin, 1925), and a number of other books by the same authors and published in the same series. For a detailed criticism of their doctrines, cf. my article "The 'Paradox' of Saving". [In the first edition Hayek cites the German version of his article, "Widersinn des Sparens".—Ed.]

[18] J. S. Mill's emphasis on the "perpetual consumption and reproduction of capital" [cf. *Principles of Political Economy*, book 1, chapter 5, paragraph 7, ed. Ashley, p. 74; reprinted, ed. Robson, *Part 1*, p. 74—Ed.], like most of his other penetrating, but often somewhat obscurely expressed observations on capital, has not had the deserved effect, although it directs attention to the essential quality of capital which distinguishes it from other factors of production. More recently the misplaced emphasis which some authors, particularly Professors J. B. Clark, J. Schumpeter, and F. H. Knight, have put on the tautological statement that so long as stationary conditions prevail capital is *ex definitione* permanent, has further contributed to obscure the problem. [Here Hayek refers to the past debates between Böhm-Bawerk and Schumpeter and Clark, respectively, as well as the ongoing controversy between himself and Knight. The main point emphasised by Hayek is that capital is non-permanent and thus, even in stationary equilibrium, the maintenance of capital is the result of and must be explained by recourse to individual decisions. Cf. on this Avi J. Cohen, "The Mythology of Capital or of Static Equilibrium? The Böhm-Bawerk/Clark Controversy", *Journal of the History of Economic Thought*, vol. 30, June 2008, pp. 151–71. Frank H. Knight (1885–1972), professor of economics at the University of Chicago, 1928–52, author of the classic *Risk, Uncertainty and Profit*. On Clark and Schumpeter, see above, pp. 76 and 222. This footnote does not appear in the first edition.—Ed.]

tude which, once it is brought into existence, will necessarily last for ever independently of human decisions. Quite the contrary: whether the structure of production remains the same depends entirely upon whether entrepreneurs find it profitable to re-invest the usual proportion of the return from the sale of the product of their respective stages of production in turning out intermediate goods of the same sort.[19] Whether this is profitable, again, depends upon the prices obtained for the product of this particular stage of production on the one hand and on the prices paid for the original means of production and for the intermediate products taken from the preceding stage of production on the other. The continuance of the existing degree of capitalistic organisation depends, accordingly, on the prices paid and obtained for the product of each stage of production and these prices are, therefore, a very real and important factor in determining the direction of production.

The same fundamental fact may be described in a slightly different way. The money stream which the entrepreneur representing any stage of production receives at any given moment is always composed of net income which he may use for consumption without disturbing the existing method of production, and of parts which he must continuously re-invest.[20] But it depends entirely upon him whether he re-distributes his total money receipts in the same proportions as before. And the main factor influencing his decisions will be the magnitude of the profits he hopes to derive from the production of his particular intermediate product.[21]

[19] [In *Preise und Produktion*, p. 46, the passage reads, perhaps more intelligibly, "whether entrepreneurs find it profitable to re-invest the same amount from the sale of the product of their respective stages of production into the production of the same intermediate goods as hitherto".—Ed.]

[20] [In *Preise und Produktion*, p. 47n., Hayek adds a quotation from Joplin's *Outlines of a System of Political Economy*, pp. 157–58, notable for its aquatic metaphors:

"The money in circulation may be divided into two descriptions; that which is employed in exchanges of consumable articles, and that which is employed in making transfers of capital and property. The first may be termed its consumptive, the last its abstract circulation.

Money in Consumptive Circulation composed of Individual Currents

From that great lake, if it may be so termed, or mass of money in consumptive circulation, each individual has a stream of its [his] own, that continually flows in to him, and from him. The magnitude of this stream is proportioned to his income and expenditure; or if he does not expend it himself, he lends it, which is the same, to others who do.

This mass, or lake, is entirely formed of these streams, which are in continual motion. It is not all the money that passes through the hands of a merchant or trader, however, which forms his own particular stream of circulation. In general, only a very small part of it does so. That part alone which becomes his, in the shape of profit, belongs to his own current. With the rest, he is only an agent, by which it is advanced forward in the respective streams to which it belongs . . ."—Ed.]

[21] [In *Preise und Produktion*, pp. 48–49, Hayek inserted an additional paragraph, of which he reproduced the following translation in his "A Rejoinder to Mr. Keynes", p. 402n.5; reprinted, p. 163n.12: "Whether production will retain its present capitalistic structure will therefore depend

9.

And now at last we are ready to commence to discuss the main problem of this lecture, the problem of how a transition from less to more capitalistic methods of production, or vice versa, is actually brought about, and what conditions must be fulfilled in order that a new equilibrium may be reached. The first question can be answered immediately: a transition to more (or less) capitalistic methods of production will take place if the total demand for producers' goods (expressed in money)[22] increases (or decreases) relatively to the demand for consumers' goods. This may come about in one of two ways: either as a result of changes in the volume of voluntary saving (or its opposite), or as a result of a change in the quantity of money which alters the funds at the disposal of the entrepreneurs for the purchase of producers' goods. Let us first consider the case of changes in voluntary saving, that is, simple shifts of demand between consumers' goods and producers' goods.[23]

As a starting point, we may take the situation depicted in fig. 2, and suppose that consumers save and invest an amount of money equivalent to one fourth of their income of one period.[24] We may assume further that these savings are

---

upon whether the proportion between the amount of money used to demand producers' goods and the amount of money used to demand consumers' goods remains the same. How any change of this proportion will lead to a change in the capitalistic structure of production will be shown in following paragraphs of this chapter and in the following chapter. There is, however, one more point which needs some clearing up before we can enter upon that discussion. One might be tempted to consider any new investment in a firm as a net increase in the means available for production, and to overlook the fact that in the normal course of business always a great number of firms not only make no profit but suffer actual losses, and are therefore unable to reinvest in its production constantly an amount equivalent to the cost of their current output. This will, for instance, be regularly the case in industries which decline as a consequence of a change in technique or in fashion. In this case, in order to maintain the relative demand for producers' goods at its existing level it is necessary that these losses be made up by new savings, for instance from the industries which gain in consequence of the same change. Only the part of the current savings which exceeds the amount necessary to make up for these losses, or net savings, must therefore be considered as an addition to the demand for producers' goods, and where I use the expression savings in the following pages this means always only net savings in this sense."—Ed.]

[22] [In the first edition, the following footnote appears at this point: "For the purposes of this discussion it will be remembered that we are supposing this demand to be expressed in money, but of course this is only a matter of convenience."—Ed.]

[23] I am deliberately discussing here the 'strong case' where saving implies a reduction in the demand for *all* consumers' goods, although this is a highly unlikely case to occur in practice, since it is in this case that many people find it so difficult to understand how a general decrease in the demand for consumers' goods should lead to an increase of investment. Where, as will regularly be the case, the reduction in the demand for consumers' goods affect only a few kinds of such goods, these special difficulties would, of course, be absent. [This footnote does not appear in the first edition.—Ed.]

[24] [As will become apparent from the argument in the text, with regard to saving and income Hayek does not refer to net, but to gross magnitudes, that is, inclusive of depreciation allowances;

made continuously, exactly as they can be used for building up the new process of production. The proportion of the demand for consumers' goods to the demand for intermediate products will then ultimately be changed from 40:80 to 30:90, or 1:2 to 1:3. The additional amounts of money available for the purchase of intermediate products must now be so applied that the output of consumers' goods may be sold for the reduced sum of thirty now available for that purpose. It should now be sufficiently clear that this will only be the case if the average length of the roundabout processes of production and, therefore, in our instance, also the number of successive stages of production, is increased in the same proportion as the demand for intermediate products has increased relatively to the demand for consumers' goods, i.e., from an average of two to an average of three (or from an actual number of four, to an actual number of six) stages of production. When the transition is completed, the structure of production will have changed from that shown in fig. 2 to the one shown in fig. 3. (It should be remembered that the relative magnitudes in the two figures are values expressed in money and not physical quantities, that the amount of original means of production used has remained the same, and that the amount of money in circulation and its velocity of circulation are also supposed to remain unchanged.)

If we compare the two diagrams, we see at once that the nature of the change consists in a stretching of the money stream flowing from the consumers' goods to the original means of production. It has, so to speak, become longer and narrower. Its breadth at the bottom stage, which measures the amount of money spent during a period of time on consumers' goods and, at the same time, the amount of money received as income in payment for the use of the factors of production, has permanently decreased from forty to thirty. This means that the price of a unit of the factors of production, the total amount

---

in particular, in the example he is going to employ, gross income is equivalent to the total money stream. Thus, consumers are assumed to fix the proportion of the money spent on consumers' goods (30) to the money spent on producers' goods (90), or to the total money stream (120). Accordingly, at the beginning of the transition all of the increase in gross saving will become net investment, yet gradually turn into reinvestment until the new equilibrium (stationary state) is reached. In the new stationary state gross saving is maintained at a higher proportion of gross income with net saving again at zero. For a contemporary exposition cf. Ragnar Frisch, "The Interrelation Between Capital Production and Consumer-Taking", *Journal of Political Economy*, vol. 39, October 1931, pp. 646–54, and the reference in Hayek, "Profits, Interest and Investment", reprinted, p. 242. Note that in correspondence Fritz Machlup criticised the obscurity of the passage in the text along these lines (cf. Machlup to Hayek, March 10, 1935, Fritz Machlup Papers, box 43, folder 15, Hoover Institution Archives, Stanford University). Fritz Machlup (1902–83), Austrian economist and a friend of Hayek from their student days in Vienna, immigrated to the United States in 1935 and taught at the University of Buffalo, John Hopkins University, and finally at Princeton. During the 1930s and 1940s Hayek and Machlup led an extensive correspondence on many issues topical to Hayek's writings.—Ed.]

ORIGINAL MEANS OF PRODUCTION

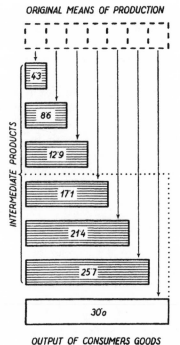

OUTPUT OF CONSUMERS GOODS

Figure 3

of which (if we neglect the increase of capital) has remained the same, will fall in the same proportion, and the price of a unit of consumers' goods, the output of which has increased as a consequence of the more capitalistic methods of production, will fall in still greater proportion. The amount of money spent in each of the later stages of production has also decreased, while the amount used in the earlier stages has increased, and the total spent on intermediate products has increased also because of the addition of a new stage of production.[25]

[25] [In effect, the addition of *two* new stages of production.—Ed.] To avoid misunderstandings I have now substituted the terms 'earlier' and 'later' stages used by Professor Taussig in this connection [cf., e.g., Frank William Taussig, *Principles of Economics*, 3rd ed. (New York: Macmillan, 1921), vol. 2, chapter 38, in particular p. 14—Ed.], for the expressions 'higher' and 'lower' which are unequivocal only with reference to the diagrams but are liable to be confused with such expressions as 'highly finished' products, particularly as A. Marshall has used the terms in this reverse sense (cf. *Industry and Trade*, 2nd ed. (London: Macmillan, 1919) [reprinted in *The Collected Works of Alfred Marshall* (1997)—Ed.], p. 219). [This footnote does not, of course, appear in the first edition, where the final sentence of the paragraph reads, "The amount of money

231

Now it should be clear that to this change in the distribution of the amounts of money spent in the different stages of production there will correspond a similar change in the distribution of the total amount of goods existing at any moment. It should also be clear that the effect thus realised—given the assumptions we are making—is one which fulfils the object of saving and investing, and is identical with the effect which would have been produced if the savings were made in kind instead of in money. Whether it has been brought about in the most expeditious way, and whether the price changes which follow from our assumptions provide a suitable stimulus to the readjustment are not questions with which we need concern ourselves at this juncture. Our present purpose is fulfilled if we have established, that under the assumptions we have made, the initial variation in the proportional demand for consumers' goods and for intermediate products respectively becomes permanent, that a new equilibrium may establish itself on this basis, and that the fact that the amount of money remains unchanged, in spite of the increase of the output of consumers' goods and of the still greater increase of the total turnover of goods of all kinds and stages, offers no fundamental difficulties to such an increase of production, since total expenditure on the factors of production, or total costs, will still be covered by the sums received out of the sales of consumers' goods.

But now the question arises: does this remain true if we drop the assumptions that the amount of money remains unchanged and that, during the process of production, the intermediate products are exchanged against money at equal intervals of time?

10.

Let us begin by investigating the effects of a change in the amount of money in circulation. It will be sufficient if we investigate only the case most frequently to be encountered in practice: the case of an increase of money in the form of credits granted to producers. Again we shall find it convenient to start from the situation depicted in fig. 2 and to suppose that the same change in the proportion between the demand for consumers' goods and the demand for intermediate products, which, in the earlier instance, was supposed to be produced by voluntary saving, is now caused by the granting of additional credits to producers. For this purpose, the producers must receive an amount

spent in each of the lower stages of production has also decreased, while the amount used in the higher stages has increased, and the total spent on intermediate products has increased also because of the addition of a new stage of production." On the Mengerian origin of the terms 'higher' or 'lower order goods', see above, p. 83n.13.—Ed.]

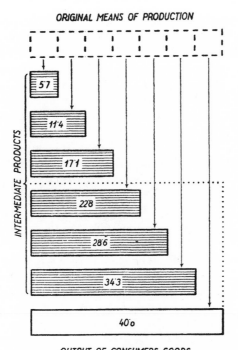

ORIGINAL MEANS OF PRODUCTION

INTERMEDIATE PRODUCTS

5·7

11·4

17·1

22·8

28·6

34·3

40·0

OUTPUT OF CONSUMERS GOODS

Figure 4

of forty in additional money.[26] As will be seen from fig. 4, the changes in the structure of production which will be necessary in order to find employment for the additional means which have become available will exactly correspond to the changes brought about by saving. The total services of the original means of production will now be expended in six instead of in four periods; the total value of intermediate goods produced in the different stages during a period will have grown to three times instead of twice as large as the value of consumers' goods produced during the same period; and the output of each stage of production, including the final one, measured in physical units will accordingly be exactly as great as in the case represented in fig. 3. The only difference at first apparent is that the money values of these goods have grown by one-third compared with the situation depicted in fig. 3.

[26] [In *Preise und Produktion*, p. 51, Hayek adds the explanation that thereby the proportion of the demand for consumers' to that for producers' goods is changed from 40:80 to 40:120, that is, the same proportion 1:3 as formerly brought about by voluntary saving.—Ed.]

There is, however, another and far more important difference which will become apparent only with the lapse of time. When a change in the structure of production was brought about by saving, we were justified in assuming that the changed distribution of demand between consumers' goods and producers' goods would remain permanent, since it was the effect of voluntary decisions on the part of individuals. Only because a number of individuals had decided to spend a smaller share of their total money receipts on consumption and a larger share on production was there any change in the structure of production. And since, after the change had been completed, these persons would get a greater proportion of the increased total real income, they would have no reason again to increase the *proportion* of their money receipts spent for consumption.[27] There would accordingly exist no inherent cause for a return to the old proportions.

In the same way, in the case we are now considering, the use of a larger proportion of the original means of production for the manufacture of intermediate products can only be brought about by a retrenchment of consumption. But now this sacrifice is not voluntary, and is not made by those who will reap the benefit from the new investments. It is made by consumers in general who, because of the increased competition from the entrepreneurs who have received the additional money, are forced to forego part of what they used to consume. It comes about not because they want to consume less, but because they get less goods for their money income. There can be no doubt that, if their money receipts should rise again, they would immediately attempt to expand consumption to the usual proportion. We shall see in the next lecture why, in time, their receipts will rise as a consequence of the increase of money in circulation. For the moment let us assume that this happens. But if it does, then at once the money stream will be re-distributed between consumptive and productive uses according to the wishes of the individual concerned, and the artificial distribution, due to the injection of the new money, will, partly at any rate, be reversed. If we assume that the old proportions are adhered to, then the structure of production too will have to return to the old proportion, as shown in fig. 5. That is to say production will become less capitalistic, and that part of the new capital which was sunk in equipment adapted only to the more capitalistic processes will be lost. We shall see in the next lecture that such a transition to less capitalistic methods of production necessarily takes the form of an economic crisis.

But it is not necessary that the proportion between the demand for consumers' goods and the demand for intermediate products should return exactly

---

[27] It is important to bear in mind that, though the total money income would diminish, the total real income would increase. [Note again that for the sake of consistency the "proportion" must refer to gross income or the total money stream. See note 24 above.—Ed.]

ORIGINAL MEANS OF PRODUCTION

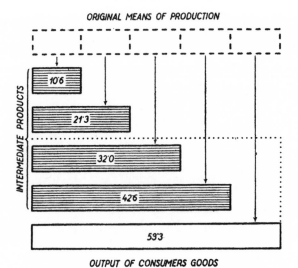

Figure 5

to its former dimensions as soon as the injection of new money ceases. In so far as the entrepreneurs have already succeeded, with the help of the additional money, in completing the new processes of longer duration,[28] they will, perhaps,[29] receive increased money returns for their output which will put them in a position to continue the new processes, i.e., to expend permanently a larger share of their money receipts upon intermediate products without reducing their own consumption. It is only in consequence of the price changes caused by the increased demand for consumers' goods that, as we shall see, these processes too become unprofitable.[30]

But for the producers who work on a process where the transition to longer roundabout processes is not yet completed when the amount of money ceases to increase, the situation is different.[31] They have spent the additional money

[28] It should, however, be remembered that a process cannot be regarded as completed in this sense, just because an entrepreneur at any one stage of production has succeeded in completing his section of it. A complete process, in the sense in which this concept is used in the text, comprises *all* the stages of any one line of production, whether they are part of one firm or divided between several. I have further elaborated this point in my article on "Capital and Industrial Fluctuations". [This footnote does not appear in the first edition.—Ed.]

[29] [The word "perhaps" does not appear in the first edition.—Ed.]

[30] [In the first edition, this sentence reads, "It is only when the rate of interest for borrowed money rises that these processes too become unprofitable."—Ed.]

[31] [In the first edition this sentence reads, "But for the producers who have not yet completed the transition to longer roundabout processes when the amount of money ceases to increase, the situation is different."—Ed.]

which put them in a position to increase their demand for producers' goods and in consequence it has become consumers' income; they will, therefore, no longer be able to claim a larger share of the available producers' goods, and they will accordingly have to abandon the attempt to change over to more capitalistic methods of production.

11.

All this becomes easier to follow if we consider the simpler case in which an increase in demand for consumers' goods of this sort is brought about directly by additional money given to consumers. In recent years, in the United States, Messrs. Foster and Catchings have urged that, in order to make possible the sale of an increased amount of consumers' goods produced with the help of new savings, consumers must receive a proportionately larger money income.[32] What would happen if their proposals were carried out? If we start with the situation which would establish itself as a consequence of new savings if the amount of money remained unchanged (as shown in fig. 3), and then assume that consumers receive an additional amount of money sufficient to compensate for the relative increase of the demand for intermediate products caused by the savings (i.e., an amount of 15) and spend it on consumers' goods, we get a situation in which the proportion between the demand for consumers' goods and the demand for producers' goods, which, in consequence of the new savings, had changed from 40:80 to 30:90 or from 1:2 to 1:3, would again be reduced to 45:90 or 1:2. That this would mean a return to the less capitalistic structure of production which existed before the new savings were made, and that the only effect of such an increase of consumers' money incomes would be to frustrate the effect of saving follows clearly from fig. 6. (The difference from the original situation depicted in fig. 2 is again only a difference in money values and not a difference in the physical quantities of goods produced or in their distribution to the different stages of production.)

12.

It is now time to leave this subject and to pass on to the last problem with which I have to deal in this lecture. I wish now to drop the second of my original assumptions, the assumption, namely, that during the process of production the intermediate products are exchanged against money between the firms at successive stages of production in equal intervals. Instead of this very

[32] [Cf. Foster and Catchings, *Profits*, and Hayek's critique in "The 'Paradox' of Saving".—Ed.]

ORIGINAL MEANS OF PRODUCTION

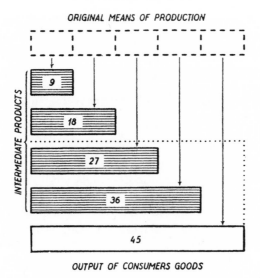

Figure 6

artificial assumption, we may consider two possible alternatives: we may suppose (*a*) that in any line of production the whole process is completed by a single firm, so that no other money payments take place than the payments for consumers' goods and the payments for the use of the factors of production; or we may suppose (*b*) that exchanges of intermediate products take place, but at very irregular intervals, so that in some parts of the process the goods remain for several periods of time in the possession of one and the same firm, while in other parts of the process they are exchanged once or several times during each period.

13.

(*a*) Let us consider first the case in which the whole process of production in any line of production is completed by a single firm. Once again we may use fig. 1 to illustrate what happens. In this case the base of the triangle represents the total payments for consumers' goods and the hypotenuse (or, more correctly, its horizontal projection) represents the amounts of money paid for the original means of production used. No other payments would be made and any amount of money received from the sale of consumers' goods could immediately be spent for original means of production. It is of fundamental importance to remember that we can assume only that any *single* line of production is in this way integrated into one big firm. It would be entirely inappropriate in this connection to suppose that the production of *all* goods is concentrated in one enterprise. For, if this were the case, of course the manager of this firm could, like the economic dictator of a communistic society, arbitrarily decide what part of the available means of production should be applied to the production of consumers' goods and what part to the production of producers' goods. There would exist for him no reason to borrow and, for individuals, no opportunity to invest savings. Only if *different* firms compete for the available means of production will saving and investing in the ordinary sense of the word take place, and it is therefore such a situation which we must make the starting point of our investigation.

Now, if any of these integrated industries decides to save and invest part of its profits in order to introduce more capitalistic methods of production, it must not immediately pay out the sums saved for original means of production. As the transition to more capitalistic methods of production means that it will be longer until the consumers' goods produced by the new process are ready, the firm will need the sums saved to pay wages, etc., during the interval of time between the sale of the last goods produced by the old process, and the getting ready of the first goods produced by the new process. So that, during the whole period of transition, it must pay out less to consumers than it receives in order to be able to bridge the gap at the end of this period, when it has nothing to sell but has to continue to pay wages and rent. Only when the new product comes on the market and there is no need for further saving will it again currently pay out all its receipts.

In this case, therefore, the demand for consumers' goods, as expressed in money, will be only temporarily reduced, while in the case where the process of production was divided between a number of independent stages of equal length, the reduction of the amount available for the purchase of consumers' goods was a permanent one. In the present case, the prices of the consumers' goods will, accordingly, fall only in inverse proportions[33] as their quantity has increased, while the total paid as income for the use of the factors of production will remain the same. These conclusions are, however, only provisional as they do not take account of the relative position of the one firm considered to all other firms which will certainly be affected by a change of relative prices and interest rates which are necessarily connected with such a process. Unfortunately, these influences are too complicated to allow of treatment within the scope of these lectures, and I must ask you, therefore, to suspend judgment upon the ultimate effects of the price changes which will take place under these conditions.

But there is one point to which I must particularly direct your attention: The reason in this case why the unchanged amount of money used in production remains sufficient, in spite of the fact that a larger amount of interme-

---

[33] [In the first edition, this word is "proportion".—Ed.]

diate products now exists, whereas in the former case the use of an increased amount of intermediate products required the use of an increased quantity of money is this. In the former case the intermediate products passed from one stage of production to the next by an exchange against money. But in the present case this exchange is replaced by internal barter, which makes money unnecessary. Of course, our division of the continuous process of production into separate stages of equal length is entirely arbitrary: it would be just as natural to divide it into stages of different lengths and then speak of these stages as exhibiting so many more or less instances of internal barter. But the procedure which has been adopted serves to bring out a concept, which I shall need in a later lecture, the concept of the relative volume of the flow of goods during any period of time, as compared with the amount of goods exchanged against money in the same period. If we divide the path traversed by the elements of any good from the first expenditure of original means of production until it gets in the hands of the final consumer into unit periods, and then measure the quantities of goods which pass each of these lines of division during a period of time, we secure a comparatively simple measure of the flow of goods without having recourse to higher mathematics. Thus, we may say that, in the instance we have been considering, money has become more efficient in moving goods, in the sense that a given amount of exchanges against money has now become sufficient to make possible the movement of a greater volume[34] of goods than before.

14.

(b) Perhaps this somewhat difficult concept becomes more intelligible if I illustrate it by supposing that two of the independent firms which we have supposed to represent the successive stages of production in our diagrams 2 and 6 are combined into one firm. This is the second of the alternative possibilities I set out to consider. Once this has happened, the passage of the intermediate products[35] from the one to the next stage of production will take place without money payments being necessary, and the flow of goods from the moment they enter the earlier of the two stages until they leave the later will be effected by

---

[34] Even if this total of goods moving towards consumption during each period is not actually exchanged against money in each period, it is not an imaginary, but a real and important magnitude, since the value of this total is a magnitude which continually rests within our power to determine. It probably stands in close relation to what is commonly called free capital, and it is certainly the supply of this factor which—together with new saving—determines the rate of interest; the capital which remains invested in durable instruments affects the interest rate from the demand side only, i.e., by influencing opportunities for new investment. [On the notion of 'free capital' cf. p.19n.72, above.—Ed.]

[35] [In the first edition, this word is "intermediate product".—Ed.]

so much less money. A corresponding amount of money will thus be released and may be used for other purposes. The reverse effect will, of course, be witnessed if the two firms separate again. An increased amount of money payments will be required to effect the same movement of goods and the proportion of money payments to the flow of goods advancing towards consumption will have increased.

15.

Unfortunately, all names which might be used to designate this kind of monetary effectiveness have already been appropriated for designating different concepts of the velocity of money. Until somebody finds a fitting term,[36] therefore, we shall have to speak somewhat clumsily of the proportion between the amount of goods exchanged against money and the total flow of goods or of the proportion of the total movements of goods which is effected by exchange against money.

Now this proportion must on no account be confused with the proportion of the volume of money payments to the physical volume of trade. The proportion I have in mind may remain the same while the volume of trade increases relatively to the total of money payments and the price level falls, if only the same proportion of the total flow of goods is exchanged against money, and it may change though the proportion of the total of money payments to the physical volume of trade remains the same. It is, therefore, not necessarily influenced either by changes in the amount of money or by changes in the physical volume of trade; it depends only upon whether, in certain phases of the process of production, goods do or do not change hands.

So far I have illustrated this concept only by instances from the sphere of production. It may be applied also to the sphere of consumption. Here, too, sometimes a larger and sometimes a smaller share of the total output of consumers' goods is exchanged for money before it is consumed. Accordingly, here, too, we may speak about the proportion which the total output of consumers' goods in a period of time bears to the output which is sold for money. And this proportion may be different in the different stages of production.[37]

---

[36] [In *Preise und Produktion*, p. 66, Hayek refers in a note to Holtrop's introduction of the term 'co-efficient of differentiation' (in *De Omloopssnelheid van het Geld*, p. 112; cf. "Die Umlaufsgeschwindigkeit des Geldes", p. 129). Later on in lecture 4 (see below, p. 276) Hayek eventually uses the term 'co-efficient of money transactions'.—Ed.]

[37] [As noted by Machlup (in the letter cited above), the last two sentences are prone to be misunderstood. Possibly, the "proportions" in question are those of the monetary transactions relative to all transactions, where the penultimate sentence refers to the stage of consumption, while the last sentence to all the other stages of production.—Ed.]

But in its effect upon the structure of production, the efficiency of a given amount of money spent in any stage of production (including the last stage—consumption) is determined by the proportion in that stage; and any change in that proportion has the same effects as an alteration in the amount of money spent in this particular stage of production.

So much for the complications which arise when we drop the assumption that production is carried on in independent stages of equal length. It has been necessary to discuss them here at some length in order to clear the way for an investigation, into which I wish to enter in the last lecture, in connection with the arguments for and against an elastic money supply. But for the tasks which I shall have to face tomorrow, it will be expedient again to make use of the simplest assumption and to suppose that production is carried on in independent stages of equal length, as we did in our schematic representations, and that this proportion is not only the same in all stages of production, but also that it remains constant over time.

THE WORKING OF THE PRICE MECHANISM IN THE COURSE OF THE CREDIT CYCLE

"The first effect of the increase of productive activity, initiated by the policy of the banks to lend below the natural rate of interest is . . . to raise the prices of producers' goods while the prices of consumers' goods rise only moderately . . . But soon a reverse movement sets in: prices of consumers' goods rise and prices of producers' goods fall, i.e., the loan rate rises and approaches again the natural rate of interest."

—L. v. Mises, *Theorie des Geldes und der Umlaufsmittel*, 1912, p. 431[1]

1.

In the last lecture I dealt with the problems of changes in the structure of production consequent upon any transition to more or less capitalistic methods of production, in terms of the total sums of money available for the purchase of the product of each stage of production. It might seem, therefore, that now I come to the problem of explaining those changes in relative prices which bring it about that goods are directed to new uses—the central problem of these lectures[2]—the explanation should run in terms of sectional price

---

[1] [This is Hayek's translation. Cf. for an almost identical formulation the second German edition (1924), p. 372, and the translation in *The Theory of Money and Credit*, p. 401.—Ed.]

[2] As has already been mentioned in the first chapter, the effects of a divergence between the money rate and the equilibrium-rate of interest on relative prices were originally shortly discussed by Professor Mises. On the actual working of the price mechanism which brings about the changes in the structure of production his work contains however hardly more than the sentences quoted at the beginning of this lecture. It seems that most people have found them difficult to understand and that they have remained completely unintelligible to all who were not very familiar with Böhm-Bawerk's theory of interest on which they are based. The main difficulty lies in Professor Mises' short statement that the rise of the prices of consumers' goods is the cause of the crisis, while it seems natural to assume that this would rather make production more profitable. This is the main point which I have here tried to clear up. So far the most exhaustive previous exposition of these inter-relationships, which anticipates in some points what is said in the following pages, is to be found in Richard Strigl, "Die Produktion unter dem Einfluß einer Kreditexpansion", in *Schriften des Vereins für Sozialpolitik*, vol. 173, part 2: *Beiträge zur Wirtschaftsthe-*

levels, that is to say in terms of changes in the price levels of the goods of the different stages of production. But to do this would mean that at this stage of the explanation I should fall back upon just that method of using price averages which I condemned at the outset.

At the same time, it should by now be clear that, at this stage of the explanation, a treatment in terms of price averages would not be adequate to our purposes. What we have to explain is why certain goods which have thus far been used in one stage of production can now be more profitably used in another stage of production. Now this will only be the case if there are changes in the proportions in which the different producers' goods may be profitably used in any stage of production, and this in turn implies that there must be changes in the prices offered for them in different stages of production.[3]

2.

At this point, it is necessary to introduce the new[4] distinction between producers' goods to which I alluded in the last lecture: the distinction between producers' goods which may be used in all, or at least, many stages of production, and producers' goods which can be used only in one, or at the most, a few stages of production. To the first class belong not only almost all original means of production, but also most raw materials and even a great many implements of a not very specialised kind—knives, hammers, tongs, and so on.[5] To the second class belong most highly specialised kinds of machinery

---

orie, Konjunkturforschung und Konjunkturtheorie, ed. Karl Diehl (Munich and Leipzig: Duncker and Humblot, 1928), particularly pp. 203 et seq. [pp. 203–6]. More recently Professor Strigl has further developed his views on the subject in a book, *Kapital und Produktion* (Vienna: Springer, 1934) [translated as *Capital and Production,* trans. Margaret R. and Hans-Hermann Hoppe (Auburn, AL: Ludwig von Mises Institute, 2000)—Ed.]. Some references to earlier anticipations of the ideas developed in this lecture will now be found in an additional note at the end of this lecture. [This footnote does not appear in the first edition.—Ed.]

[3] [In the first edition, the passage reads, "that there must be changes in the prices they obtain in different stages of production".—Ed.]

[4] Since the publication of the first edition of this book my attention has been drawn to the fact that this distinction is clearly implied in some of Böhm-Bawerk's discussions of these problems. Cf. his *Positive Theorie des Kapitalzinses* [*Kapitales*], 3rd ed. in two parts (1909, 1912), pp. 195 and 199. [The pagination refers to the excursus of part 2; cf. also the 4th ed. (1921), part 2, pp. 143 and 145, translated as *Capital and Interest,* trans. Huncke and Sennholz, vol. 3, pp. 86 and 88. This footnote does not appear in the first edition.—Ed.]

[5] This class will, in particular, comprise most of the goods which at one and the same time belong to different stages. "Of course", says Marshall (*Principles of Economics,* 1st ed., p. 109n. [cf. the 9th variorum edition, vol. 2, p. 193—Ed.]), "a good may belong to several orders at the same time. For instance, a railway train may be carrying people on a pleasure excursion, and so far it is [and so far is] a good of the first order; if it happens to be carrying at the same time

or complete manufacturing establishments, and also all those kinds of semi-manufactured goods which can be turned into finished goods only by passing a definite number of further stages of production. By adapting a term of von Wieser's, we may call the producers' goods which can be used only in one or a few stages of production, producers' goods of a specific character, or more shortly 'specific' goods, to distinguish them from producers' goods of a more general applicability, which we may call 'non-specific' goods.[6] Of course, this distinction is not absolute, in the sense that we are always in a position to say whether a certain good is specific or not. But we should be able to say whether any given good is *more or less* specific as compared with another good.

3.

It is clear that producers' goods of the same kind which are used[7] in different stages of production cannot, for any length of time, bring in different returns or obtain different prices in these different stages. On the other hand, it is no less clear that temporary differences between the prices offered in the different stages of production are the only means of bringing about a shift of producers' goods from one stage to another. If such a temporary difference in the relative attractiveness of the different stages of production arises, the goods in question will be shifted from the less to the more attractive stages until, by the operation of the principle of diminishing returns, the differences have been wiped out.

Now, if we neglect the possibility of changes in technical knowledge, which may change the usefulness of any particular producers' goods, it is obvious that the immediate cause of a change in the return obtained from producers' goods of a certain kind used in different stages of production must be a change in the price of the product of the stage of production in question. But what is it which brings about variations of the relative price[8] of such products? At first glance it might seem improbable that the prices of the succes-

---

[to be carrying also] some tins of biscuits, some milling machinery and some machinery that is used for making milling machinery, it is at the same time a good of the second, third and fourth order[s]." In cases like this a transfer of its services from a later to an earlier stage (or, to use Menger's terminology, from a lower to a higher order) is, of course, particularly easy. A plant manufacturing equipment for the production of consumers' goods as well as for the production of further machinery will sometimes be used mainly for the former and sometimes mainly for the latter purpose. [This footnote does not appear in the first edition.—Ed.]

[6] Cf. Friedrich von Wieser, *Social Economics*, trans. A. Ford Hinrichs (New York: Adelphi, 1927), book 1, chapter 15 [cf. pp. 81–85—Ed.].

[7] [The word "used" does not appear in the first edition.—Ed.]

[8] [In the first edition, this word is "prices".—Ed.]

sive stages of one and the same line of production should ever fluctuate relatively to one another because they are equally dependent upon the price of the final product. But, having regard to what was said in the last lecture concerning the possibility of shifts between the demand for consumers' goods and the demand for producers' goods, and the consequent changes in the relation between the amount of original means of production expended and the output of consumers' goods, and how an elongation[9] of the process of production increases the return from a given quantity of original means of production—this point should present no difficulty.

Now so far I have not expressly referred to the price margins which arise out of these relative fluctuations of the prices of the products of successive stages of production. This has been because I have intentionally neglected interest, or, what amounts to the same thing, I have treated interest as if it were a payment for a definitely given factor of production, like wages or rent. In a state of equilibrium these margins are entirely absorbed by interest.[10] Hence my assumption concealed the fact that the total amount of money received for the product of any stage will regularly exceed the total paid out for all goods and services used in this stage of production. Yet that margins of this kind must exist is obvious from the consideration that, if it were not so, there would exist no inducement to risk money[11] by investing it in production rather than let it remain idle. To investigate the relationship of these margins to the peculiar advantages of the roundabout methods of production would lead us too far into the problems of the general theory of interest. We must therefore be content to accept it as one of the definite conclusions of this theory that— other things remaining the same—these margins must grow smaller as the roundabout processes of production increase in length and vice versa. There is one point, however, which we cannot take for granted. The fact that in a state of equilibrium those price margins and the amounts paid as interest coincide does *not* prove that the same will also be true in a period of transition from one state of equilibrium to another. On the contrary, the relation between these two magnitudes must form one of the main objects of our further investigations.

The close interrelation between these two phenomena suggests two different modes of approach to our problem: Either we may start from the changes in the relative magnitude of the demand for consumers' goods and the demand for producers' goods, and examine the effects on the prices of individual

[9] [In the first edition, this word is "prolongation".—Ed.]
[10] [That is, Hayek is considering a long-period equilibrium, where in each stage the rate of profit is equal to the rate of interest.—Ed.]
[11] [Note that Machlup in his correspondence with Hayek (cited above) criticised that the term "risk" might erroneously suggest an explanation of interest as "risk premium" or as "profit due to uncertainty".—Ed.]

goods and the rate of interest; or we may start from the changes in the rate of interest as an immediate effect of the change in the demand for producers' goods and work up to the changes in the price system which are necessary to establish a new equilibrium between price margins and the rate of interest. It will be found that whichever of these two alternatives we choose as a starting point, our investigation will, in the end, lead us to those aspects of the problem which are the starting point for the other. For the purposes of this lecture, I choose the first as being more in line with my previous argument.

4.

I begin, as I began in the last lecture, with the supposition that consumers decide to save and invest a larger proportion of their income. The immediate effect of the increase in the demand for producers' goods and the decrease in demand for consumers' goods will be that there will be a relative rise in the prices of the former and a relative fall in the prices of the latter. But the prices of producers' goods will not rise equally, nor will they rise without exception. In the stage of production immediately preceding that in which the final touches are given to consumers' goods, the effect of the fall in the prices of consumers' goods will be felt more strongly than the effect of the increase of the funds available for the purchase of producers' goods of all kinds. The price of the product of this stage will, therefore, fall, but it will fall less than the prices of consumers' goods. This means a narrowing of the price margin between the last two stages. But this narrowing of the price margin will make the employment of funds in the last stage less profitable relatively to the earlier[12] stages, and therefore some of the funds which had been used there will tend to be shifted to the earlier stages. This shift of funds will tend to narrow the price margins in the preceding stages, and the tendency thus set up towards a cumulative rise of the prices of the products of the earlier stages will very soon overcome the tendency towards a fall. In other words, the rise of the price of the product of any stage of production will give an extra advantage to the production of the preceding stage, the products of which will not only rise in price because the demand for producers' goods in general has risen, but also because, by the rise of prices in the preceding stages, profits to be obtained in this stage have become comparatively higher than in the

---

[12] [As pointed out above, p. 231n.25, in the first edition Hayek distinguished between higher (for earlier) and lower (for later) stages of production. As such, in the first edition this word is "higher". Accordingly, whenever in the following the text refers to "earlier" and "later" stages, the words in the first edition are "higher" and "lower".—Ed.]

later stages. The final effect will be that, through the fall of prices in the later stages of production and the rise of prices in the earlier stages of production, price margins between the different stages of production will have decreased all round.

This change of relative prices in the different stages of production must inevitably tend to effect[13] the prospects of profits in the different stages, and this, in turn, will tend to cause changes in the use made of the available producers' goods. A greater proportion of those producers' goods which can be used in different stages of production—the non-specific goods—will now be attracted to the earlier stages, where, since the change in the rate of saving, relatively higher prices are to be obtained. And the shifting of goods and services of this type will go on until the diminution of returns in these stages has equalised the profits to be made in all stages. In the end, the returns and the prices obtained for these goods in the different stages of production will be generally higher and a larger proportion of them will be used in the earlier stages of production than before. The general narrowing of the price margins between the stages of production will even make it possible to start production in new and more distant stages which have not been profitable before, and in this way, not only the average time which elapses between the application of the first unit of original means of production and the completion of the final product, but also the absolute length of the process of production—the number of its stages—will be increased.[14]

But while the effect on the prices of non-specific producers' goods has been a general rise, the effect on the prices of goods of a more specific character— those goods which can only be used in one or a very few stages of production—will be different. If a good of this sort is only adapted to a comparatively late stage of production, the relative deficiency of the non-specific producers' goods required in the same stage of production will lower its return, and if it is itself a product, its production will be curtailed. If, on the other hand, the good belongs to a relatively early stage of production, its price and the amount of it produced will increase. At the same time, the additional stages of production which have been started as a consequence of this transition to

---

[13] [In the first edition this word is "affect", which has been changed, mistakenly, to "effect" in the second edition.—Ed.]

[14] This lengthening of the structure of production need, however, by no means take exclusively or even mainly the form that the methods used in any individual line of production are changed. The increased prices in the earlier stages of production (the lowered rate of interest) will favour production in the lines using much capital and lead to their expansion at the expense of the lines using less capital. In this way the aggregate length of the investment structure of society might in the extreme case take place without a change of the method employed in any one line of production. [This footnote does not appear in the first edition.—Ed.]

more capitalistic methods of production will probably require new goods of a specific character. Some of these will be new products, some natural resources which formerly it was not profitable to use.

Exactly the reverse of all these changes will take place if the demand for consumers' goods increases relatively to the demand for producers' goods. This will cause not only an increase of the difference between the prices of consumers' goods or products of the last stage of production, and the prices of the products of the previous stage, but also an all round increase of the price margins between the products of the successive stages of production. Prices in the later stages will rise relatively to prices in the earlier stages, producers' goods of a non-specific character will move from the earlier stages to the later, and the goods of specific character in the earlier stages of production will lose part of their value or become entirely useless, while those in the later stages of production will increase in value. I shall discuss certain exceptions to this parallelism later on.

It will, perhaps, facilitate the understanding of these complications if we think of production in its successive stages as a fan, the sticks of which correspond to the prices of the different stages.[15] If more demand is concentrated towards the one extreme—consumers' goods—the fan opens, the differences between the stages become larger, and goods gravitate towards the stages where higher prices are obtained, that is, towards the stages nearer consumption. The most distant stages are abandoned, and within the remaining stages more goods are concentrated toward the one end. The opening of the price fan is thus accompanied by a reduction of the number of stages of production, i.e., of the number of sticks.[16] If, however, a shift of demand from consumers' goods towards producers' goods takes place, the price fan will close, i.e., the differences between the stages will become smaller and goods will tend to gravitate towards the higher[17] stages where prices are now relatively higher, and new and hitherto unused possibilities of further extension of the process of production will be exploited. The closing of the price fan has brought a greater number of stages of production within the range of practical possibilities and thus initiated the transition to longer roundabout methods of production.

---

[15] [The simile of the 'price fan' appears already in Hayek's early typescript "Investigations", p. 129.—Ed.]

[16] At this point the simile becomes liable to mislead and it is important to keep in mind all the time that the 'fan' refers to price relationships only, but that the length of the structure of production will move in the reverse direction compared with the width of the fan. When the price fan opens, the structure of production is shortened, and vice versa. [This footnote does not appear in the first edition.—Ed.]

[17] [According to the terminology introduced in the second edition, this should read, "earlier".—Ed.]

5.

A more exact representation of this process can be given by means of a diagram.[18] This has the special advantage of making quite clear a point which is of considerable importance but on which a merely verbal explanation is likely to mislead. It is necessary in such an exposition, if one wants to avoid too cumbersome expressions, to speak of actual changes in the relative prices of goods in the different stages, where it would be more correct to speak of tendencies towards such a change, or of changes in the demand function for the particular commodity. Whether and to what extent such changes in demand will lead to an actual change in price will of course depend on the elasticity of supply, which in the particular case depends in turn in every stage on the degree of specificity of the intermediate products and the factors from which they are made.

The way in which this shifting of the demand curves for any single factor in the different stages of production operates can be illustrated in the following way. In the diagram below[19] the successive curves represent the marginal productivity of different quantities of one factor in the successive stages of production, the earlier stages being shown on the left and the later stages towards the right. To make the main point come out clearer it has been assumed that the physical quantity of the product due to every additional unit of the factor decreases at the same rate in all stages and that in consequence the general shape of the curves is the same.

The value of the marginal product attributable to every unit of factors will, however, be equal to the value of the physical product which is due to it only in the very last stage where no interval of time elapses between the investment of the factors and the completion of the product. If we assume, then, the curve on the right to represent not only the physical magnitude but also the value of the marginal product of successive units of factors applied in that stage, the other curves representing the physical marginal product of the factors invested in earlier stages will have to be somewhat adjusted if they are to represent the discounted value of the marginal product of successive units of factors applied in the respective stages. And if we assume the points to which these curves refer, to be equidistant stages as were those discussed before, the adjustment necessary at any given rate of interest can be shown by drawing a discount curve (or a family of discount curves) connecting every point on the curve on the right with the corresponding points of the curves further on the

[18] [All of section 5 is new to the second edition. Other than in the preceding section, here Hayek makes use of the second of the modes of approach sketched above, pp. 246–47, concentrating on the effect of changes in the rate of interest.—Ed.]

[19] [Hayek used the same diagram later on in *The Pure Theory of Capital*, reprinted, fig. 26, p. 271.—Ed.]

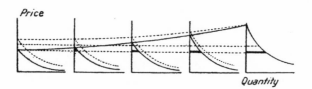

Figure 7

left, and lowering each of these curves by the amount indicated by the discount curves. (Since every point on these curves will have to be adjusted separately, i.e., will have to be lowered not by the same amount but by the same percentage, this will involve a change not only of the position but also of the shape of these curves.) The set of fully drawn curves in the above diagram shows the position at a given rate of interest indicated by the one discount curve which is also fully drawn. And since these curves show the discounted value of the marginal product of one kind of factor which must of course be the same in the different stages of production, they enable us to determine how much of this factor will be used in every stage if either its price or the total quantity of it to be used in this process are known. This distribution of the factor between the different stages at an arbitrarily assumed price is shown by the fully drawn horizontal lines.

Assume now that the rate of interest is reduced. The new position is indicated by the dotted discount curve and the correspondingly changed shape and position of the marginal productivity curves for the individual stages. Under these conditions the old distribution of factors between the stages would evidently not represent an equilibrium position but one at which the discounted value of the marginal product would be different in every stage. And if the total quantity of the factor which is available remains the same the new equilibrium distribution will apparently be one at which not only the price of the factor will be higher but at which also a considerably greater quantity of it is used in the earlier stages and correspondingly less in the later stages.

This accounts for the change in the price and the distribution of factors which can be used in different stages. To what extent and in what proportion the prices of different factors will be affected by a given change in the rate of interest will depend on the stages in which they can be used and on the shape of their marginal productivity curves in these stages. The price of a factor which can be used in most early stages and whose marginal productivity there falls very slowly will rise more in consequence of a fall in the rate of interest than the price of a factor which can only be used in relatively lower stages of reproduction[20] or whose marginal productivity in the earlier stages falls very rapidly.

[20] [According to the terminology of the second edition, this should read, "later stages of production".—Ed.]

It is essentially this difference between the price changes of the different factors which accounts for the changes of the relative prices of the intermediate products at the successive stages. At first it might seem as if, since relative prices of the different intermediate products must correspond to their respective costs, they could change only to the relatively small extent to which the direct interest element in their cost changes. But to think of interest only as a direct cost factor is to overlook its main influence on production. What is much more important is its effect on prices through its effect on demand for the intermediate products and for the factors from which they are produced. It is in consequence of these changes in demand and the changes in cost which it brings about by raising the prices of those factors which are in strong demand in early stages compared to those which are less demanded there, that the prices of the intermediate products are adjusted.

6.

As the initial changes in relative prices which are caused by a change of the relative demand for consumers' goods and producers' goods give rise to a considerable shifting of goods to other stages of production, definite price relationships will only establish themselves after the movements of goods have been completed. For reasons which I shall consider in a moment, this process may take some time and involve temporary discrepancies between supply and demand. But there is one medium through which the expected ultimate effect[21] on relative prices should make itself felt immediately, and which, accordingly, should serve as a guide for the decisions of the individual entrepreneur: the rate of interest on the loan market. Only in comparatively few cases will the people who have saved money and the people who want to use it in production be identical. In the majority of cases, therefore, the money which is directed to new uses will first have to pass into other hands. The question *who* is going to use the additional funds available for investment in producers' goods will be decided on the loan market. Only at a lower rate of interest than that formerly prevailing will it be possible to lend these funds, and how far the rate of interest will fall will depend upon the amount of the additional funds and the expectation of profits on the part of the entrepreneurs willing to expand their production. If these entrepreneurs entertain correct views about the price changes which are to be expected as a result of the changes in the method of production, the new rate of interest should correspond to the system of price margins which will ultimately be established. In this way, from the outset, the use of the additional funds which have become available will be confined to those entrepreneurs who hope to obtain the high-

---

[21] [In the first edition, the word is "effects".—Ed.]

est profits out of their use, and all extensions of production, for which the additional funds would not be sufficient, will be excluded.

7.

The significance of these adjustments of the price mechanism comes out still more clearly when we turn to investigate what happens if the 'natural' movement of prices is disturbed by movements in the supply of money, whether by the injection of new money into circulation or by withdrawal of part of the money circulating. We may again take as our two typical cases, (a) the case of additional money used first to buy producers' goods and (b) the case of additional money used first to buy consumers' goods. The corresponding cases of a diminution of the amount of money we may neglect because a diminution of the demand for consumers' goods would have essentially the same effects as a proportional increase of the demand for producers' goods, and vice versa.[22] I have already outlined in the last lecture the general tendencies involved in such cases. My present task is to fill in the details of that rough sketch and to show what happens in the interval before a new equilibrium is attained.

As before, I commence with the supposition that the additional money is injected by way of credits to producers. To secure borrowers for this additional amount of money, the rate of interest must be kept sufficiently below the equilibrium rate to make profitable the employment of just this sum and no more. Now the borrowers can only use the borrowed sums for buying producers' goods, and will only be able to obtain such goods (assuming a state of equilibrium in which there are no unused resources) by outbidding the entrepreneurs who used them before.[23] At first sight it might seem improbable that these borrowers who were only put in a position to start longer processes by the lower rate of interest should be able to outbid those entrepreneurs who found the use of those means of production profitable when the rate of interest was still higher. But when it is remembered that the fall in the rate will also change the relative profitableness of the different factors of production for the existing concerns, it will be seen to be quite natural that it should give a relative advantage to those concerns which use proportionately more capital. Such old concerns will now find it profitable to spend a part of what they previously spent on original means of production, on intermediate products produced by ear-

---

[22] As I have tried to show in another place ("Capital and Industrial Fluctuations", p. 164 [reprinted, p. 202—Ed.]) it is even conceivable, although highly unlikely to occur in practice, that hoarding of money income before spent on consumers' goods, might give rise to some additional investment. [This footnote does not appear in the first edition.—Ed.]

[23] [The phrase in parentheses, "(assuming a state of equilibrium in which there are no unused resources)", does not appear in the sentence in the first edition.—Ed.]

lier stages of production, and in this way they will release some of the original means of production they used before. The rise in the prices of the original means of production is an additional inducement. Of course it might well be that the entrepreneurs in question would be in a better position to buy such goods even at the higher prices, since they have done business when the rate of interest was higher, though it must not be forgotten that they too will have to do business on a smaller margin. But the fact that certain producers' goods have become dearer will make it profitable for them to replace these goods by others. In particular, the changed proportion between the prices of the original means of production and the rate of interest will make it profitable for them to spend part of what they have till now spent on original means of production on intermediate products or capital. They will, e.g., buy parts of their products, which they used to manufacture themselves, from another firm, and can now employ the labour thus dismissed in order to produce these parts on a large scale with the help of new machinery.[24] In other words, those original means of production and non-specific producers' goods which are required in the new stages of production are set free by the transition of the old concerns to more capitalistic methods which is caused by the increase in the prices of these goods. In the old concerns (as we may conveniently, but not quite accurately, call the processes of production which were in operation before the new money was injected) a transition to more capitalistic methods will take place; but in all probability it will take place without any change in their total resources: they will invest less in original means of production and more in intermediate products.

Now, contrary to what we have found to be the case when similar processes are initiated by the investment of new savings, this application of the original means of production and non-specific intermediate products to longer processes of production will be effected without any preceding reduction of consumption. Indeed, for a time, consumption may even go on at an unchanged rate after the more roundabout processes have actually started, because the goods which have already advanced to the lower[25] stages of production, being of a highly specific character, will continue to come forward for some little time. But this cannot go on. When the reduced output from the stages of production, from which producers' goods have been withdrawn for use in higher[26]

---

[24] [In the first edition, this sentence reads, "They will, e.g., buy parts of their products which they used to manufacture themselves from another firm, and this now can employ the labour thus dismissed in order to produce these parts on a large scale with the help of new machinery." The deletion of "this" in the second edition is probably due to a misprint. In *Preise und Produktion*, p. 83, Hayek had added after "machinery" in parentheses, "(for the production of which another part of dismissed labour will be used)".—Ed.]

[25] [According to the terminology of the second edition, this word should read, "later".—Ed.]

[26] [According to the terminology of the second edition, this word should read, "earlier".—Ed.]

stages, has matured into consumers' goods, a scarcity of consumers' goods will make itself felt, and the prices of those goods will rise.[27] Had saving preceded the change to methods of production of longer duration, a reserve of consumers' goods would have been accumulated in the form of increased stocks, which could now be sold at unreduced prices, and would thus serve to bridge the interval of time between the moment when the last products of the old shorter process come on to the market and the moment when the first products of the new longer processes are ready. But as things are, for some time, society as a whole will have to put up with an involuntary reduction of consumption.

But this necessity will be resisted. It is highly improbable that individuals should put up with an unforeseen retrenchment of their real income without making an attempt to overcome it by spending more money on consumption. It comes at the very moment when a great many entrepreneurs know themselves to be in command—at least nominally—of greater resources and expect greater profits. At the same time incomes of wage earners will be rising in consequence of the increased amount of money available for investment by entrepreneurs. There can be little doubt that in the face of rising prices of consumers' goods these increases will be spent on such goods and so contribute to drive up their prices even faster.[28] These decisions will not change the amount of consumers' goods immediately available, though it may change their distribution between individuals. But—and this is the fundamental point—*it will mean a new and reversed change of the proportion between the demand for consumers' goods and the demand for producers' goods in favour of the former.* The prices of consumers' goods will therefore rise relatively to the prices of producers' goods. And this rise of the prices of consumers' goods will be the more marked because it is the consequence not only of an increased demand for consumers' goods but an increase in the demand as measured in money. All this must mean a return to shorter or less roundabout methods of production if the increase in the demand for consumers' goods is not compensated by a further proportional injection of money by new bank loans granted to producers. And at first this is probable. The rise of the prices of consumers' goods will offer prospects of temporary extra profits to entrepreneurs. They will be the more ready to borrow at the prevailing rate of interest. And, so long as the banks go on progressively increasing their loans it will, therefore, be possible to continue the prolonged methods of production or perhaps even to extend them still further. But for obvious reasons the banks cannot continue indefinitely to extend credits; and even if they could, the other effects of a rapid and con-

---

[27] [In the first edition, this sentence reads, "When the reduced output from the stages of production from which producers' goods have been withdrawn for use in higher stages has matured into consumers' goods, a scarcity of consumers' goods will make itself felt, and the prices of those goods will rise." Thus two commas were added to the sentence in the second edition.—Ed.]

[28] [This sentence and the one that precedes it are new to the second edition.—Ed.]

tinuous rise of prices would, after a while, make it necessary to stop this process of inflation.[29]

Let us assume that for some time, perhaps a year or two, the banks, by keeping their rate of interest below the equilibrium rate, have expanded credit, and now find themselves compelled to stop further expansion. What will happen? (Perhaps it should be mentioned at this point that the processes I shall now describe are processes which would also take place if existing capital is encroached upon, or if, in a progressive society, after a temporary increase in saving, the rate should suddenly fall to its former level. Such cases, however, are probably quantitatively less important.)

Now we know from what has been said already that the immediate effect of the banks ceasing to add to their loans is that the absolute increase of the amount of money spent on consumers' goods is no longer compensated by a proportional increase in the demand for producers' goods. The demand for consumers' goods will for some time continue to increase because it will necessarily always lag somewhat behind the additional expenditure on investment which causes the increase of money incomes.[30] The effects of such a change will, therefore, be similar to what would happen in the second case we have to consider, the case of an increase of money by consumers' credits. At this point, accordingly, the two cases can be covered by one discussion.

8.

Speaking generally, it might be said that the effects of a relative increase in the demand for consumers' goods are the reverse of the effects of an increase in the relative demand for producers' goods. There are, however, two important differences which make a detailed account necessary.[31]

The first effect of the rise of the prices of consumers' goods is that the spread between them and the prices of the goods of the preceding stage becomes greater than the price margins in the higher[32] stages of production. The greater profits to be obtained in this stage will cause producers' goods in use elsewhere which may be used in this stage to be transferred to it, and the all round increase of price margins between the stages of production which will follow will cause a widespread transfer of non-specific producers' goods

[29] For a fuller discussion of the reasons why this process of expansion must ultimately come to an end, whether the banks are restricted by reserve regulations, etc., or not, and of some of the points alluded to in the next paragraphs, see my article on "Capital and Industrial Fluctuations", p. 161 [reprinted, pp. 198–99. This footnote does not appear in the first edition.—Ed.]

[30] [This sentence does not appear in the first edition.—Ed.]

[31] [In the first edition, there is no paragraph break at this point.—Ed.]

[32] [According to the terminology of the second edition, this word should read, "earlier".—Ed.]

to lower[33] stages. The new demand for these goods will cause a relative rise of their prices, and this rise will tend to be considerable because, as we have seen, there will be a temporary rise in the price of consumers' goods, due to the transient discrepancy between demand and supply, greater than will be the case after the supply of consumers' goods has caught up with demand. These temporary scarcity prices of consumers' goods will, furthermore, have the effect that at first production will tend to shrink to fewer stages than will be necessary after equilibrium prices of consumers' goods have established themselves.

Very soon the relative rise of the prices of the original factors and the more mobile intermediate products will make the longer processes unprofitable.[34] The first effect on these processes will be that the producers' goods of a more specific character, which have become relatively abundant by reason of the withdrawal of the complementary non-specific goods, will fall in price. The fall of the prices of these goods will make their production unprofitable; it will in consequence be discontinued. Although goods in later stages of production will generally be of a highly specific character, it may still pay to employ original factors to complete those that are nearly finished.[35] But the fall in the price of intermediate products will be cumulative; and this will mean a fairly sudden stoppage of work in at least all the earlier stages of the longer processes.

But while the non-specific goods, in particular the services of workmen employed in those earlier stages, have thus been thrown out of use because their amount has proved insufficient and their prices too high for the profitable carrying through of the long processes of production, it is by no means certain that all those which can no longer be used in the old processes can immediately be absorbed in the short processes which are being expanded. Quite the contrary; the shorter processes will have to be started at the very beginning and will only *gradually* absorb all the available producers' goods as the product progresses towards consumption and as the necessary intermediate products come forward. So that, while, in the longer processes, productive operations cease almost as soon as the change in relative prices of specific and non-specific goods in favour of the latter and the rise of the rate of interest make them unprofitable, the released goods will find new employment only as the new[36] shorter processes are approaching completion.[37] Moreover, the final

[33] [According to the terminology of the second edition, this word should read, "later".—Ed.]

[34] [In the first edition, this sentence reads, "Very soon the relative rise of the prices of the producers' goods will make the longer processes unprofitable."—Ed.]

[35] [This sentence replaces the following two sentences, which appear in the first edition: "Goods in the lower stages of production will generally be of a more specific character: the brunt of the price-fall there will therefore be borne by them. It will still pay to employ original factors in these stages."—Ed.]

[36] [The word "new" does not appear in the first edition.—Ed.]

[37] The reason for this asymmetry between a transition to longer processes of production, which need not bring about any of these peculiar disturbances, and a transition to shorter processes, which will regularly be accompanied by a crisis, will perhaps become more evident if it is

256

adaptation will be further retarded by initial uncertainty as regards the methods of production which will ultimately prove profitable once the temporary scarcity of consumers' goods has disappeared. Entrepreneurs, quite rightly, will hesitate to make investments suited to this overshortened process, i.e., investments which would enable them to produce with relatively little capital and a relatively great quantity of the original means of production.

It seems something of a paradox that the self-same goods whose scarcity has been the cause of the crisis would become unsaleable as a consequence of the same crisis. But the fact is that when the growing demand for finished consumers' goods has taken away part of the non-specific producers' goods required, those remaining are no longer sufficient for the long processes, and the particular kinds of specific goods required for the processes which would just be long enough to employ the total quantity of those non-specific producers' goods do not yet exist. The situation would be similar to that of a people of an isolated island, if, after having partially constructed an enormous machine which was to provide them with all necessities, they found out that they had exhausted all their savings and available free capital before the new machine could turn out its product. They would then have no choice but to abandon temporarily the work on the new process and to devote all their labour to producing their daily food without any capital. Only after they had put themselves in a position in which new supplies of food were available could they proceed to attempt to get the new machinery into operation.[38] In the actual world, however, where the accumulation of capital has permitted a growth of population far beyond the number which could find employment without capital, as a general rule the single workman will not be able to produce enough for a living without the help of capital and he may, therefore, temporarily become unemployable. And the same will apply to all goods

---

considered that in the former case there will necessarily be time to amortise the capital invested in the existing structure before the new process is completed, while in the latter case this will evidently be impossible and therefore a loss of capital and a reduction of income inevitable. (In all these discussions it is assumed that technical knowledge remains the same; a shortening of the structure of production which is due to technical progress has an altogether different significance from that due to an increase of consumption.) [This footnote does not appear in the first edition.—Ed.]

[38] Cf. the very similar example now given by Carl Landauer, *Planwirtschaft und Verkehrswirtschaft* (Munich and Leipzig: Duncker and Humblot, 1931), p. 47. [A translation of Hayek's review of Landauer's book appears as an addendum to chapter 1 of *Socialism and War: Essays, Documents, Reviews*, ed. Bruce Caldwell, vol. 10 (1997) of *The Collected Works of F. A. Hayek*, pp. 79–84. This footnote does not appear in the first edition.—Ed.]

[In this specific example, Hayek follows Böhm-Bawerk in identifying the stock of capital with a subsistence fund, that is, a stock of necessities like food for bridging the period of time during which, due to the means needed for the construction of capital goods, the production of consumers' goods will decrease. Yet, in general, and definitely in *The Pure Theory of Capital*, Hayek eschewed the idea of the subsistence fund.—Ed.]

and services whose use requires the co-operation of other goods and services which, after a change in the structure of production of this kind, may not be available in the necessary quantity.[39]

In this connection, as in so many others, we are forced to recognise the fundamental truth, so frequently neglected nowadays, that the machinery of capitalistic production will function smoothly only so long as we are satisfied to consume no more than that part of our total wealth which under the existing organisation of production is destined for current consumption. Every increase of consumption, if it is not to disturb production, requires previous new saving, even if the existing equipment with durable instruments of production should be sufficient for such an increase in output. If the increase of production is to be maintained continuously, it is necessary that the amounts

[39] [At this place, *Preise und Produktion*, pp. 91–92, adds two footnotes, worthwhile to be reproduced:

First footnote: "Theoretically, this situation of a depression (*Absatzstockung*) can be characterised in the following way: The usual demand curves presuppose that any arbitrary quantity of the means of production can be sold at some price. Yet, capitalistic production implies that every definite quantity of the original means of production requires also a definite equipment of specific, and as a rule, durable producers' goods, the production of which takes time. Thus, it will become impossible to find a corresponding demand for the total supply of non-specific producers' goods, and in particular of labour, so long as the required equipment does not yet exist. And as due to the steady use of capital goods the supply of labour has risen to such an extent that it cannot obtain any price without those capital goods, it is possible that in such a situation no wage could be low enough to employ all the labour supplied." For a similar argument cf. Hayek's 1931 Cambridge lecture, "The Purchasing Power of the Consumer and the Depression", reprinted in F. A. Hayek, *Business Cycles, Part II*, p. 153.

Second footnote: "For those who know the modern literature on the business cycle, it need not be emphasised how far the theses expounded above conform to the teachings of A. Spiethoff. In his view the scarcity of capital, which is the cause of crises, expresses itself in the 'quantitative disproportions within the totality of goods', and his explanation of crises can be summarised in that it is the scarcity of circulating capital that is the cause of crises. (Cf. Arthur Spiethoff, "Krisen", in *Handwörterbuch der Staatswissenschaften*, 4th ed. rev., vol. 6, pp. 75–80, in particular p. 78 [cf. the abridged translation "Business Cycles", in *International Economic Papers*, vol. 3, 1953, reprinted in *Business Cycle Theory: Selected Texts 1860–1939*, vol. 2: *Structural Theories of the Business Cycle*, ed. Hagemann, pp. 189–94, in particular p. 193—Ed.].) The conformity with Spiethoff rests in particular on the idea that basically industrial fluctuations are nothing but reverse fluctuations in the capitalistic structure of production. Concurrently with variations in the disposable amount of capital there is a stretching or shortening in the total length of the process of production, like—to use another simile—a concertina. Moreover, to every length of the process of production there corresponds a definite composition of the productive apparatus, so that any change in this length will generate the phenomenon of 'simultaneous scarcity and abundance' [Spiethoff, "Krisen", p. 78; translated, p. 193—Ed.], that is, abundance of those goods that due to the changed method of production cannot be used in the same quantity as before, and scarcity of 'complementary goods' [Spiethoff, "Krisen", p. 77; translated, p. 192—Ed.]." The rest of this footnote has been incorporated into the appendix to lecture 3, this volume, pp. 262–65. Notably, in the second footnote Hayek introduces the simile of a concertina, of which later on Nicholas Kaldor made use in his critique "Professor Hayek and the Concertina Effect", *Economica*,

of intermediate products in all stages is proportionately increased; and these additional quantities of goods in process are of course no less capital than the durable instruments. The impression that the already existing capital structure would enable us to increase production almost indefinitely is a deception. Whatever engineers may tell us about the supposed immense unused capacity of the existing productive machinery, there is in fact no possibility of increasing production to such an extent. These engineers and also those economists who believe that we have more capital than we need, are deceived by the fact that many of the existing plant and machinery are adapted to a much greater output than is actually produced. What they overlook is that durable means of production do not represent all the capital that is needed for an increase of output and that in order that the existing durable plants could be used to their full capacity it would be necessary to invest a great amount of other means of production in lengthy processes which would bear fruit only in a comparatively distant future. The existence of unused capacity is, therefore, by no means a proof that there exists an excess of capital and that consumption is insufficient: on the contrary, it is a symptom that we are unable to use the fixed plant to the full extent because the current demand for consumers' goods is too urgent to permit us to invest current productive services in the long processes for which (in consequence of 'misdirections of capital') the necessary durable equipment is available.[40]

9.

Here then we have at last reached an explanation of how it comes about at certain times that some of the existing resources cannot be used, and how, in such circumstances, it is impossible to sell them at all—or, in the case of durable goods, only to sell them at very great loss. To provide an answer to this problem has always seemed to me to be the central task of any theory of industrial fluctuations; and, though at the outset I refused to base my investigation on the assumption that unused resources exist, now that I have presented a tentative explanation of this phenomenon, it seems worth while, rather than spending time filling up the picture of the cycle by elaborating the process of recovery, to devote the rest of this lecture to further discussion of certain

---

n.s., vol. 9, November 1942, pp. 359–82, reprinted as chapter 10 of F. A. Hayek, *Business Cycles, Part II.*—Ed.]

[40] [This entire paragraph, which begins with the phrase "In this connection . . .", is new to the second edition. Hayek returned to the problem of unused capacity later on in "Technischer Fortschritt und Überkapazität", *Österreichische Zeitschrift für Bankwesen*, vol. 1, 1936, pp. 9–23, translated as "Technical Progress and Excess Capacity" and reprinted as chapter 8 of F. A. Hayek, *Money, Capital and Fluctuations.*—Ed.]

important aspects of this problem.[41] Now that we have accounted for the existence of unused resources, we may even go so far as to assume that their existence to a greater or lesser extent is the regular state of affairs save during a boom. And, if we do this, it is imperative to supplement our earlier investigation of the effects of a change in the amount of money in circulation on production, by applying our theory to such a situation. And this extension of our analysis is the more necessary since the existence of unused resources has very often been considered as the only fact which at all justifies an expansion of bank credit.

If the foregoing analysis is correct, it should be fairly clear that the granting of credit to consumers, which has recently been so strongly advocated as a cure for depression, would in fact have quite the contrary effect; a relative increase of the demand for consumers' goods could only make matters worse. Matters are not quite so simple so far as the effects of credits granted for productive purposes are concerned. In theory it is at least possible that, during the acute stage of the crisis when the capitalistic structure of production tends to shrink more than will ultimately prove necessary, an expansion of producers' credits might have a wholesome effect. But this could only be the case if the quantity were so regulated as exactly to compensate for the initial, excessive rise of the relative prices of consumers' goods, and if arrangements could be made to withdraw the additional credits as these prices fall and the proportion between the supply of consumers' goods and the supply of intermediate products adapts itself to the proportion between the demand for these goods. And even these credits would do more harm than good if they made roundabout processes seem profitable which, even after the acute crisis had subsided, could not be kept up without the help of additional credits. Frankly, I do not see how the banks can ever be in a position to keep credit within these limits.

And, if we pass from the moment of actual crisis to the situation in the following depression, it is still more difficult to see what lasting good effects can come from credit-expansion. The thing which is needed to secure healthy conditions is the most speedy and complete adaptation possible of the structure of production to the proportion between the demand for consumers' goods and the demand for producers' goods as determined by voluntary saving and spending. If the proportion as determined by the voluntary decisions of individuals is distorted by the creation of artificial demand, it must mean that part of the available resources is again led into a wrong direction and a definite and lasting adjustment is again postponed. And, even if the absorption of the

---

[41] [In the first edition, the first part of this sentence reads, "To provide an answer to this problem has always seemed to me the central task of any theory of industrial fluctuations; and, though at the outset I refused to make the assumption that unused resources exist the basis of my investigation, now that I have . . ."—Ed.]

unemployed resources were to be quickened in this way, it would only mean that the seed would already be sown for new disturbances and new crises. The only way permanently to 'mobilise' all available resources is, therefore, not to use artificial stimulants—whether during a crisis or thereafter—but to leave it to time to effect a permanent cure by the slow process of adapting the structure of production to the means available for capital purposes.

10.

And so, at the end of our analysis, we arrive at results which only confirm the old truth that we may perhaps prevent a crisis by checking expansion in time, but that we can do nothing to get out of it before its natural end, once it has come. In the next lecture I shall be dealing with some of the problems connected with a monetary policy suitable for the prevention of crises. Meanwhile, although so far our investigation has not produced a preventive for the recurrence of crises, it has, I hope, at least provided a guide to the maze of conflicting movements during the credit cycle which may prove useful for the diagnosis of the situation existing at any moment. If this is so, certain conclusions with regard to the methods commonly used in current statistical analysis of business fluctuations seem to follow immediately. The first is that our explanation of the different behaviour of the prices of specific and non-specific goods should help to substitute for the rough empirical classification of prices according to their sensitiveness[42] a classification based on more rational considerations. The second, that the average movements of general prices show us nothing of the really relevant facts; indeed, the index-numbers generally used will, as a general rule, fail even to attain their immediate object because, being for practical reasons almost exclusively based on prices of goods of a non-specific character, the data used are never random samples in the sense required by statistical method, but always a biased selection which can only give a picture of the peculiar movements of prices of goods of this class. And the third is that for similar reasons every attempt to find a statistical measure in the form of a general average of the total volume of production, or the total volume of trade, or general business activity, or whatever one may call it, will only result in veiling the really significant phenomena, the changes in the structure of production to which I have been drawing your attention in the last two lectures.

---

[42] [For example, the Austrian Institute for Business Cycle Research distinguished in its reports between 'free' and 'fixed prices', see, e.g., the table in *Monatsberichte*, vol. 7, February 1933, p. 23. Oskar Morgenstern, Hayek's successor as its director, dealt with this issue in "Free and Fixed Prices during the Depression", *Harvard Business Review*, vol. 10, October 1931, pp. 62–68.—Ed.]

Appendix: A Note on the History of the Doctrines Developed in the Preceding Lecture[43]

The central idea of the theory of the trade cycle which has been expounded in the preceding lecture is by no means new. That industrial fluctuations consist essentially in alternating expansions and contractions of the structure of capital equipment has often been emphasised. At one time, at the beginning of the second half of the last century, such theories even enjoyed considerable vogue and the financial journalists of those days frequently used a terminology which, intelligently interpreted, seems to imply essentially the same argument as that used here. The creation of 'fictitious capital', it was said, leads to the conversion of too much circulating into fixed capital which ultimately brings about a scarcity of disposable or floating capital which makes it impossible to continue or to complete the new undertakings and so causes the collapse. The reason why these theories did not prove more fruitful seems to have been that the concepts employed, particularly the concepts of the different kinds of capital, were too uncertain in their meaning to give a clear idea of what was really meant. But even if for this reason their popularity in the 'sixties and 'seventies was of a transient nature, they are of considerable interest as an expression of a fairly long and continuous strand of thought which occasionally came very near to modern ideas and in some instances leads very directly to some of the best known theories of today.

I have made no special study of the development of these doctrines (which they would well deserve) and I can therefore do no more than give a brief sketch of the main lines of development as I see them.[44] It seems that all these doctrines trace back to Ricardo's doctrine of the conversion of circulating into fixed capital, developed in the chapter "On Machinery" in the third edition of his *Principles*.[45] A relatively early attempt to apply these ideas to the explanation of crises was made in 1839 by the American Condy Raguet.[46] But the author who mainly developed and widely popularised it was James Wilson, the first editor of the *Economist*.[47] It seems to be from him that a host of English and French writers adopted it. In England it was particularly the group of econo-

---

[43] [The appendix and its accompanying footnotes do not appear in the first edition.—Ed.]

[44] [For a discussion of the 'conversion of circulating into fixed capital' cf. also F. A. Hayek, *The Pure Theory of Capital*, reprinted, appendix 2, especially p. 381n.4, for another account of the history of this idea.—Ed.]

[45] [Ricardo, *Principles of Political Economy*, 3rd ed., chapter 31.—Ed.]

[46] Condy Raguet, *A Treatise on Currency and Banking* (London: Ridgway, 1839 [2nd ed., Philadelphia: Grigg, 1840; reprinted, New York: Kelley, 1967]), pp. 62 et seq. [pp. 62–63. Condy Raguet (1784–1842) was an American politician and an advocate of free trade.—Ed.]

[47] James Wilson, *Capital, Currency and Banking* (London: The Economist, 1847; 2nd ed., London: Aird, 1859), articles 11, 13, and 16, particularly pp. 152 et seq. [pp. 152–54] (articles 11, 13, and 17 in the second edition of 1859). [James Wilson (1805–60), liberal politician and economist, was the founder of the *Economist*, and its editor from 1843 to 1857.—Ed.]

mists connected with the Manchester Statistical Society who took up the idea. Mr. T. S. Ashton in his recent Centenary History of this Society[48] quotes several extremely interesting extracts from lectures given to this society by T. H. Williams in 1857 and John Mills in 1867 which show clearly the great importance which they all attached to the "excessive conversions of floating into fixed capital";[49] and he particularly draws attention to a significant passage in W. St. Jevons's early tract on the *Serious Fall in the Value of Gold*, published in 1863 soon after he came to Manchester, where he says that the remote cause of the commercial tides "seems to lie in the *varying proportions which the capital devoted to permanent and remote investment bears to that which is but temporarily invested soon to reproduce itself*".[50] From the author who later on was to be the first to provide the basis for that modern theory of capital which now enables us to give more definite meaning to these ideas, this statement is of special interest and makes one wonder whether it may not be due to his early preoccupation with the problem of the trade cycle that he was led to a correct appreciation of the rôle the time element played in connection with capital.

A little later Bonamy Price developed these ideas in considerable detail[51] and from him they were taken over in France, where other authors like J. G. Courcelle-Seneuil and V. Bonnet[52] had been working on similar lines, by Yves Guyot, who not inappropriately summarised this theory by saying that "com-

[48] Thomas S. Ashton, *Economic and Social Investigations in Manchester, 1833–1933: A Centenary History of the Manchester Statistical Society* (London: King, 1934 [reprinted, Brighton: The Harvester Press, 1977]), pp. 72 et seq. [pp. 72–79].

[49] [Cf. Williams's lecture "Observations on Money, Credit and Panics", *Transactions of the Manchester Statistical Society* (1857–58), reprinted in Ashton, *Economic and Social Investigations*, p. 72, for the phrase "excessive conversion of floating into fixed capital". John Mills (1821–96), banker, president of the Manchester Statistical Society, 1871–73, in his paper on "Credit Cycles, and the Origin of Commercial Panics", *Transactions of the Manchester Statistical Society* (1867–68), pp. 9–40, propagated a theory of the credit cycle based on the changing mental moods of businessmen.—Ed.]

[50] William Stanley Jevons, *A Serious Fall in the Value of Gold Ascertained and Its Social Effects Set Forth* (London: Stanford, 1863), p. 10, in the reprint in the *Investigations in Currency and Finance* (London: Macmillan, 1884), p. 28 [cf. the 2nd ed. (1909) reprinted as vol. 7 of *Writings in Economics*, p. 24—Ed.].

[51] Bonamy Price discussed these problems on numerous occasions. Cf., however, particularly his *Chapters on Practical Political Economy* (London: Kegan Paul, 1878), pp. 110–24. [Bonamy Price (1807–88), English economist, from 1868 Drummond Professor for Political Economy at Oxford University.—Ed.]

[52] On these authors, cf. Eugen von Bergmann, [*Die Wirtschaftskrisen.*] *Geschichte der nationalökonomischen Krisentheorien* (Stuttgart: Kohlhammer, 1895), where the reader will find references to still further authors belonging to the same category. [Cf. for Jean Gustave Courcelle-Seneuil (1813–92) his *Traité théorique et pratique des opérations de banque* (Paris: Guillaumin, 1852; 10th ed. rev., 1909), and for Victor Bonnet (1814–85) his *Questions économiques et financières à propos des crises* (Paris: Guillaumin, 1859).—Ed.]

mercial and financial crises are produced, not by over-production, but by over-consumption".[53]

In the German literature similar ideas were introduced mainly by the writings of Karl Marx. It is on Marx that M. v. Tougan-Baranovsky's work[54] is based which in turn provided the starting point for the later work of Professor Spiethoff and Professor Cassel. The extent to which the theory developed in these lectures corresponds with that of the two last-named authors, particularly with that of Professor Spiethoff, need hardly be emphasised.

Another contemporary author who is evidently indebted to the same strand of thought and whose views on these problems are even more closely related to those taken in these lectures, but with whose work on this point I have unfortunately only become acquainted since he has collected his earlier scattered articles in book-form, is Professor C. Bresciani-Turroni. His monumental study of the German inflation[55] appears to me to be one of the most important contributions to the study of money which have appeared in recent years. Particularly the chapters on the influence of inflation on production and on the scarcity of capital after the stabilisation[56] seem to me of extraordinary interest and to contain a wealth of concrete illustrations of these difficult theoretical questions which is not to be found elsewhere. Few other foreign books on economic problems would equally deserve being made available in an English translation.[57]

In view of the importance which so many theories of the trade cycle attach to the inter-relationships between the different forms of 'capital' one might

---

[53] Yves Guyot, *La science économique* (Paris: Reinwald, 1881; 6th ed., Paris: Costes, 1928), English translation as *Principles of Social Economy* (London: Sonnenschein, 1884), p. 249. [Yves Guyot (1843–1928), a disciple of liberal French economists like Say and Bastiat and one of the most notable politicians of the Third Republic, succeeded Courcelle-Seneuil as the editor of the famous *Journal des Économistes*.—Ed.]

[54] [Cf. for example Tugan-Baranovsky, *Studien zur Theorie und Geschichte der Handelskrisen in England* (Jena: Fischer, 1901; reprinted, Aalen: Scientia, 1969), chapters 1 and 8 translated and reprinted in *Business Cycle Theory: Selected Texts 1860–1939*, vol. 2, ed. Hagemann, pp. 1–44. Mikhail Ivanovich Tugan-Baranovsky (1865–1919), Russian economist with Marxist, yet revisionist, leanings, originated a disproportionality theory of crises.—Ed.]

[55] *Le vicende del marco tedesco* (Milan: Univ. Bocconi ed., 1931). [Costatino Bresciani-Turroni (1882–1963) was professor of statistics at Palermo, 1909–17. After some years spent in Germany at various positions in the Reparations Commission he occupied a chair for political economy at the University of Milan, 1927–57, yet from 1927 to 1940 taught at the University of Cairo, outside fascist Italy.—Ed.]

[56] Ibid., chapters 5 and 10, an abridged German version of the latter appeared in the *Wirtschaftstheorie der Gegenwart*, ed. Hans Mayer, vol. 2 (Vienna: Springer, 1931). [Hayek's reference is inaccurate: the German version, titled "Kapitalmangel und Währungsstabilisierung", appeared 1932 in *Die Wirtschaftstheorie der Gegenwart*, a series jointly edited by Hans Mayer, Frank A. Fetter, and Richard Reisch, vol. 2, pp. 391–403.—Ed.]

[57] [Eventually the book was translated by Millicent E. Sayers as *The Economics of Inflation: A Study of Currency Depreciation in Post-War Germany*. With a foreword by Lionel Robbins (London: Allen and Unwin, 1937; reprinted, Routledge, 2003).—Ed.]

expect that investigations in this field should have received considerable help from the theory of capital. That this has hitherto been the case only to a very limited degree is mainly due to the rather unsatisfactory state of this theory which was mainly concerned with barren terminological debates or the question whether capital was to be regarded as a separate factor of production and how this factor was to be defined, instead of making its main task the general question of the *way* in which production was carried on. It would not be surprising if it would ultimately be that theory of the trade cycle, which consciously utilises the results of the only satisfactory theory of capital which we yet possess, that of Böhm-Bawerk, which should prove to be successful. It must be admitted, however, that, so far, the further elaboration of the ideas of Böhm-Bawerk, apart from two notable exceptions, have not helped us much further with the problems of the trade cycle. The two exceptions are Knut Wicksell and his pupil, Professor G. Åkerman.[58] Particularly the difficult but important investigations in the *Realkapital und Kapitalzins* of the latter author, which I did not yet know at the time when I wrote these lectures, seems to me to deserve particular attention as one of the few attempts to clear up the difficult problems which arise out of the existence of very durable capital goods.

It seems, however, not improbable that in the future the relationship between the theory of capital and the theory of the trade cycle may be reversed and that the former will be benefited by the progress of the latter. Only by studying the changes of the capitalistic structure of production will we learn to understand the factors which govern it, and it seems that the trade cycle is the most important manifestation of these changes. It is therefore not surprising that the study of the problems of the trade cycle should lead to the study of the theory of capital. As has been suggested before, this may have been the case with Jevons, and more recently it has certainly been true of Professor Spiethoff.[59]

[58] [Johan Gustaf Åkerman (1888–1959), Swedish economist, professor at the University of Gothenburg, contributed to capital theory in the tradition of Böhm-Bawerk and Wicksell.—Ed.]

[59] Cf. already his "Vorbemerkungen zu einer Theorie der Ueberproduktion", Schmoller's *Jahrbuch für Gesetzgebung, Verwaltung und Volkswirtschaft im Deutschen Reiche*, vol. 26, no. 2, 1902, particularly p. 299 [translated by Vincent Homolka as "Preliminary Remarks to a Theory of Overproduction", in *Business Cycle Theory: Selected Texts 1860–1939*, vol. 2, ed. Hagemann, pp. 71–72—Ed.], and his essay on "Die Lehre vom Kapital", in *Die Entwicklung der deutschen Volkswirtschaft[slehre] im 19. Jahrhundert. Gustav Schmoller zur 70. Wiederkehr seines Geburtstages*, vol. 1 (Leipzig: Duncker and Humblot, 1908), chapter 4.

THE CASE FOR AND AGAINST
AN 'ELASTIC' CURRENCY

"The notion common . . . to 90 per cent of the writings of monetary cranks is that every batch of goods is entitled to be born with a monetary label of equivalent value round its neck, and to carry it round its neck until it dies."
—D. H. Robertson, *Economica*, no. 23, June 1928, p. 142[1]

1.

If the considerations brought forward in the last lecture are at all correct, it would appear that the reasons commonly advanced as a proof that the quantity of the circulating medium should vary as production increases or decreases are entirely unfounded. It would appear rather that the fall of prices proportionate to the increase in productivity, which necessarily follows when, the amount of money remaining the same, production increases, is not only entirely harmless, but is in fact the only means of avoiding misdirections of production. So far as an increase of production caused by a transition to more capitalistic methods of production is concerned, this result bears some resemblance to the theory underlying certain proposals[2] for stabilising the value of money so as to keep, not the prices of consumers' goods, but incomes, or the prices of the factors of production constant, the prices of consumers' goods being allowed to fall as costs fall and vice versa.[3] Complete invariability of the effective money stream

[1] [Dennis H. Robertson, "Theories of Banking Policy", *Economica*, no. 23, June 1928, p. 142, reprinted in *Essays in Monetary Theory* (London: King, 1940), p. 54, and in *Essays in Money and Interest*, ed. John Hicks (London: Collins, 1966), p. 37.—Ed.]

[2] [In the first edition, Hayek uses the words "recent plans" instead of "proposals".—Ed.]

[3] That there is no harm in prices falling as productivity increases has been pointed out again and again, e.g., by A. Marshall, N. G. Pierson, W. Lexis, F. Y. Edgeworth, F. W. Taussig, L. Mises, A. C. Pigou, D. H. Robertson, and G. Haberler. (For more detailed references see my article on "The 'Paradox' of Saving", p. 161 [reprinted, p. 112—Ed.].) Cf. also the stabilisation proposal made by Dr. Maurice Leven, mentioned by W. J. King in the *Journal of the American Statistical Association*, vol. 23, supplement, March 1928, p. 146 [the name of the author is, correctly, Willford Isbell King and the article is titled, "The Best Index for Use in Stabilizing the Price Level"—Ed.], and the article by Ralph G. Hawtrey, "Money and Index Numbers". [This footnote is a

would, as we have seen, however, have the further effect that any transition to more capitalistic methods of production would also make a reduction of money income necessary, except in the case of complete vertical integration of production.[4] This necessity, which in view of the notorious rigidity of wages is certainly very undesirable, could however only be avoided without causing misdirections of production, if it were possible to inject the required additional quantities of money in such a way into the economic system that the proportion between the demand for consumers' goods and the demand for producers' goods would not be affected. This is no doubt a task which cannot be solved in practice. But apart from the special difficulties which may arise from the existence of rigidities I believe that the conclusion stated above holds here not only for this case of the transition to more capitalistic methods of production but also for an increase of production caused by the absorption of unused resources.[5] Furthermore, by another chain of reasoning—which is too long and complicated to reproduce here, and which I have sketched elsewhere[6]—it might be shown to apply in principle even to the particularly difficult case of an increase of production caused by the growth of popula-

revised version of the footnote appearing in the first edition, which starts with, "Cf. the proposal made by Dr. Maurice Leven", and adds the sentence, "But the theories are by no means identical."—Ed.]

[4] [To many contemporary readers in general friendly to the idea of neutral money this result appeared unwarranted and inconsistent with Hayek's own treatment of changes in the degree of vertical integration. Examples of such criticisms include Gottfried Haberler, "Der Stand und die nächste Zukunft der Konjunkturforschung", in *Festschrift für Arthur Spiethoff*, ed. Clausing, p. 90; Howard S. Ellis, *German Monetary Theory, 1905–1933* (Cambridge, MA: Harvard University Press, 1934), pp. 350–51; and again Machlup in his correspondence with Hayek. Cf. also the debate between J. C. Gilbert, "A Note on Banking Policy and the Income-Velocity of the Circulation of Money", *Economica*, n.s., vol. 1, May 1934, pp. 242–45, and Evan F. M. Durbin, "Mr. Gilbert's Defence of a Constant Circulation", followed by the former's "A Rejoinder to Mr. Durbin", *Economica*, n.s., vol. 2, May 1935, pp. 220–22 and pp. 223–25, respectively. In a final "Note" appended (pp. 225–26), Durbin remarked that with perfect price flexibility and correct foresight the concrete reaction of monetary policy should become irrelevant, a position consistent with the view that the criterion of neutral money is insufficient to determine a unique path of money prices. Curiously, this indeterminacy result was later on rediscovered by Gilbert; cf. his "The Compatibility of Any Behavior of the Price Level with Equilibrium", *Review of Economic Studies*, vol. 24, June 1957, pp. 177–84.—Ed.]

[5] [The four preceding sentences, that is, starting with "Complete invariability of the effective money stream . . .", do not appear in the first edition. In their place is a long sentence, part of which becomes the next sentence in the second edition, the one beginning with, "Furthermore, by another chain . . ." The long sentence in the first edition reads in part, "In my view—and here no doubt I should part company with the progenitors of these projects—the same conclusion holds true for an increase in production caused by the absorption of unused resources, and that, furthermore, by another chain of reasoning . . ."—Ed.]

[6] In an article, "Das intertemporale Gleichgewichtssystem der Preise" [sections 10–12; cf. "Intertemporal Price Equilibrium", pp. 210–25—Ed.].

tion, the discovery of new natural resources, and the like.[7] But however that may be, our result is in sufficient contrast to generally received opinions to require further elucidation.

2.

We can best observe how deeply the notion that it is the 'natural' thing for the quantity of money to fluctuate with fluctuations in the volume of production is ingrained in the minds of many modern economists if we look at the use they make of it in their theoretical analysis. Professor Cassel, for instance, who is of course the outstanding representative of this point of view, discussing the treatment of price problems[8] in a recent article, writes as follows: "The simplest assumption is, then, that a country has a paper currency so regulated as to keep the general level of prices constant." And again—to quote another well-known authority—Professor Pigou is expressing the same opinion when he argues[9] that if countries with paper currencies will regulate them with a view to keeping the general price level in some sense stable, there will be no impulses from the side of money which can properly be called "autonomous". Both statements imply that changes in the quantity of the circulating medium which are only just sufficient to keep the general price level steady exert *no* active influence on the formation of prices, and that, accordingly, a money so regulated would remain 'neutral' towards prices in the sense in which I have used the word. I see no foundation at all for this hypothesis, although by most it seems to be considered as an obvious platitude requiring no further justification. Everything that has been said in the earlier lectures seems to me to prove that changes in the volume of the circulation which are supposed to be justified by changes in the volume of production will have effects which are just as disturbing as those changes of the circulation which cause changes in the general price level. Prima facie, I suggest that we should expect rather that, to be neutral in this sense, the supply of money should be invariable. The ques-

[7] [Both with regard to an increase in production due to the absorption of unused resources as well as to growth of population, Hayek in "Profits, Interest and Investment", reprinted, pp. 238–40, in particular 240n.49, recanted his identification of neutral money with a "complete invariability of the effective money stream" and rather allowed for adjustments in monetary circulation as necessary for securing a stable *money income.*—Ed.]

[8] *Economic Journal*, vol. 38, December 1929, p. 589. [Gustav Cassel's article "The Treatment of Price Problems" appeared in December 1928, not in 1929.—Ed.]

[9] *Industrial Fluctuations*, 2nd ed. (London: Macmillan, 1929) [reprinted as vol. 6 of Arthur Cecil Pigou, *Collected Economic Writings* (London: Macmillan, 1999)—Ed.], p. 101. [Hayek's use of quotation marks is misleading, as not only the word "autonomous", but the whole passage is quoted from p. 101, where it reads, "will regulate them with a view to keeping the general price level in some sense stable, in which case there will be no impulses from the side of money which can properly be called autonomous".—Ed.]

tion is, can this be true? Are there not many other reasons besides a change in the volume of production which experience suggests justify changes in the quantity of money in circulation if serious disturbances are to be avoided?

I suppose that, to most economists, the idea of a circulating medium which does not vary in amount will seem perfectly absurd. We have all been brought up upon the idea that an elastic currency is something highly to be desired, and it is considered a great achievement of modern monetary organisation, particularly of the recent American Federal Reserve system, to have secured it. It does not seem open to doubt that the amount of money necessary to carry on the trade of a country fluctuates regularly with the seasons, and that central banks should respond to these changes in the 'demand for money', that not only *can* they do this without doing harm, but that they *must* do so if they are not to cause[10] serious disturbances. It is also a fact which has been established by long experience, that in times of crisis central banks should give increased accommodation and extend thereby their circulation in order to prevent panics, and that they can do it to a great extent without effects which are injurious. How are we to reconcile all this with the conclusions of my earlier lectures?

3.

To begin with certain terminological elucidations. It should be fairly clear that the magnitude which in the course of my theoretical analysis I have called 'quantity of money in circulation' and that commonly referred to under the same name in dealing with the practical problems mentioned before are not identical, but different in two respects. When, in the course of analysis, I speak of changes in the quantity of money, this is always meant to include that *total* of all kinds of media of exchange (including all so-called 'substitutes' for money) used in either a *closed* economic system (i.e., in a country which has no communication with the outside world) or in the world as a whole. But when in dealing with practical problems we speak of the quantity of money in circulation, we always mean the quantity of any particular kind or kinds of media of exchange used within one or several countries which form a part of a larger economic unit. Now, as we shall see, it follows from the definition of the quantity of money in circulation in open communities that the quantity of money thus defined will always be liable to fluctuations even if we suppose that the quantity included in the more comprehensive theoretical concept remains unchanged. It is probably this fact which makes it so difficult even theoretically to conceive the possibility or usefulness of an invariable circulation.

The fact that the monetary circulation of any one country, whatever we

---

[10] [In the first edition, this word is "incur".—Ed.]

include under the heading money, will always show natural fluctuations in conforming with an increase or decrease of the volume of local production is probably the main reason why elasticity is generally considered a self-evident necessity for the amount of money in general. But the question we have to answer is just this. Do the reasons which make fluctuations of the circulation of *any single* country necessary apply when we are considering the quantity of money as a whole?[11] The answer is simple. The increase or decrease of the quantity of money circulating within any one geographical area serves a function just as definite as the increase or decrease of the money incomes of particular individuals, namely the function of enabling the inhabitants to draw a larger or smaller share of the total product of the world. The relative magnitude of the total incomes of all individuals in an 'open' community will always stand in a definite proportion to the share of the total product of the world which the people of that community command. And, if the money circulating within that nation regularly increases as a consequence of an increase of its product, this is only one of the steps in the process of adjustment which are necessary to enable that nation to procure a larger portion of the product of the world for itself. What appears to be an *absolute* increase of the amount of money in circulation consequent upon an increase of production, if viewed from the standpoint of a single country, proves to be nothing but a change in the *relative local distribution* of the money of all nations, which is a necessary condition of a change in the distribution of the product of the world as a whole. The same thing would happen, and would be just as necessary to restore equilibrium, if the product of this country were not absolutely increased but the products of all other countries were absolutely diminished. The fact that the increase of the product of any one country is regularly accompanied by an increase of the quantity of money circulating there, is therefore not only no proof that the same would be necessary for an isolated community, it rather shows by contrast how useless would be an increase of its monetary circulation either for such a community or for the world as a whole. While for any single country among others an increase of its possession of money is only a means of obtaining more goods, for the world as a whole the increase of the amount of money only means that somebody has to give up part of his additional product to the producers of the new money.

4.

The second source of the prevalent belief that, in order to prevent dislocation, the quantity of the circulating medium must adapt itself to the chang-

---

[11] For a more detailed discussion of this problem, see my article "Das intertemporale Gleichgewichtssystem der Preise", section 12 [cf. "Intertemporal Price Equilibrium", pp. 220–25—Ed.].

ing needs of trade arises from a confusion between the demand for *particular kinds of currency* and the demand for money *in general*.[12] This occurs especially in connection with the so-called seasonal variations of the demand for currency which in fact arises because, at certain times of the year, a larger proportion of the total quantity of the circulating medium is required in *cash* than at other times. The regularly recurring increase of the 'demand for money' at quarter days, for instance, which has played so great a rôle in discussions of central bank policy since attention was first drawn to it by the evidence of J. Horsley Palmer and J. W. Gilbart before the parliamentary committees of 1832 and 1841,[13] is mainly a demand to exchange money held in the form of bank deposits into bank notes or coin.[14] The same thing is true in regard to the 'increased demand for money' in the last stages of a boom and during a crisis. When, towards the end of a boom period, wages and retail prices rise, notes and coin will be used in proportionately greater amounts, and entrepreneurs will be compelled to draw a larger proportion of their bank deposits in cash than they used to do before. And when, in a serious crisis, confidence is shaken, and people resort to hoarding, this again only means that they will want to keep a part of their liquid resources in cash which they used to hold in bank money, etc. All this does not necessarily imply a change in the total quantity of the circulating medium, if only we make this concept comprehensive enough to comprise everything which serves as money, even if it does so only temporarily.

5.

But at this point we must take account of a new difficulty which makes this concept of the total quantity of the circulating medium somewhat vague, and which makes the possibility of ever actually fixing its magnitude highly questionable. There can be no doubt that besides the regular types of the circulat-

---

[12] This confusion is particularly obvious in the writings of Thomas Tooke. Cf. Gregory, "Introduction", pp. 87 et seq. [pp. 87–89].

[13] [John Horsley Palmer (1779–1858) was governor of the Bank of England during the investigation of the Committee of Secrecy on the Bank of England Charter 1832, due to the expiration of the Bank's privilege. James William Gilbart (1794–1863), founder of the London and Westminster Bank in 1833, gave testimony as a witness to the Select Committee on Banks of Issue, appointed 1840. Cf. on this F. A. Hayek, "The Dispute between the Currency School and the Banking School, 1821–1848", chapter 12 of F. A. Hayek, *The Trend of Economic Thinking*, especially p. 233n.36.—Ed.]

[14] On this point, see, however, the recent discussion by Fritz Machlup, *Börsenkredit, Industriekredit und Kapitalbildung* (Vienna: Springer, 1931 [reprinted, Frankfurt/Main: Frankfurter Allgemeine, 2002]), particularly chapters 8 and 9. [Cf. the revised version translated as *The Stock Market, Credit, and Capital Formation*, trans. Vera C. Smith (London: Hodge, 1940), chapters 13 and 14. This footnote does not appear in the first edition.—Ed.]

ing medium, such as coin, bank notes, and bank deposits, which are generally recognised to be money or currency, and the quantity of which is regulated by some central authority or can at least be imagined to be so regulated, there exist still other forms of media of exchange which occasionally or permanently do the service of money. Now while for certain practical purposes we are accustomed to distinguish these forms of media of exchange from money proper as being mere substitutes for money, it is clear that, ceteris paribus, any increase or decrease of these money substitutes will have exactly the same effects as an increase or decrease of the quantity of money proper, and should therefore, for the purposes of theoretical analysis, be counted as money.

In particular, it is necessary to take account of certain forms of credit not connected with banks which help, as is commonly said, to economise money, or to do the work for which, if they did not exist, money in the narrower sense of the word would be required. The criterion by which we may distinguish these circulating credits[15] from other forms of credit which do not act as substitutes for money is that they give to somebody the means of purchasing goods without at the same time diminishing the money spending power of somebody else. This is most obviously the case when the creditor receives a bill of exchange which he may pass on in payment for other goods. It applies also to a number of other forms of commercial credit, as, for example, when book credit is simultaneously introduced in a number of successive stages of production in the place of cash payments, and so on. The characteristic peculiarity of these forms of credit is that they spring up without being subject to any central control, but once they have come into existence their convertibility into other forms of money must be possible if a collapse of credit is to be avoided. But it is important not to overlook the fact that these forms of credits owe their existence largely to the expectation that it will be possible to exchange them at the banks against other forms of money when necessary, and that, accordingly, they might never come into existence if people did not expect that the banks would in the future extend credit against them. The existence of this kind of demand for more money, too, is therefore no proof that the quantity of the circulating medium must fluctuate with the variations in the volume of production. It is only a proof that once additional money has come into existence in some form or other, *convertibility* into other forms must be possible.

6.

Before proceeding to investigate whether there exist any genuine reasons which would make changes in the amount of the circulation necessary in order to

---

[15] [Here Hayek refers to the notion of 'circulating' or 'circulation credit' (*Zirkulationskredit*) as put forward by Mises. See above, p. 120n.5.—Ed.]

keep money entirely neutral towards the economic process (i.e., to prevent it from exercising any active influence on the formation of prices), it is useful to ask whether, under the circumstances just described, it is at all conceivable that the quantity of the circulating medium *can* be kept invariable, and by what means a monetary authority could attain that end. I may say at once that, in spite of the qualifications that I shall introduce later, this question seems to me not merely a question of theoretical interest, but also a question the answer to which may prove very important in the shaping of a more rational monetary policy.

The credit system of a country has very often been compared to an inverted pyramid, a simile which serves very well for our purpose. The lowest part of the pyramid corresponds of course to the cash basis of the credit structure. The section immediately above to central bank credit in its various forms, the next part to the credits of commercial banks, and on these finally is built the total of business credits outside the banks. Now it is only in regard to the two lower parts, cash and central bank credit, that an immediate control can be exercised by the central monetary authority. So far as the third part, the credits of the commercial banks, are concerned, it is at least conceivable that a similar control could be exercised. But the uppermost section of the pyramid—private credits—can be controlled only indirectly through a change in the magnitude of their basis, i.e., in the magnitude of bank credit. The essential thing is that the proportion between the different parts of the pyramid is not constant but variable, in other words that the angle at the apex of the pyramid may change. It is a well-known fact that, during a boom, the amount of central bank credits erected upon a given cash basis increases, and likewise the amount of credits of the commercial banks based on a given amount of central bank credit, and even the amount of private credits based on a given amount of central bank credit. This is certainly true on the continent of Europe, where the possibility of rediscounting takes to a large extent the place of actual cash reserves. So that, even if central banks should succeed in keeping the basis of the credit structure unchanged during an upward swing of a cycle, there can be no doubt that the total quantity of the circulating medium would none the less increase. To prevent expansion, therefore, it would not be sufficient if central banks, contrary to their present practice, refrained from *expanding* their own credits. To compensate for the change in the proportion between the base furnished by the credit and the superstructure erected upon it, it would be necessary for them actually to *contract* credit proportionally. It is probably entirely utopian to expect anything of that kind from central banks so long as general opinion still believes that it is the duty of central banks to accommodate trade and to expand credit as the increasing demands of trade require. Unfortunately, we are very far from the more enlightened times when, as John Fullarton complained, "the words 'demand' and 'legitimate demand' could not even be mentioned in Parliament in connection with this subject unaccompanied by a sneer".[16] None the less, I am strongly convinced that, if we want to prevent the periodic misdirections of production caused by additional credit, something very similar to the policy outlined above, absurd as it may seem to those accustomed to present-day practice, would be necessary. I do not delude myself that, in the near future, there will be any opportunity of experimenting with such a policy. But this is no excuse for not following the implications of our theoretical arguments right through to their practical consequences. On the contrary, it is highly important that we should become fully conscious of the enormous difficulties of the problem of the elimination of disturbing monetary influences, difficulties which monetary reformers are always so inclined to underrate. We are still very far from the point when either our theoretical knowledge or the education of the general public provide justification for revolutionary reform or hope of carrying such reforms to a successful conclusion.

7.

As a matter of fact, the course of our argument so far understates rather than overstates the real difficulties. I think that I have shown that changes in the physical volume of production offer no sufficient reason for variations in the supply of money. None the less there do seem to me to exist other causes whose operation may necessitate such changes if the 'natural' price system or the equilibrium of the economic process is not to be disturbed. So far, I have been able to neglect these causes, since what I have said has been subject to an assumption, which I expressly introduced at the outset, the assumption, namely, that the proportion between the total flow of goods and the part which takes the form of an exchange against money, or the rate at which goods are exchanged against money, remains constant. But this assumption must now be removed.

Now it will be remembered that the proportion in question is not necessarily changed by changes in the physical volume of production while the amount of money in circulation remains the same, nor by a variation of the quantity of money in circulation,[17] while the physical volume of production remains the same; it changes only if movements of goods which before have been effected without the use of money now require the transfer of money, or if movements of goods which before could only be effected by means of money payments

---

[16] John Fullarton, *On the Regulation of Currencies*, 2nd ed. (London: Murray, 1845 [reprinted, New York: Kelley, 1969]), p. 206. [The quotation is slightly inaccurate. It should read: "The words 'demand', 'legitimate demand', cannot be even mentioned in Parliament, in connexion with this subject, unaccompanied by a sneer." John Fullarton (1780?–1849), a banker, represented the position of the Banking school in the discussion of Peel's Act of 1844.—Ed.]

[17] [The comma after "circulation" does not appear in the first edition.—Ed.]

can now be effected without the use of money. It will be remembered further that changes in that proportion are caused by certain changes of the business organisation, as the amalgamation of two firms into one, or the division of one firm into two, by the extension of the money economy into spheres where before everybody had only consumed his own product, or where barter had predominated, and the like. The question to which we must now address our attention is this: Will not such changes in the proportions of money transactions to the total flow of goods make a corresponding change in the quantity of the circulating medium necessary?

The answer to that question depends upon whether, without such a corresponding change in the quantity of money, the change in business organisation would cause shifts in the directions of demand and consequential shifts in the direction of production not justified by changes in the 'real' factors. That the simple fact that a money payment is inserted at a point in the movement of goods from the original means of production to the final stage where none has been necessary before (or the reverse) is no 'real' cause in the sense that it would justify a change in the structure of production, is a proposition which probably needs no further explanation. If, therefore, we can show that, without a corresponding change in the amount of the circulation, it has such an effect, this would provide sufficient reason, in these circumstances, to consider a change in the amount of money to be necessary.

8.

Let us examine what happens when a firm which represents two different stages of production, say spinning and weaving, is divided into two independent firms. The movement of the yarn from the spinning to the weaving factory, which before required no money, will now be effected by a purchase against money. The new weaving firm, which before, as part of the larger concern, had to keep money only for the payment of wages, etc., will now require additional money balances to buy the yarns. The new owner, whom we will assume to have bought the weaving mill from the old firm, will therefore need additional capital beyond what was needed to buy the existing plant and equipment and to replace the cash balances kept by the former owner for that mill, in order to effect these new payments. If no new money is added to the amount already circulating, he will either have to take this sum from other employments where it cannot be replaced, causing an absolute reduction of the demand for capital goods, and consequently a shrinkage of the structure of production; or he will have to use new savings for that purpose, which would thus cease to be available for lengthening the roundabout processes—that is to say, to use a phrase of Mr. Robertson's, they would become

275

'abortive'.[18] The effects would be the same as if, other things remaining the same, the total amount of money in circulation had been reduced by a corresponding sum used before for productive purposes. The two cases are so far alike that the change in the proportion between the demand for consumers' goods and the demand for producers' goods, which in the second case as in the first is not determined by 'real' causes, will not be permanent: the old proportion will tend to re-establish itself. But if, from the outset, the demand of the new entrepreneur for the additional cash balances had been satisfied by the creation of new money, this change in the total quantity of circulation would not have caused a change in the direction of the demand, and would only have helped to preserve the existing equilibrium.

It would be easy to show, if time permitted, that in the contrary case, the merger of two firms, and in a number of similar changes in business organisation, money is set free and that this money, if not withdrawn from circulation, would have the same effects as if so much money were added to the circulation. But I think that what I have already said on this point will be sufficient to justify the conclusion that changes in the demand for money caused by changes in the proportion between the total flow of goods to that part of it which is effected by money, or, as we may tentatively call that proportion, of *the co-efficient of money transactions*, should be justified[19] by changes in the volume of money if money is to remain neutral towards the price system and the structure of production.

All this assumes a greater importance if we remember that this co-efficient of money transactions may not only change in time, but that, at the same moment of time, it may be different in different parts of an economic system, for instance because goods change hands at shorter intervals in the lower stages of production than they do in the higher stages.[20] If this is the case, any transfer of money from one part of the economic system to another or from one stage of production to another where the co-efficient of money transactions is different will also make a corresponding change of the amount of money in circulation necessary. If, for instance, money is transferred from a lower to a higher stage[21] of production where the interval between two successive stages is twice as long, and, accordingly, only half as much money is needed to hold the same quantity of goods in that stage, half the money so transferred would become free. In the opposite case an addition of new

---

[18] [Cf. Robertson, *Banking Policy and the Price Level*, p. 45, where he speaks of "abortive lacking".—Ed.]

[19] [In the first edition, this word is "satisfied".—Ed.]

[20] [According to the terminology of the second edition, this should read, "in the later stages of production than they do in the earlier stages".—Ed.]

[21] [According to the terminology of the second edition, this should read, "from a later to an earlier stage".—Ed.]

money of an equal amount would be necessary. In such a situation, therefore, the transition to more or less capitalistic methods of production may also require a change in the quantity of money, *not* because the physical magnitude of the goods-stream has changed, but because money has been transferred from a sphere where the co-efficient of money transactions has been higher to one where it is lower, or vice versa.

9.

And this is not the only exception to which our original maxim of policy, that the quantity of money should remain invariable, may be deemed to be subject. The case just discussed is, in fact, only a special aspect of a more general and very familiar phenomenon which so far has been entirely neglected in these lectures.[22] I refer to changes in what is commonly called the velocity of circulation. Up to this point I have treated the quantity of money in circulation and the number of payments effected during a given period of time as equivalent concepts, a method of procedure which implied the assumption that the velocity of circulation is constant. That is to say, the whole of my argument applies directly only to the *amount of payments* made during a period of time. It applies indirectly to the *amount of money* if we assume the 'velocity of circulation' to be constant. So long as we make that assumption, or so long as we are speaking only of the volume of payments made during a period of time, the case just discussed seems to me the only exception to the general rule that, in order that money should remain neutral towards prices, the amount of money or the amount of money payments should remain invariable. But the situation becomes different as soon as we take into account the possibility of changes in methods of payment which make it possible for a given amount of money to effect a larger or smaller number of payments during a period of time than before. Such a change in the 'velocity of circulation' has rightly always been considered as equivalent to a change in the amount of money in circulation, and though, for reasons which it would go too far to explain here, I am not particularly enamoured of the concept of an average velocity of circulation[23] it will serve as sufficient justification of the general statement that any change in the velocity of circulation would have to be compensated by a reciprocal change in the amount of money in circulation if money is to remain neutral towards prices.

---

[22] [This sentence replaces the following sentence, which appears in the first edition: "There is another occasioned by changes which are more familiar."—Ed.]

[23] Cf. Mises, *Theorie des Geldes und der Umlaufsmittel*, 2nd ed., pp. 111 et seq. [pp. 111–17; cf. *The Theory of Money and Credit*, pp. 153–58.—Ed.]

10.

Even now our difficulties are not at an end. For, in order to eliminate all monetary influences on the formation of prices and the structure of production, it would not be sufficient merely quantitatively to adapt the supply of money to these changes in demand, it would be necessary also to see that it came into the hands of those who actually require it, i.e., to that part of the system where that change in business organisation or the habits of payment had taken place. It is conceivable that this could be managed in the case of an increase of demand. It is clear that it would be still more difficult in the case of a reduction. But quite apart from this particular difficulty which, from the point of view of pure theory, may not prove insuperable, it should be clear that only to satisfy the legitimate demand for money in this sense, and otherwise to leave the amount of the circulation unchanged, can never be a practical maxim of currency policy. No doubt the statement as it stands only provides another, and probably clearer, formulation of the old distinction between the demand for additional money as money which is justifiable, and the demand for additional money as capital which is not justifiable. But the difficulty of translating it into the language of practice still remains. The 'natural' or equilibrium rate of interest which would exclude all demands for capital which exceed the real supply capital,[24] is incapable of ascertainment, and, even if it were not, it would not be possible, in times of optimism, to prevent the growth of circulatory credit[25] outside the banks.

Hence the only practical maxim for monetary policy to be derived from our considerations is probably the negative one that the simple fact of an increase of production and trade forms no justification for an expansion of credit, and that—save in an acute crisis—bankers need not be afraid to harm production by overcaution.[26] Under existing conditions, to go beyond this is out of the question. In any case, it could be attempted only by a central monetary authority for the whole world: action on the part of a single country would be

[24] [Probably this phrase should read, "the real supply of capital". In the first edition, the corresponding phrase is "supply of real capital" and carries the following footnote, which is not present in the second edition: "'Real capital' stands here as the only short (but probably misleading) expression which I can find for that part of the total money stream which is available for the purchase of producers' goods, and which is composed of the regular receipts of the turnover of the existing producers' goods (i.e., in the case of durable goods the reserves accumulated to make up for depreciation) plus new savings." Note also Hayek's definition of the "supply of 'real capital'" as "the output of consumers' goods not consumed by its producers", in "Profits, Interest and Investment", reprinted, p. 252.—Ed.]

[25] [The term "circulatory credit" is used here synonymously with the more usual "circulation credit".—Ed.]

[26] [In the first edition, this sentence carries the additional clause, deleted in the second edition, "even during times of general depression".—Ed.]

doomed to disaster. It is probably an illusion to suppose that we shall ever be able entirely to eliminate industrial fluctuations by means of monetary policy. The most we may hope for is that the growing information of the public may make it easier for central banks both to follow a cautious policy during the upward swing of the cycle, and so to mitigate the following depression, and to resist the well-meaning but dangerous proposals to fight depression by 'a little inflation'.[27]

11.

Anybody who is sceptical of the value of theoretical analysis if it does not result in practical suggestions for economic policy will probably be deeply disappointed by the small return of so prolonged an argument. I do not, however, think that effort spent in clearing up the conditions under which money would remain neutral towards the economic process is useless because these conditions will never be given in the real world. And I would claim for these investigations at least two things. The first is that, as I have said in my first lecture, monetary theory is still so very far from a state of perfection that even some of the most fundamental problems in this field are yet unsolved, that some of the accepted doctrines are of very doubtful validity. This applies in particular to the widespread illusion that we have simply to stabilise the value of money in order to eliminate all monetary influences on production and that, therefore, if the value of money is assumed to be stable, in theoretical analysis, we may treat money as non-existent. I hope to have shown that, under the existing conditions, money will always exert a determining influence on the course of economic events and that, therefore, no analysis of actual economic phenomena is complete if the rôle played by money is neglected. This means that we have definitely to give up the opinion which is still widely prevalent, that, in the words of John Stuart Mill, "there cannot, in short, be intrinsically a more insignificant thing, in the economy of society, than money" which "like many other kinds of machinery only exerts a distinct and independent influence of its own when it gets out of order".[28] It means also that the task of monetary theory is a much wider one than is commonly assumed; that its task is noth-

---

[27] [Notably, Theodore E. Gregory, in his comments on "Recent Theories on Currency Reform" (*Economica*, no. 11, June 1924, p. 164), surmised that "after a period of deflation" the reformers in question would "like to see 'a little inflation'" as the adequate monetary response. The focus of Gregory's critique was Keynes's *A Tract on Monetary Reform* (London: Macmillan, 1923), reprinted as vol. 4 (1972) of *The Collected Writings of John Maynard Keynes.*—Ed.]

[28] Mill, *Principles of Political Economy*, book 3, chapter 7, paragraph 3, ed. Ashley, p. 488. [Cf. reprinted, ed. Robson, *Part 2*, p. 506. Hayek's quotation of the second part is inaccurate and should read exactly, "like many other kinds of machinery, it only exerts . . ."—Ed.]

ing less than to cover a second time the whole field which is treated by pure theory under the assumption of barter, and to investigate what changes in the conclusions of pure theory are made necessary by the introduction of indirect exchange. The first step towards a solution of this problem is to release monetary theory from the bonds which a too narrow conception of its task has created.

The second conclusion to be drawn from the results of our considerations follows from the first: So long as we do not see more clearly about the most fundamental problems of monetary theory and so long as no agreement is reached on the essential theoretical questions, we are also not yet in a position drastically to reconstruct our monetary system, in particular to replace the semi-automatic[29] gold standard by a more or less arbitrarily managed currency. Indeed, I am afraid that, in the present state of knowledge, the risks connected with such an attempt are much greater than the harm which is possibly done by the gold standard. I am not even convinced that a good deal of the harm which is just now generally ascribed to the gold standard will not by a future and better informed generation of economists be recognised as a result of the different attempts of recent years to make the mechanism of the gold standard inoperative. And there is still another and perhaps no less important reason why it seems dangerous to me to overstress at the present moment the urgency of a change in our monetary system; it is the danger of diverting public attention from other and more pressing causes of our difficulties. I must say a last word on that point because it will help to prevent a misunderstanding which I am particularly anxious to avoid. Though I believe that recurring business depressions can only be explained by the operation of our monetary institutions, I do not believe that it is possible to explain in this way every stagnation of business. This applies in particular to the kind of prolonged depression through which some European countries are passing today. It would be easy to demonstrate by the same type of analysis which I have used in the last two lectures that certain kinds of State action, by causing a shift in demand from producers' goods to consumers' goods, may cause a continued shrinking of the capitalist structure of production, and therefore prolonged stagnation. This may be true of increased public expenditure in general or of particular forms of taxation or particular forms of public expenditure. In such cases, of course, no tampering with the monetary system can help. Only a radical revision of public policy can provide the remedy.

[29] [In the first edition, the word "existing" precedes the word "semi-automatic".—Ed.]

Appendix: Some Supplementary Remarks on 'Neutral Money'[1]

The term 'neutral money', as mentioned in Lecture 1, was apparently first used by Wicksell, but more or less incidentally, and without the intention to introduce it as a technical term.[2] It was only comparatively recently that it came to be more widely used, apparently first in Holland, probably owing to the influence of Mr. J. G. Koopmans, who has for years been investigating this problem. The first results of Mr. Koopmans's studies have, however, appeared only recently, since the present book was first published.[3] But Mr. Koopmans has carried his investigations considerably further than was possible in the present essay, and to anyone who is interested in that problem I can only warmly recommend Mr. Koopmans's study, with which I find myself in general agreement.

A short but earlier discussion of the problem is to be found in a German work by Mr. W. G. Behrens.[4] Mr. Behrens also points out correctly that this is only a new name for the problem which had been discussed by Carl Menger and Professor Mises under the, in my opinion rather unfortunate, name of the invariability of the *'innere objektive Tauschwert'* of money, or shortly of the *'innere Geldwert'*.[5] And it may also be added that it was essentially for the same purpose that L. Walras and the later economists of the Lausanne School used the concept of a *'numéraire'* as distinguished from that of *'monnaie'*.[6]

It is not intended here to go further into the extremely difficult theoretical problems which this concept raises. There is, however, one respect in which recent discussions devoted to it have shown a certain ambiguity of the concept, which it seems desirable to clear up. It is frequently assumed that the concept of neutrality provides a maxim which is immediately applicable to the practical problems of monetary policy. But this need by no means be the case, and the concept was certainly not primarily intended for that purpose. It was des-

---

[1] [This appendix originates from a footnote in *Preise und Produktion*, p. 30n., and from "Über neutrales Geld" ("On Neutral Money"). The appendix and its accompanying footnotes do not appear in the first edition.—Ed.]

[2] [See above, p. 211.—Ed.]

[3] Johan G. Koopmans, "Zum Problem des 'Neutralen' Geldes", in *Beiträge zur Geldtheorie*, ed. Hayek, pp. 211–359. [Johan Gerbrand Koopmans (1900–58), economist, professor of economics in Rotterdam and Amsterdam, contributed, jointly with Marius W. Holtrop (see above, p. 226n.15), to what has been called 'Dutch monetarism'.—Ed.]

[4] Walter G. Behrens, *Das Geldschöpfungsproblem* (Jena: Fischer, 1928), particularly pp. 228, 286, 312 et seq. [cf. pp. 228–30, 286–87, 312–14—Ed.].

[5] [That is, 'the inner exchange value of money'; see above, p. 109n.25.—Ed.]

[6] [The distinction in question is between money as a unit of account (*numéraire*) and money as a medium of exchange (*monnaie*). Drawing on Walras, Joseph A. Schumpeter had made extensive use of it, cf. *Das Wesen und der Hauptinhalt der theoretischen Nationalökonomie* (Leipzig: Duncker and Humblot, 1908), p. 289.—Ed.]

tined in the first instance to provide an instrument for theoretical analysis, and to help us to isolate the active influences, which money exercised on the course of economic life. It refers to the set of conditions, under which it would be *conceivable* that events in a monetary economy would take place, and particularly under which, in such an economy, relative prices would be formed, as if they were influenced only by the 'real' factors which are taken into account in equilibrium economics. In this sense the term points, of course, only to a problem, and does not represent a solution. It is evident that such a solution would be of great importance for the questions of monetary policy. But it is not impossible that it represents only one ideal, which in practice competes with other important aims of monetary policy.

The necessary starting point for any attempt to answer the theoretical problem seems to me to be the recognition of the fact that the identity of demand and supply, which must necessarily exist in the case of barter, ceases to exist as soon as money becomes the intermediary of the exchange transactions. The problem then becomes one of isolating the one-sided effects of money—to repeat an expression which on an earlier occasion I had unconsciously borrowed from von Wieser[7]—which will appear when, after the division of the barter transaction into two separate transactions, one of these takes place without the other complementary transaction. In this sense demand without corresponding supply, and supply without a corresponding demand, evidently seem to occur in the first instance when money is spent out of hoards (i.e., when cash balances are reduced), when money received is not immediately spent, when additional money comes on the market, or when money is destroyed. So this formulation of the problem leads immediately to the solution of a constant money stream, with the exceptions sketched in the last lecture. The argument has, however, been developed systematically only by Mr. J. G. Koopmans in the essay mentioned above.

In order to preserve, in the case of a money economy, the tendencies towards a stage of equilibrium[8] which are described by general economic theory, it would be necessary to secure the existence of all the conditions, which the theory of neutral money has to establish. It is however very probable that this is practically impossible. It will be necessary to take into account the fact that the existence of a generally used medium of exchange will always lead to the existence of long-term contracts in terms of this medium of exchange, which

---

[7] Cf. Friedrich von Wieser, "Der Geldwert und seine [geschichtlichen] Veränderungen", *Zeitschrift für Volkswirtschaft, Sozialpolitik und Verwaltung*, vol. 13, no. 1, 1907, p. 54, also reprinted in the same author's *Gesammelte Abhandlungen*, ed. F. A. Hayek (Tübingen: Mohr, 1929 [reprinted, Saarbrücken: VDM Verlag Müller, 2006]), p. 178. [The "earlier occasion", to which Hayek alludes, is his *Geldtheorie und Konjunkturtheorie*, p. 56, cf. *Monetary Theory and the Trade Cycle*, this volume, p. 104.—Ed.]

[8] [Probably, this is a misprint and should read instead, "state of equilibrium".—Ed.]

will have been concluded in the expectation of a certain future price level. It may further be necessary to take into account the fact that many other prices possess a considerable degree of rigidity and will be particularly difficult to reduce. All these 'frictions' which obstruct the smooth adaptation of the price system to changed conditions, which would be necessary if the money supply were to be kept neutral, are of course of the greatest importance for all practical problems of monetary policy. And it may be necessary to seek for a compromise between two aims which can be realised only alternatively: the greatest possible realisation of the forces working toward a state of equilibrium, and the avoidance of excessive frictional resistances. But it is important to realise fully that in this case the elimination of the active influences of money has ceased to be the only, or even a fully realisable, purpose of monetary policy; and it could only cause confusion to describe this practical aim of monetary policy by the same name, which is used to designate the theoretically conceivable situation, in which one of the two competing aims was fully obtained.

The true relationship between the theoretical concept of neutral money, and the practical ideal of monetary policy is, therefore, that the former provides one criterion for judging the latter; the degree to which a concrete system approaches the condition of neutrality is one and perhaps the most important, but not the only criterion by which one has to judge the appropriateness of a given course of policy. It is quite conceivable that a distortion of relative prices and a misdirection of production by monetary influences could only be avoided if, *firstly*, the total money stream remained constant, and *secondly*, all prices were completely flexible, and, *thirdly*, all long term contracts were based on a correct anticipation of future price movements. This would mean that, if the second and third conditions are not given, the ideal could not be realised by any kind of monetary policy.

INDEX

actual rate of interest, equilibrium rate of interest and, 153–55
Aftalion, Albert, 84n.14
Åkerman, Johan Gustaf, 265
amount of money in circulation, 213–14, 214n.69
anti-Semitism, 5n.10
Ashton, T. S., 263
Austrian capital theory, 25
Austrian Economic Association, 2
Austrian Institute for Business Cycle Research, 2, 6, 7
Austrian school of economics, 1–2

banks, credit creation by, 123–25
barter economy, 16, 17–18, 17n.64, 40
Behrens, Walter G., 281
Bentham, Jeremy, 206–7, 207n.45, 207n.47
Beveridge, William H., 10
Böhm-Bawerk, Eugen von, 25–26
Bonnet, Victor, 263
Bresciani-Turroni, Costatino, 264
Bullion Report, 202–3, 203n.35, 209
business cycle: monetary causes of, 19–25, 53; structure of production and mechanism of, 25–33

Cairnes, John Elliot, 199, 199n.16
Cantillon, Richard, 193, 193n.1, 198, 199
Cantillon effects, 37
capital idleness, 32
capital markets, interest rates in, 159–61
capital shortages, 32

central banks, credit creation by, 123–25
Clark, John Bates, 222, 222n.11
consumers' goods, conditions of equilibrium between production of producers' goods and production of, lecture on, 217–41
Courcelle-Seneuil, Jean Gustave, 263
credit: assumption of variability of, 95–97; cessation of, 137; expansion process of, 135–36; reaction of banks to increased demand for, 133–35
credit creation, 22, 23, 123–25
credit cycle, working of price mechanism in, lecture on, 242–65
credits: bankers arbitrarily creating, 131–33; origin of additional, 128–31
credit systems, as inverted pyramids, 273–74
crises. *See* economic crises
currency, elastic, case for and against, lecture on, 266–83
currency doctrine, 203
cycles, 19
cyclical fluctuations: elasticity in volume of circulating media as cause of, 137–40; equilibrium rate of interest and, 119–21; exogenous and endogenous monetary theories of, 121–23; fundamental cause of, 119–44; impact of, on policy, 142–44; monetary causes of, 53

deflation, 54–55
Degenfeld-Schonburg, Ferdinand, 5
Dobretsberger, Josef, 5

285